YOU AND YOUR

ADOLESCENT

ALSO BY LAURENCE STEINBERG

The Life Cycle: Readings in Human Development, New York: Columbia University Press, 1981

When Teenagers Work: The Psychological and Social Costs of Adolescent Employment, New York: Basic Books, 1985 (co-written with Ellen Greenberger)

Adolescence (2nd edition), New York: Alfred A. Knopf, 1989

ALSO BY ANN LEVINE

Social Problems, New York: Harcourt Brace Jovanovich, 1982 (co-written with Michael Bassis and Richard Gelles)

Understanding Development, San Diego: Harcourt Brace Jovanovich, 1986 (co-written with Sandra Scarr and Richard A. Weinberg)

Sociology: An Introduction (3rd edition), New York: Random House, 1988 (co-written with Michael Bassis, Richard Gelles, and Craig Calhoun)

YOU AND YOUR ADOLESCENT

A PARENT'S GUIDE FOR AGES 10 TO 20

LAURENCE STEINBERG

AND

ANN LEVINE

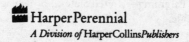
HarperPerennial
A Division of HarperCollins*Publishers*

Grateful acknowledgment is made for permission to reprint:

Excerpt from *The Quicksilver Years: The Hopes and Fears of Adolescents* by Peter L. Benson et al. Copyright © 1987 by Search Institute. Reprinted by permission of Harper & Row, Publishers, Inc.

Excerpt from "Personal Health" column by Jane E. Brody, June 3, 1987. Copyright © 1987 by The New York Times Company. Reprinted by permission.

The table "Major Drugs: Their Uses and Effects" is reproduced by special permission of *Playboy* magazine. Copyright © 1987 by *Playboy*.

First HarperPerennial edition published 1991.

Designed by Patricia Dunbar

The hardcover edition of this book has been catalogued by the Library of Congress as follows:

Steinberg, Laurence D., 1952–
    You and your adolescent : a parents' guide for ages 10 to 20 / Laurence Steinberg and Ann Levine.—1st ed.
        p.   cm.
    Includes index.
    ISBN 0-06-016241-4
    1. Adolescence.   2. Parenting—United States.   3. Teenagers—United States.
I. Levine, Ann.   II. Title.
HQ796.S8263   1990
305.23'5—dc20   89-45720

0-06-272002-3 (paperback edition)

94 95 96 97 98 RRD H 10 9

To our parents
Mollie and Irwin Steinberg
Estelle and Louis Sickles

Contents

THE PRETEENS: FROM 10 TO 13

Physical Health and Development

Acknowledgments

We gratefully acknowledge the encouragement, support, and counsel of our agent, Virginia Barber; our editor, Carol Cohen; and most of all, our spouses, Wendy Steinberg and Stacy Holmes.

Good News about Adolescence

*R*elax! The horror stories you have heard about adolescence are false.

Adolescence has long been a synonym for trouble in our society. "Everyone knows" that the road from childhood to adulthood is stormy. Extreme moodiness in adolescence is normal. Rebellion is an inevitable and necessary part of growing up. If your teenager doesn't get involved in drugs, crime, and risky sex, consider yourself lucky.

The idea that adolescence equals trouble has been part of our folklore, handed down from generation to generation, and accepted by psychologists, educators, and parents alike. Psychologists attempted to explain the storm and stress of adolescence through theory. Sociologists concentrated on delinquents, dropouts, drug users, and other problem teenagers. Few questioned the conventional wisdom. In the 1970s and 1980s, however, a new wave of research swept through the field. Psychologists began to study adolescents themselves—how they think, what they think about, how they feel about their lives, why they behave as they do, and how they respond to different types of parents. They looked not only at troubled young people, but also at ordinary, everyday kids. As a result of this research, common assumptions about adolescence have been exposed as myths.

• *Adolescence is not an inherently difficult period.* Psychological problems, problem behavior, and family conflict are no more common in adolescence than at any other stage of the life cycle. To be sure, some adolescents are troubled and some get into trouble. But the great majority (almost nine out of ten) do not. The problems we have come to see as a "normal" part of adolescent development—drugs, delinquency, irresponsible sex, opposition to any and all authority—are not normal at all. They are both preventable and treatable. The bottom line is that good kids don't suddenly go bad in adolescence.

• *The evils of peer pressure have been overrated.* To be sure, adolescents *are* concerned about what their friends think; they *do* want to fit in; and they *are* susceptible to peer pressure. But peer pressure is not a monolithic force that presses all adolescents into the same mold. Adolescents are as varied as adults are. In some adolescent crowds, earning academic honors is the "in" thing; in others, it's dressing to the nines or excelling in sports. In some, it's doing drugs. Peer pressure can be a force for good or evil, positive or negative attitudes toward family and school, depending on the source. Which crowd a teenager associates with is not random. Adolescents generally choose friends whose values, attitudes, tastes, and families are similar to their own. In short, good kids rarely go bad because of their friends.

• *The decline of the family has also been overstated.* In today's world, the story goes, parents have little or no control over their teenagers. The decline of neighborhoods, high divorce rates, women working, the youth culture, and the media all combine to undermine parental authority. This is nonsense. Parents remain the major influence on their child's attitudes and behavior through adolescence and into young adulthood. Adolescents care what you think and listen to what you say, even if they don't always admit it or agree with every point. The majority of teenagers like their parents, respect them, agree with them on the big issues (though they might disagree over matters of taste and style), and want to please them. Good parent-child relationships do not deteriorate because of adolescence. (And this is true whether parents are married, divorced, single, or remarried: Good parent-adolescent relationships do not depend on household arrangements.)

By and large, the good news about adolescence has not reached the public. One reason is that good news isn't news. Adolescents only appear in the news when a study finds a dramatic increase in teenage pregnancy, police discover that youth gangs are involved with drug rings, or a teenager kills her stepfather or commits suicide. The many, many adolescents who have good relationships with their parents, are doing well in school, do not use drugs, and do not get pregnant aren't news. You don't hear about them.

A second reason adolescence continues to equal trouble in the public mind is that cultural stereotypes die hard. An apron declares, "Mother Nature, in all her wisdom, gave me 13 years to love my son before he became a teenager"; a mug asserts, "Insanity is hereditary; you get it from your children"; the "terrible teens" is as much a part of our language as the "terrible twos." When parents of adolescents get together, they often play "Can you top this?" The parents who have survived the worst battles with their teenager get the most medals. Parents who haven't run into serious problems, who actually *enjoy* their teenagers, end up being apologetic: "I guess we are just lucky." It is not luck.

PARENTS CAN MAKE A DIFFERENCE

Your relationship with your child will not change for the worse in adolescence, but it will change. How you view this change can lay the groundwork for healthy or unhealthy development, good or bad times in your family.

When your child was small, you were responsible for directing and controlling an immature creature who saw you as all-knowing and all-powerful. In the near future, your young adult will take responsibility for his or her own life, and you will be more like friends. The adolescent still needs you, but in a different way. The parent-adolescent relationship is like a partnership in which the senior partner (the parent) has more expertise in many areas but looks forward to the day when the junior partner (the adolescent) will take over the business of running his or her own life. Parents who see the adolescent partnership as a losing proposition, or resist the adolescent's desire for self-determination, are asking for trouble.

When parents expect the worst from their adolescent, they often get it. The most common adolescent response to suspicion and surveillance is rebellion: If the adolescent's parents don't trust her, why should she try to prove that she is trustworthy?

Parents who assume that all teenagers are troubled also run the risk of overlooking the warning signs of serious problems that require immediate, professional attention.

When parents take the attitude that teenagers are teenagers and there's nothing a parent can do, their child concludes that they don't care. He may turn to his peers for guidance, or take unnecessary risks in the effort to discover for himself what his limits are, thus confirming his parents' worst nightmares.

Parents who refuse to accept the fact that their child is maturing and attempt to keep everything as it was run into similar problems. Like it or not, your child is going to try to grow up. The adolescent doesn't want you to solve every problem any more. If you don't make room for her friends, grant her privacy, and let her make her own decisions about clothes and music, when to do her schoolwork, and participation in extracurricular activities, she will find other, less benign ways to assert her independence.

In contrast, when parents welcome signs that their child is growing up and expect the best from their child, they often find adolescence the most rewarding time in their parental career. It's interesting to have a child with whom you can have an adult conversation (the kind of open-ended, all-nighters you haven't had since you were their age); exciting to be in touch with the latest fashions in clothes and music; fun to be able to share activities with a teenager (if you don't mind the fact that your daughter can beat you in tennis or knows more about computers than you do); and liberating to know that your child can take care of herself most of the time.

KNOWING WHAT TO EXPECT IS HALF THE BATTLE

Many parent-adolescent conflicts are the result, not of holding on too long or giving up too soon, but of misinformation. For example, parents tend to think of adolescence as beginning at age 13 or 14. When their son begins playing the hi-fi full blast and otherwise acting like a stereotypical teenager at age 11, they assume things can only get worse. In fact, things get better: Most families find the teenage years easier than the preteens. Parents often read interest in friends as *dis*interest in family. In reality, friends don't subtract from the adolescent's affection for his family but add to his circle of significant others. When the adolescent begins questioning their rules and their wisdom, many parents think "Oh, no; my son is the one in ten who is going to be trouble." In fact, challenging the old order is a sign of intellectual growth: You've raised a thinker!

Adolescence is a complicated time, but it is no more mysterious than infancy and toddlerhood. Like these earlier stages in development, it is a period of rapid growth and change. Some of the changes are biological, some intellectual, some emotional and social. Each individual adolescent develops according to an individual timetable. But the sequence of changes is more or less predictable. Preteens (roughly age 10 to 13) have different needs and concerns than teenagers (about age 14 to 17), and young adults (age 18 to 20) have needs and concerns of their own. If you know what to expect at each of these stages, you are in a much better position to understand why the adolescent behaves as he does and what he needs from you.

THE PURPOSE OF THIS BOOK

When your child was small, you probably kept one or more baby books on the shelf. These books told you what to expect at three months, six months, and a year and a half. You skimmed the book to get a preview of what lay ahead, pulled it out when something came up you hadn't anticipated, and reviewed it now and then to reassure yourself that your child was developing normally. When the book did not give you the answer you needed, you called your pediatrician. This book is written in the spirit of those baby books.

One purpose of this book is to describe the *normal* developmental changes young people undergo as they enter and move through adolescence. We will talk about what adolescents at a given age are likely to be thinking and feeling, what is probably happening at school and in their social world, how they are likely to perceive you and why. One obvious difference between small children and adolescents is that adolescents are able, and often eager, to tell us what is going on in their minds and their worlds, so that much of our information on this stage of life is first-hand.

The second purpose is to suggest effective ways of relating to your teenager. There is no magical formula for raising a healthy, well-adjusted teenager—and indeed, no one definition of *well-adjusted*. But research does show that some strategies are more effective than others. We suggest general guidelines, offer concrete suggestions, and highlight mistakes parents often make. But you know your child better than anyone. The best advice anyone can give you is to get as much information as you can, then follow your intuition.

In line with this view, the third purpose of this book is to provide practical information that both you and your adolescent should have. For example, we tell you what happens in an adolescent's body during puberty, what the dangers of unprotected sex are, including sexually transmitted diseases and early pregnancy, and how teenagers can protect themselves. Likewise, we talk about how the demands on students change as they move from middle school, or junior high, to high school and on to college. Much of this information is intended for parents to *share* with their child. There is nothing in this book an adolescent should not see.

The fourth purpose is to alert you to potential problems and tell you when you should be concerned and what you should do. There are many professionals trained to deal with the special medical and psychological needs of adolescents and their families. Help is available if and when you need it.

THE ORGANIZATION OF THIS BOOK

The first section of the book, "The Basics," deals with issues that come up throughout the adolescent decade. We introduce the basic principles of effective parenthood, discuss how you can improve the climate of communication and resolve conflicts to everyone's benefit, talk about when and how to get professional help, and address the special concerns of working parents, divorced parents, and stepparents. Our goal in this section is not to "sell" a philosophy of parenthood but to report what psychologists have learned about adolescents and their families.

The main body of the book is organized chronologically into sections on early and middle adolescence and young adulthood. Each section includes discussions of physical health and development, psychological and intellectual growth, and the adolescent's school and social world. The topics within each section are geared toward that particular stage of adolescence. For example, young adolescents are interested in learning about sex, but most teenagers do not begin having sexual intercourse until middle or late adolescence. For this reason, we discuss how to talk to your child about sex in the section on early adolescence but do not cover sexual decision-making, contraception, or pregnancy until middle adolescence. The last chapter deals with special issues of young adulthood.

Parents should not take the boundaries between stages of adolescence too literally, however. Adolescents develop at different rates. Labeling ages 10 to 13 the preteens, ages 14 to 17 the teens, and ages 18 to 20 young adulthood is not a statement about what is normal or expected. The correlation between chronological age and levels of development is much weaker in adolescence than in earlier stages. For example, we discuss puberty in the section on early adolescence because some teenagers begin developing at age 10 or 11. Others do not show signs of puberty until age 15 or 16. This does not mean the latter are "late developers" in the sense that a child who hasn't begun talking by age 3½ is a late developer. Either pattern is normal. We discuss questions about cigarettes, alcohol, and marijuana in the section on early adolescence, use and abuse of these and harder drugs in middle adolescence. But in some communities, young people are exposed to illicit drugs and experiment with them at an early age. If this is the case in your community, or if you and the young adolescent simply want to know more, by all means skip ahead. (Cross-references in the text will tell you where the subject is continued.)

The book can be used either as an introduction and guide to adolescent development or as a reference book. We believe it will be most useful if you read through a section as your child enters this stage of development, to get a general sense of what to expect, then refer back to specific topics as questions arise. The index will guide you to specific information when you need it. If your child is already in middle adolescence, however, we recommend at least skimming the chapters on early adolescence. Much of what is happening now builds on what went before.

No single book can say everything there is to say about adolescence. A list of resources appears at the end of most chapters; the notes at the end of the book provide suggestions for further reading.

A note on the pronoun problem. Like most authors today, we object to using the male pronoun *he* as a generic term to refer to people of both sexes. Nor are we comfortable with always using the plural forms, or constantly resorting to the cumbersome *he or she*. Our solution is to refer to the adolescent sometimes as male and sometimes as female. In either case, what we say about one sex applies to the other. For the most part, the concerns of female and male adolescents are similar. If we are talking about something of special concern to one or the other sex, we say so.

THE BASICS

CHAPTER 1

What Makes a Good Parent?

Americans have long been divided on the question of how best to rear children. On the one hand were traditional parents, who believed in laying down the law for their offspring. Parents always knew best in these families, and children were expected to do as they were told, no questions asked. The worst thing parents could do was to *spoil* a child. On the other hand were permissive parents, who believed in allowing their children freedom of expression and action. According to these parents, imposing rules and regulations on children stifled creativity. The worst thing parents could do was to *inhibit* a child. We now know, from hundreds of studies and decades of research, that neither of these extremes brings out the best in young people.

RESPONSIVE PARENTS

The most effective parents are loving but also demanding. They are accepting, affectionate, and involved. In Carl Rogers' phrase, they give their child "unconditional positive regard." They enjoy doing things with their child and take pride in her accomplishments. They believe that parents have an obligation to understand their child's needs and feelings, treat the child's interests and problems as meaningful, and show genuine concern. At the same time, they set well-defined limits. They hold their child to high standards, establish clear rules for behavior, and enforce these strictly and consistently. They are democratic in the sense that they solicit the child's opinion on such matters as bedtime hours and family plans. Because they do not consider themselves infallible, they allow their child to voice disagreements and can be persuaded to reconsider. They value curiosity and self-direction, and they want their child to understand the reasons for their demands and restrictions. When the child misbehaves, they make every effort to explain why the behavior was inappropriate. When reasoning fails, however, they do not hesitate to assert their authority. We call these mothers and fathers *responsive parents*.

Responsive parents do not demand unquestioning obedience from their children; nor do they give their children free rein. Their rules are based on reasoning, and their limits built on love.

HOW TO BE A RESPONSIVE PARENT

Nobody is perfect, not even parents. The best of us have bad days. When parents are under stress, tired, or preoccupied, they often slip into domination ("Just do it because I say so") or permissiveness ("Do whatever you want"). Moreover, some young people are easier to reason with than others. A bad day or a pressured decision will not have a profound effect on a child. What matters is the general pattern, over time.

Responsive child-rearing takes time and energy, but it's worth the effort. Parents who have always had a good relationship with their child have a head start on good relations with their adolescent. But all is not lost for parents whose style tends to be permissive, dictatorial, or even neglectful. You can learn to be a responsive parent, and your adolescent's behavior will improve as a result.

Start with Love and Trust

It is impossible to "spoil" an adolescent with too much love and affection. Even more than younger children, adolescents need to know that you are there for them. Consciously or unconsciously, many teenagers worry about whether their parents will continue to love them when they are no longer little and cute. They demand freedom from parental control, yet fear their parents will abandon them (psychologically if not physically) as they become more grown-up. Parents may inadvertently feed these fears by talking about how adorable the adolescent was as a baby, or how much fun they had when he was a small boy. Adolescents need to be reassured that nothing—neither their growing maturity, their moods, their misbehavior, nor your anger at something they have done—can shake your basic commitment to them. This is what Rogers meant by *unconditional* positive regard.

There is a difference, though, between showing that you care and that you want to understand and indulging the adolescent's every wish. As long as you maintain your authority, you can't be too loving. How can you remain close?

• *Spend time together.* Parents often misinterpret the adolescent's heightened interest in friends as *dis*interest in the family. They assume that a 14-year-old couldn't care less about going bowling with Dad, shopping with Mom, or on a family picnic. In fact, studies show that most teenagers would like to spend *more*, not less, time with their parents than they do now. Time together can mean going to a special event, sharing an activity you both enjoy, getting a job done together, or just spending time at home, with no particular plans. (Watching TV side by side doesn't count.)

• *Spend time alone together.* To get to know the teenager your child is becoming, you also need to spend time with her individually, one-to-one. When you and your spouse are both present, the teenager tends to be ignored; when other children are around, they compete for your attention.

• *Talk about the teenager's interests and concerns.* One thing almost all teenagers like to do is talk. If you show *genuine* interest in what is happening in your teenager's life, and what he thinks about issues and events, he is much more likely to open up. If you merely go through the motions—a routine "How was your day?" or "That's very interesting, dear" as you open the newspaper—he'll know. Too often parent-teenager conversations focus on household chores, schedules, grooming, and other mundane subjects. "When are you going to clean your room?" "What time do you have to be at practice?" and "Stop picking your face" are hardly conversation starters.

CONVERSATIONS TEENS CRAVE

When educational psychologist Torey Hayden asked several hundred young people what they really wished they could talk about with their parents, they named eight topics.

- *Family matters.* Adolescents want to be in on decisions that affect the whole family (like moving and vacations) as well as decisions that affect them (like allowance, curfew, rules). If there is a problem in the family (money problems, job pressures, an impending divorce, a serious illness), they want to know about it.
- *Controversial issues.* Adolescents are full of questions. Is it ever right to tell a lie? What does sex feel like? What do people mean when they say drugs make you high? What does *homo* mean? They wish their parents would talk with them about these controversial subjects instead of saying "You're too young" or "It's too complicated to explain."
- *Emotional issues.* Adolescents would like to know how their parents really feel about things. And they would like their parents to tell them "I love you" more often than most do.
- *The big whys.* Why do people go to war? Why does God let people go hungry? On the verge of philosophical thinking, adolescents wish their parents would talk about the big questions.
- *The future.* Children want to know what it's like to be a teenager, and teenagers want to talk about college and careers.
- *Current affairs.* Adolescents are often more aware of, and concerned about, current events than parents realize. When something happens in the world or in their community, they want to talk about it.
- *Personal interests.* Adolescents wish their parents would show more interest in them—in their sports, hobbies, and friends.
- *Parents themselves.* Adolescents want to know more about what their parents were like at their age. They particularly like stories that reveal their parents' emotional side and human frailties.

- *Share your own feelings and concerns.* One way to help your child become an adult is to let her into your world. This doesn't mean that you and your adolescent should become "pals"; she still needs you as a parent. It's not appropriate to dump all of your problems with your mother, your marriage, and your boss onto her lap. What it does mean is letting her see that you are a person with feelings, hopes, dreams, frustrations, and disappointments.

Knowing that you are not always sure of yourself makes adulthood seem a less formidable goal.

• *Trust your child.* Many parents enter upon their child's adolescence expecting their child to act up and their relationship to deteriorate. These parents are looking for trouble, and often find it. If you accuse your daughter of being promiscuous because she dates a lot, she may decide, Why not? If you constantly tell your son that his friends are a bunch of good-for-nothings who are going to get him into trouble, he'll stop bringing friends home. Instead of suspecting the worst, assume the best. When something goes wrong, believe that your child had good intentions.

• *Treat your child with respect.* Most adults would not dream of belittling, humiliating, or bullying (verbally or physically) another adult. But many of the same adults think nothing of treating their adolescent child like a nonperson. One of the authors was staying with friends she hadn't seen since high school. The occasion was the twenty-fifth reunion of their high-school class. When the class party ended at 2 A.M., three couples came back to the house for a last beer and found the refrigerator empty. The host stormed upstairs, dragged his sleeping 17-year-old son out of bed, marched him downstairs, and in front of everyone, pushed him toward the cellar stairs with a command that he get two six-packs from the downstairs refrigerator. The next morning the father learned that several of his neighbors had stopped by for a swim and helped themselves to the last beers. Would he have stormed into their house at 2 A.M. and demanded that they replace the beer? Never. Did he apologize to his son? No. Adolescents deserve the same civility their parents routinely extend to total strangers.

• *Be supportive.* When you're struggling with adult-sized problems, it's easy to see the teenager's problems as trivial. "You don't know what trouble is. . . ." Don't let hindsight make you insensitive. As an adult, you know that you're not the smartest person in the world, but that you have other qualities (persistence, humor, imagination) that pull you through. You know that on occasion you've been positively rotten to a close friend, or he to you, but that the two of you worked it out. You enjoy the friends you have, and don't worry about being popular. You don't like getting bald, but you don't fret about it day and night either. The teenager who just got a *D* on an algebra test after years of *A*s in arithmetic, whose best friend won't talk to him, or who is the last one of his friends who doesn't shave doesn't have your experience and sense of proportion. He may feel it *is* the end of the world. Let the adolescent know you understand how much it hurts.

• *Don't be alienated by gender.* When their child begins to look like a man or woman, parents tend to slip into sex stereotypes. Fathers often become distant with their adolescent daughters. They feel awkward about expressing affection to someone who is beginning to look sexy. They can't imagine that their daughter still wants to throw around a football or go on a weekend fishing trip. Daughters feel hurt and rejected by their withdrawal. Mothers often worry that they won't have anything in common with their adolescent sons and expect the father to take over for them. Gender shouldn't determine how you relate to your child: She is still her father's daughter, and he, his mother's son.

When parents back off, because they think the adolescent doesn't want or need their affection any more, teenagers feel abandoned. When they crack down, because they expect adolescents to act up, teenagers feel abused. Trite as it may sound, love is the most important thing you can give your adolescent. But love alone is not enough.

Set Clear, Reasoned Limits

The belief that adolescents rebel against any and all attempts to control them is a myth. In fact, the majority of adolescents feel that their parents are reasonable and patient with them most of the time. More than half admit, "When my parents are strict, I feel that they are right, even if I get angry."

What causes adolescents to rebel is not the assertion of authority but the *arbitrary* use of power, with little explanation of the rules and no involvement in decision-making. "Do it because I say so" simply doesn't work with adolescents. If you insist on laying down the law—no ifs, ands, or buts—the adolescent will continue to nag and whine (if you're lucky) or go ahead and do what he wants to do behind your back (if you're not).

When parents show respect for their teenager's point of view, are willing to discuss rules and regulations, and explain why they have to insist on this or forbid that, the adolescent is much less likely to rebel. She may not always *like* your final decision. But if she sees that you have thought about her point of view and have good reasons for saying no, she will at least see you as fair. Studies show that young people whose parents are willing to engage in discussion with them are more affectionate and respectful, and more likely to say they want to be like their parents, than are young people whose parents insist on always being right.

Involving the adolescent in decisions doesn't mean that you are giving up your authority. It means acknowledging that the teeanger is growing up and has the right to participate in decisions that affect *his* or *her* life.

Where to Draw the Line   There are times, however, when you have to draw the line. Parents and adolescents should be clear about which family rules are negotiable and which are not.

Issues that relate to *physical and emotional safety* and to *deeply held family values* fall into the category of non-negotiable rules. These are areas in which parents should not—indeed, must not —allow adolescents to make decisions for themselves. Some examples are: "You're not allowed to go to parties when there is no adult in the house"; "No riding in a car with a driver who is drinking"; and, if your family is religious, "You are expected to go to church or temple."

Adolescents may challenge these rules, but they are much more likely to comply with them if you limit non-negotiable rules to issues that really matter; you have solid, logical reasons for these rules and are willing to explain your reasons whenever you are asked; and you are willing to negotiate some of these rules, such as attending unchaperoned parties, as the adolescent becomes older and more mature.

When to Be Flexible   Issues relating to household responsibilities and personal behavior should be worked out by adolescents and their parents together, taking into account the needs and desires of both. For example, how the adolescent keeps her room, how she dresses, what time she is expected home, when she does her homework, how much time she spends on the phone, and when she'll be allowed to use the family car should be negotiable. None of these are matters of life and death. But unless you and the adolescent reach an understanding, you may find yourself constantly quarreling. (We discuss techniques for resolving conflicts in chapter 2.)

One mistake we all sometimes make is to confuse behavior with values. Suppose religion is important to your family: You are as concerned about your son's spiritual development as you are about his physical well-being. When he complains about going to church with the family every Sunday, you get angry. His resistance feels like an attack on *you*. Your first reaction is "Going to church is not open for discussion." He complies with your command but goes out of his way to let everyone see how disinterested he is in the service. If you take the time to discuss the issue with him, you may find he isn't rejecting your values at all. The reason for his complaints may be that Sunday is the only day in the week when he can sleep late (he has to be at work at 8:30 on Saturday mornings), so that the problem can be resolved by attending the 11 A.M. service. He may prefer to sit with his friends rather than with his family. (Aren't you glad he has friends who belong to your church and whose families share your religious values?) Or he may want to attend another church that has a more active youth program or a special choir—that is, he wants to be more involved in religion, not less involved. Of course, he may be questioning the value of organized religion, in which case you might ask him to speak with your minister. The minister might recommend that, for a time, your son substitute volunteer work in the church's program for the homeless for church attendance The point is that even non-negotiable rules should be open to discussion.

On one level, the goal of discussion and negotiation is to arrive at rules that you, the adolescent, and the rest of your family can live with. On another, the goal is to teach the adolescent responsibility for his own behavior and consideration for others.

Balance Control with Independence

While it is not possible to give adolescents too much love and support, it is possible to be too controlling. Adolescents need freedom as well as direction. They want to experiment with new looks, try on new feelings, and practice being themselves, *without your help*.

• *How much control is too much?* Reflexively declaring "No!" every time your teenagers ask for more autonomy, without taking time to find out what he really wants and why, invites rebellion. Control is overly restrictive when it does not take into account the adolescent's age, needs, and capabilities. A 16-year-old should not be subject to the same parental controls as a 13-year-old, and a mature 13-year-old deserves more privileges than one who shows poor judgment and little self-control. When you insist on rules that were established years earlier, you are being unreasonable and arbitrary. Because the adolescent is constantly changing, your expectations have to be revised regularly.

• *Grant freedom in stages.* The ultimate goal of the parent-adolescent partnership is autonomy. But you wouldn't hand your daughter the keys to the car on her sixteenth birthday and wish her "Bon voyage," even if the state allowed this. Rather, you see that she takes Driver's Ed, gets her learner's permit, and practices driving with an adult. Even after she's gotten her license, you wait to see how she handles short drives in the afternoon before you permit her to drive at night or take a 500-mile trip on superhighways. The same principle applies to other adult privileges. Autonomy should be granted gradually, in stages. With clothes, you might start by allowing children to choose which sneakers and what type of shirts they want to buy; progress to letting them make specific purchases by themselves but making sure they check with you before they remove the price tags; and end by giving them a clothes allowance to spend as they like. Your child should have a number of experiences being home alone in the afternoon before you dismiss baby-sitters at night.

• *Tie privileges to responsibilities.* Autonomy does not mean a "free ride." Adolescents need to learn that privileges carry responsibilities. If your son wants to use the family car, you should expect him to refill the gas tank before he comes home and to check the oil and tires periodically. You might give him the keys on Saturday nights in exchange for his washing the car and helping to keep the garage in order. If your daughter wants to have some friends over when you're going out, she should be responsible for enforcing family rules (no alcohol or drugs, no smoking, no crashers, no mess left for you to clean up).

• *Stand back.* When parents know that their adolescent is making a mistake, the temptation to intervene is strong. But unless health and safety are at stake, try to resist. Adolescents need to learn from their own mistakes. When you are tempted to take charge, ask yourself "What would happen if I didn't interfere?" Even if the consequences are serious (your son's bike will be stolen if he keeps forgetting to lock it; your daughter will get a *D* if she turns in another paper late), allow them to happen. When you take charge, you are preventing your adolescent from developing and exercising a sense of personal responsibility.

Suppose your daughter is chronically late for school. You are tired of talking the bus driver into waiting day after day. You could drag her out of bed, march her to the breakfast table, and threaten to ground her all day Saturday if she's late one more time. When you do ground her, she will be angry and resentful and look for a way to punish you back (like sulking all day or refusing to do chores). All she has learned is that you can make her weekend miserable. Instead, why not knock on her door at 7, give her a fifteen-minute warning, but let her be late and bear the consequences: no breakfast, walking to school, paying carfare out of her allowance, being shut out of her first class or kept after school. Let her "suffer," but don't rub it in. Autonomy also means the right to make mistakes occasionally, without being humiliated and belittled by your parents ("Didn't I tell you?").

Over the course of adolescence, the situations in which you should stand back will increase, and those in which you must step in, decrease.

Be Firm and Fair

Every adolescent breaks the rules on occasion. How should parents respond?

• *Don't overreact.* You've turned out the lights and are heading upstairs to bed when your 16-year-old son stumbles in the door. It's obvious he's drunk. Your 13-year-old daughter is not allowed to have a boy in the apartment when neither you nor your spouse is home. You leave work early one day and find her alone with Tom. Don't explode. Wait to hear their side of the story. There may be a perfectly reasonable explanation: He didn't know the punch was spiked. She and Tom are working on a joint school project and the library closed early. Unless the adolescent has a history of getting into trouble, presume innocence until you discover otherwise.

• *Punishment is not the only answer.* As one child put it, "A punishment is something a parent does to you. A consequence is something you do to yourself." Punishment is one of the *least* effective means of getting an adolescent to cooperate.

Often the best course is to stand back and let adolescents suffer the natural consequences of their behavior (a hangover, her friends' teasing her about Tom, or whatever the outcome may be).

Another alternative to punishment is simply to say "I'm disappointed and don't want this to happen again." Adolescents who have good relationships with their parents want their approval and generally try to avoid letting them down. Suppose your daughter took some friends for a ride in the family car when she only had her learner's permit. Telling her how you feel about what she did can be more effective than taking away her permit, postponing her driver's test, or some other concrete punishment. We're not suggesting that parents try to make the adolescent feel guilty: "I've always trusted you; how could you do something like this?" But express your displeasure with the act, not with the adolescent as a person: "I'm very angry that you drove before you had your license; it was a foolish, dangerous thing to do."

A third alternative to imposing a punishment is to ask the adolescent what he thinks the consequences of his misbehavior should be. The morning after your son comes home drunk, have a talk about drinking in moderation. If he agrees that he will not have more than one drink or one or two beers in the future, and will not drink at all when he is driving, and two weeks later comes home drunk again, point out that he has broken your agreement and ask him what he thinks would be a fair consequence. Parents who use this approach often find that adolescents impose stiffer penalties on themselves than their parents would. You might be thinking of grounding him for a week; he may propose that he not be allowed to go to parties for the next month. The severity of the penalty is not as significant as the fact that he imposes it on himself. When parents unilaterally decide on a penalty, the adolescent's contrition will be mixed with resentment. When adolescents decide on their own penalty, they can't cry "unfair."

• *Take action when you must.* When the adolescent's misbehavior is habitual or dangerous, however, you should take action. Discuss with the adolescent the reasons why you can't permit this behavior and try to work out an agreement. If you can't agree, let your child know in advance what the penalty for breaking the rules will be.

The penalty should "fit the crime." If the adolescent stays out beyond curfew again, she will be grounded; if she refuses to follow rules about car safety, she won't be allowed to use the car; if she uses money in ways you have forbidden (going to a disco you have declared off limits), you will cut back her allowance; if she repeatedly fails to do her household chores, you will give her additional chores; and so on.

Save stiff penalties for major violations. When you bring out the heavy artillery for such minor infractions as forgetting to mow the lawn, you lose credibility. The penalty for drinking and driving should be more severe than that for staying out beyond curfew; the penalty for coming in late more painful than that for failing to clean up a bedroom. Working out a schedule of punishments in advance encourages teenagers to think about the seriousness of different acts.

• *Never use physical punishment,* no matter what the teenager has done. Study after study has shown that violence begets violence. Smacking your daughter in the face or hurling your son against the wall isn't discipline, it's child abuse, even if the adolescent is as big as you are, or bigger. Physical punishment is not only wrong, it's counterproductive. Research shows that beatings do not stop undesirable behavior; on the contrary, they promote adolescent rebellion and aggression. Verbal abuse—calling adolescents names, denouncing them as no good—has similar effects. Parents who resort to these tactics are not helping, they are contributing to the problem.

Postpone discussions when you or the adolescent are angry. When emotions are boiling over, someone is bound to get hurt, psychologically if not physically. Let the adolescent know how you feel ("I'm too angry to talk right now"), but put off discussion and decisions until both of you have calmed down. If you lose control once, don't try to justify your behavior but apologize: "I never should have hit you; it was wrong; I'm sorry; it will never happen again." If you or your adolescent regularly lose control, your family needs professional help. (See chapter 2.)

• *Be consistent.* This means

Consistent in enforcement. Don't enforce a rule one time but let it slide the next time because you're tired or you want to avoid a confrontation. When you're not consistent, the adolescent will see any discipline as arbitrary.

Consistent with your spouse. If you and your partner disagree about what you should expect from the adolescent, work out your differences in private and present a united front to the child. Don't let the adolescent play one of you against the other.

Consistent with your values and beliefs. If you stress the importance of honesty, don't blow up when your son is being honest and tells you that he cut school for three days in a row. Sit down and talk about why he cut school and what the two of you can do to solve the problem. (If he cuts school and doesn't tell you—you get a call from the school—that's another matter.)

Consistent in the face of pressure from your child. All adolescents test the limits on occasion. They may complain that everybody else's parents are more liberal, accuse you of picking on them, and whine and sulk when you don't give in. Sometimes parents do give in because, consciously or unconsciously, they are afraid their adolescent won't like them if they stick to their principles. But what adolescents don't like is the *arbitrary* use of power. Don't be afraid to be unpopular for a day or two.

Accept Your Adolescent as an Individual

Adolescents are as individually variable as any other age-group in our society. Parents who accept stereotypes about teenagers and apply them to their own child, regardless of that child's particular needs and capabilities, end up behaving in stereotypical ways themselves. One common pattern is for parents who have had an easy-going relationship with their child to suddenly, without provocation, clamp down when that child becomes an adolescent. Why? Because they expect adolescence to be trouble. Not surprisingly, the adolescent sees this change in the parent's behavior as unfair. The parents' hypervigilance has the opposite effect of what they intended: The adolescent rebels, and the parents' assumption that all teenagers are rebellious is confirmed.

This vicious cycle can be avoided if you

• *Treat your child as your child, not as a stereotypical adolescent.* The 13-year-old who is grinding out her own version of a rock video in front of her mirror is the same person who tore her clothes and skinned her knees practicing stunts on her bike five years ago. Puberty doesn't cause changes in personality. If your daughter was a show-off in elementary school, she will be a show-off in high school, though in different ways. If she pushed herself too hard as a child, she will probably do the same as an adolescent. If she was timid and needed a lot of support and encouragement at 8, she will still need stroking at 18. If she was gregarious as a child, she will be outgoing as an adolescent. There may be temporary disruptions as the adolescent adjusts to new situations—junior high, dating, and the like. But her basic orientation toward people and new experiences will not change very much.

If you and your child have learned to adapt to one another's personalities in childhood, you will probably work well together in adolescence. If your child was difficult during the elementary-school years, your problems won't go away during adolescence, and may get worse. Most of the teenagers who fit the stereotype of a "rebel without a cause" did not become that way at puberty; they were difficult all along.

• *Treat your child as a person, not as a member of one or the other gender.* Many parents today want their children to escape the sex stereotypes of the past: They encourage boys to be sensitive and artistic and girls to excel in math and competitive sports. When their children become adolescents, however, parents' neutrality fades. Shared household tasks are now assigned according to gender: "Young men" aren't expected to help set and clear the table, and "young ladies" are excused from sweaty, dirty yardwork and car repairs. The message? Males can expect to be waited on; girls should expect to be provided for. If the adolescent is a boy, parents tend to become more permissive; if the adolescent is a girl, they tend to become more controlling. This is unfair to both sexes.

• *Let your child be the teenager he or she wants to be, not the adolescent you were or wish you had been.* Parents see their children as extensions of themselves, at all ages. But the tendency to live vicariously through your offspring is heightened in adolescence. One reason is that it is easier for adults to remember their own adolescence ("When I was your age . . ."); another, that parents tend to see the choices the adolescent makes now as irrevocable ("If you don't get into the orchestra now, you'll never become a musician").

Looking back as parents, it is easy to see how we could have made better choices, seized more opportunities, taken better care of our bodies, and put our heart in the right place. We are nostalgic, not so much for adolescence as we experienced it, but for how we would relive our youth with what we know now. The expression "Youth is wasted on the young" captures this feeling. It's tempting to see your child's adolescence as *your* second chance. But it's unfair to expect an adolescent to behave as you would, given your experience and maturity.

Adolescents have the right to be themselves. The fact that you were the belle of the ball, the captain of the lacrosse team, the president of your senior class, Phi Beta Kappa, or a political activist doesn't mean that your teenager will be or should be the same. Likewise, the fact that you were a wallflower, uncoordinated, and a *C* student shouldn't mean that you push your child to be everything you were not. Teenagers need to develop their own strengths and pursue their own interests. If you and your adolescent share a passion for baseball or Bach, so much the better. If your teenager finds baseball a drag and Bach a bore, don't take this as a rejection of who you are.

• *Let your child be him- or herself, not a copy of (or compensation for) an older brother or sister.* It's unrealistic to expect Johnny to follow in Billy's footsteps, or Susan to make up for all of Carolyn's faults. When adolescents feel they are constantly being compared to someone else (a sibling, the teenager across the street, the way you were, an ideal, a stereotype), their self-confidence drops. Whether the comparisons are negative ("Why can't you be more like Rachel?") or positive ("If I had had your talent . . ."), the underlying message is that the adolescent is loved for measuring up to some arbitrary standard, not for being him- or herself.

CHAPTER 2

Family Communication and Problem-Solving

*F*ew parents are totally prepared for the onset of adolescence. The idea that your child doesn't want you to have all the answers any more can be hard to accept. You understand that she doesn't need you to run her life or solve her problems, but you worry that she will make the wrong decisions, get mixed up with the wrong people, and throw her youth and talent away. Quarrels about family rules, household chores, personal habits, friends (yours and hers), the telephone, the TV, money, and a host of other large and small issues are all but inevitable. At times, you will get on each other's nerves. Even an "easy" teenager will sometimes do things that seem foolish, thoughtless, and hurtful.

You can't avoid disagreements, but you can prevent them from damaging your relationship with the adolescent. Everyday hassles become major problems when family members talk *at* one another instead of communicating *with* one another, avoid or escalate conflict instead of working out constructive ways of resolving disagreements, and fail to get professional help when they need it. In this chapter we introduce techniques for improving communication and resolving conflict and tell you how to get professional help if the need arises.

COMMUNICATION

All of us know instinctively that communication is an essential part of a healthy relationship. In our business and social lives, we try to be careful about what we say and how we say it. Within our families, however, we sometimes forget.

Obstacles to Communication

The first step toward establishing good communication within the family is reducing negatives. Without realizing it, parents sometimes speak to adolescents in ways that are all but guaranteed to cut off communication. In his classic book *People Skills,* Robert Bolton calls these *roadblocks.* Some of the most common roadblocks to communication are

• *Criticism and ridicule.* Negative evaluations of the listener are communication-killers. Labeling ("You *jerk,*" "When are you going to stop being such a *whiner?*" "Just like a *teenager*"), personal attacks ("The trouble with you is you're lazy," "You look ridiculous"), sarcasm ("That's a great [meaning terrible] idea," "Thanks a lot [for nothing]"), and put-downs ("Why don't you watch where you're going?" "When I want your opinion, I'll ask for it," "You're acting like a child") all fall into this category. Parents sometimes feel that if they do not criticize their child, their child will never learn. Criticism doesn't make people want to change; it makes them defensive.

• *Giving too many orders or too much advice.* Commands ("Do it now!" "Turn that off!" "How many times have I told you not to do that?"), threats ("Do it now, or else!" "Don't make me lose my temper," "Wait till your father hears about this!"), and sermons (statements that begin with "You should/should not") are obvious turn-offs, especially to adolescents who are struggling for autonomy. So is unsolicited advice. When you tell adolescents "If I were you, I'd do X, Y, or Z" or "What you should do is . . . ," you are communicating that they aren't capable of solving their own problems.

• *Treating the adolescent's problems lightly.* When parents attempt to reassure the adolescent ("Cheer up, things will look better tomorrow," "Don't worry, I'm sure it will all work out for the best"), or to divert him ("There's no point dwelling on it," "You think you have it tough, when I was your age . . ."), they may have the best of intentions, but the underlying message is that the adolescent's worries are trivial.

Instead of promoting communication, put-downs, orders, and blithe reassurance trigger defensiveness, resistance, and resentment and undermine self-esteem. A good rule is to avoid saying things to your adolescent that you would not say to another adult.

Saying What You Mean

It is surprising how often parents don't speak their minds. Especially when they are frustrated or angry, parents tend to read meaning into the adolescent's behavior rather than simply saying how they feel.

Saying how you feel—"*I* get frustrated/angry/upset when . . ."
—is much more effective with adolescents than shaming and blaming—"*You* never think of anyone but yourself." The first statement gives the adolescent the option of changing her behavior so that you won't feel that way again. Because you aren't imposing a solution, the adolescent is less likely to feel that going along with you is giving in. She can change her behavior without losing face. The second statement, in contrast, backs her into a corner where she has only two choices: knuckling under or fighting back. Saying how you feel also closes off rebuttals. The adolescent can argue with a statement about her motives and intentions: "I *do* care what you and Dad think." But you are the expert on your feelings: She may think your reaction is crazy or illogical, but she cannot deny what you are feeling.

Psychologists call these *I-messages* and *you-messages*. I-messages are nonjudgmental statements of how we feel about a particular action or situation. You-messages are evaluations of the other person's motives, attitudes, or character.

There is a simple formula for I-messages: **When you** _____ [describe the behavior nonjudgmentally], **I feel** _____[disclose your feelings], **because** _____[clarify the effect of this behavior on your life].

I-MESSAGES VS. YOU-MESSAGES

Situation: The teenager talks on the phone for an hour.

You-message: "You never think of anyone but yourself."
I-message: "When you stay on the phone for an hour [behavior], I feel frustrated [feeling], because nobody else can get through [effect]."

Situation: The teenager makes a snack in the afternoon and does not clean up afterward.

You-message: "You're not doing your share."
I-message: "When you don't clean up the kitchen after a snack [behavior], I get annoyed [feeling], because it makes extra work for me [effect]."

Situation: The teenager comes home an hour after curfew.

You-message: "You are trying to make me angry."
I-message: "When you don't come home by curfew [behavior], I get upset [feeling], because I lose sleep worrying that you might have had an accident [effect]."

In describing the behavior that bothers you, try to be *specific:* "When you leave your clothes on the floor" rather than a fuzzy "When your room is a total mess." *Be objective* and avoid character attacks ("You're a slob") and generalizations ("You always/constantly/never"). *Be brief.* If you say to your son "I feel angry when you get so wrapped up in a football game that you forget about the family and come home late and all dirty," it's hard for him to know what is making you angry. Are you saying that you don't want him to play football or that you don't want him to care so much about sports? That you don't want him to spend so much time with his friends or that you want the family to be more involved in the games? (What does "remember your family" mean?) That you object to his being late? Or that you wish he'd clean up before he comes to the table (which would make him later)? You're much more likely to get your message across if you stick to one issue at a time. With practice, you should be able to fit an I-message into one sentence.

In disclosing your feelings, try to use a word that accurately reflects your inner experience: *Angry* is stronger than *annoyed*; *upset* is different from *frustrated*; *worried* and *afraid* carry different messages. Parents tend to overuse *angry*. When the adolescent forgets to tell you that he is spending the night with a friend, your first reaction is likely to be fear. When your fear is relieved, you get angry because he caused you such a fright. The adolescent is more likely to see your point of view when you are able to communicate your first reaction: "I feel frightened when I don't know where you are."

In describing effects, be as concrete as you can. Focus on the way the adolescent's behavior cost you money, damaged your possessions, wasted your time, caused you extra work, or interfered with your activities. Adolescents are much more likely to change their behavior if they can *see* that something they did interfered with your legitimate rights.

Using a formula to communicate with your child might seem awkward at first. Indeed, the adolescent may well pick up on what you are doing and ask you to stop "psychologizing." But if you persist, saying what you mean will become more and more natural. Understanding in your family will increase, and fewer little issues will escalate into major battles.

Active Listening

Getting your message across is only one side of communication; the other side is listening.

Adolescents sometimes say words to the effect that "My friends listen to me, but my parents only hear me talk." Often they are right. Familiarity breeds inattention. Typically, family members are so convinced they know what another family member is going to say that they don't bother to listen. They finish the speaker's sentences, give an answer before they've heard the question, or just tune out. Other times they may hear what the person is saying but pay little attention to what the person is feeling.

Listening is not a passive process but an active one. How can parents be better listeners with their adolescents?

• *Pay attention.* You can't really listen to the adolescent if you're cooking dinner, flipping through the newspaper, or washing the car at the same time. Genuine listening requires stopping other activities, tuning out other thoughts, giving the speaker your full attention, and showing that you are interested. Put the paper down, lean forward, establish eye contact, and use nods and brief phrases ("Mmm-hmmm," "Really?" "Then what happened?" "I see," "I hear you," "What a drag!") to let the adolescent know you are with him. If you can't really listen now, suggest another time when you can. "I want to hear about it, but I'm in a rush. Can we talk after dinner?"

· *Listen with your eyes and your ears.* Words tell only half the story. To learn how the adolescent feels about what he is saying, and what he is letting slip between the lines, you have to pay attention to body language. The adolescent may say he doesn't care, but his downcast eyes and slumped posture tell you otherwise. When you get different messages from his words and his body language, believe the body language.

· *Don't interrupt with questions and comments.* Like adults, adolescents need to sound off. When they are angry or upset, they don't want advice, they want understanding. Don't jump in when you think you get the gist of what your child is saying. Let her speak her piece. When she pauses, let her know you are still there, but try to hold your tongue. Most of us are uncomfortable with silence; we feel a compulsive need to keep the conversation going. But attentive silence allows the speaker to collect her thoughts. It can nudge the adolescent to go deeper into herself and follow up her expression of what she thinks she should feel with what she really feels.

· *Rephrase the adolescent's comments in your own words.* Your first response to your adolescent should be to briefly rephrase what he said in your own words. "It sounds like you're not sure whether to try out for the play." "You're angry at Sammy because he left you out." "So now you're confused." Psychologists call this *reflective listening.* Rephrasing the adolescent's message serves three purposes: It allows you to check on whether you understand your child correctly; it tells him that you are paying attention and trying to understand; and it allows him to "rehear" what he has communicated.

The goal of active listening is to understand another person's point of view, to see things through that person's eyes, to "walk a mile in his shoes," and to share his feelings. This doesn't mean that you and your adolescent will always agree. You won't. But when family members stop assuming and start listening, the climate for communication in your home will improve.

"But My Teenager Won't Talk to Me"

One common complaint among parents is that their child stops talking to them during adolescence. Adolescents do have a greater need for privacy than small children do. Having thoughts and feelings of their own is part of becoming independent. There are times when they don't want to talk about it because they want to work it out for themselves, whatever "it" may be. But other times the adolescent's silence is a sign that the wires of communication in your family are somehow crossed. What can you do?

Listen to what you say and how you say it. Your adolescent comes home from school looking blue. How do you respond? Are you critical? ("What did you do this time?") Do you offer empty reassurances? ("This time next week you won't even remember what happened today.") Are you too quick to give advice? ("Moping around won't help; why don't you go jogging?") All of these responses close the door to communication. They make it sound as if you think you have all the answers without knowing the questions.

You can open the door by commenting on the adolescent's body language ("Looks like you had a bad day" or "Your face is beaming") and inviting her to tell you more ("Want to talk about it?" "I'd like to hear about it," or "What's on your mind?") Use eye contact and an involved posture to show that you are interested, and silence to give her time to decide whether she wants to talk or not. If she seems to be hesitant—doesn't speak up, but doesn't leave the room either—let her know you understand her ambivalence: "It must be pretty hard to talk about." If her response to your invitation of "Feel like talking?" is "Not really," don't push ("You know you can always talk to me," "It's better to get it off your chest," and the like). The adolescent has a right to keep her thoughts and her problems to herself. Compelling her to talk is an invasion of privacy, a denial of her individuality and separateness. Let her know you're there if she wants you. If you are just beginning to work on communication skills, it will take some time to build mutual trust.

In some families, the problem is not that family members don't trust one another to listen, but that they are all so busy there is hardly ever time for a good heart-to-heart talk. If this is the case in your family, you need to create times when you are available. Breakfast if you are all early risers, the dinner hour for issues that concern the whole family, and bedtime are obvious choices. The fact that your adolescent is growing up doesn't mean he won't appreciate your stopping by his room to see how things are going before lights out. But be sure to knock first.

RESOLVING CONFLICTS

Conflict is part of life. It's impossible for people to live or work together without ever experiencing differences in values, opinions, desires, needs, and habits. Everyone is aware of the negative aspects of conflict, but we tend to forget the positive ones. Conflict prods us into expressing, rather than suppressing, our feelings. It shocks us out of our passivity, forcing us to think about what we have taken for granted, to change our customary ways of doing things, and to invent solutions to our problems. To go through life avoiding conflict is to confine oneself to superficial relationships and stagnation. Conflict is, in Bolton's words, "a dangerous opportunity."

Conflict occurs when

- One family member feels that others are threatening his or her values, perceptions, life-style, sense of fairness, or "territory."
- Family members agree on the final goal but disagree on how to arrive at that point.
- There is not enough of something to go around. The "something" may be tangible—money, space, telephones—or intangible—time, attention, affection.
- Communication among family members has broken down.

For one or more of these reasons, you have reached an impasse. Unless you get beyond that impasse, hostility and resentment are likely to build, and nit-picking, teasing, criticism, yelling, avoidance of one another, and stony silences will increase.

Conflict can improve and invigorate family relationships by helping family members to understand one another better and to be more tolerant of their individual differences, leading them to clarify issues and ideas in a way that clears the air, and forcing them to redefine their goals or set new goals that are more satisfactory to everyone. When conflicts are resolved in a positive way, everyone wins.

Conflict harms family relationships when it takes the form of personality attacks and power struggles. Negative conflict leads to resentment and hostility; causes confusion, insecurity, and diminished self-esteem; and makes productive, rational discussion of issues and behavior in the future difficult, if not impossible. When family members are at war, nobody wins.

Your goal as a parent should be to resolve conflicts in a positive way, not to avoid or control them. Before you reject as wishful thinking the idea that conflicts can be useful, read what psychologists have learned from studying conflict in all kinds of settings, including families.

No-Win Solutions

The most common ways parents attempt to resolve conflicts with their adolescents are cracking down, giving in, avoiding the problem, and compromise. Although each of these strategies has its uses, each also has drawbacks. There is an alternative: collaboration, which we will discuss shortly. First let's look at the others.

One way to end an argument with an adolescent is to crack down. Like a military officer pulling rank, parents lay down the law. When parents refuse to consider the adolescent's needs and desires and/or refuse to let her participate in the decision-making process, she is not going to be highly motivated to make the solution work. To the contrary, domination fosters resentment. It should be used only in emergencies, when quick, decisive action is vital (and parents do know best).

A second way to end conflict is to give in to the adolescent's wishes. Giving in or accommodation is appropriate when parents realize that the adolescent was right and they were wrong: It shows the adolescent that they are willing to listen and to learn, and that they are reasonable. Accommodation is also appropriate when the issue is trivial to the parents but not to the adolescent (for example, how your son dresses for a party). But it shouldn't become a habit. As one psychologist noted, "If you want to hate your child, just let him win all the time. That's a sure formula."

Avoidance is also common: Parents do everything they can to escape a confrontation with the adolescent. When a problem comes up, they change the subject, suggest the family member is making mountains out of molehills, or simply withdraw. Avoidance is useful when the issue is trivial (the adolescent forgot a minor chore), when parties to a conflict are under too much stress to deal with the issue now (the adolescent has an exam the next day), or when they simply need time to cool down. But avoidance doesn't heal wounds; it allows them to fester.

The fourth strategy is compromise: Parents and the adolescent meet each other halfway. Most of us were taught that compromise is the best solution to conflict. This is only partly true. Compromise is useful when the issue is not worth much time and effort (where to eat dinner tonight). It's also useful when time pressures force a quick solution (for example, when you're expecting a long-distance call, the adolescent needs to call a friend, and you compromise by limiting his call to five minutes). But compromise is not a lasting solution to serious differences. Neither party's needs are fully met: Both settle for less than they want.

The problem with all these responses is that they don't resolve the conflict. The issue is left up in the air, and needs and feelings are pushed under the rug. Moreover, with each of these strategies somebody loses. With cracking down, it's the adolescent; with giving in, it's the parent; with avoidance, it's both. Although compromise is preferable to the other three, both parties give up something (what Bolton calls a mini-lose/mini-lose outcome). There is an alternative to these no-win approaches.

Collaborative Problem-solving

The goal of collaborative problem-solving is to find a win/win solution that satisfies everyone. This approach takes more time and energy than the others we have described. It requires the unhappy family members to confront one another, which isn't always pleasant. But in most cases it minimizes hostility and hurt feelings and maximizes the chances that you will truly resolve the issue.

There are six basic steps to collaborative problem-solving. Again, the formula may seem awkward at first, but after you've used it several times it will begin to seem more natural. This approach works best if you choose a time and place when both you and the adolescent will not be distracted, limit the discussion to a specific issue, and secure in advance the adolescent's agreement to try to work out a solution.

• *Step 1. Establish ground rules.* The ground rules for conflict resolution are essentially the rules of a fair fight. Each party agrees to treat the other party with respect—no name-calling, sarcasm, or put-downs—and to listen to the other person's point of view. Parents can set the stage by stating at the beginning their desire to be fair. Let's use the most frequent cause of conflict between parents and adolescents, the state of the adolescent's room.

MOTHER: Susan, we're arguing a lot about your room. I'd like to sit down and see if we can come up with a solution that both of us consider fair. Is this a good time to talk?

SUSAN: Yeah, I guess so.

MOTHER: I want you to understand how I feel about this, but I also want to understand how *you* feel.

SUSAN: Sure you do.

MOTHER: No sarcasm, okay? We're trying to solve this together.

SUSAN: Okay.

• *Step 2. Reach mutual understanding.* The next step is to take turns being understood. This means that each of you will have the opportunity to say what you think the real problem is and how you feel about it. It's important that you get it off your chest. But it's also important to avoid loaded words and phrases, accusations and evaluations, and to focus on the issue, not on personalities. Each of you also has the right to be understood. This is where reflective listening comes in. When you've described the problem as you see it, let the adolescent speak her piece. Then rephrase the adolescent's point of view and ask her to restate yours, so that you are sure you understand one another.

MOTHER: The way you leave your room really bothers me, because I can't get in there to vacuum and dust and it looks so sloppy. Besides, things are always getting lost . . .

SUSAN: That's not fair, how do you know things "always" get lost?

MOTHER: You're right, but I worry things will be misplaced. You were late the other morning because you couldn't find your blue sweater.

SUSAN: I suppose you never lose anything?

MOTHER: Well, you've got me there. Now tell me how you feel.

SUSAN: I don't think my room is all that bad. I know where most of my stuff is, and I don't see the point of cleaning up all the time. I get so tired of you nagging me about it.

MOTHER: Let me make sure I understand. You don't think your room is that messy, you know where to find things, and you don't like me telling you to clean up all the time.

SUSAN: Right.

MOTHER: And how do I feel about it?

SUSAN: You think my room is a disaster area, you can't clean up, and things get lost.

MOTHER: Yes, that's how I see it.

• *Step 3. Brainstorm.* The next step is for each of you to think of as many solutions to the problem as you can. The goal of brainstorming is quantity, not quality. At this stage, no idea should be rejected because it's crazy, or too expensive, or one of you thinks it is dumb. Zany ideas can reduce tension and keep creative juices flowing. Set a time limit (five minutes should be enough) and write down everything you can think of. A list of solutions to the messy room problem might include:

Susan's mother will stop bugging her about her room.

Susan will put her dirty clothes in the laundry hamper every night and make her bed every morning.

Susan will clean the room, but only when company is coming.

Susan will close the door when company comes.

Susan's mother will limit room checks to once a week.

Susan will move to an apartment over the garage.

Susan and her dad will build a wall-size storage unit so she has someplace to put all her stuff.

Susan's mom will clear some space in the hall closet for things Susan doesn't use that often (like sports gear and off-season clothes).

The family will hire a maid.

Susan will straighten, vacuum, and dust her own room.

• *Step 4. Agree to one or more solutions.* The best way to go about this is for each of you to select the options you like best. (Don't discuss each and every option; this can lead to endless, often fruitless, debate.) Then see where your interests coincide. Have you chosen any of the same options? Some give and take, or negotiation, will be necessary at this stage (Susan's mother may agree to stop nagging if Susan picks up her clothes and makes the bed daily). And you need to think through the practical consid-erations (the family can't afford a maid). But neither of you should agree to something you still find unacceptable.

• *Step 5. Write down your agreement.* This may sound excessively formal, but memory can be faulty. If either of you thinks the other has broken the agreement, you can refer to your contract.

> *Susan* will put her laundry in the hamper and make her bed each morning, straighten up once a week (not every day), and put clean clothes away promptly (the same day her mother does the laundry).

> *Mom* will stop bugging Susan about her room; clean once a week, after Susan straightens; not put things away for Susan without asking her first; and give Susan two shelves in the hall closet.

• *Step 6. Set a time for a follow-up discussion to evaluate your progress.* This is as important as the first five steps. One of you might not live up to the agreement, or the solution might not be as elegant as you thought, and you will have to work out the bugs.

This six-step formula can be applied to a variety of situations, from arguments over the adolescent's curfew to decisions about family vacations. In some cases you won't be able to reach an agreement. When it comes to health and safety, you may have to make a unilateral decision. But adolescents are far more likely to go along with you when they participate in the decision-making process and when they see that you are taking their needs and desires seriously.

GETTING PROFESSIONAL HELP

There are times when families cannot solve their problems by themselves and need professional help. Unfortunately, some peo-ple still view "seeing a shrink" as a sign that they have failed as parents. Going to a physician when your child has a persistent headache or a high fever isn't a blot on your character. What would your neighbors (and your mother-in-law) think if you ignored these symptoms? Seeking professional attention for chronic or acute behavioral or emotional problems is no different.

Knowing when a problem is beyond your capabilities is part of being a good parent. (It might help to know that you are not alone: At any given time, some 34 million Americans are receiving professional therapy or counseling.)

Other parents put off getting help because they don't know where to turn, a situation we hope to remedy.

When to Look for Help

Here are some common reasons why families with adolescents seek counseling:

- The adolescent is suffering from a severe disorder, such as depression, anorexia, drug addiction, or school phobia. Parents cannot—and should not try to—treat these problems themselves. Throughout this book we will alert you to the warning signs that a young person needs professional attention.
- You know the adolescent has a problem, but you don't know what it is. An example would be a young person who is withdrawn socially and doesn't seem to have any friends. This might be due to extreme shyness, depression, stress at school, involvement with drugs, or any number of other causes. If you don't know what the problem is, how can you help? A professional can make specific "diagnoses" and recommendations.
- You have tried to solve the problem, without success. Frequent truancy, chronic running away, or opposition to any and all authority are examples of such problems. Wise parents seek help *before* the adolescent gets into serious trouble with the authorities.
- You realize that you are part of the problem. Constant, bitter fighting among family members is a good example. It is extremely rare for one person to be the cause of chronic dissension in the family. As the saying goes, it takes two to fight. A third party—the therapist—can help you see why you are fighting and how to stop.
- When the family is under a lot of stress (for example, because of a death or serious illness in the family or because the parents are in the midst of a divorce) and one or more family members are not coping well (for example, are depressed or

drinking heavily). Therapists are trained to help individuals cope with short-term crises in healthy ways.

Recognizing that your family needs help is an important step. What then?

Finding the Right Therapist

How do you find the right therapist for your problem? Start with people whom you know and trust and who know you and your family well. If someone you are close to has been in therapy, ask whether he or she would recommend that person. Even if the therapist is not right for you, he or she may be able to make an appropriate referral. A friend who works in mental health, your family physician, your minister, or a school counselor are also good sources. These professionals will have had experience with a number of therapists and will be able to identify two or three who might work well with you. Community mental health centers and agencies are also good resources.

Many reputable therapists advertise in the Yellow Pages (under *Mental Health, Physicians—Psychiatrists, Psychologists,* or *Marriage and Family Counselors*). We don't recommend that you pick names at random from the phone book, but you might check the listings there for qualifications . . . and disqualifications (see What to Avoid, below).

What to Look For   Before you commit yourself to treatment, you should interview the therapist to determine, first, whether the person is qualified to handle your problem and, second, whether you feel comfortable with him or her. Some therapists will answer your initial questions by phone. Others will request an appointment. This doesn't mean they are evading you: Many therapists feel they can only evaluate your needs and their ability to work with you in a face-to-face meeting. Whether by phone or in person, your questions should include the following:

• Are you licensed?
• What are your educational training and background?
• What type of therapy do you offer or prefer? (What are the therapist's theories? How does he or she work with clients?)
• Do you have experience with my particular problem?
• How will I know the treatment is working?

- How often do you see clients (how many sessions per week) and how long do sessions last?
- When do you see clients? (Can the therapist accommodate your schedule?)
- What will treatment cost? (Most therapists charge a per-session fee, so the cost will depend in part on the length of treatment.)
- Will some or all of the cost be covered by my health insurance? (Have the policy with you.)

Ideally, you should talk to two or three therapists before making a decision. Their answers to your questions, and the questions they ask you, will give you a better sense of the differences in approach and personality among therapists and who makes you feel comfortable. If your personal inquiries have only produced one name, you should not be embarrassed to ask this therapist for the names of others who might be able to help you.

What to Avoid   Every profession has its share of charlatans and quacks, and the field of mental health is no exception. Some warning signs:

- The therapist makes a quick diagnosis without asking for much information from you. (No therapist can make a diagnosis over the phone; at most, the therapist might tell you to seek immediate help.)
- The therapist offers a quick or guaranteed solution to your problem.
- The therapist seems uncomfortable with questions about his or her educational background, experience, and license.
- The therapist is vague or noncommittal about fees.
- The therapist says he or she has the answer and turns down your request for additional referrals.
- The first interview includes intimate questions about sex or other matters not related to your problem.
- The therapist's ad in the Yellow Pages makes extravagant claims. (Professional ethics limit advertising to a listing of name, degree, credentials, address, and telephone number.)

Common Questions about Therapy

How do I know whether I/my family/my adolescent needs help? There is no simple answer to this question. Everyone feels blue, indecisive, discouraged, out of control, dissatisfied with their family life from time to time, including adolescents. And all families go through spells when no one seems to be getting along. Usually these feelings and quarrels pass. If they persist, the emotional pain is acute, or the fights are getting out of hand, it might be time to seek help. (We will point out warning signs at many points in this book.) The basic rule is, When in doubt, speak to someone.

Is what I say to my therapist confidential? Yes, except in two situations: When the therapist suspects that a child is being abused, physically or sexually, and when the therapist learns that someone's life is in danger (either the client or someone the client wishes harm). In these cases the therapist has a moral and legal obligation to notify appropriate authorities. Otherwise, professional ethics dictate that anything you say is strictly confidential.

Parents should know that *confidentiality applies to adolescents as well as to adults.* If your son is seeing a therapist, either individually or as part of family therapy, the therapist will not divulge anything about his private sessions to you without his consent. Many parents find this hard to accept, but it is important that the adolescent be able to trust the therapist completely. If something comes up that the therapist thinks you should know, he or she will work out a way to tell you with the adolescent.

What if the therapist recommends family therapy, but one family member will not cooperate? While it is desirable for everyone in the family to be motivated to participate in family therapy, it isn't necessary in order for the treatment to be effective. In most cases, uninterested parties later decide to come along, if only because they worry about what is being said in their absence. If you feel your family needs help and you've found someone you would like to see, make an appointment and invite everyone involved to come. If the most important actor in your family problem isn't willing or interested, go anyway. The therapist has encountered this situation many times before and will help you decide how best to deal with it.

RESOURCES

The following professional organizations publish information on getting professional help and can assist you in obtaining a list of therapists in your area.

American Psychological Association. The American Psychological Association has chapters in every state (e.g., the Wisconsin Psychological Association) and suggests that you call the local chapter for a list of referrals. The organization also publishes *A Guide to Psychological Health Services,* which contains general information about psychologists and psychotherapy. It can be obtained free of charge by writing to the Office of Public Affairs, American Psychological Association, 1200 17th Street, N.W., Washington, DC 20036.

American Psychiatric Association. Like the American Psychological Association, the American Psychiatric Association recommends that you call the chapter in your area for assistance in locating a psychiatrist nearby. These chapters are in every state and, in New York and California, in several major cities as well. They are listed in the phone book as psychiatric societies (e.g., the Pennsylvania Psychiatric Society). In addition, the organization publishes pamphlets on a variety of mental health problems, such as depression and schizophrenia. These can be obtained free of charge by writing to the Division of Public Affairs, American Psychiatric Association, 1400 K Street, N.W., Washington, DC 20005. When you write, you should specify the problem you wish to receive information about.

American Association of Marriage and Family Therapists. This organization maintains a listing of specialists organized by zip code. You may call or write to their national office for a free listing of marriage and family specialists in your area. In addition, AAMFT publishes *The Consumer's Guide to Marriage and Family Therapy,* which is also free for the asking. Its address is 1717 K Street, Suite 407, Washington, DC 20006. Phone: 202-429-1825.

National Association of Social Workers. NASW publishes a listing of clinical social workers (a clinical social worker specializes in the treatment of psychological and social problems through therapy), entitled *The NASW Register of Clinical Social Workers.* It is available in many public libraries. The register lists clinical social workers by region, specialization, and certification.

CHAPTER 3

Today's Families

*F*amilies are not what they used to be. Households in which the wife and mother is a full-time homemaker, the husband and father is the sole breadwinner, and neither has been married to anyone else are in the minority today. The facts are: More than 50 percent of mothers of school-age children and 60 percent of mothers of adolescents work. Before their 18th birthday, 40 percent of all children of the 1990s will see their parents separate or divorce, and 50 percent will live in a single-parent family, at least temporarily (a higher figure because of children born to unmarried mothers). About 20 percent will have a stepfamily.

What impact do these changes in the ways adults live and love have on adolescents?

A growing body of research shows that maternal employment, divorce, remarriage, and single parenthood, by themselves, do not interfere with psychological health and development. *What matters is the quality of the parent-child relationship, not the type of family in which a child lives.* Adolescents thrive on a balance of love and discipline. With responsive parents, adolescents from nontraditional homes can be just as well adjusted as those from traditional families. It is more difficult for working mothers, single parents, and stepparents to establish responsive relationships with their adolescents, however. In this chapter we look at some of the challenges these families face, and how to handle them.

WORKING MOTHERS

On the whole, having a mother who works is good for adolescents. This is especially true for girls whose mothers have successful careers in business or the professions. The daughters of career women tend to be higher in self-esteem, better adjusted socially, and more achievement-oriented than other girls. The sons of career women tend to be more independent and to have more positive attitudes toward women and work than those whose mothers stay at home. But two-wage-earner families do have special problems.

Balancing Careers and Family

One problem is housework. Neither parent has much free time, so adolescents usually are expected to do more around the house than they might be otherwise. Adolescent girls generally take this in stride. But adolescent boys, who are anxious to demonstrate their masculinity, sometimes resist. Their mothers may feel funny about asking them to help cook and clean. Hassles can be avoided if parents

- Assign children of both sexes household responsibilities when they are still small, before boys begin to worry about being seen with a vacuum cleaner.
- Treat housework as a joint undertaking, not as women's work or the mother's responsibility.
- Emphasize the benefits of the mother's working (more exciting vacations, more money for college, Mom in a better mood) rather than the costs.
- Adjust their expectations to their realities. Your house does not have to qualify for *House Beautiful*.

After-School Supervision and Latchkey Teens

A second problem for working parents is after-school supervision, especially of young adolescents. Children 10 to 13 years old are too grown-up for playgroups and may resent having a *baby*-sitter in the afternoons. But few schools have extracurricular activities (team sports and the like) for preteens.

Research shows that the "latchkey syndrome" has been exaggerated. Children need to know that someone is there for them psychologically, but that adult need not be physically present. Returning to an empty house after school has no ill effects on emotional, social or academic adjustment *if* the child knows his parents care about where he is and what he is doing. The latchkey children who do tend to get in trouble are those who are allowed to wander freely after school, and feel that no one cares.

Older adolescents can take care of themselves, but younger adolescents should not be left to their own devices. Parents should work out a plan with their child in advance. Specifically, the pre-teen should

• *Go directly home from school or to an adult-supervised activity.* Young adolescents are better off at home alone than with unsupervised groups of peers. You might permit the adolescent to invite a friend over for the afternoon occasionally if she clears this in advance. But if she wants to be with friends every day, you should look into a supervised youth group.

• *Check in with a parent or other adult every day.* Although this is not necessary for high-school students, young teenagers should be required to call a parent, neighbor, or other adult when they arrive home from school. This not only lets you know your adolescent arrived safely, it reinforces in her mind the idea that you are still supervising her, even if you do so from a distance.

• *Know what to do in an emergency.* Make sure your adolescent knows what to do in case of fire, injury, suspicious strangers, or other emergencies. Have the telephone numbers for the police, fire, and paramedic departments, two or three neighbors, as well as for you and your spouse, by the phone. Some neighborhoods have designated "block parents" who are usually home in the afternoon and available to help a teenager with a problem.

• *Have a plan for the afternoon's activities.* You and the adolescent should agree on an after-school schedule. The agenda might be homework, household chores, hobbies, or simply watching TV. What he plans doesn't matter so much as the fact that he has a plan. Young adolescents are most likely to get into trouble, or to feel lonely, when they are looking for something to do.

DIVORCE

Divorce *is* painful for young people; there is no point denying this. But study after study has found that living in an unhappy home is more harmful for young children and adolescents than going through a divorce. When parents are constantly fighting or coldly indifferent, no one benefits. How parents handle the divorce and life after the divorce make all the difference. Caught up in their own troubles, newly divorced parents often have less time for their children, are less sensitive to their children's needs, and provide less discipline. If children of divorce carry lasting scars, it is because of this diminished parenting, not divorce per se. For the sake of the children, parents should be honest in discussing the divorce with their children; not enlist their children in their marital battles; make sure the children understand that they are divorcing each other, not their children; and live up to this promise by remaining involved in their adolescents' lives.

Preparing Your Adolescent

How should you tell your adolescents that you are going to separate? When should you tell them? What should you say?

• *Give adolescents advance warning.* Even if they have long suspected you were not getting along and might split up, they need time to adjust. If you tell them while you are still living together, they will have an opportunity to reassure themselves of the departing parent's love through daily experience. With adolescents, the best time to tell them is after you have made a *definite* decision to separate and agreed on custody and future living arrangements. We emphasize *definite*. Most couples go through more than one cycle of deciding to divorce, then trying to work things out. It is cruel and unnecessary to drag your children through these changes of heart. On the other hand, if it's obvious that you are meeting with lawyers, deciding what belongs to whom, and the like, it's wrong to keep adolescents in the dark. If you have young children in the family, however, you should wait until a few weeks before one parent plans to move out. Small children have only a vague sense of time, and may believe you've changed your minds if the delay between the announcement and the departure stretches into months.

What should you do if the adolescent asks, point blank, whether you are planning a divorce? Unless you're certain, we recommend that you tell the adolescent "We are having difficulties, but we are trying to work things out." Adolescents need to know that it is normal for people to argue, even—perhaps especially—if they love one another. This doesn't mean that you should engage in knock-down, drag-out fights in front of your children, any more than you would in front of your friends and neighbors. But children know when you are fighting. Denying this will undermine their confidence in your honesty.

• *Break the news of a divorce together.* When one parent takes responsibility for informing the children, it implies that the other parent is already disengaging from the family. The fact that you are telling them together reassures them that you will both be available as parents in the future. Tell all of your children at the same time, even if they are years apart. Holding separate, private discussions with each individual child creates an air of secrecy and feeds suspicion that you are withholding something. Now, more than ever, your children need to know that they can trust you. Later, you can answer individual children's questions.

• *Explain why you are getting divorced.* Young people have a right to honest answers. Even small children see through half-truths, not to mention whole lies, and a divorce is not a time to undermine their faith in you. Without going into the gory details, tell them the truth, even if it hurts. "Mom has fallen in love with someone else," "Dad and Mom fight so often that it's impossible to go on living together," or "Dad has problems he needs to solve by himself" are appropriate. Try to avoid assigning blame and making angry accusations. "Your mother is sleeping with Jimmy's father" or "Your father is a drunk, and I just can't put up with it anymore" are not appropriate. The basic message might be that you once loved each other but have grown apart. Knowing they were the products of love is important to young people's feelings of self-worth. Or the message might be that you thought you were right for one another, but you made a mistake. Learning that their parents aren't infallible and sometimes make mistakes is an important part of growing up.

• *Tell your children as much as you can about future living arrangements*—where they will be living, with which parent, where the other parent will move, and when they will see him or her. Don't overwhelm them with details, but help them to form a mental picture of their future. Reassure them that their material needs will be met. Adolescents may wonder what a divorce will do to their plans for college, for example.

Your first discussion of the upcoming divorce will not be your last. A major goal in this first meeting is to create an atmosphere of open communication. Your children should feel that they can ask you anything they like and that you will answer their questions as honestly as you can.

How Adolescents React

It is common and normal for adolescents to feel angry, confused, upset, or even depressed at first. It's impossible to say how a given adolescent will react, but here are some possibilities.

Adolescents tend to be egocentric (see chapter 7): They see divorce as something you are doing to them. How dare you disrupt their lives! But getting angry at the parent who is moving out is dangerous, because that parent may not want to see them anymore. Getting angry at the parent with whom they will be living is also dangerous, because that parent might abandon them, too. So they may express their anger in indirect ways. Some adolescents use denial: They throw themselves into outside activities and act as if nothing were happening. The reason is not that they don't care about the divorce, but that they care so much. They can't handle their feelings and so repress them.

Some adolescents revert to childish, immature behavior (what psychologists call *regression*), in an unconscious attempt to return to the time when you and your spouse got along and thus reassure themselves that they will be cared for. For example, the adolescent may develop headaches or stomach aches as an excuse to stay home from school, be put to bed, and be cared for. The adolescent with psychosomatic complaints may not be faking illness deliberately: He may truly feel feverish and out of sorts, even though there is nothing physically wrong with him.

Other adolescents express anger by taking risks or "acting out." For example, the adolescent might run away, in the spirit of "I'll show you!" Running away gives her the illusion of being in control: She is the one who is leaving home, not the parent. In effect she is punishing her parents for making her feel threatened and insecure by invoking those same feelings in them. Running away is not a common response to divorce, but some acting out is. The adolescent might come home drunk, leave cigarettes, rolling papers for marijuana, or birth control pills where you are certain to find them, or start hanging out with a crowd you won't like—all to test your commitment to him or her.

Sadness is also a common reaction. The adolescent is experiencing a compound loss, of the noncustodial parent, the home life he's grown accustomed to, and of his innocence and childhood. A period of grief and mourning is natural and healthy. Sometimes, however, sadness deepens into depression. The adolescent experiences the divorce as a rejection and abandonment of himself, not of the remaining parent. He feels unloved and unlovable.

These initial reactions are usually short-lived. The adolescent stops thinking about divorce and picks up his old interests in friends, social life, and extracurricular hobbies where he left off. There may be times, over the next year or two, when events open old wounds (his father forgets his birthday, or his mother introduces a serious boyfriend). But nearly all studies find that two years later, adolescents whose parents divorced are no more likely to be troubled than are adolescents whose parents are still married—and less likely to be disturbed than those whose parents stayed together in an angry marriage.

There have not been many studies of the long-term impact of divorce on children. One ten-year study found that some parents are still in emotional disarray years after the divorce; they haven't gotten their lives back together. In these families, children may be forced prematurely into the role of psychological caretaker. These overburdened children feel responsible for preventing their parents from slipping into depression, and in some cases may take over daily management of the household. Their own emotional and social development may suffer as a result. This study also found delayed or sleeper effects, especially in some girls. In high school they seemed to be coping well. But when they reached their college years and become involved in their first serious relationships with the opposite sex, they fell apart. The feelings of abandonment they had denied in middle adolescence now surfaced as intense, unmanageable fear of betrayal.

We caution readers against taking these portraits of doomed children of divorce too literally. The findings are based on case studies. The researchers did not compare these young people to others who came of age in intact but unhappy families. There is no way of knowing whether they would have fared the same, or even worse, if their parents had stayed married. What is clear is that when parents stop being parents, when parents are emotionally troubled, or when parents constantly fight, whether they are married or divorced, children of all ages suffer.

In short, parents should expect strong, troubled reactions to divorce. If the adolescent's behavior is extreme (running away) or persists beyond two months, however, the adolescent might need counseling or therapy.

Decisions about Custody and Living Arrangements

In the past, parents were forced to go to court to obtain a divorce and settle child custody. But many states recognize "no fault" divorce today, and many also recognize joint custody. This term is often misunderstood, however. Joint *legal* custody does not mean that children spend half their time with one parent and half with the other; that is joint *physical* custody (discussed below). Rather it means that both parents have equal rights and obligations as parents. Legal custody is not a trivial matter. We believe strongly that parents with children should consult with an attorney or divorce mediator to make sure they understand the full implications of custody decisions, and not rely on do-it-yourself divorce kits. But in terms of the adolescent's immediate well-being, the most important decision is where and with whom he or she will live.

Physical custody is one area in which parents must put their children's interests ahead of their own. Adolescents' best interests are served if *their life outside the family is disturbed as little as possible.* Ideally, they should remain in their old neighborhood and school district so that their friendships are not disrupted at the same time that their family breaks apart. Friends are an important source of support, especially in adolescence. Ideally, all the children in the family should live together. Siblings may be at each other's throats, but these familiar quarrels provide continuity and comfort when the rest of the adolescent's daily life is in flux. Ideally, adolescents shouldn't have to give up extracurricular activities they enjoy, like piano lessons on Tuesdays or Little League games on Saturdays.

There is no evidence that children are necessarily better off living with either their mother or their father. It depends on the family. In some cases, one parent clearly has more interest in the nitty-gritty details of parenting than the other does. Or one is eager to return to a single life-style, without adolescents to worry about. Other times, however, this is not the case. When both parents love the children, both are competent parents, and both want their children to live with them, decisions should be based on the practicalities of everyday life. Which parent will best be able to monitor the adolescent's behavior? A parent whose career involves frequent business trips or last-minute business dinners will not be a good choice. Which parent's life-style is most appropriate for an adolescent? Which parent has adequate space?

Should adolescents have a say in where they live? Yes and no. You should not put adolescents on the spot, asking them to choose between their parents. But if adolescents express a strong preference—directly or indirectly, through a family counselor—and other considerations are equal, parents probably should respect their wishes. Certainly, you should listen to the adolescent's reasons for selecting one home over the other. It's not unusual for an adolescent who has been forced to live with one parent against her wishes to "run away" to the other parent at the first opportunity, or after a disagreement with the first parent. While you don't want the adolescent to play one of you against the other, you do want her to feel she has some control over her life. Family counseling, including the adolescent, is often helpful in making the decision. Once a joint decision is made, you should stick to it unless there are compelling reasons not to.

Because more mothers are working and more fathers want to be active, not visiting, parents, some couples are attempting to share their children after divorce. The result is a new phenomenon: the two-household or "shuttle" child, who moves back and forth every week, every month, or once a year. This arrangement may be convenient and reassuring for the parents, neither of whom wants to give up their children and neither of whom can handle the job of parent full-time. Besides, isn't it better for children to have two parents? The available evidence suggests that joint physical custody does not benefit children, and may actually be harmful, especially if the parents do not get along.

It's easy to see why. Shuttling back and forth between two households makes it more difficult for a young person to settle into a regular schedule of activities. Each household has its own personality and set of rules: No sooner has the adolescent begun to adapt to one setting than he is required to shift gears and return to the other. When problems arise, the adolescent may simply pick up and move (or be moved) rather than trying to resolve them. Since adolescents are working on developing a personal identity, this can be especially trying. One 16-year-old, who alternates weeks with her divorced parents, became known as "the bag lady" to her classmates because she so often brought her suitcase to school. Another lamented, "I don't really feel like I have a home. You have to be different for each parent . . . I don't have any sense of stability." In our view, joint living arrangements are less than ideal. Adolescents (and other people) need a home base. Would you want to live out of a suitcase, moving every week or every month?

Life after Divorce

How quickly and how well adolescents adjust to divorce depends on whether they are able to maintain good relationships with *both* of their parents. The wounds of divorce take much longer to heal when the parents are at war, or when a parent abandons the adolescent, either physically or psychologically.

Warring Parents Parents' feelings about each other do not disappear the day the divorce decree comes through. But it's important to separate your own feelings toward your ex-spouse from your adolescent's feelings toward her parent. Don't inflict your views on the child. There is a world of difference between saying "Your father doesn't think about anyone but himself" and "Your father and I have different ideas about how to handle money," or "Your mother will never grow up" and "Your mother and I enjoy different life-styles; that's why we couldn't get along." The adolescent needs to learn about each of her parent's strengths and weaknesses (just as an adolescent in an intact family does). Your input is important, but you shouldn't draw her conclusions for her.

However you feel about your ex, support your child's relationship with his other parent. Don't use your adolescents as spies (questions about whom the ex-spouse is dating or how he or she is spending money are most common), messengers ("Tell your father you need money for camp uniforms" or "Tell your mother it's none of her business whom I invite to my house"), allies ("Now you see why I divorced him: How could he . . . ?"), or scapegoats ("You're acting just like your mother; you're even beginning to look like her!"). If, as a concerned parent, you feel your ex is introducing your adolescent to the wrong kind of people, being a tightwad or spendthrift, tell your ex, not your child. If you need an ally, someone to agree that your ex is a rotter and a slob, turn to an adult friend.

Actual Abandonment   A great deal has been written about "weekend Santas"—divorced fathers who have ceased to be the head of their children's household and the disciplinarian and become the gift-givers instead. In reality, weekend Santas—with or without bags of toys—are the exception to the rule. Most non-custodial parents have very little contact with their children. They may be very attentive for the first six months or year after the divorce, but they gradually become less and less involved, especially if they or the children's mother remarries. They may make an obligatory visit once a year or disappear altogether.

When a parent abandons them, adolescents often blame themselves for being unworthy of love, rather than the parent for being unable to love. Empty reassurances—"Your mother loves you, even though she is too busy to see you right now"—are not very helpful. The adolescent has a right to be angry. Try to help the adolescent see that, just as in any other relationship, a parent has to earn love and respect.

Psychological Abandonment   In some cases, a parent is there physically, but so distraught by the separation, so overwhelmed by new responsibilities, or so busy starting a new life that he or she has little time and energy for the child. The adolescent may be left to his own devices. Or he may be allowed or required to take on responsibilities that properly belong to an adult, such as seeing that younger siblings are fed and clothed or dealing with bill collectors. In extreme cases, when parents cannot pull themselves together emotionally or begin drinking heavily after a divorce, the adolescent may become the adult's caretaker, rather than the reverse.

Even parents who are able to cope may lean on the adolescent after a divorce more than they would otherwise. One common pattern is for a mother to treat an adolescent daughter as her best friend. The adolescent may be flattered at first but troubled later on. One of the ways adolescents establish their independence is by creating some emotional and social space between themselves and their families. It is difficult enough for adolescents to seek independence; they shouldn't have to feel that they are losing or betraying their best friend at the same time.

Being close to your adolescents is important, and asking them to pitch in is reasonable. But parents must remember that, whatever their situation, they are parents first and foremost. Adolescents should be able to lean on their parents, not vice versa. Adolescents need time to develop social lives of their own and time to just be kids.

Visitation Visiting children are a special challenge. Both parent and child may have fantasies about their reunions. The father wants to make up for lost time and may forget how much work it is being a parent. The children may see visiting Dad as a vacation, forgetting how demanding he can be. Or they may resent having to leave their friends, their room, and their daily lives every other weekend or every summer. The stepmother and her children (if the father has remarried) may see the honored guests more as an invading horde. When the visit is over, everyone may be disappointed—and exhausted.

Noncustodial parents should try to make their visits with their children as much like ordinary homelife as possible, complete with homework and housework. This means welcoming your children, but not overwhelming them with gifts and excursions; creating opportunities for heart-to-heart talks, but not expecting every second of every visit to be "meaningful"; treating your children like members of the family, not like special guests who are exempt from house rules; and supporting your ex-spouse's regulations, or if you can't, settling differences with the ex-spouse directly, not through the children. A tall order, but not an impossible one.

SINGLE PARENTS

Single parents lead complex lives. Juggling the roles of wage earner, housekeeper, and parent, and making time for some semblance of a personal life as well isn't easy. Most, though not all, single parents are women. Most work but have not been employed steadily; they took time off when their children were small. Most have less money than the average two-parent family and, if they are divorced, less than they had when they were married. Many are coping with the emotional aftermath of a divorce and the social awkwardness of becoming single again.

Maintaining Authority

The biggest issue for single parents with adolescents is *control*. Single parents tend to grant more independence to their children than other parents do. This can be good for adolescents—up to a point. Adolescents need firmness as well as freedom. Responsive parenting takes time and energy, both of which are in short supply in single-parent homes. Establishing rules and monitoring the teenager's activities are much easier when there are two adults in the home. Single parents have to be "the heavy" all the time. In part to make up for their feelings of guilt, divorced parents may bend over backward to make their children happy. In the absence of other adults in the house to support their decisions, they may give in to their child in order to be accepted. Adolescents may try to step into the absent parent's shoes and present themselves as more mature than they really are. The overburdened single parent may not supervise the mature-seeming adolescent as closely as she would otherwise.

Because single parents are more likely to be permissive, their adolescents are somewhat more likely to get into trouble. If a single parent maintains a responsive relationship, however, any problems that might develop can be averted.

Dating, Sex, and Live-In Lovers

It's natural for a divorced parent to want to begin dating and entering into sexual relationships. How much of their personal life should single parents reveal to their adolescent? In our view, very little.

Adolescents are only beginning to formulate their ideas about dating, sexuality, and intimacy. Just as parents have a hard time accepting the development of sexuality in their adolescents, so adolescents find it hard to deal with the emergence or reemergence of sexuality in their parents. Whether because of unconscious desires for the parent of the opposite sex (the Oedipal triangle), or simply because they are insecure about the whole

subject, adolescents don't like to think about their parents' having
sex. When parents stay married, adolescents tend to write off
their expressions of physical intimacy as affection. When parents
are single and dating, this self-deception is more difficult.

The best way to deal with the adolescent's mixed feelings is
not to bring home every person you have dinner (or more) with.
Instead, meet new dates outside your home and tell your adolescent you are going out with a friend. If you begin seeing someone
frequently, you might invite him or her to dinner, preferably with
a group of friends the first time. Introduce your date as a friend,
and ask him or her to act like one. If the adolescent asks whether
Bill is your boyfriend, or Sandy your girlfriend, just say that you
are friends and have a good time together. If the adolescent asks,
point blank, whether you are going to bed together, we recommend saying something like "My sex life is not something I want
to discuss with you. But if I'm getting seriously involved with
somebody, don't worry, we'll talk about it."

There are several reasons for not parading every date
through your home, not to mention your bed. One is that it makes
everyone (you, your date, and your adolescent) uncomfortable. A
second reason is that your adolescent might jump to conclusions.
If the adolescent is hoping you will remarry, each date will raise
her hopes unnecessarily. If the adolescent dreads the thought
that you will remarry, each date will plunge her into needless
despair. These reactions may seem silly to you—"It's only a date"
—but your dates may seem far more significant to the adolescent
than they do to you. A third reason is that, as an adult, you may
engage in more sexually advanced behavior than you want for
your son or daughter. As a newly single woman, you may sleep
with someone on a first date, but do you want your daughter to
do the same? Do you want your son to expect this with his dates?
As a newly single man, you may go out with someone to whom
you are sexually attracted but nothing more. Do you want your
daughter to think this is all men want from a woman? Do you
want your son to emulate your behavior?

The time to introduce someone to your adolescent as a boyfriend or girlfriend is when you and that person are becoming
serious. You may or may not be contemplating marriage, but if
the relationship is loving, significant, and steady, it is time for the
people who are important in your life to meet one another. Leading a double life at this point is foolish. Moreover, before the

relationship grows deeper, you will want to know how your adolescents and your lover get along. If the relationship continues to grow, you will want to include this person in your family life.

Certainly, you should not invite someone you just met or someone you are dating casually and do not see as a potential mate to spend the night. What if you are serious? This is a personal decision. In our view, there is nothing intrinsically wrong with a lover sleeping over or even moving in, after some time, *if* the two of you care deeply for one another and are contemplating a life together. Many adults who have been through a divorce want to try living with someone before risking a second marriage. If the relationship is tentative, however, or if moving in is a way to hold someone who may not want to be held, this is a serious mistake. Your adolescent has already lost daily contact with one parent; don't subject him to another loss.

Everything we've said here applies to fathers as well as mothers and to noncustodial as well as custodial parents. It also applies to parents who are having homosexual relationships. Adolescents are usually more accepting of homosexuality than their occasional, unthinking remarks suggest. If you are going to be openly gay, your child should find out from you. When young people learn that a parent is homosexual from a third party, they are often deeply hurt—not because the parent is gay, but because the parent didn't trust the adolescent enough to discuss this significant matter.

STEPFAMILIES

The term *stepparent* used to refer to someone who married a widow or widower, replacing a parent who had died. Today, the term more often describes someone who has become an *additional* parent, stepping into a position that is still filled. Because there are no established norms for this new social role, and because the role itself is ambiguous, each stepfamily has to write its own rules.

If control is the biggest issue for single parents, divided loyalties are the major problem for stepfamilies. When the family stays together, there is no conflict between the husband and wife loving each other and also loving their children. Stepfamilies are caught up in crosscurrents. Should the mother side with her new husband or her children in a dispute? Is liking your stepmother a betrayal of your natural mother? A request to help repair a bike or solve a chemistry problem reminds a stepfather that he is not there for his own children. A mother wants her son to like her new husband, but not *that* much. . . . The first year or two can be difficult. But if parent and stepparent know what to expect, some problems can be avoided and others minimized. Parents and stepparents should also know that these difficulties are usually short-lived: After a year, or at most two, everyone usually settles down into a routine.

Becoming a Stepparent

Couples often enter into second marriages with unrealistic expectations, only to crash against postmarital realities. The children make it abundantly clear that *they* did not promise to love, honor, and obey their parent's new spouse. The wife may begin to feel more like Cinderella's wicked stepmother; the husband wonders if his adolescent stepson is auditioning to play Hamlet.

The Wicked Stepparent Syndrome In the early stage of a new marriage, adolescents often say and do hostile things. This reaction is understandable. The adolescent has already lost one parent (the one with whom he no longer lives); now he fears he will lose the other to the new spouse. Adolescent girls who have had very close relationships with their mothers take remarriage especially hard; they feel they are being replaced as their mother's ally and confidante.

The natural parent and new spouse are entering into a partnership. But the relationship between an adult and an adolescent is not supposed to be equal. No matter how much they like the new stepparent, adolescents wonder "Will he start telling me what to do?" "Will she begin commenting on my clothes, my friends, my room?" From the adolescent's perspective, it's like discovering that another layer of management (the stepparent) is being thrust between you and the boss (parent) you've reported to for twelve, fourteen, or even sixteen years. Or worse, that the business (the home) has been bought out from under you. From the teenager's perspective, remarriage can feel like a hostile takeover.

Add to this the fact that adolescents are struggling with their own identity and changing relationship to adult authority, and the stepparent becomes a natural target. Expressing anger toward natural parents is dangerous: They have already abandoned one another, and might abandon you. With a stepparent, you have little to lose. We do not mean to suggest that all adolescents go out of their way to antagonize their stepparents. Many welcome the presence of another, more neutral adult in their lives. But couples should not be surprised if the adolescent is difficult at first; nor should they take alienating remarks and behavior personally.

During the early stages of a new marriage, adolescents need to be reassured that nothing can shake their parent's ongoing commitment to them. Remarried parents should make an extra effort to spend time alone with the adolescent, doing things they did before the remarriage, and *occasionally* side with the adolescent in disputes with the stepparent. If adolescents are slow to warm up to a new spouse, parents should err on the side of patience, tolerance, and forgiveness. Trying to rush the relationship along will create more problems than it solves.

Building Trust Close relationships need time to develop. Trust has to be earned, affection shared, differences faced and resolved, and the relationship tested and retested before everyone feels secure.

The first rule for stepparents is that they cannot, and should not try to, replace the natural parent; nor should the stepparent compete with the natural parent. Rather, the stepparent has to develop his or her own relationship with the child. If the natural parent tends to be formal, for example, don't try to prove how much more fun you are. If the natural parent is artistic, don't feel you have to develop equal expertise. Just be yourself. If comparisons come up (and they usually do), try to be neutral. "Your father and I are different people, Eric; I think you can learn from both of us."

The second rule is, don't push. Adolescents do not respond well to people who pretend a closeness they don't really feel, or to people who try to be ingratiating. Be friendly and available, but wait for the adolescent to come to you. Like any friendship, stepparent-stepchild relationships thrive on common interests. If you and your stepchild love Westerns (and your spouse doesn't), rent an old John Wayne film on a night your spouse has to work late. Invite your stepson or stepdaughter along on a fishing trip. The more you do alone together, the sooner you will come to know one another. Your spouse can help by *not* tagging along every time you and the stepchild go somewhere and *not* intervening every time you have a disagreement, but letting the two of you learn to work things out together. It takes guts for the natural parent to step aside, but this pays off in the long run.

Don't feel guilty if you don't immediately love your stepchildren as you do your own, or as much as you think you should. Everyone needs time to adjust to the new family, adults included. There is no such thing as an "instant parent."

Establishing Authority   As an adult, it may seem only natural for the stepparent to offer the young person guidance and advice. Adolescents, however, may see the stepparent's attempts at direction as an arbitrary assertion of power: "You're not my father/mother; what right do you have to tell me what to do?" To some extent they are right. Emotional rapport is a prerequisite to authority. A natural parent-child relationship begins, in infancy, with basic love and trust. Only after this foundation is laid do natural parents begin to deal with control and discipline. They have all of middle childhood to get to know one another as individuals before issues of control resurface in adolescence. The stepparent and stepchild do not have a history of love and closeness. Attempting to control a stepchild before you have built a solid relationship is domination. A stepparent's first job is to establish emotional rapport. In matters of discipline, the stepparent should tread softly.

Discipline is most likely to become a problem when the natural parent and the stepparent have different styles. The mother may lean toward permissiveness; the stepfather may come from the old school and believe that children should be respectful and obedient. Some psychologists counsel a united front. We believe that in the early stages of a second marriage, and especially with adolescent children, stepparents should defer to the natural parent. This doesn't mean that they should let stepchildren walk all over them; rather, they should abide by, and expect to be treated according to, preexisting house rules. Whatever standards the natural parent has set, she has worked to convince her children that they represent the right way, *our* way. For her to suddenly change the rules just because another adult has entered her life would be arbitrary. For her new husband to take over would be an invasion. There is a world of difference between saying "Johnny, you know your mother expects you to clean up you room today" and shouting "I won't stand for that mess in your room, I don't care what your mother says!"

Combining Families

All these issues are more complicated when the new household includes not just one set of children but two. Each parent-child team has its own history and its own rules; they may be as different as cricket and baseball. You like your children to flop on your bed to watch TV or just talk; your spouse has always declared the bedroom off limits. You expect your children to show up promptly for dinner each night; your spouse sees no reason why adolescents shouldn't be permitted to eat what, where, and when they like. You supervise your children's schoolwork closely; your spouse doesn't. You have a dog; your spouse has two cats. Now you have to play ball in the same house.

The first step in combining families is for you and your spouse to talk things over, alone, and decide which of your house rules are negotiable and which are not. Let's say your new spouse insists on his private space; you feel eating together is part of what it means to be a family. The next step is to discuss problem areas with your adolescents and see if, together, you can work out solutions. "You know how you feel about someone going through your desk? That's how Bill [your new husband] feels about you coming into our room anytime you like. What do you think we should do?" You might agree to make one of your teenager's rooms your family's late night gathering place; in exchange, your teenagers might agree to knock before they barge into your room. "Ann and Bob and Susan [your new wife and her children] always have dinner together as a family. I think it's a nice idea, but what do you think?" You might agree to move the dinner hour from 6:30 to 7:30 on weeknights, so that the teenagers don't have to rush home from practice or interrupt their homework. Or you might decide to make some nights family nights and others free nights, for adults as well as adolescents.

In some areas, negotiation may not be possible or advisable. Siblings do not have the same needs and requirements; neither do stepsiblings. Some teenagers are able to handle a clothing allowance responsibly, for example, while others are not. Older adolescents, who are dating, probably need more allowance than younger children, who are not. Stepfamilies need to respect and tolerate individual differences. "Sheila and her children go to temple every Saturday. I'd like to join them now and then, and I hope you'll come, too. But it's up to you." "Alice has put a lot of effort into decorating the house, and her children are as tidy as she is. I won't ask you to meet her standards in your own room, but I do want you to respect her wishes for the rest of the house."

In terms of purchases and privileges, however, it's critical that stepsiblings be treated equally. This doesn't mean that every time you buy one child a pair of jeans, every other child has to get a pair of jeans the same day. But all should have about the same budget for clothes. If 16-year-old Adam has a midnight curfew on weekends, 14-year-old Josh should know that he will have the same hours when he is Adam's age. The same rules of fairness apply to siblings, of course. But stepsiblings will be more sensitive to inequalities.

Parents who are merging households often say that their biggest worry is whether their children will get along. What if they hate each other? How stepsiblings get along will depend on their personalities, interests, ages, sex, and other factors. Some do hate each other; others become fast friends; and still others simply coexist more or less peacefully.

RESOURCES

For more information and advice, the following groups and organizations might be useful.

For Families in Which Both Parents Work

Phone Friend. A program started by a group of psychologists in 1982 for children whose parents are not available after school, Phone Friend links the child with an adult he or she can call in the afternoons for help in dealing with minor crises. As of this writing, Phone Friend has 365 chapters nationwide.

For Single Parents

Parents Without Partners. Many communities now have chapters of Parents Without Partners and similar organizations, which organize meetings and outings for single parents. For information, write or call International Headquarters, 8807 Colesville Road, Silver Springs, MD 20910. Phone: 301-588-9354.

For Single Mothers of Boys

Big Brother. Single mothers who are having problems with an adolescent son might contact the local chapter of Big Brother. This program is designed to provide boys who do not have a father in their lives with an adult "brother" who will spend at least one afternoon every other week with the boy, take him to ballgames and the like, and generally be available when a boy needs to talk male-to-male. Big brothers are carefully screened and supervised by a social worker.

THE PRETEENS
From 10 to 13

PHYSICAL HEALTH
AND DEVELOPMENT

CHAPTER 4

Puberty

*A*dolescence begins much earlier than parents expect, at least in terms of internal physiology. By age 8 or 9, the average child has entered the stage of biological development called puberty, during which his or her childish body will be transformed into that of a mature man or woman, capable of reproduction. The outward signs of sexual maturation may not appear for several years, but children need to be prepared in advance. Puberty is different from anything they've been through before.

GROWING UP AND FILLING OUT

In childhood, growth is slow and steady; in puberty, change is rapid and dramatic. During the adolescent growth spurt, the average young person gains 12 inches in height and 20 to 30 pounds. It's not unusual for a boy or girl to grow 3 to 5 inches in a single year, literally bursting out of last season's clothes. "I'm opening up like the largest telescope that ever was!" exclaimed that famous adolescent, Alice in Wonderland. "Good-bye, feet!" To complicate matters, all parts of the body do not grow at the same time or rate. Typically, the hands and feet spurt before the arms and legs, the arms and legs before the torso. If adolescents feel awkward and gawky, it is because their bodies *are* out of proportion (temporarily). "Curiouser and curiouser," said Alice. Today's teenagers are more likely to use "weird" or "gross" to describe their changing bodies.

GROWING PAINS

About one in five young people experience actual growing pains, in the form of aches in the shins, calves, or thighs of both legs. The attacks are usually short (lasting a few minutes or at most a half hour) and most often happen at night, waking them up. Intermittent attacks over a period of months, or even years, are not a cause for concern. The pain can be relieved through massage or heat or (if frequent) with a dose of aspirin at bedtime. If a young person experiences severe or chronic leg pain, however, parents should consult the child's physician.

At a stage when young people want more than anything to be like everyone else, they find themselves the *least* alike. Everyone their age is growing and changing, but each at his or her own pace. For a start, girls show the outward signs of development two years earlier, on the average, than boys do. In sixth grade, a girl may tower over most boys her age, unwillingly violating the rule that males should be bigger and stronger than females. Differences within each sex are just as great. Some girls begin to develop as early as age 8 and others as late as age 13; in boys the outward signs of puberty may appear at age 10 or not until age 14 or 15. Some young people race through puberty in a year and a half, while others take five or six years to mature. This means that one teenager may complete puberty before another the same age begins. Best friends may look and feel worlds apart.

As if this were not enough, the outcome of puberty is uncertain. Some young women develop large breasts and others small; some men have long penises and others short; some individuals have dense pubic hair and others sparse. Adults know that bodies come in all shapes and sizes, that almost anyone can look attractive if they keep in shape and dress for their particular build, and that everyone has what it takes to make a good sexual partner. Young adolescents know no such thing.

Finally, puberty follows an independent biological timetable, which bears little relation to other aspects of maturation. A girl may look like a woman long before she feels like one inside. A boy may be mature in almost every way but still look like a child.

No wonder young people in the throes of puberty often feel that their bodies are out of control, that they will never start (or stop) growing, and that everything about the way they look is wrong. The most urgent question for young adolescents is *"Am I normal?"* Virtually all are. But knowing what to expect may relieve some of the young person's anxieties.

Becoming a Woman

For girls, the first outward sign of puberty is swelling around the nipples. Most, if not all, girls are thrilled at the appearance of "breast buds." But full breast development takes several years. At midpuberty, the breasts are soft and shapeless; only later do they become firm and full. Pubic hair begins to appear shortly after breast buds. The growth spurt begins and ends earlier in girls than in boys. At 8, the average girl is about the same height as the average boy; at 12, she is 3 or 4 inches taller; by 15, when the growth spurt in boys is taking off, she has reached her full height. The growth spurt adds inches not only to a girl's height but also to her hips. Both sexes lose most of their "baby fat," and both gain muscle during puberty. But boys acquire relatively more muscle, especially in their chest, shoulders, and arms, and girls retain relatively more fat, especially in their breasts, arms, buttocks, and thighs. Filling out is a normal part of female development. But given our culture's emphasis on thinness, girls in this stage of puberty may fret that they are becoming "obese." (See Changing Shape, later in this chapter.)

The onset of menstruation (called menarche) is a relatively late development, occurring several years after puberty has begun. The girl's internal sex organs (ovaries, fallopian tubes, and uterus) have been growing all along, but invisibly. Her first period is a developmental milestone, a sign that she is beginning to ovulate and is capable of becoming pregnant. The other changes girls experience during puberty are gradual and progressive; the onset of menstruation is sudden and dramatic. If a girl is prepared, if you treat menstruation as a normal and natural part of becoming a woman, and if you respect her desire for privacy, or celebration if that is what she wants, the chances are she will take menstruation in stride. Girls are much less likely to have negative attitudes toward menstruation today than they were twenty years ago. Even so, most have mixed emotions. There is no point denying to your daughter that menstruation is a nuisance; every woman knows it is.

In most girls, the vaginal opening is covered by a membrane called the hymen. This membrane is flexible, and usually has an opening that is large enough for a finger or tampon to pass through. In most cases, the hymen remains intact until a girl has sexual intercourse, and its rupture may cause slight pain and bleeding the first time she has sex. But in some cases the membrane is very thin and ruptures spontaneously during such exercise as horseback or bike riding.

Other nuisances and embarrassments associated with puberty are oily skin, perspiration, and odor. The glands work overtime in adolescence. Most girls do not develop acne, but many do break out from time to time. And nearly all stain the underarms of their clothes occasionally. Keeping clean is even more important now than it was in childhood. Frequent showers, washing the face several times a day, and using a mild antiperspirant/deodorant are all good ideas. Most adolescents do not need to be told this. Young people who acted as if they were allergic to soap in childhood monopolize the bathroom in adolescence.

THE SEQUENCE OF DEVELOPMENT IN GIRLS

Characteristic	Age Range
Breast development begins	8–13
Pubic hair appears	11–14
Growth spurt starts	9½–14½
Menstruation begins	10–16½
Underarm hair appears	13–16
Breast development complete	13–18

Becoming a Man

For boys, the first outward sign of puberty is development of the testicles. In childhood the testicles are small and close to the body;

during puberty, they become larger and "drop" between the legs, and the scrotum, the sac that holds the testicles, becomes darker. If a boy is modest, parents may not notice these changes. But locker room comparisons will tell a boy exactly where he stands. To their embarrassment, some boys also develop swellings under their nipples in the early stages of puberty. This is normal and usually disappears within a year. As hormone production in the testes accelerates, other developments follow. Pubic hair appears; the penis begins to grow; a light down spreads across the upper lip; and the boy's voice begins to "break." In terms of overall growth, boys are slow starters. But once their spurt starts, they grow faster (4 to 5 inches a year) than girls do and for a longer period. At 14 or 15, the average boy is taller, heavier, and stronger than the average girl—and still growing. Coarse facial and body hair and a deeper voice are the finishing touches of male development, and occur relatively late in puberty.

Just as menstruation is concrete evidence that a girl is becoming a woman, ejaculation is a sign that a boy is maturing sexually. Technically, the boy has been capable of an erection since birth. But only when testosterone begins circulating in his system in sufficient amount can his body manufacture sperm. Some boys discover this new capacity through masturbation; others have their first experience as a nocturnal emission or "wet dream." Most boys also have spontaneous, involuntary erections, often in the most inconvenient situations (when they have just been called on in class, or lying in the sun at the beach).

Boys are somewhat more likely than girls to have problems with oily skin, perspiration (including sweaty palms), and odor (especially smelly feet). As with girls, good hygiene and frequent changes of underwear and socks should do the trick. Acne, however, may require special treatment.

HELPING YOUR ADOLESCENT COPE WITH PUBERTY

Puberty is one case where ignorance is *not* bliss. Girls who are taught nothing at all about menstruation, or taught that it is a nasty, messy, shameful business, are far more likely to have severe cramps, heavy bleeding, and other physical problems than are girls who know in advance what to expect. In general, the more a young person knows about puberty, the easier time he or she will have.

THE SEQUENCE OF DEVELOPMENT IN BOYS

Characteristic	Age Range
Growth of testes and scrotum begins	10–13½
Pubic hair appears	10–15
Growth spurt starts	10½–16
Growth of penis begins	11–14½
Change in voice begins	11–14½
Growth of penis and testes complete	12½–17
Facial and underarm hair appear	12–17

• *"When should I begin talking to my child about puberty?"* Children should be informed about puberty *before* it begins—9 is a good age (remember, many girls begin menstruating at age 10). Discussing menstruation and nocturnal emissions is particularly important, since these occur suddenly, whereas other changes they will experience are gradual and cumulative. The young person who is taken by surprise is likely to be upset and frightened. If you have been answering your children's questions about why boys and girls are different and where babies come from all along, you've laid the groundwork. Now you want to talk directly about what is going to happen to their bodies. "But my son/daughter is only a *child*!" All the more reason to protect him or her from potentially scary, unpleasant experiences and from misinformation.

• *"How should I begin?"* The best approach is to discuss issues informally, as they arise, and not make too big a deal of them. Say you and your daughter are setting the table and she casually asks, "Mom, how old were you when you got your period?" This isn't idle curiosity on her part. Use the opportunity to discuss variations in the rate of maturation. "I was almost 14, and terrified that I would never start. Isn't that silly?" or "I was only 10, and my friends teased me a lot. I think they were just jealous." Or "I was 12. Have any of your friends begun to menstruate? What have they told you about it?"

• *"My child never asks."* Some preteens are embarrassed to say what is on their minds. Others don't know what questions to ask. This means that you may have to take the initiative. A visit from a family with young adolescents can provide an opening. "Did you notice that Jane is beginning to fill out? I was flat as a board at her age. Are you wondering when you will start to develop?" Or you may overhear your son making a crude comment about menstruation to a friend. After the friend leaves, speak to him. "Do you know why girls menstruate?" A magazine article on health, premenstrual syndrome, or male-female relationships can be an opener. Many of the women's and family magazines regularly feature self-knowledge tests; ask your son or daughter to question you, or read it together and question your spouse.

Be sensitive to indirect or disguised questions. A boy who asks his father whether he reads *Playboy* may be looking for a way to talk about masturbation. A girl who asks what brand tampon her mother uses may be worried because her periods haven't started yet. Asking "Is that all you want to know?" may reveal that the teenager is totally bewildered by something he read, a pronouncement by one of his friends, or his own feelings.

Don't be put off if the reaction to your attempts to discuss puberty is "I know all about that, Ma" or "Yuk, that's sick." The adolescent who pretends to be disinterested, bored, asleep, or stone deaf may be memorizing every word.

• *"Ask your father/mother."* Many parents assume that it's the father's responsibility to talk to their son about puberty, the mother's duty to talk with their daughter. Some teenagers agree. A boy who talks freely to his father about masturbation might be mortified to learn that his mother knows he is masturbating. A girl may go to extreme lengths to prevent her father from seeing that she is developing pubic hair. But other young people feel that the parent of the opposite sex suddenly abandoned them in puberty. Find out how your child feels. When your son asks a question about girls, suggest "I'm not really sure; let's ask your mother." If he says "Never!" respect his wishes. In the long run, you want your son or daughter to feel comfortable with the opposite sex, but it may take a while for a young person to develop this level of self-confidence. Whichever parent the child chooses, don't limit your discussions to matters affecting his or her own sex. Boys need to learn about girls, and girls about boys.

What Preteens Want (and Need) to Know

Children entering puberty need facts. Try to anticipate their questions and provide them with as much accurate information as you can. It helps to have at least one detailed, illustrated book on puberty on your shelf. When your child asks a question, don't hand him the book and send him to his room. That's a cop-out. Read sections together and leave it on the shelf for later reference. Your child will probably want to do some private reading when you're not around.

In general, it's a good idea to give adolescents a little more information than they ask for (menstruation *and* ovulation, erections *and* ejaculation, for example). Mix questions with answers: "Did you ever wonder about . . . ?" "Have any of your friends told you. . . ?" Don't dismiss their questions because you think they are too young to be thinking about such matters. Encourage them to think ahead.

Young teenagers not only want facts, they want to know how it feels. Your own experiences and those of your friends are a rich source of anecdotes. Your high-school yearbook may do more than anything you can say to convince the young person that individuals who were short or gawky or pimply in adolescence can become attractive, successful adults.

Above all, adolescents need reassurance. It *is* awkward to be taller or shorter than anyone in your class; embarrassing to have pimples; difficult to adjust to menstruation; strange to experience sexual excitement for the first time; and frightening not to know how you will look a year or two from now. Preteens and older teens need to be reassured that puberty isn't weird or painful or "gross" but a natural process and a sign that they are growing up. They won't be "invaded by alien forces"; they've had the equipment to become men and women since before birth, and sex hormones have been circulating in their bodies all along, though in less quantity than now. They won't suddenly change into new and unfamiliar people; they will remain themselves, even though their bodies are changing. And they will still be your son or daughter, long after they've grown up.

Menstruation   Menstruation deserves special attention and sensitivity. Girls may have learned the biological reasons for menstruation in health class, but they are also exposed to mixed cultural messages. "Congratulations, you're a woman now" is offset by "Poor thing, you've got this awful curse to deal with each month." Ads for feminine products promise "new freedom" but also imply that a girl needs to fill an entire medicine cabinet with products that will make her feel fresh and keep her spirits up at "that time of the month."

Here are the questions girls ask most often.

• *Why do girls have periods?* By now, your daughter should know the basic facts of reproduction, but it won't hurt to go over them again.

Girls are born with some 400,000 egg cells in their ovaries. Each egg cell is enclosed in its own follicle or sac. These cells lie dormant until puberty, when the girl's body begins to manufacture the hormones that govern her reproductive cycle. In the first phase of this cycle, one, or occasionally two, egg cells begin to mature, and the follicle starts to produce the hormone estrogen. Estrogen has two effects. First, it causes the lining of the uterus to grow and thicken, in preparation for a pregnancy. Second, when it reaches peak levels, about fourteen days after the cycle begins, it triggers ovulation. The now ripe egg cell bursts from its follicle, floats to a fallopian tube, and drifts down the fallopian tube toward the uterus. This journey takes two to three days, and these are the days when a girl can become pregnant. Meanwhile, the empty follicle stops producing estrogen and begins secreting progesterone, the hormone that sustains pregnancy. If the egg cell is not fertilized before it reaches the uterus, it disintegrates, hormone production drops, the blood vessels in the uterus pinch off, and the lining of the uterus is expelled as menstrual flow, about fourteen days after ovulation. The low levels of hormones in the girl's system signal another egg cell to begin growing, and the cycle starts again.

While a young adolescent may not need to know all about hormones, she should know when she is likely to ovulate—*and* that the exact timing of ovulation varies from woman to woman and cycle to cycle.

• *When will I get my period?* There is no normal or right or best age for menstruation to begin. Each girl's body develops at its own rate. The age at which she begins menstruating will not affect her figure as an adult, her ability to have children, her enjoyment of sex, or anything else. Any age between 10 and 16 is within the normal range. Make sure your daughter understands this.

If a girl has not shown any sign of puberty (breast buds, pubic hair) by age 13, or not gotten her period by age 16, you should consult a physician. And if she is within the normal range, but upset that she is ahead or behind her friends, a visit to a physician may reassure her that she is developing normally. '

• *How long does a period last and how much blood will I lose?* This varies from woman to woman and cycle to cycle. The flow may consist of a few teaspoons or half a cup over a period of three days to a week. Typically, it is brownish-red at the beginning, dark red as the flow becomes heavier, then a rusty color near the end. The girl may notice what looks like clots of blood; these are loosened pieces of the uterine lining. During the first few years after she has begun to menstruate, a girl's periods may be heavier and last longer than they will when she is older. You might point out that she isn't actually "bleeding"; her body produced extra blood that it doesn't need unless she becomes pregnant.

• *What is a "regular" cycle?* This varies, too. Some women menstruate every twenty-eight days, some every thirty-five, others somewhere in between. For the first year after menstruation begins, a girl's periods often are irregular. In some cases, there is no pattern. In others, a girl has several regular periods every twenty-eight days or so, skips a month or more, then experiences heavier and more prolonged bleeding than she did before. Missed periods (called amenhorrhea) may be caused by a change in environment (a summer trip, a shift to boarding school), sudden and rapid weight loss (because of illness or extreme dieting), *very* strenuous physical exercise (daily ballet classes or long-distance running), emotional stress (trouble at home, a broken friendship), or, of course, pregnancy. Sometimes they just happen. Usually there is no cause for concern. As the girl matures, her periods will become more regular and predictable. If amenhorrhea persists for as long as six months—and you are certain that your child isn't pregnant—it would be wise to see a physician.

• *Is it better to use pads or tampons?* This is a matter of personal choice. Most women find that tampons are both more reliable (pads rarely stay in place, so accidents are likely) and more convenient (tampons slip easily into a purse, don't show under tight clothes, don't smell, and flush down the toilet). Contrary to what many people believe, there is no reason why a young girl who hasn't had intercourse shouldn't use tampons. As noted above, the hymen usually has a natural opening large enough to admit a tampon. Contrary to what many girls believe, a tampon cannot get lost "up there." The vaginal passage is closed at the top by the cervix. If the tampon string disappears, she can always find it with her finger. A tampon can't fall out (except perhaps while she is going to the bathroom). Once a girl learns how to get a tampon into place, she won't feel it's there. The main problem with tampons is remembering to change them frequently (four to five times a day). Some girls don't like the idea of inserting something into their bodies, however. And some like to use a tampon and a pad, particularly on heavy days.

• *What is toxic shock syndrome?* It's a rare but deadly bacterial infection that develops in the vagina and seeps into the bloodstream. The toxic-shock-syndrome scare, caused in part by a particular tampon product since removed from the market, has subsided. Only about one in 25,000 women develops this problem, usually because she forgot she was using a tampon. With current products, the risk is slight. However, if a girl suddenly develops a high fever, vomiting, and diarrhea, she should remove the tampon and get to a doctor immediately. To be extra safe, a girl might want to use pads instead of tampons at night.

• *Does menstruation smell?* Menstrual blood does have a strong odor when it is exposed to the air, another reason why many women prefer tampons. If a girl who is using pads changes them regularly, disposes of them immediately, showers frequently (perhaps twice a day during her period), and changes her underwear regularly, there shouldn't be a problem.

Underlying this question may be a more general fear that "everyone will know" she is menstruating. Everyone won't know. But ads for various forms of "feminine deodorants" may feed a girl's anxieties. These products are not only unnecessary, but may cause irritation and rashes. An unusual discharge between periods, with a particularly strong smell, may be a sign of infection, however, and the girl should see her doctor.

• *What if I have an accident?* Because the flow is sometimes heavier in the first years of menstruation, and because the girl is still learning how to use pads or tampons, she probably will stain her underpants, clothes, or sheets now and then. Suggest that she can avoid embarrassment in the locker room by wearing dark-colored panties and buy her several pairs. Explain that the way to treat menstrual or other blood stains is to soak the garment in cold water as soon as possible. If she stains her bed clothes during the night, tell her to let you know and you'll take care of it discreetly, when her father and siblings aren't around.

• *What causes cramps?* No one knows for sure. The best guess is that overproduction of hormonelike substances called protaglandins causes the uterus to contract, blocking menstrual flow. Whatever the cause, most women experience discomfort at some point in their life, ranging from dull aches to intermittent but severe abdominal cramps. The old remedies—two aspirin and a heating pad applied to the abdomen at night—are still the best. The fact that a girl had cramps this month does not mean she will have them the next, however, and cramps usually become less frequent and severe as a girl gets older.

A few girls and women experience extreme discomfort— headaches, backaches, pains in the inner thighs, nausea, and severe cramps—during their periods. Dysmenorrhea, as this is called, is not normal. A girl who has such extreme pain before or during her period should see a physician. Dysmenorrhea may be caused by hormonal imbalances, pelvic infection, or the growth outside the uterus of tissue that should be lining the uterus (endometriosis). All of these problems can be treated. Many young women find that menstrual discomfort subsides when they take birth control pills.

• *What activities are okay during menstruation?* Any activities she likes—hiking, tennis, gymnastics, horseback riding, swimming, what have you. In the "old days" (twenty-five years ago), girls were often excused from gym class when they had their period. This was probably a mistake: Many girls and women find that exercise prevents or reduces the intensity of cramps.

• *What is PMS?* PMS, or premenstrual syndrome, refers to a range of emotional disturbances some women may experience just before they get their periods, including moodiness, depression, irritability, and lethargy. PMS is highly controversial. No one knows whether all women experience at least mild forms of PMS, or only some women; whether PMS is caused by fluctuations in hormone levels or by learned (that is, culturally induced) anxieties about menstruation. Some experts think PMS is a myth; others cite PMS as the reason why a woman shouldn't be elected president! Given this confusion, we recommend playing down PMS with your daughter. You might tell her that some women get "touchy" before their periods, but many do not. If she thinks that she is one of the few, she should go easy on herself when she is expecting her period. But don't let her use PMS as an excuse to pick on her younger sister or be rude to you.

• *Can you get pregnant before you've started having your period?* Yes, you can. Ovulation takes place about fourteen days *before* menstruation.

Conception is unlikely in the early stages of puberty. Most girls do not ovulate regularly for a year or two after their periods begin, a phenomenon known as adolescent subfertility. But this does *not* mean that pregnancy is impossible. There is no way of anticipating whether a girl who has just begun to menstruate will or will not ovulate in a given cycle. Girls need to be warned that the fact that they are immature or have skipped periods does not mean that they are "safe." (See Talking to Young Adolescents about Sex, chapter 5.)

• *Can you skip periods even if you are not pregnant?* Yes, especially in the first years of menstruation, as explained above. If there is any chance the girl might be pregnant, however, consult a physician immediately.

• *Do you menstruate for the rest of your life?* No, most women stop menstruating in their fifties (menopause).

In addition to explaining the biology of menstruation to your daughter and answering her questions, you should help her prepare for the event. Go to the drug store together and select the pads and/or tampons she'd like to use. When you get home, decide on a convenient and private place to store her supply. Then go over the directions, making sure she knows how to use and dispose of them. Plan in advance what she will do if she gets her first period when she's away from home. Are there vending machines in her school? If not, she can go to the school nurse. Does she know which friends are likely to have a pad or tampons in their lockers or purses? Remind her that frequent changes and showers will make her feel fresher. Finally, if she is the first or last of her friends to get her period, reassure her that each individual develops according to her own biological timetable.

The Forgotten Boy Parents are more likely to prepare girls for puberty than they are boys, for several reasons. First and most obviously, girls need to deal with menstruation. Second, and equally obviously, girls can become pregnant. Although boys make girls pregnant, the risk may not seem as urgent or direct. Third, menstruation is not tied directly to sexuality. Talking to a preadolescent daughter about her period is no more difficult than explaining "the birds and bees" to a younger child. Erections and ejaculation bring up potentially embarrassing questions about sexual fantasies, erotic dreams, and masturbation, topics many parents hope to avoid. Finally, gender stereotypes hold that boys are all too eager to achieve sexual maturity. Yet a substantial minority of boys (perhaps one in five) are frightened the first time they ejaculate or have a wet dream. Some are afraid that their body has "sprung a leak"; others that they have contracted a venereal disease.

What do boys want to know?

• *How are males and females different inside?* Males and females not only have different sex organs, but also different sex hormones. After puberty, the boy's testes manufacture sperm continuously. Sperm are stored in coiled tubes on top of the testes. If they are not "used" (if the boy or man does not ejaculate), the sperm simply disintegrate. Sperm cannot be "used up," no matter how often a male ejaculates. The testes produce billions of sperm each month. (If this seems excessive, a single ejaculation may contain anywhere from 300 to 500 million sperm.) And whereas females can only become pregnant on two or three days of the month, a male can father a child at any time.

• *Why do boys get erections?* When males are stimulated, veins in the penis fill with blood and the penis becomes hard and erect. Erections may be caused by touching, rubbing, sexual thoughts, or sexual dreams. An erection may subside slowly, by itself, or quickly, if the male has an orgasm and ejaculates. (We're assuming the boy already knows that the "purpose" of an erection, in strictly biological terms, is to enable him to have intercourse.)

During adolescence, it takes very little stimulation for a boy to get an erection. Some boys find that wearing a jock strap makes erections less noticeable and saves them from embarrassment. By the middle of adolescence, spontaneous, unwanted erections become less and less likely, probably because hormone levels are more stable and the boy has more regular sexual outlets (masturbation, petting, intercourse, or some combination).

• *What is ejaculation?* It's the spurt of whitish liquid from the penis when a male reaches a sexual climax. This liquid, called semen, contains sperm and fluids that protect the sperm as they travel through the female's vagina, into her uterus, and up the fallopian tubes "in search of" an egg cell. Sperm can live inside the female's body for as many as four or five days.

Males urinate and ejaculate through the same opening, but during a climax the ducts for urination are closed off. Urine cannot mix with semen.

• *Do girls ejaculate?* No. When a girl becomes sexually aroused, the walls of her vagina become wet to enable the penis to slip in, and some of this lubricating fluid may drip down. But she does not ejaculate when she has an orgasm.

• *Does ejaculation sap your strength?* No. After an orgasm, a boy usually experiences a deep sense of relaxation, which may feel like weakness. He may not be able to have another erection for twenty minutes to an hour. But ejaculation, however frequent or infrequent, does not affect his overall vitality.

• *Is it dangerous to have an erection and not ejaculate?* No. It may be frustrating to become excited and not be able to relieve sexual tension there and then. But it will not cause sperm to "back up," the boy's testicles to swell ("blue balls"), or any other outcome he might imagine.

• *Where do wet dreams come from?* Because adolescent boys are easily aroused, a dream may cause them to have an erection and ejaculate in their sleep. (Girls may also have sexy dreams and reach a climax in their sleep.) Wet dreams are caused by the combination of an erotic dream and friction or pressure from the boy's pajamas or sheets. A boy cannot have a spontaneous emission while he is awake; an erection will simply go away if he doesn't touch himself. And the content of his dreams says nothing about his future sexual orientation and behavior (see Feelings and Sexual Fantasies, chapter 5). Like involuntary erections, wet dreams become less and less frequent as a boy matures and becomes more sexually active (masturbating and/or having intercourse). But grown men may have wet dreams now and then.

Parents should tell their son that there is nothing to be ashamed about; he isn't "wetting his bed," he is simply growing up. Tell him that if his pajamas or sheets are stained, he should simply drop them in the hamper and you'll supply new ones.

• *Is my penis big enough?* Yes. A look around the locker room tells a boy that there are many variations in size and shape. In part, this is because boys are in different stages of puberty; in part, because of inborn individual differences. When erect, however, most penises are from 4 to 6 inches long and quite adequate for intercourse. Contrary to what many boys believe, neither masturbation nor frequent intercourse affect the size of the penis. And there is no reason to try to make the penis grow. Any woman can tell the boy that his "rating" as a lover will depend on his sensitivity and sexual technique, not on the size of his equipment.

• *Why are my nipples swollen?* Perhaps two-thirds of boys develop a swelling around the nipple in the early stages of puberty. This does *not* mean that the boy is developing breasts. The swelling will disappear in a year to eighteen months. Why does this occur? Both sexes have the same hormones circulating in their bodies. The difference lies in the proportions: Females' bodies produce more estrogen and progesterone, males' bodies more androgen and testosterone. During puberty, however, hormone levels fluctuate. For a time the boy's body may manufacture too much estrogen and too little androgen. This has no long-term effect on appearance, no effect on sexual functioning, and eventually the male balance will be restored. If a boy is concerned—if he won't take his shirt off at the beach, for example—a visit to a physician can assure him that there is nothing wrong and he is not developing breasts.

Notes for Parents   Puberty can take parents by surprise, too. Here are some guidelines.

• *Don't confuse muscles with maturity.* Puberty follows a biological timetable that has little or no relation to social, emotional, and intellectual development. The fact that a young person looks grown-up tells you nothing about his ability to make intelligent decisions, behave responsibly, exercise self-control, or other measures of maturity. Parents as well as peers tend to admire boys who look mature early in their teens and to baby those whose physical development is slower. This is unfair to both. Early maturers may be forced into adult roles at too early an age (for example, being assigned extra chores around the house because of their size) and denied needed opportunities to be childish and playful ("If you're old enough to shave, you're old enough to know better"). Late maturers may be denied privileges at home and responsibilities at school simply because they still look like children.

• *Avoid the "Lolita assumption."* The fact that a girl is biologically advanced does not mean that she is sexually precocious. Don't presume her "guilty" until she proves herself innocent. She may or may *not* be interested in dating. If she does want to go out with an older boy, base your decision on the same criteria you would use for another child (her level of maturity, what you know about

the boy, where they plan to go, whether there will be adult supervision, and the like). When you decide that she's too young to go
on a camping trip with an older, mixed crowd, she may be relieved.

• *"I hate myself!"* At times all adolescents feel uncomfortable
with their changing bodies. Don't dismiss their anxieties by saying
"You'll grow out of it"; that won't help now. Listen to the teenager's complaints. When he has calmed down a little, try to determine if there was something specific that plunged him into
despair. Then deal with that specific issue. If an early-maturing
girl is unhappy with her bust, help her find bras and clothing
styles that will make her shape less obvious. Don't force a boy who
is growing by leaps and bounds to wear pants that stop 4 inches
above his ankle. Look for opportunities to remind the adolescent
who is late maturing physically that he or she is growing up emotionally.

HEALTH AND HEALTH CARE IN ADOLESCENCE

As children enter adolescence, they become more and more conscious of their looks but tend to take their health for granted.
How can parents help their adolescent look and feel good?

Diet, Exercise, and Sleep

During periods of rapid growth such as puberty, the body needs
extra nutrition—especially protein to build muscles, calcium to
build bones and strengthen teeth, vitamins, and minerals. Girls in
particular need iron, calcium, and protein. A girl's diet during
puberty will affect both her own health and that of her infant
many years later. But both sexes need three square meals a day,
plus healthy snacks of milk, fruit, and the like.

At the time when young people need a balanced diet most,
they are slipping away from the family table. Studies show that
adolescents, and especially adolescent girls, are one of the most
poorly nourished groups in America. The chief culprits in adolescent subnutrition are skipping meals, mainly breakfast, going on
crash diets, and filling up on junk food. Candy bars and fries
don't cause acne, and Twinkees don't cause violent mood swings.
But neither do they provide the young adolescent's body with the
building materials it needs to grow.

Changing Shape   Most adolescents are unhappy with their shape. Typically, boys worry about being skinny and underdeveloped; girls more often worry about not being thin enough. This new self-awareness can lead to healthy attempts to trim down or build up—or to an unhealthy preoccupation with eating and/or dieting.

It's important for both parents and teenagers to know what is normal. Changes in weight and proportion are to be expected during puberty—the average teenager puts on 10 pounds a year between the ages of 10 and 14. But development is not always even. A girl may fill out before she reaches her full height and so look chubby for a time; a boy may grow before he fills out and appear skinny.

The charts on pages 86–89, developed by the National Center for Health Statistics, show height and weight percentiles for children and adolescents of different ages, separately for boys and girls. For example, a 10-year-old boy who weighs 70 pounds is at the 50th percentile in weight for his age, whereas a 13-year-old girl who stands 5 feet 3 inches tall is at the 75th percentile in height for hers. By using the height and weight charts together, you can determine whether your adolescent's weight is out of synch with his or her height.

Begin by measuring your adolescent's height and finding, on the appropriate height chart, the corresponding percentile for a boy or girl of that age. Now, using that percentile, look on the weight chart to see how much the adolescent's weight is over or under what might be expected. For example, a 14-year-old girl who is 5 feet 3 inches tall is at about the 50th percentile in height for her age. The 50th percentile in weight for 14-year-old girls is about 110 pounds. This is the figure against which a 14-year-old girl of this height should compare her actual weight.

Averages, of course, do not reflect differences in build and activity level. In general, an adolescent who is within 10 percent of the expected weight for someone of the same height and age (in the case of the 14-year-old girl above, between 99 and 121 pounds), is well within the normal range. If an adolescent's weight is 20 percent or more above the expected figure, parents should be concerned (see Obesity, below). While being slightly underweight is less cause for concern, sudden or dramatic weight loss may be a sign of serious medical problems, or if self-induced, psychological problems (see Eating Disorders, chapter 8).

Keeping Fit For many adults, fitness has reached the level of a fad. In contrast, today's children and adolescents are fatter and flabbier than the children of two decades ago. A surprising number lag behind their active, middle-aged parents in cardiovascular fitness. One reason for this is that adolescents lead more sedentary lives today. They are less likely to walk to school or bike to their friends' houses and more likely to spend hours in front of the TV. Another problem is that schools emphasize competitive sports. The minority of adolescents who make a team spend hours after school in training. But the average student gets only two or three hours of physical education a week, and much of that time is spent standing around. Moreover, participation in football, basketball, hockey, and other competitive sports is usually limited to the school years. It is a good idea for parents to encourage physical activities outside school that offer *lifelong* participation—swimming, tennis, hiking, jogging, biking, walking, and the like. In addition to promoting physical fitness, sports help adolescents relieve tension, build self-confidence, make friends, and generally feel good about themselves.

Getting Rest Many adolescents have trouble getting up in the morning, fall asleep in the afternoon, and generally seem to have less energy than they did as children. Part of the reason, of course, is that they are staying up later (watching TV, talking to friends, reading, or studying). But part of the reason is biological: Growing consumes energy. Furthermore, many of the hormones that stimulate pubertal development are released during sleep. Sleep is as important to adolescent health as diet and exercise.

Obesity: Causes and Treatments

Causes Approximately 15 percent of American teenagers are seriously overweight. Obesity rarely begins in adolescence, but often becomes more pronounced in the teenage years. Why? Basal metabolism rate (the rate at which the body burns up calories) drops by about 15 percent in adolescence. Add to this the fact that teenagers have easier access to fast foods and snacks than children do, and the results of poor eating habits developed in childhood are magnified.

Experts used to trace obesity to psychological causes: People

Weight for Age

BOYS FROM 2 TO 18 YEARS

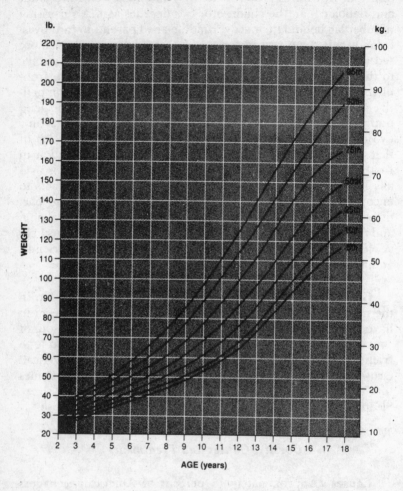

Height for Age

BOYS FROM 2 TO 18 YEARS

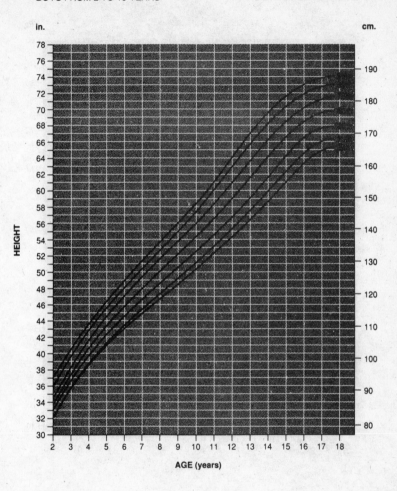

Weight for Age

GIRLS FROM 2 TO 18 YEARS

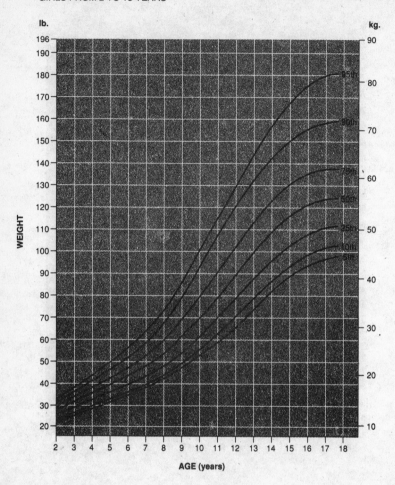

Height for Age

GIRLS FROM 2 TO 18 YEARS

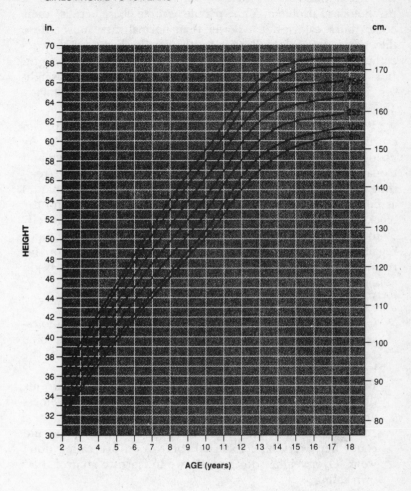

became fat because they ate to fill unmet psychological needs. Current thinking holds that obesity is more a medical than a psychological problem. Many people become obese because their bodies burn calories at a slower than normal rate, not because they gorge themselves. Because of their body chemistry, they accumulate more and larger fat cells than people of normal weight. It is also much harder for them to lose weight or to keep weight off. The tendency to become obese is at least in part hereditary.

What to Do   Virtually all overweight teenagers want to trim down. The problem is, they don't know how. There are many good weight management programs for overweight children and teenagers. Most combine diet with self-awareness training (realizing when and why you eat), behavioral change (such techniques as putting down your fork between bites or walking around the block before you have a snack), and peer support. Unfortunately, 50 to 70 percent of teenagers who lose weight on these programs regain the unwanted pounds when the program stops. For this reason, most experts agree that weight management must begin at home. How can parents help?

Parents should *not*

- Constantly call attention to the teenager's weight. The adolescent knows all too well that she is fat, and doesn't need to be reminded. Don't talk about the adolescent's weight unless she brings it up first.
- Berate the young person for being fat. Nagging will only deepen the overweight adolescent's feelings of unworthiness and self-distrust.
- Insist that the adolescent go on a highly restrictive diet and count her every bite. External controls on overeating don't work. Overweight adolescents have to learn to control their own eating.

Parents *should* encourage sensible eating and exercise patterns for everyone in the family. Your goal should be to discourage overeating, not to deprive or shame the overweight child. In her column, "Personal Health," Jane Brody writes:

- Establish dependable mealtimes and plan nutritious meals that are low in fat. . . . Urge your child to eat every meal, especially breakfast. Overweight children are notorious meal-skippers, which undermines their self-control at the next meal.

- Serve the same foods to the entire family rather than preparing special foods for the child with the weight problem. Be sure to include foods the child likes.
- Do not eliminate any category of food. Rather, substitute lean meats for fatty sausages, ribs or steaks; broil or bake chicken and fish rather than fry it. . . .
- Provide plenty of bulky, low-calorie foods and foods that take a long time to eat or that require lots of chewing [salads, crunchy vegetables, soups]. . . .
- To control portion size, dish up individual servings from the stove rather than setting platters on the table. Encourage your child to eat to the point of satiation but not beyond, and to wait at least 20 minutes from the start of the meal before asking for seconds (it takes that long for fullness to register). . . .
- Plan two or three low-calorie, nutritious snacks a day: fruit, vegetables with dip, hot-air-popped corn, a small homemade muffin, a frozen juice bar. . . .
- Insist that food be eaten in only one or two places in the house —the kitchen and dining room, for instance. Allow no eating in bedrooms, while watching television or while doing homework.
- Keep food—especially tempting, high-calorie foods—out of sight. . . .
- Don't forbid fast foods, takeout foods and dining out. But you can discuss choices that are reasonable in calories, like a plain burger rather than a cheeseburger, a baked potato rather than fries, chocolate milk rather than a shake. . . .
- Don't ban high-calorie treats, especially at social occasions where everyone else is indulging. Depending on what your child loves most, you might suggest that two cookies . . . a small candy bar or ice cream be the dessert or snack once a week. . . .
- Many youngsters (and adults) with weight problems do not overeat, but rather underexercise. A heavy child might not fare well in competitive and team sports, but could shine in individual activities like cycling, skating, swimming, jumping rope, jogging, hiking or weight-training. Encourage children to walk rather than ride whenever feasible. Plan some physically active family outings for weekends.

- Help [your] child develop hobbies that can keep the hands busy and the mind off food.
- Above all, be sure to let your children know that they are loved and appreciated [no matter what] their size and shape.

Many overweight adolescents are tempted by crash diets that promise miracle results. These should be discouraged. A teenager might lose 10 pounds on a two-week liquid diet, but this won't teach her how to eat sensibly under normal conditions. In addition, severe dieting may increase the appetite and lower the metabolism rate, making further or sustained weight loss more difficult.

A realistic goal is losing about 2 pounds a week. Most experts recommend a combination of diet and exercise. *Not* stopping for a burger, fries, and a shake several times a week, eating sensible meals and snacks, walking the half-hour to and from school at a good pace, and doing forty-five minutes of strenuous exercise three times a week should lead to slow but steady weight loss. To a teenager who needs to lose 30 pounds or more, a loss of 2 pounds may seem unnoticeable and a diet extending over many months, impossible. Help the adolescent set specific goals for the not-too-distant future—returning to school after summer vacation 20 pounds lighter, or losing 15 pounds before Christmas and shopping in the regular junior, not the "chubby" department, for a size 13 or 11 dress.

Acne: Myths and Facts

Acne is not a "normal" part of adolescence; it is a medical problem that deserves serious attention. What causes acne? All of the glands become more active during puberty, including the oil glands just under the surface of the skin. Acne develops when oil and bacteria get trapped in an oil gland and infect the surrounding tissue. The first sign of acne is an inflammation, or pimple. Over time, the inflammation develops into a pustule or yellowhead, or into a cyst or boil if the infection is well below the skin surface. Acne most often develops on the face, especially around the hairline, neck, shoulders, and back, where oil glands are most numerous.

Having described what acne is, we need to say what it is not. Acne is *not* caused by slovenliness; adolescents do *not* get pimples because they are not bathing or washing their faces often enough.

The infection is under the skin, and no amount of scrubbing can wash it away, though regular washing can prevent the infection from getting worse. Acne is *not* caused by eating junk food. Cutting back on chocolate and french fries may be good for health in general, but it won't improve an adolescent's complexion. Finally, acne is *not* related in any way to sex. Among themselves, adolescents may joke that a friend has acne because of too much sexual activity (especially masturbation) or too little ("he isn't getting any"). They're wrong.

To date, there is no known way of preventing acne. But it *can* be controlled. In mild cases, a good soap keeps oil from sitting on the skin and dust or makeup from clogging pores, making acne worse than it already is. Frequent shampooing helps cut down on pimples along the hairline. Over-the-counter preparations containing benzoyl peroxide, applied each night, can prevent oil from building up overnight and reduce the number of blackheads or whiteheads. Benzoyl peroxide creams do not work quickly; to be effective, they must be used steadily. An occasional blackhead or whitehead can be removed by gentle squeezing with clean fingertips. But performing this "operation" with dirty fingernails, or working on an area that is already inflamed, will cause more harm than good and should be avoided. Scrubbing, as well, is not recommended, since it only irritates an already inflamed area.

In severe cases, or in cases where the over-the-counter preparations do not work, we strongly recommend taking the teenager to a dermatologist. Untreated, acne can leave permanent scars on the young person's face, not to mention his or her psyche. Why make the child suffer? A dermatologist may prescribe a preparation that includes benzoyl peroxide, but in higher concentration than is available over the counter; tretinoin, a derivative of vitamin A marketed under several different product names, including Retin-A; or topical antibiotics, including erythromycin or clindamycin. Steroids, applied as a cream or injected directly into severe red pimples, kill infections that have already started and lessen the probability of permanent scars. Topical treatments are typically quite effective, although different ones work better than others for particular sorts of skin problems.

In very bad cases, a dermatologist may consider prescribing an oral medication called isotretinoin (Accutane). Although highly effective, this drug carries two risks: If a woman becomes pregnant while using it, there is a high risk the baby will suffer birth defects; and if she does not use strong sun screens, she stands a slightly higher than average risk of developing skin cancer. As a last resort, a dermatologist or plastic surgeon can remove the top layer of skin and some or all of the scars (a procedure called dermabrasion). This can only be done in late adolescence, after the acne itself has abated, and can be avoided by earlier treatment.

Finally, there is evidence that birth control pills cut back on the production of skin oil and hence reduce the likelihood of acne. Obviously, this doesn't help boys, and most girls would not start taking the pill for acne alone.

Cosmetic Concerns

A tiny imperfection that went unnoticed in childhood may suddenly become a source of constant misery in adolescence. Some youngsters are convinced that they will not be happy (or popular, which amounts to the same thing) until they have changed their looks. There is no point in arguing that looks aren't important. They are, and not only to adolescents. For some adolescents dissatisfaction is a passing phase; others, however, truly feel "deformed." Dismissing adolescents' complaints outright may only convince them that you don't want them to be attractive.

The cosmetic changes adolescents frequently request include

- Removing excess facial or body hair (for girls).
- Pierced ears and sometimes multiple piercings for boys as well as girls. Pierced ears on boys are not, as some adults believe, a symbol of homosexuality; they are simply a fashion statement.
- Removing birthmarks and moles.
- Tattoos.
- Rhinoplasty (or a "nose job").

If your adolescent brings up a cosmetic change, here is what you should consider:

- *How bad is the problem?* Is his nose or her mole really disfiguring? Parents tend to minimize their children's imperfections, having grown used to their looks. But adolescents want their peers' approval, not their parents' unconditional love—on this issue. To get an objective opinion, ask a friend or relative whom you know to be honest, or a physician who would not perform the procedure him- or herself.

How safe is the procedure? Home cures are generally to be avoided. It's much safer to have your ears pierced by a doctor or in a reputable jewelry store than by a friend.

• *How permanent is the change?* The more permanent the change, the more thought should go into the decision. Tattoos, for example, are impossible to remove without leaving a scar or discoloration.

• *Is the timing right?* Some procedures should wait until the young person has grown. Many youngsters "grow into" their noses, for example. But others, such as braces for protruding teeth, are better taken care of now.

• *Does the youngster understand the costs and benefits of the change?* Youngsters sometimes pin all their anxieties and problems onto a small blemish. Your daughter may imagine that removing that mole will magically transform her into a ravishing beauty and the most popular girl in seventh grade. Before agreeing to a procedure, make sure the youngster has informed and *realistic* expectations.

Feeling good and looking good are important to a youngster's self-esteem; parents shouldn't belittle an adolescent's cosmetic concerns.

RESOURCES

Some young people "graduate" from their pediatrician in their preteens. If you are seeking a new physician for your teenager, information about and assistance in locating a specialist in the field of adolescent medicine can be obtained from *The Society for Adolescent Medicine,* 10727 White Oak Avenue, Granada Hills, CA 91344. This organization maintains listings of health care providers around the country who specialize in adolescence.

CHAPTER 5

Sexual Awakening

*L*earning to think of oneself as a sexual being, deal with sexual feelings, and enjoy a new kind of relationship with another human being are among the central developmental tasks of adolescence. Helping young people develop attitudes toward sex and sexuality that are realistic, positive, informed, and responsible is a key task for parents.

QUESTIONS YOUR CHILD MAY NOT ASK

All young adolescents are curious about sex, but many are too modest or shy to speak up. What is on their minds? Here are some of the most common questions young adolescents ask:

- Am I crazy for thinking about sex?
- Do all people feel this way?
- Am I normal to want to masturbate?
- Could I become a homosexual?
- How will I know when and how to do it?

Sexual Feelings and Fantasies

Feeling pleasure is not a new experience for adolescents, but feeling "horny" is. In the early stages of puberty, especially, many young people wonder where these feelings come from, if they and they alone are experiencing these cravings, and what to do about them.

There is no easy answer to the question of where sexual feelings come from. Undoubtedly hormones play a role. And because the body's production of hormones is accelerating in adolescence, sexual feelings may seem more intense, more urgent, than they do in adulthood. But hormones are only half the story. The cultural belief that boys are supposed to be horny and girls, if not horny, romantic, plays an equal role in sexual awakening. Perhaps children have been experiencing tinglings and longings all along, but only in adolescence do they begin to label these sensations as sexual.

What we do know is that sexual desires and fantasies are normal and common. Everyone has them, not just teenagers, and not just boys. The most important thing for teenagers to know is that *no thought, by itself, is sick or weird or wrong*. Fantasies cannot harm you, no matter how bizarre or "far out" they are. At some time in their lives, almost everyone imagines making love to a member of the same sex, seducing a sibling, joining in an orgy, fornicating in a church, watching a neighbor undress, forcing or being forced to engage in sexual acts. Rape is wrong; incest is wrong; feeling aroused *only* when you are spying (the Peeping Tom syndrome) is sad. But *thinking* about forbidden acts is normal.

The only real harm in sexual fantasies is guilt. Young people who believe that their fantasies and dreams reveal something hidden and horrible about themselves are the most likely to be upset about their sexuality and also the most likely to become obsessed by a fantasy. It is important that young adolescents understand that fantasies are just that—fantasies.

In a survey of 1,067 teenagers, more than three-quarters of the boys and about two-thirds of the girls said they had sexual fantasies. The most common object of their desire was their current girl- or boyfriend, followed by TV or movie stars, friends and acquaintances, strangers, rock stars, made-up people, and relatives. Today, as in the past, girls' fantasies tended to be romantic, while boys' fantasies tended to be sexually explicit. Girls still dream of being swept off their feet. They do not, however, fantasize about a stranger forcing them to have sex. Teenagers' fantasies do not support the myth that "all women secretly want to be raped." Because boys' fantasies are often graphic, boys are somewhat more likely to feel guilty about them. And because their urges and fantasies may lead to unwanted erections and wet dreams, they are more likely to be embarrassed. Because many girls have been socialized to think that "nice" women don't think about sex, they are somewhat more likely to feel that they are the only ones having such thoughts.

Contrary to what adults believe or fear, many young people *prefer* fantasy to action. Daydreams are a safer initiation to sexuality than actual contact. In their fantasies, they are the producer, director, screenwriter, and cameraman; flaws can be swept away with the airbrush of imagination; scenes can be played and replayed until they come out right. Psychiatrist Robert Coles describes a 15-year-old boy who had every social and material advantage, but found the pressure to be top in his class, to excell at sports, and to find a girl who met his parents' exacting standards too much. He told Coles, "I want out." Instead of acting out, the boy had been carrying on a long, intimate, deeply committed, and wholly imaginary affair with a famous model. They traveled to remote islands, studied together, made love in meadows. The most important aspect of this fantasy was that it was *his*.

Parents should answer their childrens' questions about sexual desires and fantasies, but respect their privacy.

Masturbation

Woody Allen once quipped, "I enjoy masturbation. At least I know I'm having sex with someone I love." Twenty-five years ago, this remark would have been considered scandalous; today, we laugh. We also laugh about the old myths that masturbation causes warts, hairy palms, blindness, and insanity. Surprisingly, adolescents haven't gotten this message.

New myths have replaced the old ones. Many teenagers believe that masturbation means you are a homosexual. (There is no connection.) Some believe that masturbation stunts your sexual development, saps your strength, or causes acne. (It doesn't.) A few still believe tales of hairy palms and insanity. Among boys, especially, the general feeling is that masturbation isn't "real sex," that it is immature. Masturbation is still a dirty word for teenagers. The slang boys use to describe it—"jacking off," "wacking it" —is derogatory; girls seldom have slang terms for it.

Masturbation is one sexual topic adolescents do not discuss among themselves, even with their best friends. If they do bring the subject up with their parents, their questions are likely to be indirect. "Is having intercourse the only way to not be a virgin?" (Yes, that's what *virgin* means.) "Can a guy use up his sperm?" (No, as explained earlier.) "If a girl puts her finger in her vagina, will she break her hymen?" (She may, but this is unlikely.)

To set the record straight, for parents as well as teenagers: Masturbation is a natural, harmless way of feeling sexual pleasure and relieving sexual tension. Most people masturbate at times, even when they are married and have a good sex life. Some people masturbate a lot, some very rarely, and some not at all. All of these patterns are normal and healthy. If you enjoy masturbation, that's fine; if you don't, that's fine, too.

Parents should answer their children's direct or indirect questions honestly and matter-of-factly. And if they discover that a youngster is masturbating, they should not be surprised, angry, or concerned.

Homosexuality

An 18-year-old college student came to a counselor with a "terrible confession." After much hemming and hawing, he blurted out, "I'm a homosexual." The conversation continued as follows:

"Do you want to be a homosexual?"

"Of course not."

"Have you ever had a homosexual experience?"

"Of course not, what do you take me for?"

"I don't know yet. Have you ever had a heterosexual experience?"

"Of course not, I'm a homosexual. You're making fun of me."

"So far, the diagnosis is *asexual*."

It turned out that the boy had had homosexual fantasies at age 12 or 13 and was so upset by these fantasies that he avoided sex altogether thereafter. His fears and ignorance are only a slight exaggeration of common feelings.

At one time or another, almost all adolescents worry that they might be homosexual. At the age when most children enter puberty, they are still *homosocial*—that is, nearly all of their friends are members of the same sex and they spend most of their time with members of the same sex. As a result, they begin to experience sexual pangs before they have much contact with the opposite sex. A girl may find herself getting sexually excited during a tickling match with her best friend; a boy may get an erection when he thinks about all the wet naked bodies in the locker room. This does not mean they have homosexual inclinations; rather, their sexual development is temporarily ahead of their social development.

At one time or another, about half of all boys and a third of all girls play sex games (kissing experiments, group masturbation contests) with members of the same sex. These activities are motivated by curiosity, not sexual attraction. Most young people take these experiments for what they are—experiments. But some feel guilty and ashamed and begin to wonder about themselves.

In early adolescence, young people often develop "crushes" on a teacher or older child of the same sex. Some confuse hero- or heroine-worship with sexual attraction, particularly if their peers and parents tease them about their not-so-secret admiration.

Late developers (young people whose sex drive is not as strong as they think it "should" be) and older teens who are still virgins may doubt their heterosexuality, even if they have never felt attracted to a member of the same sex.

Finally, young people who do not fit sex stereotypes may be harrassed by their parents as well as their peers. Exhorting a boy who cries when his feelings are hurt, or one who is interested in theater, not football, to "act like a *man!*" is both cruel and counterproductive. Forcing frilly dresses and dates with your friends' sons on a girl who is most comfortable in a sweat suit and more interested in horses than boys right now won't change her interests, but it will create conflict. The world puts enough pressure on young people to behave in sex-stereotyped ways; they don't need more at home. Besides, these interests are not a "symptom" of "underlying" homosexuality.

There is no such thing as latent homosexuality—a trait many adolescents attribute to themselves, even if they don't know the term. Exaggerated fear or hatred of homosexuality, or a prurient interest in homosexuals, does not mean that a person "really is one." It simply means that the person is afraid or hostile or nosy. To say someone is a latent homosexual makes about as much sense as saying all women are latently pregnant.

Looking back, many adult homosexuals say that they always knew or that they remember the day they realized that they were gay. We suspect that this "certain knowledge" only developed through hindsight. Sexuality does not suddenly turn on, like a light bulb. Adolescence is a period of wondering, fantasizing, and

experimenting, for everyone. Sexual commitments and prefer-
ences are still tentative.

No one knows why some individuals develop a homosexual
orientation whereas the great majority become exclusively heterosexual. Attempts to trace homosexuality to genetic flaws, over- or
underproduction of sex hormones, family patterns (the domi-
neering mother/weak father syndrome), or "critical experiences"
have all foundered. This should not come as a surprise. Most
human characteristics are the result of overlapping, interacting
influences. Why should sexual orientation be easier to explain
than, say, school performance?

Current thinking indicates that an individual's sexual orientation is not a conscious or voluntary decision. There is nothing a
parent can or should do to prevent a young adolescent from
becoming gay or to "cure" an older adolescent or adult son or
daughter of his or her sexual orientation. Attempts to change an
individual's sexual orientation exact a heavy psychological price.
Suspicion, lectures, and pleas will only add to the adolescent's
anxieties, whatever his or her sexual inclinations. (See also Coming Out of the Closet in chapter 18.)

Homosexuality is not an illness. Homosexuals are no more
likely than heterosexuals to suffer from emotional or psychological problems, though in our society their lives are complicated by
prejudice. Nor is homosexuality a physical illness. Some people
object to homosexuality on moral or religious grounds. But it is
important to distinguish between moral judgments and medical
diagnoses.

Adolescents' anxieties about homosexuality are a reflection of
society's judgments. Children learn at an early age that calling
someone "faggot," "queer," "fairy," "lesbo," or "dyke" is the ultimate insult. They hurl these derogatory labels at one another
without thinking, and often without knowing, what they mean.
Attitudes toward homosexuality have become more tolerant in
recent years, but tolerance is not acceptance. A person can still be
denied a visa to the United States, discharged from the armed
forces, or dismissed from a job in the FBI or CIA solely because
he or she is homosexual. Even though overt discrimination in
other areas is against the law, a great many homosexuals live in
fear of losing their jobs or their leases, not to mention their
friends and families, if their orientation becomes known. Children should know this. The best evidence we have says that individuals are no more able to choose their sexual orientation than

they are to choose their race, gender, or social class. Discrimination against homosexuals is as wrong as discrimination against racial and ethnic minorities or against women.

Young people who learn that homosexuality is simply a different way of loving, not a sickness or a perversion, are less likely to worry about their own thoughts and experiences.

Pornography

Nine out of ten adolescents get their hands on soft-core pornography at some point. As often as not, they sneak magazines from a parent's or older sibling's stockpile. Males are much more likely than females to be turned on by photographs, at all ages. This does not mean that girls have no interest in erotica; they generally prefer romantic novels with torrid love scenes.

Most experts feel that *soft-core* pornography (pictures or descriptions of nude women and men in explicitly sexual poses and situations) is relatively harmless. Used as a means of satisfying curiosity, or as an accessory to masturbation, these materials will not speed up, slow down, or otherwise disrupt a young person's sexual development. If pornography is an adolescent's main or only source of information, however, it can create problems. The advice columns in these magazines specialize in fetishes, group sex, and other unusual sexual activities, which may give young people a distorted impression of how most adults behave. They may also create unrealistic expectations for sexual performance (a man should be able to maintain an erection for 20 minutes, a woman should have multiple, earth-shaking orgasms).

In most cases, fascination with pornography is a passing phase. Getting very upset or angry when you discover magazines hidden under the mattress is only likely to make the "forbidden fruit" seem more enticing. If you feel strongly about pornography, say so and say why. Use the teenager's copy of *Playboy* or *Penthouse* or *Fanny Hill* to point out that not everyone is built like a Playboy bunny; that pornographic magazines and books sell fantasies, not reality; that most people do not behave like the people the columns describe; that pornography treats women, and more rarely men, as sexual toys; or whatever you believe. But we don't think you should make a federal case of soft-core pornographic books or magazines.

Hard-core pornography (magazines and books with graphic

pictures or descriptions of people violating sexual taboos) is a different story. There is no evidence that representations of explicit sex drive people into uncontrollable sexual frenzy or cause them to engage in acts they would otherwise condemn. Hard-core pornography is not dangerous in this sense. But there are other reasons why it is not appropriate for young teenagers. Hard-core pornography links sex to aggression (sado-masochistic imagery is common), distorts male-female relationships (nearly always men are portrayed as dominating women, and women as accepting and even enjoying this), ignores intimacy (love and sex are totally disconnected, or love is confused with lust and obsession), and presents an unrealistic picture of sexual behavior (unconventional sex acts and fetishes greatly outnumber more conventional forms of arousal). In our view, parents should banish hard-core pornography from the home for all these reasons—and say why.

Pornographic films, now readily available as home videos and on some cable channels, are problematic for other reasons. Magazines and books leave room for imagination; pornographic films, even of the soft-core variety, do not. The actors are often chosen for their unusual builds; the scripts usually emphasize exceptional sexual prowess and exotic sexual tastes. At a stage when young people have many doubts about their own bodies and sexual competency, it isn't helpful to watch women with enormous breasts and men with huge penises mimicking sexual ecstacy. Such films are likely to raise unsettling questions (Am I supposed to moan and groan? Will I be able to perform eight times a night?) that adolescents will be embarrassed to ask, if only because asking means admitting they watched the video. Adult entertainment is for adults.

TALKING TO YOUNG ADOLESCENTS ABOUT SEX

Study after study shows that teenagers want more information about sex than they are getting. When asked how they would choose to learn about sex, nine out of ten say from their parents —yes, their *parents*—not from their friends or a health class or books. When asked if they actually talk to their parents about sex, however, only about *one* in ten says yes. The reason, according to most teenagers, is that their parents hold back. "Whenever I ask her something, she tells me 'later.' "

The Obstacles

Why are parents reluctant to discuss sex with their teenagers?

• *"I don't want to encourage sex."* Many parents believe that talking to young people about sex will lead to premature sexual activity; that children will interpret their parents' willingness to talk as permission to become sexually involved. Both beliefs are false. Learning about government didn't transform your children into political activists; why should learning about sex make them promiscuous? Researchers who have studied this question extensively find no evidence—repeat, none—that sex education, from whatever source, increases sexual activity. What they do find is that *lack* of education increases teenage pregnancy. The message children get from discussions of sex is the message you communicate. If you say that you do not think teenagers should have sex, your child will hear you. He or she may not agree with you, of course. But if you say nothing, you will never learn what your child thinks.

• *"My child knows more than I do."* Some parents believe that they don't need to discuss sex because their children already know whatever they need to know, from sex education in school or other sources. And some young adolescents are convinced they "know it all." They don't.

The sex education provided in a typical junior or senior high school consists of a total of five to ten hours of instruction and/or discussion. The emphasis is usually on anatomy and physiology. Teenagers sometimes refer to these classes as "organ recitals"— everything you ever wanted to know about the biology of human reproduction, and then some. Sexual feelings and sexual relationships—the issues that concern adolescents most—are rarely mentioned. If contraception and STDs (sexually transmitted diseases) are introduced, it is often in the eleventh and twelfth grades, which may be after the fact. In short, sex education in school tends to be too little, too late, and boring. So young people turn to their friends, older siblings, and whatever books, magazines, and TV shows are available, and they come up with a few facts, a good many half-truths, and almost as many untruths. Your adolescent may have an advanced sexual vocabulary, but this doesn't mean he knows what he's talking about.

Today's teenagers present a surprising mixture of sophistication and ignorance about sex. It is up to parents to find out what their children know, or think they know, and to correct misinformation. Early adolescence is not too soon to be talking about sex, relationships, conception, and pregnancy.

COMMON MYTHS

All of the following statements are FALSE.

- A boy's sex drive is stronger than a girl's.
- The larger a girl's breasts, the stronger her sex drive.
- When a girls says no, she really means yes.
- It is okay to tell a girl with whom you want to have sex that you love her when you really don't.
- A girl can't get pregnant if
    she is under twelve
    she has intercourse standing up
    she doesn't have an orgasm
    she douches with Coke after intercourse
    she takes a birth control pill the day before or morning after she
        has intercourse
    the boy pulls out before he reaches a climax
- Plastic wrap around the penis is as effective as a condom.
- Condoms are not a reliable form of birth control because they often break.
- It is illegal for minors to purchase over-the-counter contraceptives (such as condoms or vaginal foams).
- You don't need birth control if you only have sex occasionally.
- Birth control is the girl's responsibility.

Some parents avoid discussions about sex because they are afraid they won't know all the answers and will look foolish. If your own sex education left something to be desired, do some advance reading. Lut don't think you have to become an instant expert. If you don't know the answer, say so.

- *"I get embarrassed!"* Most parents feel somewhat uneasy talking about sex with adolescent children. Some imagine that the adolescent is really asking about what they do in bed with their spouse. Although adolescents may be curious about how you felt and what you did at their age, most do not think of their parents as having a sex life—one reason they say things like "You can't know what I'm feeling." For better or worse, they are more interested in themselves than anyone else at this age.

Some parents say that they feel like hypocrites when they try to tell their children sex is okay for adults but not for teenagers, especially if the parent is single and dating. But asking young adolescents to delay sex is no more unfair than requiring them to wait until age 16 to drive or age 18 to vote. Like driving and voting, entering into sexual relationships demands a level of maturity and responsibility that 12- and 13-year-olds simply don't have.

Some parents are just uncomfortable talking about sex, period. Young people are very good at reading nonverbal signals. If you are embarrassed, your child will pick this up. But she won't know whether your discomfort comes from her questions (because they are silly or nasty) or from you. Be honest. "My parents didn't tell me very much, so I'm really not sure how to explain things to you. I guess we'll have to learn together." The child will be relieved to know that the anxiety she senses isn't coming from her alone.

• *"I don't know how to begin."* Perhaps the main reason parents feel awkward about discussing sex is that they don't know *how*. Today's parents come of age during the sexual revolution of the 1960s and 1970s, but sex was still a taboo subject in their homes. When the time comes to talk with their children, they don't have role models for being parents of sexually open teenagers. In spite of what they think they should do, a part of them feels it is inappropriate to include frank sexual discussions in their child's upbringing. One generation's prohibitions have a way of becoming the next generation's inhibitions.

Guidelines

How can parents overcome their own hesitations and their young adolescent's resistance?

• *Don't postpone discussions of sex until you think the adolescent is involved in a relationship.* Ideally, you should start talking to your child *before* he or she has become sexually active. Ten- to 12-year-olds are less likely to take the discussions personally and react defensively and more likely to say what is on their minds. It is much less embarrassing to ask and answer a hypothetical, "what if" question than one based on last night's experience or tomorrow night's expectations. If you wait until your daughter is 15 or 16 to bring up contraception, for example, she may feel that you are accusing her of being sexually active or invading her privacy. A younger adolescent won't take your views as a judgment of his or her maturity. Conversations are less likely to become emotional, and doors to future conversations (and the teenager's room) will not be slammed shut.

Having said this, we must add that it is never too late to start. If you've put this off, say so. "We should have talked before now; you've grown up so fast I just didn't realize. That's my fault, but I'd like to start now."

• *Don't try to say everything at once.* Many readers will remember the Big Talk. Out of the blue, your father folded his newspaper, glanced knowingly at your mother, and said, "Let's go for a walk, son." Or your mother came to your room, closed the door, and announced solemnly, "It's time you and I talked woman-to-woman." If you remember anything about the Big Talk, it is probably that you and your parent were both horribly embarrassed. (Besides, you had already discovered where your father kept his "rubbers" or your mother her diaphragm.) Heart-to-heart talks have their place, but the Big Talk tends to over-dramatize sexuality, making natural developments seem like momentous, mysterious events. The adolescent won't learn very much from a single lecture anyway.

If you want your child to consider sex a normal—not scary or compulsive or superglorious—part of life, the most natural approach is to weave discussions of sexual topics into everyday conversation. TV shows (especially some of the more socially conscious talk shows and news specials), magazine articles, the advice columns in newspapers ("Dear Abby" and others), and even gossip columns provide ample opportunities to discuss sexual behavior and values. A program on teenage pregnancy can set the stage for talking about why (other) teenagers take chances and how much your child knows about conception and contraception. An article on AIDS, a segment from "Dynasty," or an offhand comment that someone is a "fag" can lead to a discussion of homosexuality. (Is homosexuality a disease? How can you tell if someone is homosexual? Was the TV portrayal accurate?) If your adolescent daughter walks in when you and a single or divorced friend are discussing whether she should sleep with a man she has been seeing, don't automatically shush your friend. You can talk about sexual pressures on women of all ages without getting into the details of your friend's sex life. If you and she are old friends, tell your daughter about some of the experiences and misunder-standings the two of you had at her age.

Don't overwhelm the young adolescent with information. If your son or daughter asks a question, answer it and ask if there is anything else they would like to know. Your goals should be first to find out what your child knows and correct misinformation and second to let the youngster know that it is okay to talk about sex. The best way to break the ice is to show the adolescent you are interested in his or her views on topics like teenage pregnancy and sexual harassment.

• *Respect your adolescent's privacy.* As teenagers move into adoles-cence, their desire for privacy increases. They don't want you going through their bureau drawers while they are in school, and they don't want you prying into their private thoughts. The rule that sex is private is not for adults only, even if the adolescent's sex life is all fantasy at this point.

Try to keep discussions impersonal. If you overhear your son making a crack to a friend about "jerking off," wait until you are alone to talk. Asking "Do your friends talk about masturbation?" or "What do kids today think about masturbation?" is just as ef-fective—and less threatening and prying—then asking flat out "Do you masturbate?" When you begin conversations by talking about other people, you give your son or daughter the option of talking generally or asking personal questions about his or her own experiences. The choice is theirs.

If your daughter takes you into her confidence, don't rush off to tell your husband or your best friend what she said. Let her make the decision about who she wants or doesn't want to know about her feelings.

The privacy rule works both ways, of course. If you feel com-fortable talking about your own experiences, fine. ("Would you believe that I thought girls didn't masturbate until I was in my twenties?") But if you don't, say so. You and your adolescent can have a useful, informative conversation about sex without going into intimate details.

Talking about Intercourse   Preteens have questions about sexual intercourse, even if their questions are still hypothetical. Young girls wonder if intercourse will hurt, especially the first time. It is difficult for them to imagine how an erect penis will fit into their vagina (especially a penis the size of those in porno-graphic videos!). The honest answer is that if her hymen is tight, she may experience pain and bleeding the first time she has inter-course (all the more reason to wait for a loving, concerned part-ner). But the vagina is flexible enough to allow babies to be born, and pain is not a regular feature of intercourse. Girls should also know not to expect "the moon and stars": Most young women do not have an orgasm the first time they have intercourse. Boys worry about performance: Will they know where to put it? What if they can't get an erection or come too soon? Because they are anxious and inexperienced, many boys do not live up to their own expectations at first. As a rule, these problems do not last.

To repeat, there is *no* evidence that answering the young ad-olescent's questions about sex encourages precocious activity. But it can help to prevent unhappiness. Young people deserve to know that enjoying sex takes time and experience: Early disap-pointments do not mean that they are frigid or sexual failures.

At some point, nearly all preteens ask "How old do you have to be to have intercourse?" Don't assume that your son or daugh-ter is comtemplating an affair. Most young teenagers are looking for reasons *not* to have sex, and welcome their parent's help in saying no.

Preteens do not have the emotional experience and maturity to handle sexual intimacy. They don't know how it feels to see their boy- or girlfriend flirting with someone else, to find them-selves quarreling over little things, or to discover thay they are no longer in love but don't want to hurt the other person. They are still learning about their own and other people's feelings. Falling in and out of love is painful enough without sexual complications.

Telling adolescents that they are emotionally immature or that they only *think* they are in love (if that is the case) is not likely to make much of an impression, however. The best approach with preteens is to emphasize the real risks:

• *Unprotected sex—at any age, even once—can result in pregnancy.* The only way to prevent pregnancy is to abstain from intercourse or to use effective contraception. But no form of contraception is 100 percent effective. Young adolescents are even less likely to use contraception than are older adolescents.

• *Pregnancy at an early age is both physically and psychologically risky.* Very young mothers are more likely to have complicated preg-nancies and deliveries than are women in their twenties; their babies are more likely to be underweight, sickly, and slow to develop. Girls who become mothers in their teens are far less likely than other girls to complete high school or go to college. They are also less likely than older girls to marry the father of their baby or, if they do, to stay married. Abortion also entails greater risk when the girl is very young, if only because young teens are reluctant to face the possibility that they are pregnant and delay seeing a physician.

• *The risk of STDs (sexually transmitted diseases) among teenagers is high.* STDs are a leading cause of sterility, among other health problems. Having sex now can reduce the chances of having children later in life. The only way to avoid STDs is to abstain from sexual intercourse or to use condoms.

In short, young adolescents should know that saying no until they are older is important to their health and their future. They should know that having sex doesn't prove that you are grown up, that you love someone (or they love you), or that you are glamorous, attractive, and "with it." Sex doesn't prove anything. Saying no at any age, for any reason, is okay.

Talking about Values   Deciding what is normal and permissible sexual behavior is a central part of sexual development. Although they might be the last to admit it, adolescents want to know where their parents stand. We think most parents will agree that early adolescence is too soon to become involved in sexual relationships, for the reasons given earlier. However, it might not be too soon to begin discussing how to make responsible decisions about sex, and good and bad reasons for having sex (topics we cover in chapter 12). You might also want to say that kissing, hugging, and holding hands are good ways of expressing affection that adults enjoy, too. Walking arm in arm on the beach or star-gazing with someone you care for are wonderful at any age. They needn't be a prelude to sexual intercourse (and shouldn't be at ages 10 to 13).

Answering your child's questions about what is normal is important, especially if your child has read or watched material that emphasizes sexual athletics. A standard definition of normal sex is "consenting behavior between *adults*." But that doesn't tell a young adolescent much. Normal sex is behavior that both partners enjoy, in which neither is hurt and neither feels exploited, guilty, or ashamed afterward. A good sex life does not depend on how often a couple have intercourse or what they do together. Some couples make love every night, and some are just as happy making love once a week. Some enjoy oral sex, and some don't. Some like to act out fantasies together, and some like to fantasize about each other. Good sex depends on communication and compatibility. Feeling good about yourself, comfortable with your partner, and safe are essential ingredients, and these take time to develop.

RAPE AND SEXUAL ABUSE

Young adolescents need independence; they don't want to be chaperoned and chauffeured everywhere they go. Yet almost every week, parents read of a young person who has been dragged into the woods or onto a rooftop and raped. How can parents grant their young adolescents freedom *and* protect them from sexual attacks?

Teaching Self-Protection

Girls are far more likely than boys to be the victims of sexual assaults in adolescence, if only because boys have learned to be more aggressive in defending themselves. Undoubtedly you taught your daughter to be cautious with strangers when she was a small child; now that she is growing up you need to reinforce those lessons. Adolescent girls should be taught

- *Never to open the door to a stranger when alone in the house.* If he says he is the TV repairman (or the equivalent) and she hasn't heard anything about a TV being broken, she should tell him to come at another time.
- *Never to accept a ride from a stranger.* Hitch-hiking is dangerous, even if you are with a friend.
- *Always to avoid dark, deserted, and/or unfamiliar places.* Convince your daughter that you would rather pick her up or pay for cab fare than have her take chances.
- *Some rapes take place in full daylight near public places.* If a girl suspects that she is being followed, she should not be embarrassed to walk up to a policeman, speak to the busdriver, or go into a nearby store and ask for help.

Girls also need to be assertive in rejecting unwelcome advances and sexual teasing, even—indeed, especially—from someone they know.

If rape by a stranger is devastating, sexual assault by a trusted adult is traumatic. It is also far more common: *70 to 80 percent of sexual assaults on young people are committed by someone they know, and even love.* (Here again, adolescent boys are less likely to become victims, but they are not immune). Sexual abuse of children has received a good deal of media attention in recent years. Everyone who reads the paper or watches the news knows that the unthinkable happens. But most parents find it almost impossible to believe it could happen to their child. These parents are wrong. It can.

The real tragedy with sexual abuse is that many (if not most) girls are afraid to tell anyone. As a result, the assaults may continue for months and even years. Why do girls remain silent? Many believe that if they speak up, they will be accused of misinterpreting the adult's behavior ("He's your uncle! How can you even think such a thing"), making up stories to get attention ("You're just jealous because your sister is getting married"), or leading the adult on ("If you didn't dress like a hooker, men wouldn't treat you like one"). When the approaches begin, the young girl may not believe what is happening herself. She may suspect that there is something peculiar about the way a neighbor looks at her, or something wrong about her brother wanting her to sit on his lap. But to speak up would mean saying that she thinks men find her sexually attractive. Few young adolescents have the self-confidence to make such an "admission." Her silence emboldens the offender, who may progress to more sexually aggressive acts and to bribes or blackmail to keep her quiet. When she finally does speak up, her previous silence may be taken as evidence that she was somehow to blame or cooperated with the abuser. All too often, parents respond by restricting the girl's activities, in effect punishing her for being abused.

No parent wants to think that someone they know would sexually assault their child (or any child). The first step toward protecting your child is admitting *to yourself* that such things happen, even in the best of families and communities. The second step is to arm your youngsters, without making them unnecessarily afraid. As small children, they should be taught the difference between "good touching" and "bad touching" and told to speak up *the moment* someone violates their personal space. As adolescents, they should be reminded that they and they alone have the right to decide who can touch them and whom they will touch. If a girl feels uncomfortable with someone, she should tell a parent, even if she's not sure exactly what is making her uncomfortable. Never force her to be alone with, or affectionate toward, someone she doesn't like. Make sure she knows that you will not blame her if she gets into a situation she can't control. Sexual molestation of a minor is *never* the minor's fault, regardless of what the child or teenager did or didn't do. She needs to know that you will take her side, no matter what.

Helping the Young Victim

The unthinkable happens: Your daughter tells you that she has been molested by someone close to your family. What should you do? Assure her that she did the right thing by coming to you, that you believe her, and that you are very angry at the abuser but love her very much. Make sure that she knows your response is motivated by anger and outrage at the abuser, not shame and embarrassment. Whatever you do, do *not* ask what she did to provoke the assault or invite sexual attention. Most of all, reassure her of your continuing trust.

If a young person has been raped or sexually abused, we strongly recommend contacting one of the rape crisis centers listed in the Yellow Pages of the phone book. In addition to your love and support, the adolescent needs professional guidance. She should have a physical examination (to determine if she has been injured, impregnated, or infected with an STD). She may also need the help of a psychotherapist in working out her feelings of shame, anger, and guilt. Counselors at the rape crisis centers are trained to help young people and their families get the help they need. We also believe that any case of sexual molestation of a child should be reported to the police or other appropriate authorities. Parents often cover up such incidents to protect the child from embarrassment. This reaction is understandable, but the young person who is assured "We won't tell anyone" may get the message that if peole knew they would think badly of her, as if she were soiled and disgraced. Besides, she may not be the only victim. A counselor from a rape crisis center and/or a psychotherapist who specializes in this area can help you decide what is in your child's best interest and help you deal with the courts if that is what you decide.

What if an adolescent who is being abused does not speak up? Some of the signs that a young person has a "terrible secret" are fear of being left alone or going out alone, aversion to being touched by anyone, and nightmares. Delinquency, drug use, and running away are often linked to sexual abuse in adolescence. (Even if they are not, such behavior requires action on your part.)

Although sexual abuse of adolescent boys is rarer, it does occur, and in some cases the abuser is an older male. Such boys suffer the double shame of assault and unwanted homosexual experience. They need to be reassured that they were not responsible for what happened and that there is nothing wrong with them as a result of the experience. As with girls, we strongly recommend that parents of abused boys seek professional guidance.

RESOURCES

For more information on talking to children and adolescents about puberty, sex, and sexuality, we recommend Planned Parenthood's *How to Talk with Your Child about Sexuality,* by Faye Wattleton, with Elizabeth Keiffer (Garden City, N.Y.: Doubleday, 1986).

For the pamphlet *Tune into Your Rights: A Guide for Teenagers about Turning Off Sexual Harassment* ($1.00), write to

Center for Sex Equity in Schools (CSES)
School of Education
1046 School of Education Bldg.
610 E. University
Ann Arbor, MI 48109

Child Abuse Hotline: 800-422-4453

For parents who have abused a child or think they might, Parents Anonymous has chapters in many communities. Write or call

Parents Anonymous
6733 S. Sepulveda, Suite 270
Los Angeles, CA 90045
800-421-0353

CHAPTER 6

Talking about Cigarettes, Alcohol, and Marijuana

WHY ADOLESCENTS TRY DRUGS

Studies of why young people try drugs yield consistent responses. By far the most common reason is *to fit in*, to be part of the gang, to be liked. Peer acceptance can be all-important to adolescents. And many see smoking, drinking, and/or "doing" drugs as a key to popularity.

> I thought that I would be left out or different than everybody else, and I thought that if I did drugs everybody would look up to me, and I would be happy or something.

The second most common reason (closely related to the first) is *to feel grown-up*. Teenagers see drugs as a rite of passage, a way of proving you are an adult or out from under the control of adults.

> I was only twelve and was hanging out in the neighborhood with some older kids. They asked me if I wanted to get high. I said I did because I didn't want them to think I was a baby.

> When I started junior high school, I really started feeling scared of the older kids. They intimidated me . . . So I started using pot to impress them.

A third reason, more common than parents might imagine, is *boredom*.

> We were just hanging around, with nothing to do, then Johnny said, "Let's drink some beer."

Some kids try drugs out of *defiance*, precisely because they are forbidden.

> I remember when I first smoked pot with [my cousin], I felt sneaky, and that made a sort of bond between us, against authority and against our parents.

And some kids are simply *curious:* They want to know how drinking or smoking feels.

The reasons why young people *continue* to use drugs are more complex. Cigarettes, alcohol, and marijuana are acquired tastes. The first time someone tries smoking or drinking, he typically feels dizzy and nauseous; with marijuana, he often feels nothing. Why, then, do teenagers go back for more? One possibility is that young people who lack social skills find that drugs offer relief from the discomfort and stress they feel around peers. They cannot control whether other people like them, or their own feelings of inadequacy and frustration in social situations; but they can control the feelings they get from drugs. Once they begin to use drugs, the chemical effects—the euphoria or high—become self-reinforcing.

MYTHS AND FACTS: WHAT YOU AND YOUR ADOLESCENT SHOULD KNOW

Virtually all experts agree that the key to the adolescent drug problem is prevention. The earlier young people begin using drugs, the more likely drugs will become part of their life-style, personality, and self-image, the harder it is for them to stop. How can you help your child say no to drugs? The first step is information.

The last thing adolescents want from their parents is a lecture on drugs. They already know what you're going to say: "It's bad. It's wrong. Don't do it." Most young adolescents agree. When asked what is the biggest problem facing teenagers today, the majority say drugs. In one survey, four out of five said that the laws against the sale and use of drugs (including marijuana) are not strict enough. "We have a right to be protected from drugs," declared a seventh grader in Washington, D.C. At the same time, however, young people are picking up ideas about "good drugs" and "bad drugs," safe and unsafe drug use, what is "cool" and not cool, from the media, their friends, and their parents. Few escape the drug mystique.

The trick for parents is to educate their children without alienating them. In this section we will describe common myths about cigarettes, alcohol, and marijuana and give the corresponding facts. We recommend that you share these with your adolescent.

Cigarettes

We doubt you could find a single American child who doesn't know that smoking causes cancer. But cancer is something that happens when you get "old" (age 40 and beyond), and adolescents aren't concerned about the distant future. They care about what is happening in their lives right now. Study after study has shown that exposing teenagers to the grim facts of cancer and heart disease does little or nothing to discourage smoking. The best way to keep adolescents from smoking is to address issues that are close to their hearts—namely their looks, their physical performance, and their popularity.

Myth: Smoking is sexy.
Facts. Smoking causes bad breath, yellow teeth, gum disease, hacking coughs, excess phlegm, smelly hair, stained fingers, and burn holes in your favorite clothes. Surveys show that most teenagers do not want to go out with, much less *kiss*, someone who smokes.

Myth: Cigarettes are relaxing.
Facts. In reality, the opposite is true. Just one puff on a cigarette causes heart rate and blood pressure to increase. The reason smokers feel that cigarettes are relaxing is that they are addicted to nicotine. When the nicotine from their last cigarette wears off (about a half hour after it was smoked), their body craves more and they cannot relax until they have another. Cigarettes *create* tension that only cigarettes can relieve.

Myth: Exercise counteracts the effects of smoking.
Facts. Cigarettes are poison. The only beneficial use of nicotine is as an insecticide! Every puff of cigarette smoke contains carbon monoxide (the poisonous gas that is blown out of a car's exhaust pipe), tar, and fifteen known carcinogens. Smoke paralyzes the

cilia, hairlike structures that sweep irritants and germs out of the lungs, making you more vulnerable to colds, the flu, and bronchitis. Someone who smokes a pack a day for a year has about a quart of tar sitting in his lungs. All the exercise, vitamins, and health foods in the world won't get rid of these poisons. Smoking lowers the level of oxygen in the bloodstream, causes shortness of breath, and reduces stamina, making exercise more difficult.

Myth: Smoking helps you lose weight. Girls in particular, are likely to see smoking as a way to improve their looks.

Facts. There is some truth to this; indeed, it's one of the factors the Surgeon General cited in his 1988 report as a reason why people continue smoking. On the average, smokers weigh 5 to 7 pounds less than nonsmokers. But averages disguise the range of individual differences: There are many fat smokers and just as many thin nonsmokers. The reasons smokers may weigh a little less probably are that they eat less and that smoking stimulates their metabolism so that they burn calories faster. So, yes, smoking may cause a temporary weight loss. But it also has a rebound effect: When smokers quit, they tend to gain weight even if they don't eat much more than they did when they were smoking, and they have more trouble taking that weight off.

Myth: I can always stop if I want to.

Facts. Most adults who smoke began smoking in their teens. The earlier they began to smoke, the more likely they are to be heavy smokers. When heavy smokers try to quit, they usually experience withdrawal symptoms (the jitters, irritability, sleep disturbances) for days or weeks after they quit, dream about cigarettes months later, and still experience cravings years later. To be sure, some 30 million Americans have quit. But it wasn't easy. Suggest that your teenager ask several older people who smoke, "If you had the choice today, would you start smoking?" Nine out of ten smokers will say no and go on to describe how many times they've tried to stop. Most *teenagers* (90 percent) who've been smoking for a year or two wish they had never started.

Myth: But everyone is doing it.

Facts. Everyone isn't smoking. Recent studies show that a majority of teenagers don't think smoking is "cool." Less than 10 percent of preteens, and 13 to 17 percent of older teens (depending on the survey) light up. Nonsmokers are in the majority, and smokers are the "oddballs."

Myth: At least my child is not using hard drugs.

Facts. Teenagers who smoke are more likely than nonsmoking teenagers to experiment with other drugs. According to the American Lung Association, 80 percent of teenage cigarette smokers have tried marijuana, compared to 17 percent of nonsmokers. Smokers are fourteen times more likely than non-smokers to use cocaine, amphetamines (or "speed"), and other so-called hard drugs. But whereas use of marijuana may be a passing phase, smoking usually is not.

More to the point, *nicotine is an addictive drug.* In his 1988 report the Surgeon General warned that nicotine is as addictive as heroin or cocaine. Like these other drugs, nicotine causes a high, simultaneously stimulating the brain and relaxing the muscles. Smokers develop a tolerance for nicotine: Once they get used to the drug, they need increasing amounts just to feel normal. They smoke compulsively, despite adverse effects on their health and social life.

Alcohol

The leading cause of death among young people is drinking and driving. Alcohol is also associated with delinquency, under-achievement in school, social and emotional problems, teenage suicide, and use of other drugs (75 percent of teenagers who drink moderately to heavily have smoked marijuana, compared to 14 percent of nondrinking adolescents). Drinking in adolescence is all too common. A national survey of high-school seniors found that more than 90 percent had tried alcohol; half said they drank every week; 37 percent had had five or more drinks on one occasion (in other words, gotten drunk) in the last two weeks; and 5 percent admitted to drinking daily. A high proportion of these high-school drinkers began experimenting with alcohol at an early age: 10 to 25 percent of young adolescents (ages 11 to 13) have tried alcohol. Even *fourth graders* say drinking is a big problem for kids their age.

As with smoking, adolescents will be exposed to a good deal of misinformation about alcohol. Here are some of the more common myths—and the rebuttals.

Myth: Alcohol is harmless.

Facts. Alcohol is a drug, just like nicotine or heroin. Unlike food, which needs to be digested, alcohol is absorbed directly into the bloodstream. Because adolescents are smaller than adults, the effect of alcohol on their bodies and brains is greater. Many adults are able to drink in moderation, but others become dependent on alcohol. They need this chemical in their bodies to keep from feeling sick: They are alcoholics.

Alcoholics are not the only ones who can be harmed by drinking, however. Alcohol affects the control centers in the brain, impairing coordination, reducing inhibitions, and creating a false sense of confidence, even invulnerability. When they are drinking, people may take risks they wouldn't take otherwise—such as pushing the speedometer up to 90 m.p.h., wading into the ocean at night, or having sex without protection. Because they are less mature and have less experience with alcohol, teenagers are at greater risk than adults.

Myth: Alcohol drowns your troubles.
Facts. Alcohol tends to intensify emotions. The problem is, it's impossible to predict which emotions will be released. Different people react to alcohol in different ways, and the same person may react in different ways on different occasions. Drinking may make a person feel relaxed and happy, or it may make her hostile, violent, depressed, or morose. However it makes you feel, it doesn't solve your problems, and may create new ones.

Myth: Drinking is the best way to "party."
Facts. Everyone feels shy from time to time, especially at parties where they don't know many people and want to make an impression. And some people feel that a drink makes them more at ease, more confident, and more entertaining in social situations. The problem begins when people become convinced that they won't have fun and won't be liked *unless* they have a drink. These people often find that they need, not one, but two or three drinks before they begin to relax. By the time they've had two or three, their judgment has slipped and they don't read other people's signals very well. Others may find them boring, obnoxious, or just plain drunk, but they are too intoxicated to notice. The next morning they may not remember anything about the night before . . . and have a Bloody Mary to cure the hangover. Thus a shy drinker becomes a problem drinker. The best way to avoid this downhill slide is not to start.

Myth: Drinking makes you funnier.
Facts. Drunks are neither funny nor much fun. Intoxication interferes with memory and thinking, speech and coordination. Some-

times drunks begin a story but forget what they were saying in midsentence; other times they tell the same story, or play the same record, over and over and over. Sometimes their speech is so slurred they are incomprehensible. They knock over drinks and fall over furniture. They throw up. Does that sound like fun?

Myth: Drinking improves sex.

Facts. Alcohol does lower inhibitions. But it interferes with sexual performance and pleasure. Getting drunk makes you senseless, and even a few drinks dull your senses. A boy may find that he is unable to get an erection, or unable to reach an orgasm; a girl, that she doesn't really feel anything. The morning after, both may have strong feelings, not of pleasure, but of embarrassment, shame, guilt, and fear—because he took advantage of her, she gave in to him, and they had sex without protection. There are no statistics on how many unwanted teenage pregnancies were assisted by alcohol, but we suspect the number is high.

Myth: But everyone's doing it.

Facts. Only a minority of young adolescents (10 to 25 percent) have ever taken a drink. Many older adolescents and many adults abstain from alcohol, too. Some don't drink because of religious or moral convictions; some because they don't like the taste of alcohol or the feeling of being intoxicated and out of control; some because they don't want the extra calories (booze is fattening); and some because they don't like exposing their bodies to anything that might injure their health. There are just as many reasons for *not* drinking as there are for drinking.

Marijuana

In discussing marijuana with your adolescent, it's important not to exaggerate—or underestimate—the dangers. There is little evidence that marijuana is a "gateway" drug that inevitably leads to addiction to harder drugs. Teenagers who smoke pot *daily* are more likely to use other drugs as well. But many teenagers smoke pot occasionally, at parties, and never use anything stronger, just as many adults drink in moderation. Regular marijuana users may develop a tolerance for the drug, needing more and more to get high. They may also become psychologically dependent. But there is no evidence that marijuana is physically addictive. Telling adolescents that a single joint will get them hooked is simply not telling the truth. But this does not mean that marijuana is safe.

In the 1960s and 1970s, when marijuana first became popular on college campuses, many scientists concluded that it was relatively benign. But scientific opinion has changed, for several reasons. First, the marijuana being sold today is much more powerful than that available in the 1960s and 1970s. The active, mood-altering ingredient in marijuana is the chemical tetrahydrocannaboid (THC). In the "old days," the average level of THC in marijuana was .2 percent; today it is 5 percent, making pot twenty-five times more potent. It is also more dangerous. Studies have found that when the level of THC reaches 2 percent, there is a definite risk of psychological disruption. Relatively rare in the 1960s and 1970s, "bad trips"—the feeling that people are ganging up on you, or that you are losing your mind—are more likely today.

Second, scientists have more information about marijuana, and the news isn't good. Teenagers who smoke marijuana twice a week or more have immature brain wave patterns. This side effect disappears if the teenager stops using pot, but regular users may suffer from learning problems that resemble dyslexia. They may also slip into an "amotivational syndrome," characterized by apathy and aimlessness. In the words of one adolescent, "Everything I used to like has become a drag. Even chicks. I feel bummed out all the time." Most alarming, THC inhibits the formation of DNA, the strands of genetic material that tell cells how to grow. This may not only disrupt metabolism and development, but also be passed on to the next generation.

The third reason for increased concern is the age at which adolescents begin using marijuana. Most parents were introduced to marijuana in college. Today, 15 percent of young people try marijuana before age 13, and a third before leaving ninth grade. Even if the effects of THC are temporary, marijuana may disrupt learning, motivation, personality, and physical growth at a crucial stage in adolescent development.

Myth: Marijuana is no more harmful than alcohol and less harmful than cigarettes.
Facts. Today's teenagers are no more likely than yesterday's youth to be impressed by scare tactics. But they might perk up if you explain how marijuana affects the brain and the sex organs. Alcohol is water-soluble. Although it is dangerous for other reasons, it does not stay in the body, but is passed out through urine and sweat in a matter of hours. THC is fat-soluble. When it enters the

body, it heads for the organs—including the brain and the testes or ovaries—and remains there for at least one and sometimes two weeks. THC lodged in the brain is the biological reason for "flashbacks" (the recurrence of hallucinations experienced while smoking marijuana). In the sex organs, a buildup of THC may disrupt the menstrual cycle and cause temporary infertility, in females, and reduce the sperm count and increase the number of misshapen sperm, in males. Current research indicates that smoking one joint causes as much damage to the lungs (and looks, physical stamina, and endurance) as *an entire pack* of cigarettes.

Myth: Getting high feels good.
Facts. Some people do feel euphoric when they smoke pot. But like alcohol, grass has different effects on different people and different effects on the same person at different times. Marijuana is just as likely to make you feel foggy, confused, or paranoid (people are spying on you, ganging up, plotting against you) as it is to make you feel good.

Myth: Marijuana makes me sharper.
Facts. What marijuana does is make you "spacey," literally. A study with rhesus monkeys found that when they had the equivalent of a joint's THC in their bloodstream, the spaces between the neurons (or nerve cells) in their brains became wider and fluid in these spaces more opaque. The researchers concluded that marijuana may slow down or interrupt brain messages. Tests of human motor control suggest that marijuana has a similar effect on people. Even after the high wears off, pot smokers at driving machines have trouble staying in their lane, maintaining a steady speed and distance from other cars, and braking quickly in an emergency. By extension, marijuana makes it more difficult to ride a skateboard, dribble a basketball, follow a history class, or conjugate a French verb. Adolescents who try to do homework when they are high may have the illusion that they're sharper, when in fact it is taking them much longer than it normally would, and the results may be incomprehensible.

Myth: I'm cool, I can handle it.
Facts. Because marijuana is illegal, there is no way of knowing exactly what you're buying. Dealers can claim that just about anything that looks like marijuana is marijuana. In some cases what's sold as pot is dried parsley mixed with PCP, a drug first developed as an animal tranquilizer that has unpredictable and often violent

effects. Neither your mind nor your body can handle that, no matter how cool you are.

We have focused on cigarettes, alcohol, and marijuana here because almost all young people will be offered these drugs, and perhaps pressured to try them, in their early teens. But they may be exposed to other drugs as well. Parents may want to look ahead to chapter 13.

ESTABLISHING RULES

Surveys tell us that young people who smoke are more likely to drink, that those who drink are more likely to smoke pot, and that those who use pot are more likely to smoke and drink. The most sensible policy is to *prohibit all drug use,* at least until the adolescent has graduated from high school. No exceptions.

Drugs are one area where the rules should be crystal clear. Telling an adolescent "You're too young to smoke" or "You can't drink until you're older" or even "I forbid you to use drugs" is too vague. Encouraging a preteen to puff on a cigarette because you think it will make him sick and discourage him from trying again, or allowing an older teen to drink at home on special occasions while expecting her to abstain away from home constitute mixed messages. Asking adolescents to mix or serve drinks, or to find your matches or light your cigarette, involves them in your (adult) use of drugs.

Tell the adolescent exactly what you expect, and *why.*

• *Reason 1: Drugs are dangerous for young people.* The truth is that scientists do not know the effects of drinking or of smoking cigarettes or marijuana on growing children. No scientist would experiment on children. They do know that children can be damaged before they are even born if their mothers drink while they are pregnant and that women who smoke while they are pregnant are more likely to have miscarriages or premature babies. They know that smoking marijuana can cause temporary infertility. And they know that heavy drinking and even moderate smoking have serious, harmful effects on the body over time. Don't experiment with your body. It's the only one you'll ever have.

• *Reason 2: Drugs do not mix with school, sports, and other teenage activities.* Growing up isn't easy, and young people need clear heads and healthy bodies to develop into happy, successful adults. Drugs will make it much harder for you to do well in school. They will lower your endurance and stamina and throw your timing off in sports. And they can mess you up emotionally. Don't make your life harder for yourself.

• *Reason 3: It is illegal for minors to use drugs.* Buying cigarettes is illegal for anyone under age 16; drinking is illegal for people under 18 (or 21 in most states); and selling marijuana is illegal for anyone. If you fool around with drugs, you might get in trouble with the law. Although preteens cannot be sent to adult jail, they can be taken to juvenile courts. Besides, we don't approve of breaking the law in this house.

In addition, discuss what the penalty for breaking your no-drug rule will be. Begin by asking your adolescents what they would consider appropriate. Preteens and teens who are involved in the rule-making process are less likely to break the rules, or to cry unfair when you impose a penalty. For example: "If I smoke, you will cut off my allowance for a month." "If I smoke mari-juana, I will be grounded for six weeks: No dates, no parties, no Saturday afternoon movies." "If I drink, I won't get my driver's license until six months after my 16th birthday."

You should also consider incentives for staying drug-free. One father we know promised his sons five hundred dollars each if they didn't smoke before their 21st birthdays and put them on the honor system. Now in their fifties, neither has ever smoked. And they went to Europe with their reward (five hundred dollars was a lot in the 1950s). For your adolescent, the incentive might be a room of her own at age 16, the deposit for an apartment at age 21, or something else of her own choosing. Tell her how important it is to you that she stay away from drugs and ask her to think of something that would mean a lot to her.

While you should lay down the law on drugs, it is important not to cut off communication. You don't want your son to be afraid to tell you that some of his friends are drinking beer after school and he doesn't know how to handle it. And in general you don't want adolescents to develop a pattern of keeping their ex-periences and activities secret. Tell the preteen that you are will-ing to discuss the rules and penalties at any time (and do so). If your son has one beer out of curiosity, hates it, and tells you, make an exception. "I'm glad you told me and happy you've de-cided to say no the next time. We're counting on you." (If he

comes home drunk, or beers regularly disappear from your refrigerator, that's another story. See chapter 13.) Also look for
opportunities to discuss and reinforce your policy. If you hear
about a party where kids were drinking and smoking, ask your
child how she feels about this. What would she do if she discovered that a close friend was smoking pot?

HELPING PRETEENS SAY NO

Establishing rules is one thing; enforcing them, another. Chances
are your child will be offered one or all of the drugs we've discussed during early adolescence and pressured to join in. You
can't follow your children around. But you can help them to say
no for themselves.

Practicing at Home

The inspiration to experiment with drugs may come from peers,
but drug prevention begins at home. (We discuss coping with
peer pressure in more detail in chapter 9.)

• *Listen.* Young teenagers are confused about drugs. If you get
angry or upset at the very mention of alcohol or marijuana, you
will lose opportunities to influence your child. If you use active
listening (described in chapter 2), you can help him sort out his
thoughts. Encourage him to figure out for himself why other
teenagers might drink or use other drugs (what are they trying to
prove?), why he feels pressured to join them (to be part of the
crowd?), and what a good friend should do (say, "I like you better
straight").

• *Practice.* Help your child to anticipate situations where she will
be offered drugs and plan how she can say no without losing face.
Try role playing at the dinner table. See how many ways to say no
you and other family members can come up with. Post a list on
the refrigerator and add items as you think of them.

"I'm in training for [whatever sport your child enjoys]."
"I'm saving my brains for something better."
"I'd rather sit here and watch you guys get stupid."
"I don't like the way it [beer, cigarettes] tastes."

"Do I *have* to smoke/drink to be your friend?" (Two friends might make a pact to say no to drugs. This way they will know that if they refuse, their buddy will back them up.)

"Oops, I forgot: A friend is going to call me at home, my Dad said he might come home early, I have to make dinner tonight, my Mom's going to give me a driving lesson this afternoon [or any other reason to leave or get friends to leave]." Where drugs are concerned, white lies may be excused.

In many situations, a simple "No, thanks" or "Not today" will do.

• *Be the "bad guy."* In a pinch, the adolescent can always "blame" you for his refusals. "If I come home smelling of cigarettes, my dad will lock up my bike for a month" or "If I don't drink, I'll get to use my mom's car on Saturday nights."

• *Analyze ads.* Peers are not the only pro-drug influence in our society; cigarette and liquor ads are also powerful. Analyze ads with your child. Why do cigarette ads always show a sparkling mountain lake or wide open spaces? (They don't want you to think about the dirty hot air you take into your lungs when you smoke.) Why do beer commercials show so many athletes? (They don't want you to think about how alcohol wrecks your coordination.) If you're smart, you won't fall for the advertising con game.

• *Encourage activities.* Adolescents who are involved in school clubs and committees, sports, music, and other hobbies, and who enjoy family activities are less likely to become involved with drugs than those who are just drifting through adolescence. They don't have the time and energy to waste on drugs. Encourage your child to develop special interests. Spend time together as a family (if only watching TV *and* talking about what you saw). Allow adolescents to participate in decisions about family outings and vacations, and to bring a friend along. If the adolescent loves tennis, go to a tournament together; if horror movies are more her style, rent some of the old ones to watch together.

• *Give young teens supervision.* Young people use drugs when a parent or other adult isn't around. If you don't get home until several hours after your child does, insist that you know where he goes after school, with whom, and what they do. Declare off limits shops that sell drug paraphernalia and places where you know drugs and alcohol are being used. If you are the only parent in your child's peer group who is home in the afternoons, encourage your child to bring his friends to your house. Give them space, but let everyone know you are there. Don't permit your child to go to a party unless you know there will be an adult chaperone and that drinking will not be permitted. This doesn't mean you have to act as your child's parole officer; it means being a responsible parent. Preteens are often relieved to know they can count on an adult to set the limits and won't have to handle peer pressure all by themselves.

• *Don't play the Lone Ranger.* Parents shouldn't try to fight drugs all by themselves either. Many schools have drug prevention programs. Some of the best use slightly older teenagers to teach young adolescents about the harmful effects of drugs and to model ways of resisting peer pressure. If your school, church, or neighborhood center does not have such a program, ask why. In some neighborhoods, parents have formed groups to establish a united drug policy, monitor children's activities, and petition for strict drug enforcement in school and better recreation programs and facilities out of school. If you bring the subject up at a PTA or block association meeting, you may be surprised at how many other parents would like to participate. Don't wait until your child or someone else's has developed a drug problem to take action.

For Parents Who Drink or Smoke

Parents are models for their children's behavior, even when they do not want or intend to be. Studies show that adolescents are five times more likely to smoke cigarettes if someone in their home (a parent or older sibling) smokes than if they are raised in a nonsmoking household. Adolescents whose parents drink are more likely to experiment with alcohol than those whose parents do not. And those whose parents use and abuse drugs (marijuana, valium, sleeping pills, diet pills, whatever) are more likely to use drugs than are their peers. How can these parents protect their children?

Don't think that because you enjoy drinking, or haven't been able to quit smoking, you have no right to prohibit these activities for your child. Many activities that are permitted for adults are forbidden to minors. Drugs head this list, for all the reasons we have given. Setting different rules for your adolescent children than you apply to yourself doesn't mean that you are a hypocrite; it means you're concerned about their welfare. Make this clear to your child. "We enjoy drinking occasionally, and when you're of legal drinking age, you may, too. But right now, you're too young to handle alcohol."

Do explain why and how you use drugs. "When I began smoking, people didn't realize how harmful cigarettes are. Now I'm addicted and it's very difficult to quit." Quitting is the best example you could set for your teenager, and something you should do for yourself; but if you aren't ready, at least be honest. "You hear me cough in the morning and see me huff and puff up the stairs; I don't want you to be as stupid as I was." Use the same approach with other drugs. "Your mother and I enjoy having cocktails with friends or alone together on Friday night." At the same time, be sure to mention other ways you unwind and have fun: working out, watching a good movie, playing a game of Scrabble. "I like the taste of wine and enjoy trying different kinds." But point out that there is a time and place for wine, just as there is for ice cream sundaes: If you had a banana split every day, it wouldn't be a treat any more.

Do take some time to analyze your own habits. Children learn not only from what you tell them, but from what they observe. They see when you drink, why you drink, and how much you drink. If you drink every night, when you're down, when you've had a fight, when you are alone (if you are single or your spouse travels), or almost any time you are feeling out of sorts, your child will be learning that alcohol is a kind of medication. If you offer friends a drink before they get out of their coats, push drinks on adults who say "No, thanks," make fun of nondrinkers, laugh about the times you've been smashed, and make alcohol part of every adult activity from business lunches to football parties, your child will be learning that alcohol is what distinguishes good-time Charlies from bores and nerds. If you drink and drive, boat, swim, hunt, or engage in any other potentially dangerous activity that requires coordination and judgment, your child will be learning that taking such risks is okay. Studies show that light or moderate use of alcohol by adults in nonrisk situations does not have negative effects on young people, but that frequent (everyday) or heavy use (enough to get drunk on numerous occasions) does.

Finally, if someone in your home or family is an alcoholic, don't deny this or try to hide it from your children. They know when there is a problem in the family and have a right to know what the problem is. They may feel that they are somehow responsible for the alcoholic's binges, or guilty because they are angry at that person for causing so much pain and chaos. You and your adolescent might want to join local chapters of Al-Anon and Alateen, organizations that help nonalcoholics cope with alcoholics (see Resources, at the end of this chapter).

And for Parents Who Do Not

Don't assume that because you and your spouse neither drink nor smoke, your teenager will follow your example. Research shows that a surprising one in ten alcoholics came from nondrinking homes. You are only one of many influences on your adolescent. Take time to explain why you do not drink, smoke, or use other drugs.

RESOURCES

See also the resources for chapter 13.

The following groups can provide additional information and/or assistance.

For Parents Interested in Drug Education

*American Council for Drug
    Education*
5820 Hubbard Drive
Rockville, MD 20852
301-984-5700

American Lung Association
1740 Broadway
New York, NY 10019

*Families in Action Drug
    Information Center*
Suite 300
3845 Druid Hills Road
Decatur, GA 30033
404-325-5799

*National Congress of Parents
    and Teachers* (PTA)
700 North Rush Street
Chicago, IL 60611
312-787-0977

*National Federation of Parents for
    Drug-Free Youth*
Suite 16
1820 Farnwell Avenue
Silver Spring, MD 20902
800-544-KIDS

*National Parents Resource
    Institute on Drug Education*
    (PRIDE)
Suite 1216
Robert W. Woodruff
Volunteer Center
100 Edgewood Avenue
Atlanta, GA 30303
800-241-9746

For Professionals Interested in Drug Education Programs

U.S. Department of Education
Alcohol and Drug Abuse
Education Program
400 Maryland Avenue, S.W.
Washington, DC 20202

American Council for Drug
Education (see above)

For Families of Alcoholics

Al-Anon and Alateen
P.O. Box 182
Madison Square Station
New York, NY 10159

Al-Anon and Alateen are self-help groups for relatives and friends of alcoholics. Local chapters may be listed in your telephone directory.

PSYCHOLOGICAL HEALTH AND DEVELOPMENT

CHAPTER 7

How Young Adolescents Think

*I*n adolescence young people not only begin to look more like adults, they also begin to *think* more like adults. As a result, the way they see themselves, other people, and life in general changes.

THE INTELLECTUAL GROWTH SPURT

Failure to understand changes in the way young adolescents think is a leading cause of conflict between parents and teenagers. The intellectual growth spurt of adolescence involves new ways of thinking. Adolescents are entering the world of abstract ideas, hypothetical situations, and formal logic. Unless parents know what to expect, the shift from immature to mature thinking is easy to misinterpret.

Abstract Concepts   Intellectually, children and teenagers are worlds apart. Preadolescent children think in terms of concrete actions and events, things they can see and touch and grasp in their hands. Asked to define *fairness,* an 8-year-old might say "Giving everyone a turn" or "Dividing the candy bar in half." To a child this age, being religious means going to church on Sunday and behaving properly.

In adolescence, abstract concepts like justice, honesty, and loyalty take on new meaning. Adolescents know that fairness cannot be quantified and measured. They recognize that honesty involves more than simply telling the truth; an honest person examines his own motives. For them, being religious depends on what you *believe*, not just on what you *do*. Abstractions add a new layer to the young person's thinking. The simple blacks and whites of childhood—good vs. bad, mean vs. nice, smart vs. stupid —give way to gray expanses of uncertainty, ambiguity, and debate.

Possibilities Expanding mental abilities open adolescents to possibilities. For adolescents, what is real (what exists now) is only one of many possibilities (what could or might exist). Their mental horizons are not limited to the immediate environment. They can conceive of a world without war, a society without adults, life with a different set of parents. Thinking about possibilities raises the issue of identity. Adolescents think about how their personalities and social lives might change in the future. To children, you are who you are: Identity is given. To adolescents, who you are now is only one of many possibilities: Identity is a question mark. It is only a small step from thinking about what could be to thinking about what *should* be. Visionaries and idealists one day, adolescents can be harsh social critics the next. Their harshest criticism is often directed at the ones who are nearest and dearest —themselves and their parents.

Logic and Reason Adolescence is the age of reason. The teenager's ability to think problems through and to see the logical consequences of different positions or actions is much greater than the child's.

Preadolescent children can understand logic and reason, but they rarely use these mental tools themselves. Presented with a problem, children jump right in. Adolescents stop to consider the best strategy, what they need to know, and how other participants or players might respond to their moves. In a game of Twenty Questions, for example, children typically ask specific questions: "Is it a cat?" or "Is it the Cosby show?" Adolescents ask categorical questions that progressively limit the possibilities and allow them to gain information from negative answers. "Is it alive?" "Yes." "Is it animal, not vegetable?" "No." "Is it edible?" The child's questions are random guesses; the adolescent's questions are systematic and strategic.

Logical thinking is not limited to games and schoolwork. Adolescents apply their new-found powers of reasoning to the "game" of family rules and regulations. After dinner, your son picks up his jacket and announces, "I'm going over to Billy's to watch a new video." You respond, "No, you're not! It's a school night." He retorts, "I finished my homework this afternoon. Why do I have to hang around here?" Or your daughter "casually" mentions that a classmate was suspended for smoking marijuana. When you ask what she thinks about her friend's behavior, she says, "She shouldn't have smoked in school." You snap back, "She shouldn't smoke marijuana period!" "Why?" your daughter asks. "You and Mommy have a drink before dinner every night. What's the difference?" These adolescents have anticipated their parents' reactions and prepared logical rebuttals.

Advanced thinking begins to emerge in early adolescence (or even preadolescence). By 11 or 12, most young people have some grasp of abstract concepts, possibilities, and formal logic. Often, however, these cognitive advances do not jell until middle or late adolescence. Intellectual maturity has a "now you see it, now you don't" quality. A young person may apply advanced logic in some areas (math class) but not in others (managing his allowance), seem intellectual and astute one day but dense and childish another. These inconsistencies are not deliberate. Nor do they mean the young person is mentally lazy. Just as it takes time to adjust to a new body, so it takes time to adjust to a new mind. At times the young adolescent is intellectually awkward and uncoordinated.

What to Expect

For parents, the most obvious consequence of intellectual development is that your child becomes more interesting. Conversations with young children are one-sided. The child is an amateur at life, and you are her coach. A "conversation" usually means that you listen to the child's plans or problems, then point out the logical consequences of different actions. Your teenage daughter can do this for herself (at least some of the time). More and more, your conversations lead to an *exchange* of ideas. She is better able to understand other people's points of view—including yours. Share your concerns about an elderly relative or your indecision about changing jobs. She may have valuable insights, and she will certainly like your treating her as someone whose opinions count.

At the same time, a teenager is going to challenge your positions—and your patience. Just as a baby who has learned to crawl goes into constant motion, so a teenager who has discovered the powers of reasoning will flex his intellectual muscles. He insists on debating issues you consider closed. Often he argues for the sake of arguing. Then, suddenly, he shuts the door and you haven't a clue about what's bothering him. When he maintains a stony silence all through dinner, you may long for a shouting match.

For the adolescent, intellectual development opens doors. New classes are offered in school in decidedly grown-up subjects (algebra, trigonometry, philosophy, acting). The adolescent will be learning facts and skills her parents have forgotten or never knew. What adolescent doesn't enjoy telling a parent who is totally frustrated by a new program for the family computer, "It's easy," then explaining the commands as if she were instructing a child? The rewards of advanced thinking are not confined to school subjects. The ability to think about what is going on inside people and to take another person's point of view opens new worlds of intimacy and friendship. Being able to think about a problem in one's peer group and come up with a solution—on one's own— leads to greater social independence.

Yet the realization that life is not so simple, that things are not so cut and dried, creates new anxieties. Reexamining old beliefs is one of the hallmarks of adolescence. What was certain, permanent, and unquestioned (God loves humankind, parents are all-knowing, I can do anything if I try hard) becomes tentative. We do not mean to suggest that all adolescents are closet philosophers. But this type of questioning is far more common in adolescence than in other stages of life.

How to Minimize Conflict

When your teenager acquires the logical weapons only you yourself had before, you have met your intellectual match. The adolescent's new intellectual independence can be disorienting for parents. They were used to a child who considered them all-knowing, accepted their decisions (however reluctantly), and brought them his problems. Suddenly, they are being challenged. Your adolescent may point out—correctly—that you are becoming irritable, short-tempered, irrational, and dictatorial. A few simple guidelines can make life easier for both you and your teenager.

• *Don't confuse readiness to debate with argumentativeness.* It is extremely rare for a young person who was not defiant as a child to become suddenly argumentative in adolescence. The reason your adolescent is questioning your judgment and engaging you in endless, tiresome debate is that she is maturing intellectually. She recognizes flaws in your logic and inconsistencies in your principles, and delights in pointing these out.

Your teenager is *not* undergoing a "personality change" and, for the most part, *not* trying to get your goat. Quite simply, the teenager has become a better arguer. And this requires adjustment on your part.

Once your child has begun thinking like an adult, it is unrealistic for you to expect him to go along with what you say simply because you are his parent. Like adults, young teenagers look for the rationale behind a request. If they are being asked to do, or not do, something, they want to know why. They are better able to see when a rule is arbitrary than they were as children. And, like adults, when adolescents feel that a request is unreasonable or illegitimate, they respond with defiance.

Too often parents only look at the negative side of intellectual development ("I'm losing control over my child"), disregarding the positive implications ("She's becoming an independent thinker"). Would you want your child to be unquestioning and compliant in other settings? Would you want your son to go along with friends who decide to spray-paint racial slurs on a schoolyard wall? Your daughter to give in when her boyfriend says she would go all the way if she really loved him? Of course not. Do you want your adolescent child to believe everything he sees on television? To sit quietly in class, memorizing what the teacher says, never disagreeing, never asking a question? No.

Young adolescents who are trying their new intellectual wings need a safe place in which to practice. Arguing with parents about smoking or socialism helps them to discover and develop their own positions. If adolescents learn at home how to play devil's advocate, how to stand their ground when others oppose them, and how to lose an argument without losing face, they will be better prepared to deal with peer pressures and illegitimate demands by other adults.

• *Remember that it takes two to fight.* If you and your teenager argue constantly, you may be treating her steps toward independence as threats to your authority (see Independence, chapter 8).

Say you're waiting to drive your daugher to a birthday party for her best friend. She appears in the kitchen in a thigh-length purple sweater, shocking pink leotards, and yellow sneakers. You tell her that she is *not* going out dressed like that and give her 10 minutes to change. The young thinker is ready for you. "Don't you think I'm old enough to pick my own outfits?" Before you get drawn into a battle, stop to consider your own reaction. Is it really the *clothes* you object to, or the challenge to your authority? Are you dismissing her tastes and decisions simply because they are hers, not yours?

Say it's a warm Saturday in May, and you and your spouse decide to go for a hike in a nearby state park. Your youngest child is thrilled. Your adolescent son groans "No way." He plans to spend the day with his friend Henry, who just got a new computer game. You protest, "It's such a beautiful day, it's a crime to stay inside." Your spouse chimes in, "You're still part of this family, son. You're coming with us!" Your son wants to know "Why do I always have to go along with your plans?" Before you get into a battle, ask yourself: Are you really objecting to his plans, or to the fact that he doesn't share your love of the outdoors? that he has friends and interests of his own? that he doesn't want to go everywhere with the family any more?

Giving *in* on decisions about what to wear or what to do on the weekend doesn't mean that you are giving *up* your authority as a parent. You are simply acknowledging that your child is growing up. Save arguments for issues that really count—safety, health, decisions that will open or close doors in the adolescent's future.

It might help you to know that studies find teenagers dislike fighting as much or more than their parents do.

• *Keep in mind that you want to raise a curious, inquisitive, independent individual.* How quickly a young person develops advanced thinking, and what level of thinking she attains, depend in part on her experiences. Specifically, adolescents whose families encourage lively and open discussion usually develop advanced thinking sooner than those whose families discourage intellectual dissent.

This means that parents of adolescents should encourage, not discourage, discussion and debate. No parent wants to get drawn into daily discussions about why a teenager should clean his room or the logic behind curfews. But if the issue is an interesting one, and what you were doing can wait, take advantage of the opportunity. Banter refines intellectual skills. If it's the wrong time and place, tell the adolescent you are interested in what she said and propose a time when you can talk more.

Make discussions of political and moral issues, personal and interpersonal problems, part of your family routine. You manage to fit jogging into a busy schedule; surely you can find time for intellectual exercise. Eating dinner at the table (not in front of the TV) is an obvious opportunity, but it's not the only one. If everyone in the family goes in different directions Friday night, plan to get together for milk, cookies, and talk at 11. Use Sunday mornings to debate issues in the news. When your teenager is on vacation and you're not, take him or her to lunch. Ask the adolescent to critique a letter you've written to your Congress-person or a speech you are going to give at a meeting of your community board. Don't force discussions on your teenager; home isn't school. But if you create opportunities for debates, they will probably happen. Contrary to what most parents believe, surveys find that teenagers would like to spend *more* time talking with their parents than they do currently.

Don't worry that your adolescent expects you to have all the answers. When adolescents ask "Why does God allow hunger and war?" or "Why do people smoke when they know it causes cancer?" many parents are caught off guard. How can you answer questions like these? More than answers, young adolescents want to know that you are listening and that you share their puzzlement. Knowing that you, too, find these dilemmas frustrating is reassuring.

Finally, encourage your adolescent to take challenging classes at school. Safe, easy courses may help the adolescent maintain a high grade-point average, but they won't stretch his mind. Teenagers who take advanced science courses, in particular, tend to develop a higher level of abstract reasoning than those who do not. Now is a good time to try calculus or Russian. Let your child know that you won't be angry if she gets a lower grade than usual in a difficult class. (We'll say more about the choices young adolescents face in school in chapter 10.)

EGOCENTRISM AND OTHER LIMITATIONS

Being able to think more like an adult doesn't catapult an adolescent into social and emotional maturity. The young adolescent may have the mental equipment to "think great thoughts," but he doesn't have much experience applying advanced logic to the mundane, practical realities of everyday life. Much of the behavior we think of as typically adolescent results from this gap between thought and experience.

The Imaginary Audience

One of the major intellectual advances of adolescence is the ability to think about what others are thinking. "He knows that I know that he knows . . ." In early adolescence, this revelation can become an obsession. The adolescent imagines that everyone is always thinking about him! In effect, he constructs an "imaginary audience" that observes and evaluates his every move. You know there will be three thousand teenagers at tonight's rock concert; he knows that every single one of them will notice the pimple on his nose. Not only will they notice, they'll laugh and snigger behind his back. When the family goes out to dinner, she slouches in the darkest corner, terrified that her friends will see what weirdos she has for parents. Imagine trying to work or give a small, intimate dinner party in a department store window and you'll know how self-conscious your young adolescent feels much of the time. The imaginary audience is the result of the new ability to think about other people's thoughts—coupled with the inability to differentiate between one's own preoccupations and other people's interests.

The Personal Fable

The feeling that one is the center of attention can lead to feelings of exaggerated self-importance. In early adolescence this takes the form of a personal fable. The adolescent sees herself as unique and special; social rules and natural laws that apply to other people do not apply to her. She is invulnerable, invincible, immortal. A New York City mother described her 15-year-old son this way:

Our teenager gets mighty huffy if we suggest that he's too young or too irrresponsible or too immature for anything at all.

He feels invincible. He is Rambo. He is a soldier of fortune. He is Indiana Jones and Dirty Harry.

Certainly, he feels brave enough to take the subway after dark. "No one would mess with me!"

He is courageous enough to snoop around all five boroughs, Long Island, Westchester, and the states of New Jersey and Connecticut any time, day or night. "I'll kill anyone who gets in my way."

As far as he is concerned, he can guzzle two six-packs without getting drunk, he can drive a car without a lesson or a license, he can fly without wings. He probably feels that he could smoke, snort, sniff, inhale, swallow, or inject any substance at all without overdosing, becoming an addict, or losing his grip.

He thinks he has total control over himself and his environment and over all people and events in the entire world.

His response to everything is: "I know *I know!*"

On an abstract level, young adolescents understand that playing with drugs can lead to addiction or an overdose; sex without contraception, to pregnancy; driving above the speed limit, to a ticket or an accident. But they do not have the intellectual wherewithal to integrate this abstract knowledge into everyday life. As the New York mother put this, her teenager "actually believes that he won't break out into acne because he is philosophically opposed to pimples."

The adolescent's feeling of uniqueness is another source of egocentrism: She honestly believes that no one has ever loved as deeply, hurt as badly, or understood things as clearly as she does.

Apparent Hypocrisy

Young adolescents can appear extraordinarily hypocritical. They expound lofty principles one minute, violate those same principles the next, and become indignant if an adult points out the discrepancy between their words and deeds. Your teenage son may lambaste you for caring too much about appearances, then spend an entire afternoon polishing and waxing his car. Your daughter and a friend may spend hours talking about how they can't *stand* so-and-so because she's such a gossip. A crowd of teenagers may hold a rally for the environment . . . and leave the site of their demonstration littered with soda cans and leaflets. This apparent hypocrisy is the result of intellectual immaturity, not moral weakness. When adults are hypocritical, we can assume they are aware of the connection between theory and practice. Young adolescents have difficulty making this connection. Intoxicated with the discovery of abstract ideals and principles for behavior, they can't be bothered with practical details. At this age, expressing an ideal is the same as working toward that ideal.

Overthinking

Young adolescents often get carried away with their newfound ability to grasp complexities and may overlook the obvious, simple solution to a problem. Applying complex reasoning to simple problems can make your teenager seem stubborn, even stupid. One reason young adolescents have so much trouble making decisions, for example, is that they are able to contemplate innumerable possibilities. Deciding what to wear or what to order in a restaurant or even what to say is agony, because there are so many choices. Adults have faced the agony of choice innumerable times and developed strategies of elimination. At a post-Christmas sale, you choose a tan skirt because it goes with everything or a lacy blouse because it will soften your plain suits. Your daughter is so caught up in how many different looks she could put together that she literally *can't* decide what to buy or what to wear to a party two weeks later. Being able to hold many variables in mind simultaneously is an important skill, one that will help your adolescent in chemistry and physics classes now and in business later on. But in early adolescence, young people have difficulty knowing when advanced thinking is appropriate and when it is unnecessary and counterproductive.

Living with the Young Philosopher

The traits we have just described are not confined to adolescence. Adults sometimes play to an imaginary audience, behave as if they were invulnerable, violate their own principles, and make intellectual mountains out of molehills. The difference is that in early adolescence these logical lapses are common and pervasive. As a result, your once delightful child may seem unbearably egocentric. What is a parent to do?

First, try not to get angry. Occasional or even frequent ego-centricity is *not* a sign of character flaws. Learning to apply ideals and complex reasoning to everyday life takes times. Second, be patient. These *are* phases; the adolescent *will* outgrow them.

More specifically: In most cases, overthinking is harmless. If you feel your adolescent's complicated efforts to solve a simple problem (what to do about a friend who was mean, how to arrange a room for a party) are leading toward frustration and failure, you may want to suggest an easier approach ("You could ask Barbie if anything is the matter"; "Why not start with a list of party activities?"). But proceed gently. You do not want the teenager to feel you think she is stupid. And you don't want to discourage her from recognizing and tackling complexities in the future.

Although extremely irritating, hypocrisy is also relatively harmless. Trying to reason with a hopelessly idealistic and thoroughly impractical adolescent is banging your head against the wall. The adolescent simply isn't ready intellectually to connect theory with practice. For now, he may label your practical cautions "cynical" or "cowardly." As he gains more experience with real world attempts to achieve concrete goals, he will discover the value of compromise for himself.

The imaginary audience is somewhat harder to deal with, if only because it causes so much unhappiness. Here, too, reasoning is likely to fail. If you try to convince your daughter that no one will notice the run in her stocking, you will just convince her that "you don't understand." The best approach is to be sympathetic and offer concrete suggestions, without reinforcing her narcissism. Fix the stocking or lend her a pair of yours, but don't make a fuss. If your daughter complains that she is fat, and you disagree, say so. She may be fishing for a compliment and welcome your reassurance. If she persists, acknowledge her feelings, without agreeing with her delusion. "If *you* think you need to lose weight, why not begin an exercise program?" (See also Diet, Exercise, and Sleep, chapter 4.)

Ultimately, the best cure for the teenage center-stage syndrome is developing close friendships, sharing intimate thoughts, and discovering that other people can be as self-conscious, insecure, and lonely as they are.

A note of caution: Parents should not correct or make fun of a sensitive adolescent in front of other people. Wait until you can speak to him or her alone. Public criticism or mockery is painful for anyone, and devastating for a young adolescent.

How you should respond to your teenager's personal fable depends on the nature of the fable. Often, all you need to do is encourage him to test his fantasies against reality. Your son claims that he can pass a history test without studying. Instead of telling him flatly that he's making a big mistake, ask him whether he has done this in the past or what his classmates are doing. He may insist on his fable . . . and flunk the test. But he is more likely to study the next time if he discovers this for himself than if you force him to obey you.

In some cases, personal fables are dangerous and self-destructive, and a mistake can cause irreparable tragedy. Suppose you discover that your adolescent daughter is sexually active and believes that pregnancy is something that only happens to other people. She may think that she can only get pregnant while she is having her period, or imagine that middle-class girls never get in trouble. Your son may be equally ignorant. *Now* is the time for a serious discussion of pregnancy, contraception, and sexual responsibility, and perhaps a visit to a doctor (see chapter 12). Delusions of invulnerability about drinking and driving, smoking, or drugs demand the same forceful approach (see chapter 13).

The key point is that you need to be aware of the young adolescent's predisposition to personal fables and to know what your adolescent believes. Do not construct a personal fable of your own that holds "My son or daughter is smarter than that." If you can discuss controversial issues with your teenager without becoming judgmental or confrontational, you will be in a much better position to know when action is necessary.

RIGHT AND WRONG

All parents want to raise good children—individuals who have a strong set of values and the courage to stand up for what they believe is right. In adolescence, this sometimes seems like an uphill battle. The peer group may promote norms and values that undermine what parents are attempting to teach their children. TV soaps and serials treat violence, law-breaking, and casual sex as normal everyday events. In the culture as a whole, the hippie motto of the 1960s—"Do your own thing"—acquired new, materialistic, yuppie overtones in the 1980s that made the old ethics of self-discipline, self-denial, sacrifice, and service to others seem just that—old.

Don't give up. If you understand how your adolescent thinks about moral issues, and how moral reasoning changes over the course of adolescence, you will be better able to encourage healthy values, attitudes, and behavior.

Advances in Moral Reasoning

The development of moral reasoning follows predictable patterns. The young child's morality is based on self-interest. To 6- and 7-year-olds, what's fair is getting an equal slice of the pie. They avoid temptations because they don't want to get into trouble. If they do something nice for someone, they expect something nice in return. On the other hand, if a school chum is mean, they are mean in return. Their basic operating principle is tit-for-tat, or "Do unto others as they do unto you."

Around age 8 or 9, children begin to be concerned about how others view them. What's right at this stage is living up to the expectations of people you know and care about. The reason to be good is to earn social approval. The older elementary school child and preteen are attuned to the Golden Rule: "Do unto others *as you would have them* do unto you." They look beyond the immediate consequences of an action for them, personally, to the long-term impact of a moral decision on their relationships with other people. They can put themselves into another person's shoes and imagine how they would feel if they lost five dollars, were left out of a game, or were pushed around by a bully. They see the limitations of getting even and understand the principle "Two wrongs don't make a right." They don't need to be bribed or threatened into obedience; they *want* to be good. Above all, they want others to think well of them. This has been called the "good boy/nice girl" stage of moral development.

The drawback to this way of thinking is that what is good is confused with what other people expect. This may be fine when the people the child is trying to please set high moral standards —but what if the audience applauds deception rather than honesty, defiance rather than cooperation, risk-taking rather than self-respect, and snobbery and sarcasm rather than generosity and kindness?

When the "good boy/nice girl" level of moral reasoning first appears, in mid- to late elementary school, parents are delighted. The child seems more caring, more cooperative, and generally easier to live with. The reason? She is eager to please her parents. In junior high, however, the same child may suddenly seem sullen, uncooperative, and rebellious. The reason? She is now more interested in pleasing her peers. At this age, moral decisions are likely to be based on what she thinks will make her popular. "But Mom, *everybody* does it" is a common refrain. A girl who was nice to a shy, friendless child in sixth grade, because she had been taught to be kind, may turn clannish and cruel in eighth grade to maintain her status with her peers. One who would never have considered stealing may now see petty shoplifting as a game. Thus the strength of this stage of moral reasoning—desire for approval—is also its weakness.

Fostering Moral Development

Becoming more involved with, and influenced by, peers is a normal and inevitable part of adolescent development. There is little or nothing a parent can do to stop teenagers from caring what their friends think. But they can help adolescents develop the inner strength and security to resist pressure to violate the moral standards they have learned as children. Thomas Lickona developed the following practical guidelines for bringing out the best in young adolescents.

Addressing the Highest Moral Level When young people reach the age when they stop wanting to be good boys and girls in their parents' eyes and start wanting to be cool and with it in their peers' estimation, it's tempting for parents to slip back into earlier modes of moral reasoning: "You'll do it if you know what's good for you" or "Do this for me, and I'll do that for you." Such backward-looking strategies are not only insulting to the adolescent's moral intelligence, they are often ineffective.

Appeal to the adolescent's better self:

"*Wouldn't you like to be known as* a responsible (or caring, sincere, honest) person?"

"This is a favor we are asking. Think of it as *a good deed.*"

"Try to *look at this from my point of view.* What would you do if you were the parent?"

"I'm tired and grouchy right now and *I really need your full cooperation.* Thank you."

"*How do you think it sounds* when you talk to your brother like that?"

"*We're trusting you* to do what we've asked while we're gone. Can we depend on you to do that?"

"*We expect you* to be a responsible person, even when those around you aren't. We probably do expect more of you than some other parents expect of their kids. But we expect a lot of you because we think a lot of you."

Parents are sometimes surprised to find that an appeal to the adolescent's self-image "clicks" where other strategies have failed. This won't always work, of course, but it will give the adolescent practice in more mature thinking.

Developing a Positive Self-Image   The better adolescents feel about themselves, the less likely they are to cave in to peer pressure. All adolescents experience periods of self-doubt, which is one reason why they need approval so badly. How can parents bolster a shaky self-image?

• *Praise effort and achievement.* However independent they may seem, adolescents still need your love and encouragement. *Do* tell them you love them (even if they act as if they didn't hear you). *Do* praise their efforts ("You did a great job on those posters," "You've really been helpful today," "Your piano sounds better and better"). *Try not* to use shaming ("You should know better than that"), embarrassment ("What kind of home will people think you come from?"), intimidation ("At the rate you're going, I doubt you'll make it to ninth grade"), or denigrating comparisons ("Your sister always got *A*s, why can't you?" or "At your age, your brother had a part-time job; don't you have any drive?"). Such parental statements may be designed to prod an adolescent into behaving better, but the underlying message is a negative one: "You don't measure up."

• *Encourage interests and activities the adolescent can master.* Doing especially well in an academic subject, playing a musical instrument, showing talent in individual or team sports, developing a hobby, knowing more than most people do about baseball or old movies, all make an adolescent feel good about him- or herself. Helping adolescents set *realistic* goals for themselves is also important. If an adolescent expects too much, the inevitable failure can be crushing. When a boy who is only an average athlete announces that he expects to be picked as quarterback, for example, suggest that making the team is an honor in itself.

• *Give real responsibilities.* As Lickona points out, many parents limit their demands on children to doing their homework and keeping their rooms neat. But these responsibilities are *self*-oriented. Young people should also be given responsibilities that are *other*-oriented, such as supervising a younger sibling, helping to cook dinner, taking care of a family pet, washing the family car, and working in the yard. Other-oriented responsibilities give adolescents the feeling of being a useful and important member of the family team. This needn't be limited to the family. Community work—volunteering at a nursing home or day-care center, collecting money for UNICEF or the annual cancer drive—can instill an even greater sense of accomplishment.

• *Encourage independent thinking.* Small children demonstrate a kind of unthinking independence: They say what's on their minds and stick up for their rights, even if it means getting into a fight. Adolescents are more reflective, more cautious, and, for a time, more conforming. You can't push the adolescent into independence, but you can lay the groundwork. Emphasize the value of independence. One father reports, "Whenever my kids say, 'But Dad, everybody is doing it!' I simply say, 'I don't believe in statistical morality. I don't decide what's right by what most people do.'" Another told his sons, "People will like you more if they know you have a mind of your own. They won't respect you if they see you're bending over backward to please everybody." Challenge group (or statistical) morality: "You've told me what your friends say, but what do *you* think?" "What would you decide if everyone took a secret ballot and no one would know how you voted?"

• *Support friendships.* Adolescents who have supportive friends, or even just one good friend, are less likely to be swayed by the crowd. In Lickona's words, "If you have the approval of someone, you don't need the approval of everyone." Parents may get tired of hearing how Eve said this and thinks that, goes here on vacation and goes there by herself, but try to understand that, for the moment, Eve is an island of security for your child.

Talk with the adolescent about the meaning of true friendship. A friend is someone who likes you for yourself, understands when you have a problem, tries to help, and stands by you even when other kids are making fun of you and giving you a hard time. A friend is *not* someone who judges you by what you wear or whether you go along with the crowd, tries to get you to do things that will hurt you or get you into trouble, or deserts you when the going gets tough.

CHAPTER 8

New Feelings and Emotions

Adolescence has long been seen as a period of inevitable emotional turmoil. In fact, the great majority of youngsters grow to maturity without serious problems. Some adolescents are emotionally troubled. But such disturbances rarely appear for the first time in adolescence. The troubled adolescent nearly always has a history of problems with school, peers, and adults.

This is not to deny that adolescents are moody. Early adolescence is a time of emotional highs and lows. But knowing what the adolescent is feeling and why can take the sting out of hurtful comments and thoughtless behavior, and reduce parent-adolescent conflict.

SEEKING INDEPENDENCE

"Where did you go?"
"Out."
"What did you do?"
"Nothing."

This classic exchange captures a central theme in adolescent development, the quest for independence. Teenagers want and need to take charge of their own lives, to make their own decisions, to choose their own friends, to plan their own activities, to think their own thoughts, and to dream their own dreams. Not telling you everything (or anything) is part of this process. By definition, becoming an adult means becoming independent of one's parents. For the adolescent, and often the parents, this is an exciting—and frightening—prospect.

The relationship between parent and child inevitably changes as the adolescent becomes less an extension of his family and more an individual in his own right. Psychologists call this *individuation*. Giving up his childish image of his parents as all-knowing and all-powerful, for a more realistic (and critical) appraisal of them as *people* is part of this process. The young adolescent may not know who he is, but he knows he is more than his parents' son. His family used to be the center of his emotional life; now peers and other adults are just as important to his feelings of self-worth and self-esteem—and sometimes more so. Not surprisingly, both the adolescent and his parents may feel ambivalent about these changes.

Growth toward independence is easy to mistake for rebellion. Rather suddenly, the adolescent begins questioning your values, challenging your opinions, debating the rules, and telling you in countless small ways to go away. At the same time, she may treat her friends as the ultimate authority on everything from hair styles to global politics. This doesn't mean she is breaking away from her family, throwing out her upbringing, and joining the rebel army in a war between generations. To some degree the adolescent needs to dissociate from her family, and to reject their image of her, to become her own person.

The early development of independence is almost always played out in the home. You have always had the final say; now the adolescent wants an equal voice in decisions affecting *his* life. Equally important, the adolescent knows (at least on an unconscious level) that home is a safe place, where mistakes will not be too costly.

What this means in real-life, everyday terms is that parent-child confrontations tend to increase in early adolescence. Young adolescents often express their need to be independent of their parents through criticism and quarreling, silence and secrecy. There may be a period of disequilibrium as family members adjust to the new person in their midst. In most cases, this is short-lived. Confrontations between parent and child usually peak in eighth or ninth grade, then decline. (Conformity to peers follows a similar curve.) While disagreements are normal and common in the in-between stage, constant fighting and out-and-out rebellion (running away, using drugs, truancy, delinquency) are *not*. Such behavior is a sign that the adolescent is having trouble establishing his independence, and/or that parents are exercising too much or too little control (see chapter 15).

What to Expect

The adolescent wants to control who she is as well as what she does. The problem is that the young adolescent isn't at all sure who she is at this point: She has begun to shed her total identification with her family but has not yet developed a personal sense of self. This insecurity has predictable consequences. Parents can expect some or all of the following:

• *Adolescents will see being close to, or reliant on, their parents as "babyish."* Be prepared for your adolescent to reject your efforts to be helpful, reassuring, or affectionate. Your son may fly off the handle when you offer to help him fix his tape recorder—not because he doesn't need help, but because he doesn't want to be reminded that he still does. Your 13-year-old daughter no longer wants to sit on her father's lap. Reminded to fuss over Aunt Susy, whom she hasn't seen in a year, she disappears into her room. Teenagers see familiar gestures of affection not only as childish (and therefore inappropriate for them), but also as phony. "Don't touch me" doesn't mean "go away"; it means the rules are changing. Teenagers want hugs and kisses to be spontaneous and meaningful.

• *Teenagers don't want to been seen with their parents.* Many adolescents go through a phase of not wanting to go out with their parents, especially if they might run into their friends. The reason is not that they are embarrassed by you, but that they want to look older and more independent. Ways to handle this situation are to invite the adolescent to bring a friend along; allow him to sit separately (for example, in a movie theater); choose restaurants and movie theaters that are not school hangouts (so that he won't be the only one who is with his parents); and permit him to stay home alone from time to time.

• *Adolescents have a need for emotional, as well as physical, privacy.* Small children like to tell their parents about what happened in school, at the playground, in their dreams; adolescents jealously guard their personal lives. When you ask your adolescent daughter how her day went, you get a one-word answer (if that); when you inquire whether she has seen a particular friend lately, she accuses you of prying. This doesn't mean she is hiding misbehavior. One way adolescents establish their emotional independence is by keeping their thoughts and feelings to themselves.

• *Adolescents will look for (and find) your personal weaknesses.* Small children idealize their parents; adolescents can be hypercritical. De-idealizing one's parents is part of individuation. Among other things, de-idealization makes becoming an adult seem an attainable goal; no one wants to think they have to be perfect. Be prepared for the adolescent to point out your faults more often than you'd like. At the same time, the adolescent may idealize other adults. You may hear over and over how "Coach Smith understands me," "Uncle Bob is really with it," or "Sammy's parents [unlike you] do this or that." The reason for these sometimes hurtful remarks is not that the adolescent is rejecting you, but that he is expanding his network of identifications. On some level the adolescent realizes that, unless he is to be a carbon copy of you, he needs an array of adult models.

• *Adolescents often choose friends over family.* You used to spend Saturdays with your child, driving her to the movies or skating rink, taking her along with you to the supermarket and the mall. Now she'd rather be with her friends, and you have to bargain for a share of her time. Again, this isn't a rejection of you personally, but an expression of her widening horizons. She wants to experiment with new attitudes and behavior as well as new clothing styles and nail-polish colors.

• *Adolescents turn everyday decisions around the house into tests of both their competence and your trust.* You think he should spend Saturday outdoors, playing basketball or riding his bike; *he* wants to spend all his free time at the bowling alley. *You* think she should wear her new skirt the first day of school; *she* is determined to wear an old pair of tattered jeans. Or the adolescent may suddenly announce an important decision you haven't discussed: "I'm not going to camp." Underlying most such disputes and assertions are basic questions about the adolescent's right to make independent decisions. Arguing with your son about whether he does his homework before or after dinner, for example, isn't really an argument about homework. It's an argument over whether he is mature enough to decide how to schedule his own activities and accept the consequences. It is also a test of whether and how far you trust his decision-making abilities.

How to Respond

Growth toward independence is a family affair that requires changes in the parents' attitudes and behavior as well as the adolescent's. When parents attempt to maintain the same level of control over an adolescent that they exercised when he or she was a small child, or step up controls because they believe teenagers are not to be trusted, adolescents often rebel. When parents accept the adolescent's need for increasing autonomy, the transition from dependence to independence is relatively tranquil. Adolescents who feel their parents give them "enough freedom" are more likely than other teenagers to say that they feel close to their parents, enjoy doing things with their families, have few conflicts with their mothers and fathers, seek their advice, and hope to be like their parents when they grow up.

Most parents have mixed feelings about their child's independence, however. In the preadolescent years, they grew accustomed to exercising unquestioned authority. Moving from this position of power into a more equal relationship that requires negotiation and compromise can be threatening to parents. This isn't just a "power trip." Adults know that the real world is full of dangers and disappointments. Letting an innocent, inexperienced child go out into the world on her own can be frightening, especially if the young adolescent seems blissfully unaware of potential dangers and her own vulnerability (the personal fable).

More subtly, the role of parent fulfills many of our own needs —to be in control, to be right, to be needed, to be trusted and loved beyond all others. When adolescents demand the right to control their own lives, express their own opinions, take confidences they used to bring to their parents to a best friend, and in other ways demonstrate that they don't need their parents so much anymore, it is easy for parents to feel rejected.

Finally, all parents have hopes and dreams for their children. Some are proud that they have been able to give their children all the advantages they never had; others are determined to prevent their children from making the mistakes they made as teenagers; still others dream their children will fulfill their own frustrated ambitions, by going to medical school or becoming a jazz musician. When their adolescent shows he has his own ideas about how to run his life, his parents may feel unappreciated and angry.

Some parents merely want to help, and feel wounded when the adolescent says, "No, thanks."

How can parents manage their own feelings of ambivalence? let go without losing control? grant the young adolescent freedom without exposing her to danger?

• *Don't take the adolescent's steps toward independence personally.* Try to remember that your adolescent is reacting to your *role as parent* —to what you represent—as much as to you personally. She is going to want privacy no matter how understanding you have been; seek the advice of friends no matter how "with it" you are; challenge you on day-to-day decisions no matter how democratic you have been; question your values no matter how contemporary you think you are.

• *Allow rebellion within limits.* Adolescents learn to make choices by having choices. Your job at this stage is not to solve their problems for them or to protect them from making mistakes, but to protect them from making mistakes that will cause irreparable harm.

Think about issues on which you can safely defer to your child's judgment. Some good choices are how your adolescent dresses, how he decorates his room, what music he listens to, when he does his homework, when he goes to bed, and (within reason) how he spends his allowance and what he does on weekends. A leather jacket, fatigue pants, and combat boots may not be your idea of chic, but they won't harm his health or hurt his future. Doing her homework with the TV running may seem irrational to you, but if her grades are good, what is the harm?

At the same time, be clear about the standards you expect your child to live up to within these "free zones." You won't tell him what to wear, but you do expect his clothes to be clean. You won't tell her when to do her homework, but if she falls behind, you expect her to spend part of the weekend catching up. You won't tell him how to spend his Saturdays, but you do expect him to tell you where he is going, with whom, and what they plan to do.

Just how much freedom you grant a young adolescent depends on the individual child. Some preteens are able to handle a good deal of responsibility. They do their homework without being prompted, have money left over from their weekly allowance, feed and walk the puppy they begged you to buy, say no when a friend suggests hitch-hiking downtown, and so on. Other preteens have to be pushed to think through the consequences of their choices and constantly reminded of their responsibilities. Match your level of control to the adolescent's level of maturity. For example, if a boy handles money carefully, you might give him a clothes allowance and allow him to shop for himself. If he typically spends the money you gave him for a pair of sneakers on a spangled T-shirt and then whines that he needs new sneakers, you should control the purse strings, decide what he needs, and only allow choices within these categories.

But, again, you won't know how much responsibility your adolescent can handle if you never let her make decisions and choices for herself.

• *Expect some mistakes.* In part because of their intellectual immaturity, in part because of their inexperience, all adolescents make some decisions that are hasty and foolish. Sometimes young adolescents do not think through the consequences of their actions. Your son and his friends may take a bus to the beach, spend half the afternoon playing Pac Man, and only later realize that they don't have the fare to get home. Preteens may not recognize that people who give advice sometimes have a vested interest in their decisions. Your daughter may come home from the store in tears, having spent her birthday money on an outfit that looks horrible. Why did she buy it? The salesperson told her it looked great. And sometimes young adolescents don't ask for information or advice because they feel this would be an admission that they are unable to act independently. If you get angry or ridicule them for poor judgment ("How could you be so stupid?"), you undermine their confidence in their ability to make decisions, which is already shaken.

Help the young adolescent save face ("Everybody makes mistakes") and also learn from the experience ways to avoid such mistakes in the future. Did he think about buying a round-trip ticket? Did she ask about the store's return policy? Suggest that he tuck a five-dollar bill in the back of his wallet for emergencies or that she take a friend along when she goes shopping. These safety measures may seem obvious to you, but they won't be to new decision-makers who are going places by themselves and buying things for themselves for the first time.

When you think your child is going to make a poor decision, use questions rather than orders or judgments. "Have you thought this through?" "What alternatives have you considered?" "Is there another way to solve this problem?" "Have you tried making a list of the pros and cons?" "Will you feel happy about this a month from now?" Asking questions allows you to steer the adolescent away from foolish choices without backing him into a corner where he feels he has to stick with a poor decision to assert his independence.

• *Don't be afraid to say no.* Adolescents need the freedom to make (and learn from) their own mistakes. But they also need guidelines and controls. However much they may fuss and fume, adolescents appreciate limits. If nothing else, setting limits shows you care. Teenagers whose parents do not set rules turn to their peers for advice and emotional support. Because their peers are as inexperienced as they are, little is learned, and mistakes are often repeated. These young people also tend to be crowd followers, who are psychologically dependent on peer approval and afraid to take an independent stand or to make decisions for themselves.

Decide where to draw the line. "No, you can't walk home by yourself at 10 P.M., it isn't safe." "No, you are not allowed to go to a party unless there is adult supervision." "No, you're too young to drink alcohol." A good rule with adolescents is to say yes when you can, no when you have to. But don't cut off discussion. Debating controversial issues like sex and drugs with their parents helps adolescents to develop and espouse their own (not their peers') values and beliefs.

FEELING VULNERABLE

Adolescence is the first time that young people are able to think —and worry—about what is happening to them. In the words of one writer, "Worry is the result of our knowing there is a future. When we think about that future and see that it might be uncomfortable, unpleasant, or dangerous in some way, we worry." Small children don't think very far ahead; adolescents do. A list of common worries appears on page 157.

Sources of Anxiety

Self-esteem tends to decline temporarily in early adolescense: 10- to 13-year-olds are much more likely than younger children to feel unhappy with their looks, unsure of their abilities, and

WHAT WORRIES YOUNG ADOLESCENTS?*

	%
My school performance	56
My looks	53
How well others like me	48
That one of my parents might die	47
How my friends treat me	45
Hunger and poverty in the U.S.	38
Violence in the U.S.	36
That I might lose my best friend	36
Drugs and drinking around me	35
That I might not get a good job	30
Whether my body is growing normally	26
Nuclear bombing of the U.S.	25
That my parents might divorce	22
That I may die soon	21
Sexual abuse	19
That my friends will get me into trouble	18
Drinking by a parent	15
Getting beat up at school	12
Physical abuse by a parent	12
That I might kill myself	11

* Based on a survey of 8,000 junior-high-school students

worried about their popularity. At the same time, self-consciousness increases. Young adolescents wonder *"Can* I do it?" "Will I *look* stupid?" *"Will* I make friends?" *"What* will they think of me?"

As a rule, girls experience more intense self-doubt than boys do (although there are many individual exceptions). There are several reasons for this. Female socialization emphasizes getting along with others, while male socialization stresses becoming independent. Being popular is important to girls of all ages. The in-crowds and cliques she encounters in junior high may threaten this basic part of her self-image. Second, puberty usually begins earlier for girls. Boys often have a year or two of junior high behind them before they start developing; a girl may enter junior high looking mature but still feeling like a child inside. Third, our society sends girls mixed messages about their emergent sexuality. Glamorous, sexy women are greatly admired ("Show yourself off"), but nice girls draw a line ("Cover yourself up"). The message to boys is simpler ("Be careful," implying "Go for it!"). Our society also sends girls mixed messages about achievement: Do your best in school, but don't be too competitive, brains don't attract brawn. (Being able to beat every boy in your class in tennis isn't necessarily an asset either.)

Wait a minute, you say: That's not how I've raised my daughter! But you are not the only influence on your daughter's interpretation of sex roles. TV sitcoms, ads, and rock videos still promote stereotypes. So does the peer group. Young adolescents tend to be more conservative and stereotyped than their parents in sex roles, if only because boys and girls are unsure about how to act like men and women.

Finally, the core of the male stereotype—success in a career—is postponed until early adulthood; the core of the female stereotype—success in dating—begins in junior high. No wonder adolescent girls are more likely to say negative things about themselves, feel insecure about their abilities, and worry about whether other people like them. But boys are not immune to self-doubt.

That's the bad news. The good news is that this period of increased vulnerability is temporary. By ninth grade, self-esteem has begun to stabilize; in middle and late adolescence, feelings of self-worth usually increase. In other words, vulnerability peaks during the transition into adolescence; it does not persist over the entire adolescent decade.

What to Expect

When your child is entering adolescence, you can expect some or all of the following expressions of heightened vulnerability:

- *Moodiness.* Young adolescents may be ecstatic one moment, despondent the next. The intensity of their emotions seems totally out of proportion to the events that inspire them.
- *Sulking.* Young adolescents do not have much experience talking about feelings. They may feel down but not know why, not be able to verbalize their feelings, or not want to do so. Or they may attribute all of the discomfort they are experiencing to a particular comment or event and not be able to think about anything else.

- *Privacy.* Being on stage all the time is tiring, even if the audience is imaginary. Closing the door to their room allows teens to relax. Alone, they can indulge in heroic fantasies without being observed. Or they can surround themselves with the old, familiar possessions of childhood without letting others know they are not as grown-up as they pretend to be.
- *Short tempers.* With little or no provocation, young adolescents may blow up at their parents and siblings. This is a familiar defense mechanism we all use on occasion. When we are frustrated or anxious, we displace these feelings onto another person. A boy who was the butt of a practical joke at school torments his little brother; a girl who is terrified of the upcoming tryouts for cheerleader accuses her mother of pressuring her. Parents are frequent targets of displacement because, consciously or unconsciously, the teen believes they will love him no matter how awful he is.

How to Respond

Vulnerability and moodiness are *normal* responses to the transition from childhood to adolescence. Most adolescents are able to deal with disruptions in self-image on their own—and prefer to do so. You can be supportive and sympathetic (see Developing a Positive Self-Image, chapter 7), but you cannot live through this phase for them. What you *can* do is come to grips with your own feelings about the adolescent's behavior.

- *Don't overreact.* Parents commonly react to their young adolescent's emotional unpredictability with distress and anger. They feel helpless in the face of their teenager's misery; exasperated by unsuccessful attempts to make him or her "snap out of it"; cut off from something important that is happening in their child's life. One of the hardest lessons for parents whose child is entering adolescence is that in most cases they are not the cause of his unhappiness (though they may be the target for displaced anger), and they are not responsible for bringing him out of it.

What adolescents and the rest of us want most when we are down is someone to listen, not lecture. If your daughter is upset because her boyfriend left her, declaring cheerfully "There are other fish in the sea" won't help. Right now, he's the only one who counts. Suggesting that she will fall in love again or that a year from now she won't remember him may infuriate her. After all, if this is the first time she has experienced disappointment in love, she doesn't know that she will recover. You can try empathy, describing how terrible you felt when your first romance fell apart. But don't expect to be believed. When she says, "Mom, you don't know what it means to be in love," she means it. (Recall adolescent egocentrism and the fable of being unique, chapter 7.)

Try to be supportive without being judgmental. Assure the adolescent that feeling nervous about a test or a first date, or down about a poor grade or broken romance, is normal. However independent teenagers may seem, they still want and need your approval.

• *Don't pry.* In some cases parents are the last people adolescents tell their troubles to. Try not to take your adolescent's secrecy personally. Privacy-seeking is not necessarily parent-rejection. Respect your adolescent's desire to work things out for himself. Let him know that you see he is feeling blue and that you're available if he wants to talk. But don't persist in asking what is wrong or insist that he tell you what is on his mind. The fact that he isn't talking doesn't necessarily mean he is hiding something. He may not know why he is unhappy. Or he may know but not be willing or ready to talk. What he needs to know is that you are on his side and that it is safe to be himself at home, bad moods and all.

The best strategy with moody adolescents is probably distraction. Plan activities that you know your adolescent likes, activities that will get him out of the house and force him to think about something other than his troubles. A movie or a basketball game, a new haircut or pair of sunglasses, or a free call to a friend from summer camp who lives in another city (*free* meaning that you pay), can lift the gloom. But don't try too hard to cheer him up: Being nagged about moodiness only adds to the teenager's problems.

• *But draw the line.* There is no reason to tolerate rudeness and disrespect. Feeling confused is not an excuse for the adolescent to throw out everything you have taught her about manners and civility. Respond to your child's temper or moodiness by saying how *you* feel, rather than lecturing or criticizing her. If your adolescent snaps at you for asking how her day was, for example, say, "I don't like to be jumped on for asking a simple question. If you had a bad day and don't feel like talking about it, just say so. I have days like that myself."

SERIOUS EMOTIONAL PROBLEMS

How is a parent to know the difference between ordinary vulnerability and moodiness and psychological problems? A list of danger signs appears below. If *any* of these statements describes your adolescent, talk to a school counselor, a therapist, or your physician or clergyman. One problem that may appear for the first time in adolescence is depression.

PSYCHOLOGICAL PROBLEMS: DANGER SIGNS

If your child exhibits any of these signs, you should seek professional help.

- The adolescent is withdrawn for *long* periods of time and shows *no* interest in others.
- The adolescent has *no* friends of the same age (within two years of his or her age) and is not integrated into a peer group.
- The adolescent's pattern of after-school and weekend activities *suddenly* changes (and he or she is reluctant for you to meet new friends).
- The adolescent goes *out of his or her way* to avoid you or other adults.
- The adolescent is docile, *never* acts independently, and *never* initiates activity.
- The adolescent's school behavior (attendance or performance) *suddenly* changes for the worse.
- The adolescent *continually* runs away from home or school.
- The adolescent *frequently* gets into fights and physically abuses others.
- The adolescent engages in *indiscriminate* sexual activity with a number of partners.
- The adolescent is *often* drunk or under the influence of drugs.
- The adolescent is either *frequently* or *persistently* anxious or depressed.
- The adolescent loses a *dangerous* amount of weight out of excessive concern for appearance.
- The adolescent *talks about or threatens* to commit suicide.

Depression

Emotional lows are a normal part of life. Like rainy days, they come and go. Psychologists reserve the term *depression* for a serious emotional disorder that warrants treatment. Clinical depressions are not normal and do not go away by themselves.

People in the grips of a clinical depression feel sad, helpless, worthless, guilty, inadequate, powerless, "out of things." They brood over past mistakes, see no hope for the future, and often think about ending it all. Activities and people they used to enjoy no longer interest them. They don't seem to have the energy to do anything. They lose their train of thought in midsentence and can't remember why they went from one room to another. Routine activities (brushing their teeth) seem overwhelming. On bad days, one young patient told her doctor, "I'd just like to go back to bed and creep under the covers . . . and just . . . stay there all day."

In some cases depression is a reaction to a specific event (the death of a loved one, divorce, failure to achieve an anticipated goal, or having committed a regretted act). But the response may be delayed and the individual's emotions seem out of proportion to the event. Such depressions begin suddenly and lift when the person comes to terms with the event, often through pyschotherapy. Other times depression builds slowly, with no apparent cause, and persists over time. The individual may not remember when or why he began feeling blue. The depression may lift for a day or two, then return, again without apparent reason. Recovery is slower and more difficult, even with treatment. Symptoms of depression are shown on page 163.

Recognizing Adolescent Depression

Adolescent depression is often overlooked. One reason is that the stereotype of the moody, brooding, emotionally unstable adolescent may lead parents and others to conclude that a teenager is merely "going through a phase." Another reason is that the symptoms of depression in teenagers can be different from those seen in adults. In these cases, depression may be mistaken for problem behavior. This is particularly true in early adolescence.

• *Boredom and restlessness*. Depressed adolescents may seek constant stimulation, plunging into new activities with enthusiasm but

SYMPTOMS OF DEPRESSION

During clinical depressive periods, three or more of the following symptoms are present:

- Insomnia or hypersomnia (sleeping more than is normal)
- Low energy level, chronic tiredness
- Feelings of inadequacy, loss of self-esteem, or self-deprecation
- Decreased effectiveness or productivity at school, work, or home
- Decreased attention, concentration, or ability to think clearly
- Social withdrawal
- Loss of interest in or enjoyment of pleasurable activities
- Irritability or excessive anger (in children, often expressed toward parents or caretakers)
- Inability to respond with apparent pleasure to praise or rewards
- Less active or talkative than usual, or feels slowed down or restless
- Pessimistic attitude toward the future, brooding about past events, or feeling sorry for self
- Tearfulness or crying
- Recurrent thoughts of death or suicide

quickly losing interest and searching desperately for other activities. This unending search for stimulation can be seen as an unconscious attempt to escape inner feelings of emptiness.

- *Fatigue and preoccupation with their bodies.* Other depressed adolescents feel "wiped out" much of the time. Sometimes the problem is insomnia; other times they may sleep a full eight, ten, even fourteen hours but wake feeling exhausted. Their concern with their bodies may far exceed normal adolescent worries. Many complain of headaches or stomach problems. They are not faking these physical ailments; constant tension and anxiety take a toll on the body. They may also disregard appearance and hygiene; girls, in particular, may overeat.
- *Difficulty concentrating.* Depressed adolescents frequently have difficulty focusing on the task at hand. Their schoolwork declines as a result. When asked what the problem is, they typically say that no matter how hard they try, they can't seem to remember anything. Unlike adults, they do not connect their difficulty concentrating with their emotional state. The most common reason

depressed youngsters come to the attention of school counselors is that they are having problems with schoolwork.

• *Acting out.* Youngsters may use action to ward off feelings of inadequacy and helplessness. Unable to face or express despair, they run away, experiment with drugs, steal from their parents, or vandalize a local school. Acting out serves a number of functions. It relieves the adolescent of the burden of thinking about a painful subject. It bolsters a personal fable of invulnerability. And it may be the only way an adolescent can say "I'm in pain, I need help." Defiant, antisocial behavior by a previously conforming youngster is a common response to the death of a parent or relative.

• *Flight to or from people.* Some depressed adolescents dread being alone. They may panic if a parent is five minutes late coming home from work, or feel a compulsive need to phone friends at all hours. In some cases, depression leads to promiscuity: Physical intimacy temporarily relieves their fear of abandonment. Other depressed adolescents turn away from people, rather than toward them. They stop going out and do things that seemed designed to alienate former friends. The youngster who feels out of it, worthless, and unlikeable avoids rejection by avoiding people.

While it is important not to overreact to normal emotional highs and lows of adolescence, it is vital to recognize when the problems run deeper. A *dramatic change* in school performance, patterns or levels of activity, or social behavior and friendships is a sign that something is wrong. So is sadness that is way out of proportion to the loss or disappointment the youngster experienced, particularly if it *persists over time.*

Getting Professional Help

When an adolescent first slips into a depression, parents are usually sympathetic and try to help. When the depression persists, however, they may become frustrated and angry. This is a mistake: The adolescent cannot "snap out of it." Depression is a serious emotional disorder, one parents should not attempt to treat themselves. The adolescent needs professional help.

Depression is treatable. With a combination of psychotherapy and medication, 80 percent of seriously depressed individuals recover. Unfortunately, remission rates are also high, and many individuals have second and third episodes. The sooner depression is detected, the more likely it is that the individual will respond to treatment and the less likely he or she will be to experience serious depressions in the future.

Coping with Threats of Suicide

Adults find it hard to believe that an adolescent would deliberately take his or her own life, even after a suicide or suicide attempt has occurred. Teenagers have their health, their looks, and everything to live for. Adolescents who talk about suicide are "just trying to get attention." Adults who think this way are wrong.

The suicide rate for teenagers has tripled over the last twenty-five years. Each year, approximately one in every one thousand teenagers attempts suicide. Thankfully, the vast majority of these attempts (perhaps 98 percent) do not succeed. Even so, about five thousand adolescents kill themselves each year. Suicide is a leading cause of death among young people.

Contrary to myth, adolescent suicide is rarely an impulsive reaction to immediate distress (such as breaking up with a boy- or girlfriend or having a fight with parents). Typically, the adolescents have made repeated attempts to solve their problems—perhaps with drugs, sex, or other forms of acting out. They have tried, but failed, to communicate their distress to others. (In one study, 85 percent had told someone that they intended to commit suicide, and 40 percent had made a previous unsuccessful attempt.) From an adult's point of view, their negative assessments of their lives may seem totally unrealistic; from their point of view, they have exhausted all other options. Many adolescent suicide attempts are carefully planned. It is not unusual for a teen to straighten his room and give favorite belongings to friends before taking his life—in effect, making out his will. This is not to say that adolescents who attempt suicide, "know what they are doing." Their conception of death may be hazy. They may want to "disappear" . . . but not forever. See page 166 for suicide danger signs.

Teenagers who commit suicide tend to fit one of three patterns. Some, especially boys, have a history of problem behavior: They abuse alcohol or drugs and have been in trouble with the

SUICIDE: DANGER SIGNS

- Direct suicide threats and comments ("I wish I were dead"; "You'd be better off without me")
- A previous suicide attempt, no matter how minor
- Preoccupation with death in music, art, and writing
- Loss of a family member, pet, or boy- or girlfriend (through death, abandonment, or breakup)
- Family disruptions (parental unemployment, serious illness, relocation, divorce)
- Problems with sleeping, eating, and personal hygiene
- Problems with schoolwork; loss of interest in school or hobbies that had been important
- Dramatic changes in behavior patterns (such as a shy adolescent suddenly becoming extremely outgoing)
- Prevailing sense of gloom, hopelessness, and helplessness
- Withdrawal from family members and friends; alienation of important people
- Giving away prize possessions
- A series of "accidents," increase in risk-taking, or loss of interest in personal safety

law. Some, especially girls, are depressed. And some, most often boys, are rigid, ambitious perfectionists who tend to isolate themselves from others. Nearly a third have a family history of suicide.

- *Any threat of suicide demands immediate professional attention.* Do not dismiss talk of suicide because you know that your child is not the type who would really go through with a suicide attempt, or because the threat seems theatrical or half-baked (your daughter goes to the medicine cabinet for aspirin, then asks you how many aspirin will kill a person, knowing full well that you will take the bottle away before she unscrews the top). It may well be that she is "only" trying to frighten you. But there is a reason why she's making such a desperate attempt to get your attention, and you or a therapist *must* find out what that reason is.

In addition, adolescents do not necessarily know what is and is not lethal. Your daughter may take half a dozen barbiturates in the mistaken belief that a few pills won't kill her (they can). A son who is toying with the idea of suicide may accidentally release the safety lock on your gun. After the fact, it will not matter whether or not the adolescent truly intended to kill him- or herself. Any threat of suicide is a cry for help that must not be ignored.

Many teenagers have thought about suicide. What distinguishes thinkers from doers? As a rule, those who actually attempt suicide have a history of depression and/or self-destructive behavior (the "acting out" side of depression). They have not only thought about suicide, they have planned *how* they would go about it. If they make an attempt and are lucky enough to survive, they do not know or cannot say why they did it. Adolescents who explain a suicide attempt in interpersonal terms—who recognize that they are trying to communicate something to important people in their lives—are least likely to make another, successful attempt. But there are many exceptions to these rules.

We repeat, *any threat of suicide is a cry for help.* You are no more qualified to determine if a suicide threat or attempt is serious than you are to determine whether a lump in your breast or groin is cancerous. Call the suicide hot line in your community (listed under Suicide Prevention in the Yellow Pages) for advice. If your daughter has already taken a handful of pills, take her to a hospital emergency room; don't wait to see if she pulls through.

• *How you react to a suicide attempt can be crucial.* Parents' reactions to a teenager's suicide attempt range from deep concern and remorse to disbelief, indifference, anger, scorn, and even ridicule. It is not unusual for parents to berate an adolescent for causing so much trouble or to ridicule him or her for trying to get attention. These negative reactions are understandable: Suicide is the ultimate rejection. Anger and scorn enable parents to avoid their own feelings of helplessness and self-blame. But they may also lead the adolescent to "try harder." When parents take the suicide threat or attempt seriously, show concern about the young person's problems, and demonstrate willingness to reassess the attitudes and events that led to the attempt, the chances that the adolescent will develop constructive ways of dealing with distress and respond to therapy are much greater. Parents who find it difficult to be supportive under these circumstances should seek counseling for themselves—in addition to, or in conjunction with, counseling for the adolescent.

• *If someone close to your child has committed suicide, it is important that you talk.* When a relative or classmate commits suicide, adolescents are likely to feel guilty, because they wonder if there was anything they could have done to help, and afraid, because death is a reminder of their own mortality (something adolescents do not think about very much).

On occasion, one adolescent suicide is followed by a cluster, or epidemic, of suicides. Whether these clusters of suicides are the result of media coverage (which makes teenage suicide look glamorous), personal suggestion (friends convincing one another that suicide is a viable option), common events (massive layoffs in a community might lead to widespread family problems, which in turn might trigger adolescent suicides), or some other factor is unknown. But there is some evidence that teenagers are more likely to identify with a teenager or with a celebrity who commits suicide than adults are.

Most suicides are isolated events; suicide epidemics are rare. Nevertheless, parents and schools should take the possibility of copycat suicides seriously. The worst thing to do is to pretend that nothing happened. If a suicide is receiving a great deal of media coverage, discuss it with your adolescent. Help him to form a realistic image of suicide. Media reports hardly ever discuss the pain and disfigurement that accompany suicide; as a result, it may seem like the easy way out, even glamorous. Get your teenager to think about what someone who has jumped from a 15-story window, taken an overdose, or "blown his brains out" looks like. Also, the media rarely discuss alternative ways of coping with unhappiness and stress—counseling, hotlines, self-help groups. What other alternatives can your teenager think of? If the suicide reported in the media was a teenager, talk about what your adolescent would do if a friend of his said he was contemplating suicide. Explain that suicide is a plea for help and that telling you or another responsible adult is not betraying a confidence. If someone your adolescent knows personally committed suicide, encourage him to discuss his feelings. He needs to be reassured that being a better friend, or a better son, would not have prevented the suicide; people who are contemplating suicide need professional help.

Eating Disorders

The socialite Babe Paley is credited with the motto "You can never be too rich or too thin." Unfortunately, not everyone is genetically or metabolically meant to be as thin as fashion magazines tell people they should be. Some adolescents, particularly female adolescents, become so concerned about gaining weight that they take drastic—and dangerous—measures to remain thin. Adolescents suffering from such eating disorders as anorexia and bulimia need professional attention.

Although the most important symptoms of anorexia and bulimia concern the adolescent's eating patterns, most experts believe that these disturbances have underlying causes that have little to do with food or dieting. Instead, they are better understood and more successfully treated as serious emotional problems.

Anorexia Anorexia is primarily an adolescent disorder. Nearly all of the victims are upper-class or middle-class Caucasian or Oriental girls in early or middle adolescence. Estimates are that 1 in 250 teenage girls becomes anorexic. The disorder may begin when a friend comments that the girl has put on weight, or when she discovers that a size 8 is too tight. She goes on a diet. Losing weight makes her feel good about herself, so she reduces her food intake even more and steps up her exercise program. Avoiding food becomes an obsession. Having dropped below 10 to 15 percent of her normal weight, she looks bony and gaunt to others; in her own mind she is still fat. One of the peculiarities of anorexia is that while starving herself, she remains intensely interested in food and may collect recipes, beg to do the family shopping, and prepare sumptuous meals for others. But the idea of herself eating fills her with anxiety and disgust.

We don't really know what causes anorexia. But case studies suggest that the disorder is often rooted in ambivalence about growing up and becoming independent. On the one hand, dieting makes the teenager feel in control of her life. Losing weight is an achievement that doesn't depend on other people. On the other hand, extreme weight loss enables her to remain a child. Her parents worry about her health, just as they did when she was a child. Her emaciated body looks childlike. She stops menstruating (one of the side effects of extreme weight loss). In denying herself pleasure, she denies—or at least postpones—her sexuality. Some clinicians trace the anorexic's anxieties about independence to overcontrolling, overprotective parents who demand high levels of compliance from a child and treat her achievements as their own. But the evidence for this is not strong. Whatever the cause, once anorexia is underway, parents are drawn in. The anorexic becomes the focus of family attention, forcing her parents to fuss over her. At the same time, she refuses their attempts to influence and nurture her, pushing them away.

The danger signs for anorexia are shown below. In relatively mild cases, anorexia causes nutritional deficiencies, loss of muscle strength, hormonal imbalances, cessation of menstruation, increased susceptibility to infection, low blood pressure, chronic constipation, and the growth of fine hair (lanugo) on the face, trunk, and arms. In severe cases, anorexia may lead to death by starvation. This is more common than one might think: 15 to 20 percent of anorexics die as a consequence of this illness.

DANGER SIGNS FOR ANOREXIA

- Intense fear of becoming fat that does not diminish as weight is lost
- Disturbance of body image (claiming to look "just right" or even to "feel fat" even when emaciated)
- Extreme, self-induced weight loss (25 percent or more of original body weight, or 25 percent below normal weight for someone her age and height)
- Denial that anything is wrong

Anorexia requires immediate medical attention. Parents should not attempt to deal with the problem alone, for two reasons. The first is that it is too dangerous: Parents are not qualified to determine whether a teenager is on the verge of starvation. The second is that one of the psychological "purposes" of self-starvation is to break away from parental control. Parents' efforts to change the anorexic's unhealthy behavior will feel like control to the teenager and may have the opposite effect of pushing her to greater extremes. In addition, most anorexics actively resist treatment. They do not believe that there is anything wrong with them, are terrified of becoming fat, and see anyone who encourages or requires them to eat as the enemy. A 17-year-old, hospitalized for anorexia, complained, "I feel as if everyone is making decisions for me. I feel out of control and I feel fat and . . . I don't want to eat. I almost hope I lost weight this weekend to show them [hospital staff]." Medical professionals are trained to deal with resistance and hostility; parents are too involved to handle an anorexic calmly and effectively.

The first step in treating anorexia is to stop weight loss. In many cases, the physician or psychologist will recommend that the girl be hospitalized until she recovers from malnutrition and has reached an acceptable weight. The second step is helping the anorexic develop a more realistic body image and healthier ways of achieving autonomy and control over her life. This stage of treatment may involve family therapy, especially in cases where the parents' excessive attempts to control the adolescent's behavior may be contributing to the disorder. Other anorexics benefit more from supportive individual therapy designed to help restore an accurate and healthy self-image. Because some anorexic teenagers are also suffering from depression, antidepressant medication may be recommended.

Bulimia Bulimia is a pattern of uncontrollable binging, often followed by self-induced vomiting, overuse of laxatives, strenuous exercises, or fasting. A bulimic may consume a dozen cakes and gallons of ice cream (10,000 to 50,000 calories) in the space of one or two hours, then stick her finger down her throat to purge herself of unwanted calories. Or she may go on a two-week binge, then starve herself for the next month.

Like anorexia, bulimia most often strikes relatively well-off Caucasian or Oriental adolescent girls. Although symptoms of the two may overlap (an anorexic may go on binges and a binger may go through periods of self-starvation), bulimia has distinctive features. Anorexics tend to be withdrawn and antisocial; bulimics often appear extroverted and well-adjusted. Not eating makes an anorexic feel in control (even though an outsider can see she is controlled *by* her obsession); bulimics feel out of control. Getting thinner and thinner enhances an anorexic's feelings of self-esteem. Bulimics ride an emotional seesaw: When they binge, they are filled with self-loathing; when they purge or starve, they feel elated. Anorexics are proud of their weight loss; bulimics are troubled by their eating habits and hide their behavior from others. Although their weight may fluctuate by 10 pounds or more in a given month, their average weight is usually within the normal range. As a result, bulimia often goes undetected. Although clinicians once believed that a large proportion of teenage girls are bulimic (early studies suggested a figure as high as 20 percent), new, better-designed studies indicate that the disorder is quite rare. When the strict diagnostic criteria of the American Psychiatric Association are applied (at least two binge-purge episodes weekly), as they were in these new studies, the incidence of bulimia appears to be somewhere between 1 and 3 percent.

The danger signs for bulimia are listed below. Food disappearing from the cupboard at a surprising rate and secretive eating patterns are also signs that a teenager has a problem. Although usually not life-threatening, bulimia can cause serious health problems, including erosion of teeth enamel, enlarged salivary glands, lesions in the esophagus, stomach spasms, and chemical and hormonal imbalances.

DANGER SIGNS FOR BULIMIA

- Recurrent episodes of binge eating
- Fear of not being able to stop eating during binges
- Regular use of self-induced vomiting, laxatives, rigorous diets, or fasting to counteract the effects of binges
- Awareness that one's eating patterns are abnormal

Bulimia has not been studied as closely as anorexia. But clinical studies suggest that the problem is related to general feelings of inadequacy, unworthiness, and depression, combined with the belief that being thin will provide magic relief. Bulimia may be triggered when a slightly overweight girl attempts to diet but fails to achieve her goal. Disheartened, she consoles herself with a binge of eating; binging makes her feel disgusted with herself; to restore her self-confidence, she induces vomiting and/or goes back on a stringent diet. A bulimic may settle into a more normal pattern of eating for a time but return to binging and purging when under stress. A 15-year-old bulimic went on a binge when corrected by her basketball coach. "I felt empty and angry . . . so I ate and ate. While I was eating I'd feel physical pain but soon I didn't feel anything . . . It [binge-eating] took the place of the other hurt. Vomiting hurt too but it made me lose weight . . . then

I felt better." The longer this pattern continues, the more likely she is to feel that she has no control over her behavior.

As often as not, parents do not know that their daughter (or son) is bulimic. When bulimics seek medical help, they are often in their early twenties (but report that they have been binging and purging for four to six years). Because they want help, bulimics are somewhat easier to treat than anorexics. Some psychologists work with bulimic patients in groups; others prefer to treat their patients individually. In most cases, treatment consists of a combination of insight therapy, to help the patient understand the causes of her low self-esteem, education in healthy eating habits and nutrition, stress-management techniques, and behavioral modification designed to reduce episodes of binging and purging.

RESOURCES

The following organizations publish information and/or answer questions.

Depression

The National Institute of Mental Health's D/ART (Depression/Awareness, Recognition, and Treatment) Program provides free information. Write to

D/ART Public Inquiries
Room 15C-05
5600 Fishers Lane
National Institute of Mental Health
Rockville, MD 20857

Suicide

For *Suicide in Youth and What You Can Do about It: A Guide for School Personnel* (also appropriate for parents), or a companion guide for students, prepared by the Suicide Prevention and Crisis Center of San Mateo County, California, and the American Association of Suicidology, write to

Health Information Services
Merck, Sharp & Dohme
West Point, PA 19486

For a list of crisis intervention centers, call or write to

American Association of Suicidology
2459 South Ash
Denver, CO 80222
303-692-0985

For a 24-hour hotline call or write to

The Samaritans
Suicide Services
500 Commonwealth Avenue
Boston, MA 02215
617-247-0020

Recommended reading on adolescent suicide: Frances Klagsbrun, *To Die Too Young: Youth and Suicide* (Boston: Houghton Mifflin, 1976) and John Mack and Holly Hickler, *Vivienne, the Life and Suicide of an Adolescent Girl* (Boston: Little, Brown, 1981)

C H A P T E R 9

The Social Revolution
of Adolescence

*I*n childhood, peer groups are organized and supervised by adults. Opportunities to socialize depend on who lives near whom, which parent is willing to host a pajama party, who belongs to the Cub Scouts, and the like. In adolescence, peer groups take on a life of their own.

CLIQUES AND CROWDS

Children's friendships tend to be fickle. Children may declare that so-and-so is their best friend, but most are willing to play with almost anyone. In early adolescence, young people tend to band together in tight-knit groups of three or four best friends, or cliques. Members of a clique see themselves as different and special: They draw a sharp line between "us" and "them." Within the clique, individual differences are discouraged. Insiders dress in the same styles, listen to the same music, develop their own repertoire of in-jokes and phrases, and adopt a similar posture toward school and parents.

At a stage when adolescents are wondering "Who will I become?" the clique provides an alias: "I'm a member of The

Group." What should I wear? Should I try out for the team? study all night? be nice to this person? joke with those boys? The clique provides answers.

Depending on what image they project, members of a clique will be identified with one or another crowd. Almost every junior and senior high school has its crowd of school leaders (called "elites" or "preppies"), athletes ("jocks" or "animals"), serious students ("brains," "bookhounds," or "grinds"), partiers ("populars" or "socies"), and would-be or actual delinquents ("leathers," "JDs," or "stoners" and "druggies"), as well as individuals who are pegged as outsiders ("nerds" or "goobs"). Members of a crowd do not necessarily associate with one another, or even know one another. Rather, a crowd is a social identity.

In some ways adolescent crowds resemble—and reflect—social classes and groups in adult society. Some crowds have more status than others. Depending on the school, jocks or preppies may be the top of the heap. Like social class, crowds promote snobbery: Brains don't want to be seen with JDs, and vice versa. And association with a crowd is not entirely voluntary. A boy who is slow to develop physically has little chance of becoming a jock, while a boy who matures early may be seen as a jock even though he's more interested in studying than sports. Crowd labels are stereotypes, and like other stereotypes, they stick. Once an adolescent is associated with a particular crowd, it is difficult to switch to another, unless the adolescent changes schools.

Cliques and crowds are islands of security in a rapidly changing social scene. The desire to fit in—and the fear of suddenly being dropped and becoming an outsider—is stronger in early adolescence than at any other age. The *last* thing the young adolescent wants is to stand out from the crowd. Not until middle or late adolescence do young people have the self-confidence to stand alone.

POPULARITY

Who doesn't want to be popular? But popularity has a special urgency at this age. For young adolescents, to belong, to be part of the in-group, means you are somebody—and to be shut out means you are nobody. "Am I popular?" is the young person's first identity crisis (followed by questions about "Who am I?" and

"Where am I headed?" in later adolescence and young adulthood, and "What have I done with my life?" in middle age).

Why are some adolescents popular and others not? A major reason is personality. As a general rule, popular adolescents are friendly, helpful, enthusiastic, good-natured, humorous, and intelligent. (Contrary to rumor, intelligence is a social asset, not a liability, probably because bright children are good at figuring out what will make them likable.) They perceive and respond to other kids' needs. They are confident and assertive without being cocky. They like to have fun. And they behave in ways their peers consider appropriate for someone their age. Unpopular adolescents lack these social graces. Some are conceited and self-centered, constantly drawing attention to themselves. Some are aggressive: Always on the defensive, they interpret the most innocent comments as personal attacks, and strike back first. Some are so serious, or unenthusiastic, or uncomfortable socially that they make other people edgy. In one way or another, they interfere with other kids' fun. The personality criteria for popularity at this age are much the same as they are in childhood or adulthood. But there's more.

Popularity in early adolescence also depends on fitting in, on meeting peer standards for appearance and activities. This is a frequent cause of parent-child misunderstanding and conflict. From the youngster's point of view, the costs of being the odd-kid-out are high. It's not simply a matter of being pushed to the margins of a clique or excluded from a party (both of which are painful). Adolescents type one another on the basis of superficial characteristics ("He's a nerd because he dresses funny"). And young people who are branded as losers early on find it hard to shake this label. Parents shouldn't encourage conformity, but they should be sensitive to the adolescent's concerns. The boy who insists on dressing in the latest punk outfit and the girl who won't wear anything without a designer label aren't just conforming; both are seeking social acceptance. The same is true of the boy who gives up the choir for drums or wrestling and the girl whose passion shifts from collecting rocks to listening to rock.

Conforming to sex-role stereotypes is another way young adolescents attempt to fit in. Indeed, early adolescence is one of the most sexist periods in the life span. Insecure about their sexual identities, adolescents sometimes go to extremes of femininity and masculinity in order to reassure themselves. A girl who liked to be one of the boys suddenly becomes obsessed with clothes and make-up; a boy who spent his afternoons practicing the violin shifts to hockey. This doesn't mean they are "selling out"; they are trying to fit in with what their friends want. And they're right, at least in one regard: Conforming to traditional sex roles does affect popularity at this age. Parents who hoped to raise children who were not bound by these traditions needn't despair. If the boy has a genuine interest in the violin, over time he will find a way to combine music and masculinity. The girl may or may not outgrow her interest in fashion, but many women who are highly successful in nontraditional fields (science, finance, athletics) are smart dressers, too.

Of course, if fitting in means smoking marijuana, under-achieving in school, some other harmful change in behavior, or going against what the adolescent believes, parents should step in. But allowing adolescents to go along with the crowd in matters of taste and style is important.

Rejection

Popularity is not a trivial issue. Study after study has found that unpopular adolescents are more likely than their popular peers to be low in self-esteem, do poorly in school, drop out of school, get involved in delinquent behavior, and suffer from a range of psychological problems as adults. Whether adolescents become unpopular because they lack self-esteem or lack self-esteem because they are unpopular is not known. Each probably affects the other. But we do know that having friends matters. Parents should be concerned if the adolescent

- Spends all or almost all free time alone
- Rarely mentions other adolescents or social activities
- Is awkward, aggressive, childish, or otherwise inappropriate with agemates
- Frequently complains about having no friends (with no im-mediate reason, such as changing schools)
- Has been friendless through most of childhood

If this describes your child, consider talking to a teacher or the parent of one of your adolescent's classmates whom you trust to give you an honest answer. Why isn't Johnny invited anywhere? Is he boastful, boorish, arrogant, disruptive, square? Does he "dress funny"? have a weird way of talking? turn down invitations and overtures from classmates? If you find that your adolescent is alienating his peers, you (or a psychologist) may be able to help him develop such basic social skills as asking other people about themselves, complimenting them, sharing, cooperating, and joining group activities (without trying to dominate them). If the answer is that your adolescent is shy, read on.

Shyness

It's important to distinguish between unpopularity and shyness. Although the inner experience can be similar, some shy adolescents are well liked, while some outgoing adolescents are universally disliked. Shyness is fear of other people. Shy individuals are prisoners of self-consciousness. In extreme cases they are afraid to do or say anything that might call attention to themselves, because they are sure that other people will find them ridiculous and convinced that the only reason people are nice to them is out of pity. Shyness is painful, but it need not be debilitating.

Some adolescents were "born shy": They've always been timid in social situations. Indeed, new research suggests that this type of shyness may have some genetic basis. Shy children do not suddenly become gregarious and social in adolescence. If the teenager seems happy and has one or two close friends, parents should not be concerned. Every adolescent does not have to be the life of the party.

Other adolescents are nervous and withdrawn when talking in front of a large group or meeting new people, but relaxed and outgoing with their family or close friends. And some young people who were easy-going and extroverted as children suddenly become self-conscious and tongue-tied in early adolescence. Such transient shyness is fairly common at this age and passes with time. Probably the *worst* thing parents can do is to call attention to it.

Parents should only be concerned about shyness if the adolescent expresses extreme distress, directly ("I hate parties!") or indirectly (repeated excuses for not going to a new school). In these cases, it's a good idea to talk to the adolescent about it. Point out that everyone worries about being rejected and most people have found themselves in situations where they don't know what to say. In his book *Shyness,* psychologist Philip Zimbardo quotes the advice comedienne Carol Burnett (herself a painfully shy child) gives her three daughters:

> I tell [them] that the important thing is to know that other people have the same problems you have and not to be so selfish as to think the world revolves around what people think you look like, what you're feeling and how you act, or the fact that a boy did not come up and ask you to dance. They're not always evaluating and judging you in critical ways. They're thinking about themselves and you have to come out and reach to people. . . . [T]he more you smile and are outgoing to people the more you are going to get that back—you know you reap what you sow. I mean it's a cliché, but it's a cliché because it's so true. Then just to go on and make contact with other people. If you see a kid in school who is a little shy, or who isn't getting along too well with some of the other kids and looks a little unhappy, that's when you should reach out . . .

PEER PRESSURE

Over the years, experts have blamed peer pressure for everything from delinquency and drug abuse to conformity and consumerism. Whatever the observer's particular bias, the assumption has been that left to themselves, teenagers are up to no good.

Myths and Facts

Current research suggests that peer pressure has been both overrated and misunderstood. Following are some common myths and the corresponding facts.

• *Peers are always a bad influence.* This myth is based on the assumption that teenagers are themselves uniform; on the belief that there is one and only one Youth Culture, and that this culture endorses everything adults oppose. In fact, the adolescent world is as varied as the adult world. Peer pressure can be *proso-cial* as well as antisocial. Depending on which crowd the adolescent runs with, he or she may feel pressured to be a straight arrow or to be delinquent; to achieve high marks in school or to goof off; to stay sober and turn down drugs, or to experiment; to save sex for a mature, loving relationship that might lead to marriage, or to go all the way now. The real question is not *whether* adolescents will feel peer pressure, but *what kind* of pressure they will feel.

• *Parents and peers are opposing forces.* A variation of the first myth implies that the so-called generation gap is a mile wide. In fact, adolescents agree with their parents and follow their parents' advice more often than many would like to admit. As a general rule, adolescents accept their parents' views on "big issues" (moral and religious values) but follow their peers on matters of style (music, clothes, hair, neatness, and the like). They listen to their parents more than their peers on questions relating to their future (college and career choices) but to their peers more than their parents on issues that affect their current social life (choice of friends and activities). When parents and adolescents argue about controversial issues like sex and drugs, the differences between them are often a matter of degree. For example, parents may believe that a couple should only have sex if they are married; their adolescent may feel that a couple should only have sex if they are planning to get married. Their arguments may be heated, but in terms of national norms, both generations are on the conservative or traditional side. Adolescents are most likely to turn to their peers when they believe, rightly or wrongly, that their parents have little experience or expertise about something (for example, drugs) or when their parents seem unable or unwilling to advise them (for example, about sex).

• *Peers lead the adolescent astray.* This myth implies that teenagers are as passive as sheep and as willing to self-destruct as lemmings. The fact is that adolescents, like adults, choose friends whose attitudes and values are similar to their own; friends who see them as they want to be seen. A young person who strongly opposes drugs does not befriend "druggies" anymore than one who dislikes school and gets poor grades hangs around with the top students in the class. Peer pressure is not one-directional, like a gun pointed at the adolescent's head. It's circular. The adolescent who is struggling with academic work makes friends with classmates who are having similar problems. They reassure one another that school doesn't matter, make fun of their more successful classmates ("All brains are wimps"), cut up in class or simply cut classes, and put their energy into activities where they *can* be stars (often delinquency). Their attitudes and behavior make it even more likely that they will fail academically and drop or be pushed out of school. The same mutual reinforcement occurs among druggies and preppies, jocks and brains.

Adolescents are influenced by their friends. But parents who scapegoat peers miss the point. The real question is not who is making the child go wrong, but *why* the child chose those friends in the first place. To reverse negative peer pressure, parents have to look at *both* the individual adolescent's problems (such as underachievement in school) and the peers who support this behavior.

• *Conformity to peers is part of being adolescent.* This is only half true. Everyone feels pressure to accommodate to other people's wishes, adults as well as adolescents. The idea that all adolescents are helpless conformists and all adults are rugged individualists is nonsense. The phrase "keeping up with the Joneses" was not invented to describe teenagers.

• *All adolescents succumb to peer pressure.* This is another half-truth. Adolescents differ in their vulnerability to peer pressure. As a general rule, susceptibility to peer influence climbs during early adolescence, peaks in eighth or ninth grade, and declines thereafter. Why eighth graders should be less willing than fifth or twelfth graders to say no when peers say yes is not known. But study after study yields the same pattern.

Knowing this timetable is important. Parents who see their child becoming a stereotypical teenager at age 11 or 12 often despair. Because they've always assumed that adolescence begins for real at age 14 or 15, they assume that things can only get worse: "If my child is addicted to the telephone and sporting purple, spiked hair now, what will she be like at 15 and 16?" Take heart. Conformity peaks in early adolescence: Things *will* get better.

Contrary to popular opinion, boys are more susceptible to peer pressure at every age, especially if they are being pressured into risky or delinquent activities. The reasons for this difference are not clearly understood. A good guess would be that our culture expects boys (but not girls) to prove their independence, allows boys (but not girls) to sow their wild oats, and permits girls (but not boys) to demur on the grounds, "My parents would kill me."

• *There is little a parent can do . . .* Adolescents who have warm, affectionate relationships with their parents—adolescents who like their parents and whose parents like them and *show it*—are less likely to agree to something they don't want to do than are adolescents whose relationships with their parents are cool and distant. One reason is that they tend to be higher in self-esteem, and self-esteem increases self-confidence and assertiveness. Another is that they tend to choose friends whom their parents like, friends who believe in staying out of trouble, doing well in school, and behaving responsibly.

Helping Your Adolescent Deal with Peer Pressure

Beyond being close, what can parents do to help their adolescent deal with peer pressure?

• *Build self-esteem by helping adolescents discover their strengths and special talents.* Adolescents who like themselves are less likely to give in to negative peer pressure because they want to be liked by others. The desire to be popular may override the desire to be unique at this age, but kids still need to know that their parents think they are special. One couple had their 12-year-old daughter's soccer badges mounted and framed for her Christmas present. Their 10-year-old daughter, who is equally coordinated but not very competitive, got leotards and jazz dancing lessons. These gifts showed that the parents took their daughters' play seriously and recognized them as separate but equally talented individuals.

• *Encourage independence and decision-making within the family.* Adolescents who are treated as responsible people in their homes are more likely to make responsible decisions away from home. Listen to your son's ideas about how *he* would divide up household chores; allow your daughter to make her own decision about when to study; concede that the adolescent has made a point you hadn't considered.

• *Talk about situations in which people have to choose between competing pressures and demands.* Adolescents are not the only ones who feel peer pressure; so do you, in your social life and your work. Share some of your own experiences, past and present, with your adolescent. At summer camp one year, the in-crowd in your bunk ganged up on a new girl; their practical jokes eventually drove her from the camp. What did you do? What do you wish you had done? Why?

• *Encourage your adolescent to anticipate difficult situations and plan ahead.* Talk about situations the adolescent might encounter and how he or she would handle them. Suppose your son's friends were planning to pull up a cranky neighbor's rose bushes, take the bus to a downtown area you have declared off-limits, or lock an unpopular classmate in the janitor's closet. What would he do?

(For specific ideas about how to handle peer pressure to drink, use drugs, or engage in sex, see chapters 6 and 12.)

• *Encourage your adolescent to form alliances with peers who share his or her, and your family's, values.* This does *not* mean that you should push the adolescent to make friends with a child whom you consider a model citizen. Pushing will probably backfire (she'll decide the girl is a "nerd"). But if a strong, positive friendship is developing, suggest that your adolescent invite the friend for sleepovers and take her along on special family outings. Ask about her welfare ("How did Roxanne like camp?" "Did she get the part she wanted in the school play?" and the like).

PARENTS AND THEIR ADOLESCENT'S FRIENDS

How parents respond to the adolescent's changing relationships with peers can set the stage for good times (good friendships, good fun) or bad. The key is to remain involved in the adolescent's life without interfering unnecessarily.

Guidelines for Parents

Here are some general rules for walking the fine line between involvement and interference:

• *Know your adolescent's friends.* Your teenager's selection of friends says a lot about who he is and what he is likely to be doing when you are not around. If your son's friends are "jocks," he probably feels most successful and most himself on the sports field. If your daughter's friends are "arty," or "preppie," or "brains," that's how she sees herself and wants to be seen by others. Without pressing, try to get to know her friends as individuals. This doesn't mean you should try to be one of the girls (or guys). That would be intruding. But stop by the teenager's room to chat when a friend is visiting, ask her friends how it's going, compliment them on their clothes or congratulate them on an award, and the like. When parents show genuine interest in their adolescent's friends, adolescents are less likely to maintain a secret social life outside the family than they are if their parents get irritable every time they bring friends home, or if their parents seem indifferent. They are less likely to see peers and parents as opposing forces.

• *Don't jump to hasty conclusions, based on appearance, dress, language, or interests.* At this age, especially, adolescents sometimes go to extremes to prove that they are not like their parents and that they are independent of adults. They are also experimenting with different social identities. The boy who is dressed in leather and reading motorcycle magazines this year may be sporting a jacket and tie and running for class president next year. Nasty comments will only make the adolescent feel that he can't bring his friends home.

If you honestly believe your adolescent is getting mixed up with the wrong crowd, or the wrong friend, however, make your feelings known. Say your daughter is an exceptionally good student and outstanding athlete. In junior high she begins running around with a group of girls who care only about shopping. Find a quiet time to talk. Tell her that it's her choice, of course, but you think those friends aren't nearly as bright or interesting as she is. What does she see in them? Is there something you are missing? You may find that she really agrees with your assessment but is having trouble breaking into other friendship cliques. Your support may give her the courage she needs to ask a fellow A student to work with her on a project or invite some teammates home after practice. Unless you know for certain that your child's best friend is using drugs, or that his friends have been responsible for a good deal of vandalism, you shouldn't forbid your child to associate with this or that person. But you should express your opinions. Young adolescents do listen to their parents, even though they may pretend the opposite.

• *Make room for peer activities.* Adolescents need time to be with their friends. "Hanging out" may seem like a waste of time to you. But their "fooling around" is an important part of learning about themselves and other people. Far from doing nothing, they are working on who they are and who they want to become. You may have the adolescent's best interests at heart when you fill his free hours with tennis and violin lessons, trips to museums and sporting events, weekends with interesting people, and other stimulating activities. But if you don't leave time for friends, you are depriving him of an important part of growing up.

• *Remain close to the adolescent.* Some parents unconsciously see the adolescent's blossoming interest in peers as a rejection of them and pull back. Others are secretly relieved that the adolescent doesn't need them so much any more and disappear psychologically. Still others pride themselves on letting go. All are making a mistake. Close relationships with parents are the best insurance that adolescents will choose friends their parents like and resist negative peer pressure.

When to Worry

When should parents worry about an adolescent's relationships with peers?

• *If the adolescent has no friends.* At times, every adolescent complains, "Nobody likes me." In nearly all cases, this is an exaggeration. The adolescent had a bad day (he was the butt of a joke; she heard that a friend was talking behind her back). Or the adolescent has one or two close friends but isn't as popular as he or she would like. In a few cases, the adolescent is left out and alone. (See Shyness earlier in this chapter.) Persistent friendlessness is a symptom of existing problems, however, and possibly a cause of future problems including delinquency and depression. If this is the case, parents should seek psychological counseling.

• *If the adolescent is secretive about his or her social life.* Sharing secrets with friends is one thing; keeping friends secret, another. If the adolescent never talks about his friends, never brings anyone home, refuses to identify people who call him on the phone, and goes out of his way to be alone when you pick him up, there is a reason. He may be running with kids he knows you won't like (with good reason), or he may be convinced you won't like anyone he introduces as his friend. Whatever the reason, you should find out.

• *If the adolescent suddenly loses interest in friends.* Everyone wants to be alone from time to time, including adolescents. But sudden, complete loss of interest in social activities extending over more than two weeks can be a sign of depression (see chapter 8).

• *If all the adolescent's friends are much older.* There is nothing wrong with having a few older friends who share the adolescent's interest in stamps or dirt bikes or who live nearby. But when young adolescent girls, especially, spend all their time with an older crowd, they may be pressured into mature activities (sex, drugs) before they are mature enough to make responsible decisions. Boys are more likely than girls to "run in packs" of boys of different ages. If a boy is much younger than his friends, or the only preteen in a group, he may have to prove himself in harmful ways (smoking, drinking). Older friends are not necessarily something to worry about, but something to watch.

COMMON ISSUES

Being with friends is one of the luxuries of adolescence. Parents should anticipate that their child's social life will change during the transition to adolescence. Here are some of the most common issues that arise during this transition.

Early Dating

As a rule, young people begin dating, one-to-one, in middle adolescence. The average age for girls is 14 or 15; for boys, 15 or 16. Some early-maturing girls, especially, may begin going out at 11, 12, or 13. We believe this is a mistake, for several reasons. Girls who start dating in early adolescence nearly always go out with boys several years older than they are, if only because boys their age are still in the silly stage of boy-girl relations. The older boy is more experienced in heterosexual relationships than she is, and likely to overpower her psychologically as well as physically. For her, the idea of becoming sexually involved is still a misty, romantic fantasy; for him, it may be a reality.

Early dating also affects same-sex friendships. Because she is dating an older boy, a girl may be admitted into an older clique, but only as a marginal member. To prove herself to these older friends, she may feel that she has to wear heavy make-up and provocative clothes, smoke, drink, experiment with drugs, and talk as if she were sexually experienced. This act may gain her provisional acceptance by the older crowd but alienate her from girlfriends her own age who feel she is not "one of us" any more. As a result, she may lose valuable experience with intimate friendships.

Finally, early dating can interfere with achievement. Girls who begin dating very early tend to be more self-conscious and anxious than girls who still spend their free time with girls. Eager to maintain their attractiveness to boys, they may underachieve in school. Wrapped up in the social scene or a particular boy, they have less time for school work, outside interests and hobbies, friends, and family. It is much healthier for girls to develop the social skills needed for dating gradually and in groups, with girl-friends to support them and adults to supervise. When they are a little older, are a little more secure emotionally, have had more playful experiences with boys in groups, and so feel more comfortable with the opposite sex and confident about themselves, they will be better able to handle dates and potential romance.

Although there are no data on boys who begin dating very early, we expect the impact is similar: marginal status in the older crowd, disruption of same-sex friendships, distraction from school and other activities, and sex-stereotyped behavior.

Parties

Parties can be the high points—or the low points—of the early adolescent social whirl. A survey of middle- and junior-high-school students found that most fifth and sixth graders prefer same-sex parties; in seventh or eighth grade, many adolescents begin to enjoy boy-girl parties; and by ninth grade, mixed-sex parties are "it."

What makes or breaks a party? Young adolescents (fifth through seventh grades) prefer structured parties with organized activities—indoor or outdoor games, movies, outings to a skating rink or the beach, etc. Parties fail, in their view, when there is nothing to do, the parents are too strict and bossy, things get out of hand, or some of the guests are smoking or drinking. (The latter makes young adolescents uncomfortable.) Slightly older teens prefer free-form parties with good music, good food, and space for dancing or just sitting and talking. Parties fail, in their view, when parents hang around, the lights are too bright, the guests are too "cool" (unfriendly), and there is too much pairing off or too little mingling between the sexes (boys in one corner, girls in another).

By fifth or sixth grades, adolescents should be allowed to plan parties by themselves. The teen knows better than you do what his or her friends enjoy. The young host or hostess might invite a few friends over before the party to help get ready. You role in planning should be minimal (making sure the adolescent hasn't forgotten anything important, like ice).

During a party, the majority of young adolescents want their parents to be in the house but out of sight. This is good advice. Parents should greet guests as they arrive, make them feel welcome, but then retire to another room (the kitchen, den, or bedroom). When parents mingle with the guests all through the party, it makes teenagers nervous and uncomfortable. Adolescents want their parents' help and support, but only when needed.

When are parents needed? Asked about misbehavior at parties, junior-high-schoolers came up with the following: throwing food, prank phone calls, calling the police, performing chemical experiments with the refreshments, dipping into the parents' liquor supply, breaking light bulbs, locking people in rooms, climbing on the roof, setting off firecrackers, throwing snowballs through windows, and leaving the party to roam. (Eight out of ten said that they, personally, had never participated in these activities, but they'd seen or heard about them). The adolescent host should not have to deal with misconduct alone. When a parent intervenes, the teen doesn't lose face.

Trouble is less likely to start if there are plenty of interesting things to do. But when a party gets out of control, parents should step in immediately. If possible, take the offender(s) aside and talk to them privately, so that they won't be embarrassed in front of their friends. If this doesn't work, call their parents. They would rather hear about their children's misbehavior from you than through the grapevine.

Parents should also establish ground rules with their adolescent before the party begins, including

- No crashing. Open houses are likely to attract groups of older teens who have different ideas about how to have fun, such as liquor, marijuana, and sex.
- No smoking, alcohol, or drugs. (Apply the same rules to the party that you apply to your child.)
- No conduct you wouldn't allow under nonparty conditions (except, of course, for nonstop music and noise).
- No wandering around the house. Confine the party to a specific room or rooms or the backyard. Young adolescents shouldn't be permitted to close themselves in the bedroom, no matter what they are or are not doing, or to wander around the neighborhood.

Kissing games are quite common at this age. We feel getting upset about this is a mistake. The kissing is more social than sexual, and when a group of teens is playing a game, knowing you are in the house, there is less chance that one couple will go too far. Close dancing and girls sitting on boys' laps are equally harmless. Experimenting at a party, where there are other people nearby, is safer than when there is no one else around. Turning the lights off is not a good idea (some adolescents may be pushed too far sexually, some will be left out, and things may get broken). But if you allow dim lighting from the start, adolescents will appreciate the sophisticated atmosphere and be less likely to put themselves (and you) in the dark.

When your child is going out in the evening, to a party, dance, sporting event, or the like, you should know

- Exactly where your adolescent is going and with whom
- That adults will be present (if necessary, call and check)
- What your adolescent plans to do
- When the event is scheduled to start and finish
- How your adolescent plans to get there and back

In general, parents of young adolescents should prohibit parties on school nights (though other events, such as a game or a play might be permitted occasionally); allow only one late night on weekends; and try to see that the adolescent balances big days or nights with quiet, restful times (Saturday at an all-day beach party followed by a quiet Saturday night; Friday night at home before Saturday night at a party).

The Telephone

Arranging a date, planning a party, telling a best friend what happened in trig class today or at a party last night—conversation is the heart of a teenager's social life. When teenagers tie up the phone day and night or run up the bill calling friends outside the local dialing area, parents get angry, and understandably so. The solution to constant quarreling is negotiation. Parents need to understand that the telephone is the adolescent's lifeline, the way he or she keeps in touch. And teenagers need to understand that, even though their parents' social life may not be as hectic or urgent as theirs is, adults need the phone sometimes, too. The issue isn't really the telephone, it's consideration for other family members. To prevent the phone from becoming a battleground, parents and their adolescent need to agree upon guidelines that everyone in the family can live with.

One possibility is a phone schedule. Sit down with your teen-ager(s), talk about your different schedules and needs, and decide what times of day each of you will have free or priority use of the phone and how long a given family member will be allowed to stay on the phone (five, fifteen, or thirty minutes, depending on the time of day). Talk about how to handle incoming calls during another family member's phone time (unless it's an emergency, say you will call back). Set a limit for out-of-town calls (the adoles-cent should either pay for them or get your permission in ad-vance). And write your agreement down. This works in many families, although parents and teenagers may disagree about what constitutes an emergency.

Another possibility is a second telephone line. If the teenager is willing to pay the extra charge out of allowance or earnings, or your children are willing to share the expense among themselves, this may be a good solution. If you get a lot of calls too, and you don't see how you and the teenager can share one line, you might consider paying for a second phone yourself. Another phone doesn't mean that you won't set any limits on how much time the teenager spends on the phone, but it does eliminate conflicts.

Of course, if the adolescent is spending all her time on the phone (three to four hours a night), that's another matter. A teenager who is involved in after-school activities and devoting adequate time to homework (one to two hours a night for a good student) shouldn't have that much time for conversation. If she's cutting other family members off from the outside world, the phone is not the real problem—you need to talk to her about how she spends her time and consideration for others. You may want to impose a limit on phone calls in the interim, while you resolve these other issues.

Clothing and Grooming

Clothing and grooming are issues throughout the adolescent de-cade. The way teenagers dress often drives parents to distraction. Arguments over the adolescent's appearance are at least as com-mon as quarrels about the phone. These arguments are nearly always avoidable.

It's useful to think of clothing and grooming as a form of communication. Our decisions about what to wear, what kind of car to drive, where to go on vacation, and even what we eat are based in part on our desire to send a message to others about our values, attitudes, and status—about who we are.

Like adults, adolescents want to manage the impression they make on others. The only real difference is the audience they are playing to. The adolescent who insists on wearing jams to school because all his friends are surfers is really no different from his father who insists on wearing a navy pinstripe suit to the office or a tweed jacket to his lectures at the university. The boy and the adult are both saying, through their appearance, "This is who I am."

Some parents view the adolescent's attempt to create an image as yet another reminder that their child is growing up, something they do not want to face. Others don't understand that the adolescent is playing to a different audience than they are. Still others believe that if they give in on clothes, drugs can't be far behind. These parents need to ask themselves what they are really worried about. As far as we know, dressing in current adolescent styles does not lead to problem behavior, any more than wearing tweed jackets increases one's intelligence. The parents may be assigning more significance to appearance than their adolescents do.

Adolescents have a right to wear the clothes and other paraphernalia their peers consider fashionable, within reason. Parents have a right to insist that the adolescent's appearance be clean (for reasons of hygiene), not sexually provocative (the teen might not realize that her clothes send a message that may invite sexual harassment, or worse), not likely to interfere with school and other activities (it's difficult for a girl to get around school on spike heels, and a boy who wears a T-shirt splattered with obscenities to school is not only offensive but disruptive), and within the family's budget. Even if teenagers are earning their own money, they shouldn't be spending it all on clothes (see Money and Money Management, chapter 17).

There is nothing wrong with expressing your opinion about your adolescent's appearance, but in most cases, clothes are not worth going to battle.

Music

Music has always been an expression of generational solidarity: In the 1930s and 1940s, it was jazz; in the 1950s, Elvis; in the 1960s, folk music; in the 1970s, the Beatles; and today, hard rock. Parents have rarely approved of their adolescent's tastes in music.

Today, as in the past, parents worry about the effect of music on their adolescent's behavior. Will rock turn adolescents on to drugs? Lead to promiscuous sex or unwed motherhood? There is little evidence that adolescents listen to lyrics, much less use them as a guide for behavior. Teenagers who listen to music with drug references are no more likely to take up drugs than adults who read murder mysteries are to become murderers. Like light reading, music is a harmless way of escaping from everyday life and indulging fantasies. If you find your adolescent's taste in music offensive, ask them to close the door or treat yourself to a pair of headphones for them. And don't worry about what messages are being shouted into their ears.

Rock concerts are best seen as big parties with a lot of crashers. The same rules you apply to parties apply to rock concerts: No drinking, no drugs, no driving with someone who has been drinking. One difference between parties and concerts is that the latter are policed for alcohol and drugs. An adolescent caught with either might face arrest (something that is not likely at a private party). For teenagers *under 16,* parents should consider driving them to the concert and picking them up at a designated time and place afterward. (Because concerts are sometimes held in a rough part of town, girls, especially, should not go on their own.) For all teenagers, parents should be informed about who is going, where the concert is being held, what time it will end, and how the teen will get to and from the concert.

Allowance

Going out with friends and owning the "right" clothes and "in" records cost money. Most families renegotiate allowances in the preteen years.

How much allowance you give an adolescent depends on your budget, your family's life-style, community standards, and what your adolescent needs. If you have more than one child, you must consider current prices as well as your children's different ages and needs. Often later-born children are short-changed because parents assume that the ten dollars they gave their oldest child when he was a sophomore in 1980 is perfectly adequate for their youngest child who is starting high school in 1990. Ten dollars doesn't go as far today as it did then.

One way to work out an allowance is to ask the adolescent to keep an expense record for two weeks. The teenager should write down everything she pays for herself (bus fare, snacks, movies), everything you buy for her (clothing, school supplies), things she will *need* in the coming months and approximately what they will cost (club dues, equipment for hobbies, gifts for family and friends), and a "wish list" (things she *wants* and would like to save for and buy in the coming year). While she is doing this, you should make a list of expenses she might not consider (such as the telephone bill and car insurance). Also talk to other parents about how they determine allowance levels.

At the end of this time, sit down and go over your lists. If you think he is spending too much on electronic games, discuss this. If he wants a substantial raise, will he share some of the expenses you have been carrying? If he wants to buy his own clothes and you agree, decide on a reasonable clothing budget. Discuss how he can save for some of his "wish list" items (if you approve of his wishes). Then decide on the amount of his allowance and when it will be paid (weekly, biweekly, monthly). Write down which of you will be responsible for what. Agree to review the adolescent's spending and saving plan every month or two, or whenever he runs into problems. If you have more than one child, make sure they understand why they receive different amounts.

Some parents tie the adolescent's allowance to household chores. We think this is a bad idea. Teenagers should do household chores because they are members of a family, not because they will be paid for pitching in. No one pays you to cook dinner or do the laundry. Your daughter shouldn't be paid for shoveling the walk after a snow or looking after a younger sibling occasionally. Other parents offer teenagers bonuses for good grades. This, too, is a mistake. Bonuses for good grades tend to decrease, not increase, motivation, because the teenager is working for you, not for herself (see chapter 11).

How should you handle major expenses that are beyond the adolescent's means (a computer, a car, a ski trip)? In our view, loaning the adolescent a large sum with the understanding that you will be paid back in the future or giving the adolescent an advance on his allowance are bad ideas. They depersonalize the parent-child relationship. You're a parent, not a banker. If the request is reasonable and you can afford it, consider it. Maybe you can give your son the ski trip for his birthday present or buy a second car if your daughter agrees to pay all or part of the insurance and upkeep or to help run errands and ferry younger siblings. Say you think the computer is a good idea, but if you buy it you won't be able to pay for another season at summer camp. If the teenager's request is not reasonable (a motorcycle), explain why you won't permit it (they're dangerous). If the family cannot afford the request, be honest. Adolescents often are more understanding than their parents give them credit for.

RESOURCES

Recommended reading for shy adolescents: Philip G. Zimbardo's *Shyness* (New York: Jove, 1978). Chapter 10 of this book has concrete suggestions for overcoming shyness. Although written for adults, these suggestions are easily adapted for teenagers.

Middle School and Junior High

*A*dolescents spend more time in school than in any other single setting. School is not only their "job," but also the center of their social world. Their experiences in school—whether they are passing or failing, popular or unpopular, engaged or alienated—set the tone for their daily lives.

LEAVING ELEMENTARY SCHOOL

The move from elementary school to middle school or junior high can be difficult. In elementary school the child had a single homeroom teacher, who got to know him personally; now he has different teachers for each subject. In elementary school children are rewarded for trying hard; in middle school or junior high, grades are based more on performance than on effort. In elementary school children are supervised all day; now they are on their own much of the time. As a sixth grader, the child was one of the "big kids"; in seventh grade, he is a "little kid" again, compared to the full-fledged teenagers in the ninth grade.

For all these reasons, many students are temporarily disoriented during the transition from elementary to middle or junior high school. Their self-esteem falters. Their grades may drop slightly. Their interest and participation in school activities declines. They feel anonymous, alienated, and vulnerable. The younger the students are when they change schools, the more likely they are to have problems adjusting: 10-year-olds are harder hit by the "little kid" label than 12- or 13-year-olds. Not only are the latter bigger, they have also had a few more years of being "upper classmen" in elementary school. Presumably they have mastered fractions, decimals, and basic grammar in the more protected atmosphere of elementary school and so are on more solid ground academically. The adjustment will also be harder if a child experiences other major changes (puberty, a move, separation or divorce) at the same time. Nearly all adolescents recover their former enthusiasm for school, but the transition can be difficult.

Parents can help by

- Talking to the child about how middle or junior high school will be different, so that he has an idea of what to expect.
- Getting involved with the new school. Now is *not* the time to drop out of the PTA or cut back on parent-teacher conferences; the more you know about the school, the more you can help your child.
- Encouraging the child to work independently at home and monitor her own progress, before the transition.
- Supporting the friendships the child will carry over from elementary school (finding out which friends will be in his school and class, helping them to stay in touch over the summer, and perhaps arranging for them to travel to and from school together).
- Arranging some outside school activities in which the child will be competing with peers (sports leagues, junior drama clubs) or with herself (private lessons) instead of constantly being outshone by older students.
- Talking about sex and drugs so that the young adolescent will not feel totally ignorant and left out and will have some face-saving ways of saying no.
- *Not* getting upset if the transitional student's grades are a notch lower than they were in elementary school.

VICTIMIZATION: WHAT TO DO ABOUT BULLIES

Almost everyone has vivid memories of a schoolyard bully, and how they went out of their way to avoid him. (We use the male pronoun deliberately here: Bullies and their victims are nearly always boys.) Although his face has changed, the bully is still there. Perhaps one in ten elementary and junior-high-school students live in fear of being taunted, threatened, robbed, or beaten up. What should you do if your child is one of the victims?

Some parents believe a boy must learn to "stand up and fight like a man." This is true—up to a point. Young people do need to learn how to settle conflicts with peers by themselves (nonviolently whenever possible). A boy should be able to defend himself against an opponent his size and age. But it is not reasonable to expect him to defend himself against frequent threats and attacks by someone who is older, bigger, and tougher than he is, or against group attacks.

If your child is being victimized, your first step is to speak to the school principal. The school is legally responsible for your child's safety, from the moment he leaves your door until the moment he returns home. If something happens to him or her on the way to or from school, the school can be sued. Moreover, the school has the legal right and moral responsibility to discipline students who are bullying other students outside school grounds and to call their parents in for a conference. Sometimes school officials will claim that there is nothing they can do about incidents that occur away from school. If the school is unresponsive, you should file an official complaint with the local school board. But don't wait for your complaint to be heard to protect your child.

GETTING OFF ON THE RIGHT TRACK

Under the traditional British school system, every child took a rigorous national examination at age 11. The small number of students who earned high scores were admitted to grammar schools, which prepared them for university studies. The great majority were assigned to comprehensive schools, which offered a combination of academic subjects and vocational training on the assumption that they would leave school to go to work at age 15 or 16. For these students, the possibility of higher education ended at age 11.

Your next step should be to contact the tormentor's parents. In some cases, bullies are the product of neglect: Their parents have no idea that they are running with a gang or terrorizing younger children. Your call may wake them up and prompt them to take action. In other cases, however, the parents deny that their child is the aggressor. In still other cases, the parents are bullies themselves: Many studies find that the schoolyard aggressor is the victim of physical aggression in his home. If this is the case, the parents may be as verbally abusive toward you as they are toward their child, and their child is toward yours.

If you get nowhere talking to the parents yourself, insist on a meeting with the school principal and the bully's parents. Official recognition of the problem, and the possibility that their son may be suspended from school, will usually cause parents to take their son's aggressive behavior seriously. Make sure the school follows up on the meeting.

If all else fails, you can appeal to the law. Hire a lawyer (or seek free representation from Legal Aid) and initiate court proceedings against the parents and child. This is a drastic step, to be sure. But no child should be afraid to go to school.

Some parents hesitate to take these steps because they suspect (or hope) that their child is exaggerating. While this may be true in some cases, it's far more common for youngsters *not* to tell their parents or teachers that they are being victimized, for fear of retaliation. Instead they skip school or feign illness. If a child who always liked school suddenly becomes school phobic, the reason may be a bully or gang. Parents should not hesitate to act.

The United States has never had an official national examination system. Nevertheless, our schools do practice selection. At some point, a decision is made about the student's intellectual potential, and the child is channeled onto an appropriate educational "track." Exactly when tracking decisions are made varies: Some school systems make the decision in middle or junior high school (often eighth grade); some wait until high school. What tracking means also varies. In some schools, students are assigned to separate college-bound, general, or vocational programs and begin to study different subjects. In other schools, all students take the same basic academic subjects but are assigned to different classes (advanced, average, remedial) according to perceived ability.

Effects of Tracking

Tracking has both short- and long-term consequences. In general, students in the higher tracks get better teachers, better equipment, and a better education. Their teachers emphasize conceptual learning, call on their students more often, invite discussion, and encourage independent projects. In the lower tracks, teachers tend to lecture, focus on basic skills and memorization, spend a lot of classroom time on drills and discipline, and call on students less frequently. Students in these classes have fewer opportunities to debate ideas, generate knowledge, or read or write anything substantial. To be sure, there are some dedicated teachers who choose remedial education and some uninspiring teachers on the advanced track. But students who are seen as college potential do enjoy advantages.

Assignment to a lower track limits a student's options, especially in math and science. Mathematics is cumulative: Each course is a prerequisite for the next. A student must take algebra before geometry, geometry before trigonometry, and trigonometry before calculus. A student who has not taken algebra cannot leap into calculus. Similarly, a student who takes a general science course rather than biology, chemistry, and physics will have less chance of being able to take advanced science courses in college and may struggle with the required courses. Although the distinctions between average and advanced studies are less clear-cut in the liberal arts, they do exist. For example, students who begin a foreign language in eighth or ninth grade will be better prepared for required language courses in college. Students who take advanced seminars in literature or psychology in high school have a head start in college, too.

Equally important, adolescents usually make friends with the people they see in class every day. If your child's classmates and friends place a high value on education, brag about how they stayed up all night to study for an exam or the books they read over the summer, and debate the relative advantages of Harvard and Yale, your child is likely to reflect these attitudes. If, on the other hand, classmates and friends see school as a necessary evil, brag about how little they study and how little they care, and debate the advantages of joining the army and going to secretarial school or doing construction work, your child is likely to reflect these attitudes. Next to parents, friends are the strongest influence on an adolescent's educational aspirations.

Finally, decisions about tracking are difficult to reverse. It is extremely rare for a student to be moved from one track or ability level to another. Students at different levels use different books and cover different material. To switch classes after even one semester requires learning material other students have already mastered as well as adapting to new teachers, new classmates, and new academic and social expectations.

For all these reasons, it is vital that parents be aware of tracking and keep up to date on what the school plans for their child. All students do not belong on an advanced, college-bound track. Pushing a student of average ability into difficult classes will only result in frustration and decreased motivation. Holding a student of exceptional ability back can have a similar effect. Most schools do a good job of matching students to curricula. Decisions are based on an evaluation of test scores, grades, and teacher recommendations. In large schools, however, a guidance counselor may be responsible for several hundred students and find it impossible to give individual attention to each student. This is where parents come in.

What Parents Should Ask

Parents should not be timid about asking questions and making recommendations regarding their child's academic placement. Your first job as parent is to find out when decisions about tracking are made, what criteria are being used, and what the consequences will be for your child. To help you in this, we've included a brief overview of the most common types of tests on page 202.

Your second job is to help the school see your child as an individual. Suppose your daughter is an avid reader and does very well in English but has trouble with math. The school might feed this information into a computer and come up with a schedule that places her in a remedial math class and average-level classes for other subjects. When you question this decision, you learn that the advanced section for ninth grade English is scheduled at the same time as remedial math. You suggest that summer school and/or tutoring in math would enable her to keep up with

TESTING: AN OVERVIEW

Over the course of their school careers, students usually take three types of tests. You should know what these are and how they are scored.

Intelligence (IQ) tests are designed to measure the student's level of mental ability. They require a certain degree of cultural literacy, or general knowledge. But the goal is to test overall quickness and ability to reason and learn, not specific skills. IQ tests are standardized so that a score of 100 means a student is of average intelligence for his age.

There are two common myths about these tests. One is that IQ equals intelligence. Something as complex and multifaceted as intelligence cannot be reduced to a single number. IQ tests do not measure such qualities as originality, open-mindedness, sensitivity, or thinking before acting. But they do measure potential to do well in school. The second myth is that IQ is fixed and unchanging. In fact, IQ scores may fluctuate by as many as 20 points, especially during adolescence. Parents should not view a single IQ score as an indicator of their child's intelligence, carved in stone. But several tests, spaced over two- to three-year intervals, provide useful information about a child's academic potential.

Achievement tests measure a student's present level of knowledge in a particular subject. Most schools give achievement tests to all grades once a year. They are a measure of the student's standing in relation to other students; her progress since the last test; and the school's success in teaching different subjects. Achievement test scores are usually reported in terms of grade equivalents (GEs). A GE of 8.2 in computation means that the student's performance on the test was equivalent to that of the average student in the second month of eighth grade; a GE score of 9.0 in reading comprehension, that her performance was equivalent to that of the average student at the beginning of ninth grade.

Aptitude tests are designed to predict a student's future performance both in subjects he has studied and subjects in which he has no formal training. Most schools give aptitude tests once, in eighth grade, to identify individual strengths and weaknesses. Aptitude test scores are usually reported in terms of percentiles. For example, if your son scores in the 75th percentile for mechanical ability, it means he scored higher in this area than 75 percent of the students on whom the test was standardized but lower than 24 percent.

average work in math and take the advanced class in English. Given your willingness to participate, the school would be likely to agree. Suppose your son has always been an above-average student, but the year he enters junior high, you and your spouse separate, and your son's grades slip. If the school knows the circumstances, they might be willing to give him a second chance to take advanced courses in eighth grade.

When you meet with your adolescent's counselor, here are some specific questions you might ask.

• *What is my child's IQ?* Knowing your child's IQ scores helps you to set realistic expectations. If your child's IQ is in the average range, you can expect her to do well in school, but you should not push her to get As in all her subjects. If her IQ is above average, you want to make sure that her classes are challenging so that she does not become bored. If it is below average, you want to know that she is either being assigned to classes with children of similar ability or getting special help so that she will not be bewildered or humiliated.

We do not recommend that parents barge into a school conference and demand to know their child's IQ right off. Many schools are reluctant to give parents IQ scores for fear they will attach too much importance to a single number. Instead, look for an opening. If the teacher tells you he is concerned about Sally's grades, that's a natural point to ask about IQ. Suppose her most recent IQ score was 103. Ask whether this is the only intelligence test she has taken, and if not, how this score compares to others. Let's assume her scores have ranged from 100 to 105. Your next question should be how she compares to other students in her school. If the average IQ for her school is 110, she is competing against students who tend to learn more easily than she does. In the context of this school, Sally may be in the 30th percentile, meaning that in a class of 100 students she would be 70th from the top (and 30th from the bottom). In this light, her C+ average may look quite good.

• *What are my child's results on achievement tests?* Achievement test scores provide information not only on your child's standing in relation to peers, but also on areas of strength and weakness. Say your son John took achievement tests in December of fifth grade (the fourth month of fifth grade, or grade 5.4). Most of the students in his class are four to six months ahead of statewide averages on this particular test (with scores of 5.8 to 6.0). John's score on the math section was a strong 6.4, but his scores on vocabulary and reading comprehension were 4.8 and 4.2, respectively. In this area he is below the statewide average and more than a year behind his classmates, clearly a matter of concern.

• *What are my child's results on aptitude tests?* Aptitude tests are given to help with decisions about the student's high-school track. In looking at these scores, you will be looking ahead. Say your daughter Jeanne attends a private school. At a conference mid-way through eighth grade, her counselor tells you that Jeanne's performance on the aptitude test given that year put her at the 50th percentile in math and the 60th percentile in verbal reasoning—good scores, but not great. However, on the language skills section (designed to test aptitude for studying foreign languages), she scored at the 75th percentile. Your next question should be, What standard was used in scoring this test? Was Jeanne being compared to a state- or nationwide sample or only to other independent school students? If the teacher was referring to independent school norms, which are higher than all-school norms, it means that although Jeanne may not qualify for advanced placement in her particular high school, she is above average nationally and stands a good chance of being admitted to a competitive college.

• *What are the school's plans for my child?* Lastly, you want to learn how the school plans to use this information. Given her ability, Sally is doing well. The school may recommend that she be placed on the college preparatory track but that she not attempt such difficult courses as algebra, chemistry, or foreign languages. With Jeanne the school might take a wait-and-see approach. If she maintains her B+ average through eighth grade, they might suggest that she continue with math and science, begin a foreign language in ninth grade, and take electives in English or social sciences in tenth and eleventh grade. As for John, it is not unusual for boys this age to be better at math than at reading and writing. However, in John's case the gap is too wide to be ignored. The school would very likely recommend further testing to determine exactly what the problem is, and, depending on the results, extra instruction, a different type of instruction, summer school, or a home program for improving his verbal skills.

PARENTS' LEGAL RIGHTS

You may not realize that you have a number of legal rights concerning your child's education. These include the right to

- Request a meeting with a teacher or the principal.
- Receive information about what your child is being taught, what materials and methods will be used, and how the school will evaluate achievement.
- Know what tests your child will be given, what the purposes of these tests are, what your child's scores mean, and how they will be used. The school requires your permission *in advance* if it wishes to give a child psychological tests.
- Examine your child's school record, challenge information that you believe is misleading, and insert written comments if you feel this is necessary to clarify the situation.
- Insist that your child's record be kept confidential. No one but school personnel can look at your child's record without your permission.
- Know whether your child has been assigned to a particular track or ability group and challenge that decision if you believe it is wrong.
- Be informed of school rules in advance and appeal any decision that affects your child's rights (such as suspension).
- Demand that your child be physically and emotionally safe, not only in school, but also on the way to and from school. Physical or emotional abuse by teachers or intimidation by peers is grounds for legal action.
- Expect appropriate education in the least restrictive environment possible for a child with special learning needs or one with physical or emotional handicaps.

STUDENTS WITH SPECIAL NEEDS

How young people feel about themselves reflects their experiences in school. Adolescents who for one reason or another are out of step with their classmates need special attention.

Gifted Adolescents

Gifted students are those who are way ahead of their peers in intellectual development. They learn much faster than other students their age, covering the same material in, say, half the time. Often they teach themselves, advancing well beyond the material covered in school without instruction. (Gifted children may discover the principles of advanced mathematics, grasp the structure of fugues, or learn Latin on their own.) Frequently they know more than their parents and teachers. Some are exceptional across the board; others are gifted in one area (such as math or science) but not in others (humanities).

The distinction between a very bright child and a gifted child is subtle but important. The very bright child has high test scores, earns straight *A*s, and is elected to the honor society. She is at the top of her class and finds her schoolwork challenging and rewarding. The gifted child is well beyond her classmates in knowledge and understanding. Her scores on intelligence and aptitude tests compare with those of much older students; she earns straight *A*s without even trying and puts her extra mental energy into special projects of her own. The regular school curriculum bores her.

What should you do if you believe your child is gifted? The first step is to seek an objective opinion. An experienced teacher will recognize whether your child is "merely" bright or so exceptional that he gets little out of regular classroom activities. Tests will confirm or refute this perception.

The second step is to remind yourself that a gifted child is still a child. Like other children, he needs to learn how to work and play with peers. Although he may be years ahead of them intellectually, physically and socially he is no more mature than his average classmates. Indeed, he may be socially immature. Parents are often enthralled or intimidated by gifted children and reluctant to subject them to any restrictions. As a result, the children are spoiled. Moreover, the youngster who spent his childhood playing chess, doing chemical experiments, or programming a computer may have missed ordinary opportunities to play with friends and develop everyday social skills.

The challenge with intellectually gifted children is to prevent their becoming bored. What are the options?

Enrichment   One approach is to give the gifted child more challenging work. Some schools and school districts offer special classes for gifted students. For example, Fairfax County, Virginia, has a program known as "telescoping." Students in special classes study the same subjects as other students, but the usual material for that grade level is covered in the first third or half of the semester, with the remaining time devoted to in-depth study.

In small school districts, there may not be enough gifted students to warrant special classes. Here, enrichment must be designed for the individual student. The school might recommend that the gifted student add an extra science course to her schedule. Alternatively, regular classroom teachers might give the child special assignments: advanced readings, research projects, supervised independent study in an area of special interest, or the opportunity to tutor other students. Note that enrichment within the classroom does *not* mean giving the student more of the same. Assigning a child who has mastered long division twice as many problems as other students is not stimulating, it's stifling; rather, the student should be moved on to fractions.

Enrichment need not be confined to school hours. The gifted student might get a position as a laboratory assistant at a local university, attend adult lectures at a museum, or sign up for a summer program in computer programming, geology, or marine biology.

The advantage of enrichment is that it allows the gifted student to remain with her physical and social peers and to participate in the social and extracurricular activities that others her age enjoy.

Advanced Placement   A second approach for intellectually gifted students is advanced placement. If tests show that the child has already mastered material to be covered in the coming year, the school may recommend that he skip a year or, if he is in high school, that he begin taking some college courses. In considering advanced placement, parents should ask three questions.

- Is the young adolescent truly prepared for the higher grade? (Is there any essential material he will miss by skipping sixth grade? If so, can he cover these topics in summer school?)
- Is the adolescent emotionally mature enough to handle the effects of skipping on his classmates? (Both his old and his new classmates may treat him as an outsider, at least temporarily. Is he self-confident enough to ride this through?)
- What stage of physical development has the adolescent reached? (If the gifted student has not even entered puberty, and most of his new classmates are well into their growth spurt, he may be treated as a social nobody for years to come.)

If you feel the adolescent can skip a grade without undue suffering, the best time to make this move is when other adolescents are also changing schools. (If junior high school begins in seventh grade in your school district, the gifted youngster might skip sixth grade; if high school begins in tenth grade, he might skip ninth grade.) This way the advanced student will not be the only one who has to adjust to a new learning environment.

Most educators today see advanced placement as an extreme step, especially in adolescence. "Book learning" is only part of school. The girl who skips seventh grade is also skipping a year of gossip with her girlfriends, going to dances where no one really wants to dance, fantasizing about teachers' private lives, practicing how to dress, and other early adolescent activities that ease the transition from child to teenager. In many cases, the social costs of advancement outweigh the intellectual benefits.

Special Schools   A third possibility, which may or may not be available in your community, is a special school. For example, the New York City school system has the High School of the Performing Arts, where students receive rigorous training in their artistic specialty as well as academic instruction, and the Center for Math and Science, for students gifted in these fields. If there are no special schools in your area, you might investigate independent (or private) schools. Often these schools have more resources than public schools and are better able to offer a gifted child enrichment. Independent schools are expensive, but many offer scholarships to gifted children whose parents can't afford the tuition.

Learning-Disabled Adolescents

The term *learning disabled* refers to a child of average or even above-average intelligence who for one reason or another has difficulty learning. The problem may be perceptual handicaps, brain injury, minimal brain dysfunction, dyslexia, developmental aphasia, or attention deficit. What all these formidable terms mean is that the child cannot learn *the way other children learn,* not that the child cannot learn. Learning disabilities cannot be "cured." But youngsters can be taught how to compensate for learning handicaps and go on to lead normal, even exceptional, lives. College is not out of the question; indeed, there is a special version of the SATs for learning-disabled students.

Learning disabilities do not appear for the first time in adolescence. And schools today are much more aware of these problems than they were fifteen or twenty years ago. In almost all cases, a learning disability will be identified long before the child reaches middle or junior high school. In rare cases, however, the child manages to do satisfactory work in elementary school but is overwhelmed by the volume and difficulty of assignments in upper grades. If an adolescent who likes school and studies conscientiously shows a slow but steady decline in classroom grades and test scores, learning disabilities may be the reason. Parents should request a diagnostic evaluation of their child. This usually includes a medical examination and review of family history as well as tests to measure educational stengths and weaknesses.

If this evaluation does reveal learning disabilities, the next step is for parents and school personnel to work out an Individualized Education Plan (IEP). Depending on the child's needs and the school's resources, this might consist of

- Special help in a regular classroom
- Full-time assignment to special classes
- Part-time instruction in regular classes and part-time enrollment in special classes
- Transfer to a special school

The first goal of an IEP is to help the student learn how to learn. The second goal should be to make the child's school life as normal as possible, so that the child does not feel isolated or stigmatized.

Public Law 94-142 requires states to provide "free, appropriate public education" to all handicapped children, including the learning disabled. This law also requires that parents give their consent for testing and special placement, be involved in the planning process, and be informed regularly about their child's progress. In the planning meetings, you should ask these questions:

- What exactly will be provided in terms of special classes, tutoring, counseling, and the like?
- What will the child gain from this program? (What information and skills will the child be expected to master? How will your child's level of achievement compare to that of average students?)

- Who will be responsible for working with the child or, if several teachers are involved, who will oversee the child's progress?
- When and how will the child's progress be evaluated? (Federal law requires an evaluation at least once a year, but some states and many schools provide more frequent progress reports.)

In addition, you might ask for the names of parents whose children have been placed in similar programs whom you can call for information, and how other children in these programs have fared. (Have they met their goals? Have any been returned to regular classes?) In evaluation meetings, ask not only about your child's educational progress, but also about social and emotional development. (How well is the child getting along with teachers and peers? Does the child seem comfortable with this program or often frustrated?)

Schools have a legal obligation to help the learning disabled child, but it is up to parents to see that this obligation is fulfilled. It's also up to parents to make sure the adolescent's self-esteem doesn't suffer. Let the adolescent know that you understand how difficult school is for him, and how much you admire his sticking with it, even though his grades are nothing to brag about. Praise his accomplishments in other areas. And remind yourself that success in life depends on more than good grades in school.

RESOURCES

The following organizations publish information and/or answer questions for parents.

Learning Disabilities

Academic Therapy Publications
20 Commercial Boulevard
Novato, CA 94947

Association for Children with Learning Disabilities
4156 Liberty Road
Pittsburgh, PA 15234

Closer Look
Parent's Campaign for Handicapped Children and Youth
P.O. Box 1492
Washington, DC 20013

Foundation for Children with Learning Disabilities
99 Park Avenue
New York, NY 10016

Gifted Children

Council for Exceptional Children
1920 Association Drive
Reston, VA 22091

For information on
independent schools:

*National Association of
Independent Schools*
4 Liberty Square
Boston, MA 02109

Handbook of Private Schools
Porter Sargent
11 Beacon Street
Boston, MA 02108

Parents' Legal Rights

For more information on the laws in your particular state, you
can obtain a "parent rights card" by writing to

*National Committee for Citizens
in Education* (NCCE)
410 Wilde Lake Village Green
Columbia, MD 21044

Or call the NCCE hotline: 800-NETWORK.

CHAPTER 11

Your Role in Your Adolescent's Education

When a child enters middle or junior high school, many parents feel their role in their son's or daughter's education is finished. This is a mistake. Education is *not* the sole responsibility of the school. Rather it is a cooperative venture, in which teachers and parents are (or should be) equal partners. Schools wish parents of adolescents would be more, not less, involved.

WHAT PARENTS SHOULD—AND SHOULD NOT—DO

What is an appropriate level of involvement in school and schoolwork for parents of adolescents? How can parents stay involved?

Contacts with the School

Take advantage of back-to-school days, parent organizations, parent-teacher conferences, and other school programs to keep informed about, and involved in, your adolescent's education.

In most school districts, parents can participate in several organizations designed to support and advise schools. The best known are the local PTA (a branch of the National Parent-Teacher Association) or PTO (an independent Parent-Teacher Organization). In the old days, these organizations concentrated on such things as raising money to buy band uniforms and providing volunteers for visitor's day. The PTA was (and still is) the place where you could meet your child's teachers and other parents. Today, however, many are actively involved in educational planning and keeping parents informed about testing, school financing, education for the handicapped, and other issues. In several states and many local communities, the law now requires that parents serve on the committees that plan and evaluate school programs. If you are concerned about drugs, sex education, or rising standards for college admission, these organizations allow you to make your voice heard.

Many schools also welcome parent volunteers—to work in the library, coach teams, advise clubs, provide career information in their field, use their special skills in enrichment classes for gifted children, chaperone parties, and countless other activities.

Parent-teacher and parent-counselor conferences are your opportunity to get a more detailed report on your adolescent's abilities and achievements from the school and to give the school a more intimate picture of your child's interests and problems. Ask how the school estimates your child's aptitudes, what his test scores mean, how he compares to his classmates, when decisions about tracking will be made, and what the school plans for him. Ask about homework: What kind of assignments is he being given and about how long should he take to complete them? This varies from student to student, of course, but the teacher can give you a rough idea of whether your son is working as hard as he should at home. Is he making good use of his time in school? participating in class discussions? getting along with other students? and so on. Most schools schedule regular parent-teacher conferences two or three times a year. If your child is having problems, however, don't wait. The sooner you spot a problem, the easier it will be to solve.

Homework

The first rule here is: Never *do* homework *for* your adolescent. It is better to err on the side of too little help than too much, for several reasons. First, the relationship between parent and child is based on affection. Part of the parents' "job" is to let the adolescent know they will love her no matter what. Love comes first, and evaluation second. When parents play teacher, emotions get in the way. The adolescent takes correction and criticism—and the parent takes confusion and mistakes—personally.

Second, doing homework for an adolescent fosters dependency. The child learns to see you as the expert and himself as helpless. It's hard to be enthusiastic and self-directing if you believe you are incompetent.

Third, when you check all of the adolescent's assignments before she turns them in, the teacher may get a false impression of the student's level of understanding. The fact that she hasn't grasped the different past tenses in French will come out on a quiz. But in the meantime, both student and teacher have lost valuable time.

Finally, your teaching may be faulty. Your memory of photosynthesis may be hazy; your Spanish may not be as fluent as you think; the way you learned algebra thirty years ago may not be the way it is taught today. Tutoring your adolescent in these subjects may do more to confuse than enlighten him.

It's understandable that parents want their children to do well. But by protecting them from failure (by tutoring them at home and checking their work), you are preventing them from learning from their mistakes. You may also be undercutting their motivation to achieve.

This does not mean that when your adolescent comes to you for help with homework you should say "Go away." If she has a question ("What is the capital of Yugoslavia?" "What does *incubus* mean?"), suggest where she can find the answer for herself ("Have you looked in the atlas or dictionary?"). If she can't find the word in the dictionary, write it down (but don't go over her papers looking for misspellings). If she can't solve a math problem, suggest that she do her best and then ask her teacher for help before the next class. If she's struggling with a paper and *asks* for help, make suggestions ("Remember that trip we took/the article you read to me? Why not write about that?") and help her organize her thoughts ("That's a good idea, why don't you open with that?"), but don't tell her what to say. If she is stuck on a paragraph in one of her textbooks, read it aloud and figure out the meaning together. If she asks you to test her on vocabulary words, listen to a speech she has prepared, or read a paper, do so with enthusiasm, but be cautious about judging her work before the teacher has seen it. In short, be your child's supporter and assistant, but not her tutor or her stand-in.

In addition, some adolescents need help getting organized, especially in their first year or two out of elementary school. If the student just isn't getting his work done, you may insist on regular study hours. During that time, he's expected to be at his desk and working (no TV, no stereo, no phone calls). If the student spends hours at his desk but can't seem to get anything done, you need to help him develop better study skills. On the other hand, a few adolescents do their best working lying on the floor with the TV running, isolated from the world by headphones, or between 5 and 7 A.M. on school mornings. As the saying goes, "If it ain't broke, don't fix it." Don't intervene unless you have to.

What should parents do if their adolescent isn't even trying to do homework? Getting angry won't help. Rather, you need to find out why the adolescent won't study. Talk to the adolescent and to her teacher.

When young people are asked why they aren't studying, the most common responses are "I hate the teacher" or "The class is stupid." These blanket condemnations often disguise the fact that the adolescent is confused (the subject level is over his head) or bored (the subject level is below his knowledge and abilities). If you believe this describes your child, speak with the teacher about arranging for extra help or more challenging assignments.

When an adolescent is falling behind in almost every subject, she may have a problem with reading. (As we discuss later in this chapter, this is more common than most parents imagine. Professional help is available at most schools.) A second possibility is that the adolescent is overcommitted: Family responsibilities, extra-curricular activities, and/or a job may leave her little time to study. (Many educators believe that teenagers today are putting too much time and effort into their jobs and too little into their schoolwork; see Working during the School Year, chapter 17.) A third possibility is that the adolescent sees *not* doing schoolwork as one of the only ways she can exercise control over her own life (see Overcontrol, later in this chapter).

Once you have identified the problem, you and the adolescent should sit down and work out an understanding about when homework is to be done, where, and so forth. Your job is not to see that the adolescent gets a *C, B,* or better on every assignment (that's his job), but to see that he completes his assignments on time. If the adolescent is resistant, consider working out a contract that grants the adolescent points toward privileges for completing the week's assignments in different subjects as well as points toward withdrawal of privileges for not completing assignments. Again, these points should not be based on the grade the adolescent receives but on the fact that he is doing his job.

Grades

How parents react to grades is important. On the one hand, you want to make it clear that you value achievement. A student who earns three *A*s and a *B,* or who gets a *C* on a test she was certain she would fail, deserves applause. On the other hand, you need to support the adolescent when he does poorly. Don't dwell on the failure. Acknowledge his disappointment, then talk about what he can do to improve his performance on the next paper or test.

In discussing grades with the adolescent, it's important to find out *why* the adolescent feels she did well or poorly. Research shows that successful students believe that their grades are the result of ability and effort, not chance, the position of the stars, or the teacher's disposition. They attribute their triumphs to ability ("I got an *A* because I'm smart") and their failures to lack of effort ("I got a *C* minus because I didn't study"). They assume that they can do better if they try harder.

Unsuccessful students, in contrast, feel that success or failure in school is out of their hands. They attribute their high marks to external factors ("I made a few lucky guesses" or "The test was easy") and blame their failures on personal qualities ("I got a *D* because I'm dumb") or prejudice ("The teacher doesn't like me"), none of which they can change. A student who believes his *A* was due to luck doesn't think about what he did right and how he can keep up the good work. One who believes the *D* proves she is dumb (something she suspected all along) stops trying. Why study when she'll only fail again?

Listen to your child's explanation of successes and failures. If she volunteers that she could have worked harder, relax. She has the right attitude. However, if she attributes a poor grade to the fact that her teacher is boring or doesn't like her, or to lack of ability (when all the signs say she is capable of doing the work), and she dismisses high grades or test scores as lucky breaks, she has a problem. To be sure, there are occasions when a particular teacher and student clash. If you suspect this might be the case, you should investigate. But a pattern of attributing school performance to uncontrollable factors suggest that the problem runs deeper.

Parents should also listen to their own comments. Sympathetic reactions to a poor performance ("Too bad, I know you tried hard" and "I never was any good at math either") only reinforce the adolescent's pessimism and passivity. You're implying not only that he doesn't have the ability, but also that his disability is inherited!

Parents can foster constructive attitudes by focusing on ability when the adolescent does well ("You've always been good at science" and "You have a real flair for writing"), and effort when the adolescent does poorly ("Could you have studied harder?" and "What can you do to improve?").

Parents should *not* offer their adolescent money or other material rewards for good grades. Rewarding the adolescent for good performance in school demonstrates a basic lack of trust: If you believed she wanted to do a good job, you wouldn't feel you had to bribe her. In bribing her, you deprive her of the satisfaction of doing a good job freely, by her own choice, purely for the satisfaction of doing something well. Studies show that grades tend to decrease, not increase, when parents pay young people for grades.

Your Home Environment

Finally, parents need to create a home environment that promotes learning and academic achievement.

Talk to your child about what is going on in school, just as you talk to your spouse about what is happening at work. What authors are they reading in English this semester? Who is the adolescent's favorite? Have they gotten to the Civil War in history? Is the geometry teacher interesting? How is the science project going? Don't go through the motions; see what you can learn from your child. The botany student might be able to explain why your gardening book says to do this or that. The adolescent who is studying the Constitution might help you understand the controversy over the War Powers Act. The more genuinely interested you are in the adolescent's studies, the more interesting they will seem to the student.

Talk to the adolescent about what you yourself are reading. Discuss current events at the dinner table, not just who didn't do their chores. When someone raises a question no one can answer, look it up. Plan outings to museums, historic sites, nature reserves, political rallies, and the like. Studies show that, other things being equal, adolescents from families who take advantage of community resources earn higher grades than those whose families do not.

When appropriate, talk to the adolescent about your grades (work reviews), how you deal with success (and co-worker jealousy) and failure (and temporary loss of confidence), and how you tackle difficult problems (get information, do cost-benefit analyses, list pros and cons, etc.).

All this may seem obvious. But many parents today are too stressed, too tired, or too involved in their own careers to play an active part in their child's education. They've given their child a good start and assume the school will take responsibility from now on. There's more to education than what goes on in the classroom. You can make a major difference in your child's attitudes, achievements, and aspirations.

PROBLEMS WITH SCHOOLWORK, AND HOW TO HANDLE THEM

Students who sail through elementary school sometimes falter in middle school or junior high. Here are some of the more common obstacles young adolescents encounter, and how parents can help their child prevail.

Reluctance to Read

Virtually every course the adolescent takes requires reading—not only English, history, and other "wordy" subjects, but also science and math. Adolescents who read poorly are at a serious disadvantage in every subject.

Most schools assume that children will have mastered basic reading skills by the end of fourth grade. Specific instruction in reading usually stops at that point, and teachers no longer routinely monitor the child's reading skills. They may not realize that the adolescent's problem is not being able to *read* the math problem or *comprehend* the history text. His poor performance may be attributed to lack of motivation or to a short attention span rather than to reading difficulties. (Here we say *his* deliberately; reading problems are more common in boys than girls.)

Some of the signs that a young adolescent has a reading problem are that he or she

- Doesn't read spontaneously, for pleasure or for information
- Claims he "can't find" anything to read
- Gets upset when she is assigned reading for homework and reads at a painfully slow pace
- Has trouble with ordinary, everday reading (reading signs, following the instructions on a package, using a recipe, and the like)
- When reading aloud, frequently hesitates, mispronounces words, skips words, reads them out of order, or says the wrong words (*saw* for *was, bone* for *done, man* for *men,* and the like)

There are three common causes of reading problems in the post–elementary school years.

- The child has an organic problem that makes it difficult for him to perceive and decode words, or a vision or hearing problem that has interfered with learning. Such problems are nearly always diagnosed in elementary school, but if you have any doubts, check with your own or the school physician.
- The child had difficulty learning to read, did not receive the extra help he needed, and has developed an aversive or hostile attitude toward reading as a result (a learning problem).
- The child is perfectly able to read but chooses not to (a problem in motivation).

Parents should not attempt to diagnose or to treat reading problems by themselves. If you suspect a problem, your first step should be to talk to a teacher or school counselor. Here is what to expect.

Let's assume that you rule out organic difficulties. The solution to a learning problem is learning. Some middle and junior high schools have clinics for students who need additional help in reading. If not, they will recommend a private clinic or a tutor. These programs can be quite successful: On the average, adolescents gain two years for every one-year of structured, individualized reading instruction. Attempting to tutor an adolescent in reading yourself, at home, is not recommended. To adolescents, being read to by their parents seems infantalizing, as if they were babies with a picture book.

Don't let emotions get in the way. Most parents are extremely upset when they discover their adolescent "can't read." Whereas difficulties with math may be brushed aside (lots of bright people can't decipher an equation), difficulties with reading imply that there is something deeply wrong. The adolescent, too, may feel that his struggles with schoolwork mean he is "dumb"; repeated failures in many subjects reinforce this self-defeating belief. In fact, some reading problems go undetected because the student has superior intelligence and is bright enough to bluff and guess his way through elementary school work. In junior high, which requires more independent study, bluffing becomes increasingly difficult.

What about the young adolescent who can read but doesn't? Problems in reading motivation usually begin at home. Often the parents themselves don't read; books are something they gave up when they graduated from formal schooling. If both are working, they may not have time for a good novel. One study found that only 13 percent of adult Americans borrowed books from the library; only 17 percent were currently reading a book; 25 percent of college graduates had not read a single book during the past year; and over 40 percent of homes did not have a bookcase. Sometimes the home environment just isn't conducive to reading; there are too many distractions (the TV running, people coming and going, and so on).

Again, parents shouldn't attack the problem on their own. Nagging an adolescent to read, pressing her to read classics instead of comics, and grilling her on her reading may have the opposite of the intended effect. Reading then becomes a chore, not a pleasure. If anyone pushes the child to read, it should be a teacher. But parents can help by establishing a quiet time and place for anyone who wants to read (the living or dining room for a half hour after dinner). Don't require the adolescent to read, but set an example by reading yourself, and insist on quiet. You can also set an example by talking about what you are reading with your spouse, your friends, and your child, even if all you have time for is the morning paper. Try to impress on the young adolescent that reading is a source of information. "Hey, remember what you asked me the other night? I found the answer." Read aloud. Most adolescents don't want to be read a story, much less one of Shakespeare's histories. But they will listen to an amusing letter, a passage from a book, or a magazine article on teenage runaways. And a young adolescent might get caught up in reading Sherlock Holmes as a family, with everyone guessing "who done it." Don't expect the reluctant reader to leap from no books to great books. Subscribe to a magazine that appeals to his or her special interests *(Sports Illustrated, Road & Track, Seventeen)*. Ask if he would like to look for a book on hiking while you're in the supermarket. Don't get annoyed if she develops a taste for romance novels—some reading is better than none at all. (And then, of course, there is the 11-year-old who can't put down *Moby-Dick*, doesn't hear you announce dinner, and reads straight through "Miami Vice.")

Fear of Math

Middle or junior high is a turning point in math. In most schools, arithmetic (or computation) is taught through sixth or seventh grade, and higher mathematics (using symbols, formulas, and logical deduction to solve problems) begins in eighth grade. Students who plan to go to college are usually required to take two years of algebra and one of geometry; trigonometry and calculus are treated as electives.

Difficulties with math are at least as common as difficulties with reading, probably more so. Many adolescents do not make the transition to higher mathematics, and some still do not fully grasp the basics of arithmetic. But schools, parents, and students generally do not take failure in math as seriously. After all, most adults are able to function quite well with only a basic knowledge of arithmetic and a pocket calculator. An adult can readily admit to total ignorance of higher mathematics without the slightest embarrassment. Most schools do not have clinics for students with math disabilities. Rather, the student is advised to skip higher math, especially if the student happens to be a girl (more on this below).

The symptoms of problems with math are similar to those with reading: avoidance, emotional distress ("I *hate* math!" or "The math teacher hates me," repeated year after year), and inability to do simple, everyday calculations. The causes are also similar: learning problems, lack of motivation, and, more rarely, some sort of organic impairment. Many psychologists recognize a special learned helplessness with regard to math: "Once a person has become frightened by math, she or he begins to fear all manner of computations, any quantitative idea, and words like *proportion, percentage, variance, curve,* and *exponential.*"

What is peculiar and significant about math anxiety is that it is far more common in girls than in boys. The sexes begin school as mathematical equals. By adolescence, however, girls begin to slip behind boys; their average SAT scores in math aptitude are lower than boys'; and very few earn advanced degrees in math and related subjects. There is much debate among social scientists and educators as to why this is so. A few argue that girls just don't have the same ability for math; most, that our culture defines math as unfeminine and allows, even encourages, girls to be complete dunderheads with numbers. This would explain why the "math gap" makes its first appearance in adolescence, when girls are becoming concerned about sex roles. For girls, but not boys, math anxiety is a double-edged sword: They worry that they will not be able to understand advanced mathematics and worry that they will seem unfeminine if they do.

Whatever the reason for sex differences in math, it is clear that girls need extra support and encouragement in this area. Often schools track a boy with only average aptitude into higher mathematics but pack a girl with the same aptitude off into art history or a foreign language. The girl may agree with this decision, or even request it. It's important for girls to know that failure to pursue math closes off many majors in college—not only physics, engineering, economics, and computer science, but also premedicine, psychology, business, architecture, and a host of others. And closing off majors means closing off careers in these fields.

We strongly recommend that both sexes take at least the required courses in higher mathematics and more advanced courses if they are able. (Colleges will admire a $B+$ student for taking calculus, even though she only earns a C; see chapter 17.) Certainly, every student should be competent in basic arithmetic.

If you suspect that your child has problems with arithmetic, consult with the school. Again, home tutoring is not a good idea. But you can foster interest in math by making adolescents aware of everyday uses and applications. Like Molière's *bourgeois gentilhomme,* who spoke prose for forty years without knowing it, we use math all the time without thinking about it. Sports statistics are an obvious example: What does a batting average mean? But you also need math to adapt a recipe for twelve servings to your family of four or to shop for a party and adapt how much you buy to the number of people who will attend. Carpentry requires a knowledge of geometry and even trigonometry for advanced woodworking. So does design: How can you arrange the furniture to maximize the space in your livingroom? plot an herb garden in a symetrical pattern? Comparative shopping is an exercise in arithmetic. Get your adolescent to help you with everyday applications. If you enjoy mathematical puzzles, do them as a family.

PARENTAL PRESSURES (FOR BETTER OR WORSE)

All parents want their children to do well in school, of course. But parents may undermine their adolescent's motivation by placing too many or too few demands on the child or by making the wrong kinds of demands.

Constructive Pressure

When parents place a high value on education, set high standards for achievement, praise their child for doing well, and encourage intellectual curiosity and independence, adolescents thrive in school. Responsive parenting (a combination of warmth and demands) pays off in self-confidence and high motivation.

The children of responsive parents tend to be self-directing. They strive to do their best, enjoy an intellectual challenge, persist when the going gets rough, and bounce back from failures. They set high but realistic standards for themselves. (The adolescent with a talent for science sets his sights on a science prize; the adolescent of average ability aims for three *C*s and a *B*.) They develop strategies for achieving their goals (the girl who is gettings *B*s in other subjects but struggling with French decides to study with a friend who has a flair for languages; the boy who is dedicated to photography makes good use of study halls so that he can spend after-school hours in the darkroom). They are able to concentrate on schoolwork when they would rather be doing something else. They work to please themselves, not their parents, teachers, or friends. They try their best, even when a project will not be graded. In short, they are motivated by a *need to achieve*.

Excessive Demands

Overly demanding parents treat high grades as a moral imperative. They expect their child to be near the top of every class, regardless of his or her abilities and interests. When the child earns "only" *B*s and *C*s, they feel angry and betrayed. In some cases, these parents were straight A students themselves and just assume their child can do as well. In other cases, the parents did not have the educational opportunities their child has, or feel they wasted their years in school, and want the child to make up for their disappointments. Or they may be comparing the child to a sibling who has exceptional aptitude. They exhort, bribe, and threaten the adolescent to do better, ignoring the school's evaluation—that the child is doing well, considering her aptitude. All the adolescent knows is that she does not measure up.

Adolescents caught in this no-win situation may react in several ways. Some set unrealistically high goals for themselves, goals that virtually guarantee failure. Having set unattainable goals, they work only halfheartedly to meet them. When their results are mediocre, they have two alibis: "Nobody could keep up with the work I had this semester. I'm surprised I did as well as I did," and "I didn't really try my best; I'm sure if I'd studied harder I would have done well."

Other adolescents react to unrealistic parental pressures by avoiding any and all risks. In class, they sit in the back of the room, hoping they won't be noticed. They never enter into classroom discussions voluntarily. When called on, they choke. They are afraid to say they don't understand an assignment or to ask for help after class. The slightest criticism ("That's a good point, John, but it doesn't answer my question") causes intense feelings of shame. With homework, they are perfectionists. But they become so obsessed with memorizing all the facts and figures that they miss the point of the assignment. Tests often throw them into panic.

These youngsters are motivated not by a desire to achieve, but by *fear of failure*. Aware that they can never please their parents, they devise strategies for avoiding risk, or at least avoiding blame.

Overcontrol

A variation on the overdemanding parent is the overcontrolling parent, who sets rigid standards, dictates what school the adolescent will attend and what courses she will take, and reacts harshly and punitively when the adolescent does not fall into step. The adolescent isn't admonished to try harder; rather, she's told in no uncertain terms, "You're a disgrace!" These parents take the child's academic performance personally. School achievement becomes a battle of wills, with the parent insisting "You will!" and the adolescent proving "I won't."

A common adolescent reaction to overcontrol is rebellion of a passive-aggressive sort: The adolescent hits back, but in ways that cannot be seen as a direct blow for independence. The student "forgets" to write down assignments, reads the wrong chapter, turns in papers late, oversleeps the day of an exam, daydreams through class, and in other ways manages to underachieve. In effect, he has gone on academic strike. A psychologist recalls a bright 14-year-old named Paul, who was about to be expelled from boarding school. Paul came from a wealthy, socially prominent family. His father was the kind of parent who saw no reason to discuss anything with his son; his word was law. The father had attended the same elite prep school and gone on to a distinguished university. He expected—no, demanded—the same of his son. In a therapy session aimed at discovering why Paul was failing, the psychologist suggested that Paul might see this as one way he could stand up to his father: "Paul smiled broadly, fully the Cheshire cat: 'You said it; there's not a darn thing he can do about it; when he got the call from the headmaster he hit the ceiling, but he can't do a thing about it.' "

Overprotection

Parents can err in the opposite direction, too. Recent studies of achievers suggest that, although parental warmth is important, what really distinguishes achievers' parents is that they train their children for independence: From early childhood, they encourage exploration, experimentation, curiosity, initiative, thinking for oneself, and doing for oneself.

This suggests that parents can nip achievement motivation in the bud by being overprotective. Answering all the child's questions instead of suggesting how she can find the answer for herself, checking each homework assignment before it's turned in instead of letting the teacher find errors in spelling or grammar, and taking over every time the child seems to be struggling isn't helpful in the long run. Neither is stepping in each time the child has a disagreement with a playmate or a sibling instead of allowing them to work things out themselves. However well intentioned, this "help" conveys the message that the child is not capable of functioning on her own. These young people avoid challenges not because they are afraid of being slapped down, but because they haven't had opportunities to test themselves and develop confidence in their own abilities.

Overprotection can be especially harmful in early adolescence, when young people begin to actively seek autonomy. Adolescents don't want or need a parent who is all-knowing and ever-ready to intercede.

Lessons for Parents

An adolescent's attitude toward school achievement is the product of countless, cumulative childhood experiences. But attitudes *can* change and motivation *can* improve if parents follow five basic rules:

- Base your demands and expectations on a *realistic* appraisal of your adolescent's abilities.
- Don't impose your goals on the adolescent and treat his somewhat different ambitions as a threat to your authority.
- Remain interested in your adolescent's school career but don't become overinvolved. School is her job, not yours.
- Examine your own attitudes toward education to be sure you aren't sending the adolescent mixed messages ("Do well in school—but not that well"; "School is important—but not that important.")
- Make sure your adolescent knows you love him for who he is, not for what he achieves.

UNDERACHIEVERS

Of all students, the most frustrating for parents and teachers are underachievers—students who have average or superior intelligence but perform well below their potential. Adolescents whose achievement test scores are 35 percentile points or more below their aptitude test scores, and students whose grades drop by more than one point (from As to Bs and Cs, or from Bs to Cs and Ds), fall into this category. Note that a temporary drop in grades is not uncommon during the transition from elementary to secondary school, for all the reasons discussed in chapter 10: Grading is stiffer; the transition itself can be stressful; and social activities compete for the student's attention. Eighth graders have more on their minds than pleasing their teachers. Parents should be concerned only if

- The decline in school performance is *extreme*—from straight As to Cs, solid Bs to Ds
- The problem *persists* for more than one marking period

Parents whose adolescent is a persistent underachiever typically begin by pleading: "You're so bright. Your teachers say you could be getting As. You used to love school. Why aren't you trying?" When pleas fail, they put on the pressure. The adolescent is sent directly to his room to study after supper, forbidden to use the phone, banished from the TV room, confined to the house on weekends, and threatened with cuts in his allowance, removal from athletic teams, or summer school. When the results are nill, parents search for a scapegoat (the school or his friends).

The first problem with the pleas-and-pressure approach is that it is accusatory. Telling the student he is bright may be intended as a compliment, to build self-confidence and incentive. But the underlying message is "You're a lazy, careless, good-for-nothing; you're wasting your own talents and my efforts as a parent." The second problem is that the pleas-and-pressure approach assumes that the adolescent can do better if he is told he can (and chained to his desk). This may not be the case.

What to Do

As junior-high-school principal Eric Johnson suggests: Don't accuse, *investigate*.

Step 1: Elimination Identifying the reasons for underachievement is a process of elimination. Start with things the adolescent can't control.

- *Arrange for a physical examination.* If the adolescent hasn't had a checkup during the last year, arrange one now. An easily correctable problem with vision or hearing might be holding the child back. The physician might also discover that the adolescent is upset about puberty, acne, or real or imagined obesity, any of which can interfere with concentration on schoolwork.
- *Talk to the school.* Make sure the adolescent has been given tests that would identify a learning disability or a specific problem with

reading or math. Make sure your expectations for the adolescent are realistic. If the school thinks the child is exceptionally bright, are her classes stimulating enough? If she is not as bright as the average student in her school, is the school taking this into account? Ask why the counselor or teacher thinks the child is having problems.

• *Examine your own attitudes and behavior.* Are you too demanding? too critical? too managing? Do you show interest in her interests? listen to her point of view? sympathize with her problems? praise her accomplishments (in and out of school)? Are you setting a good example, by reading, talking, investigating, yourself? Do you believe school is as important as you say it is? Or are you sending mixed messages about achievement?

Step 2: Communication   Next, have a quiet, unpressured talk with your adolescent. Don't accuse him of not trying; rather, assume that he is as troubled by his poor grades as you are. "I know you want to do well in school. Let's see if we can find out why you are having problems this year." Ask what *he* thinks is wrong. Here are some common responses and what they might indicate:

• *"The work's too hard; I can't keep up."* This indicates that the adolescent may need help with study skills or tutoring in one or more subjects.
• *"It's soooo boring."* The adolescent is telling you her mind is on other things. Why is she so nonchalant? Fear of failure? Fear of her friends?
• *"I try, but I just can't concentrate."* This may be a sign of underlying anxiety; see step 4 below.
• *"The kids all laugh at me."* Social problems can translate into disaffection with school (see Popularity, chapter 9).
• *"My teachers hate me."* A student may have a personality conflict with one teacher, but it's unlikely that all of his teachers actively dislike him. The adolescent may be projecting his anxieties about schoolwork, or your approval, onto his teachers.
• *"You're always bugging me."* This may be true, or half true. Ask what you do that annoys her and listen to her complaints.

Don't expect to get to the heart of the matter in one conversation. But if you communicate concern, rather than anger and hurt, future conversations may enable you to pinpoint specific problems your adolescent can solve, with a little help from you.

Step 3: Goals and Rewards Underachievement is often a matter of self-discipline. Parents can help by teaching adolescents how to set short-term goals and reward themselves for meeting those goals.

• *For the student who avoids reading assignments.* Some adolescents avoid reading because they haven't developed such basic study skills as breaking long assignments into small steps, underlining, and stopping at the end of a paragraph or section to review what the author has said. They may go through the motions of reading but not absorb very much. As a result, reading seems like an exercise in futility. Go over basic study skills with your child (see Resources at the end of the chapter). Then establish a schedule of rewards. If he completes his assignments every night for two weeks and gets a note from his teachers saying he came to class prepared during that time, his reward might be going to a concert, getting new posters for his room, or watching whatever he likes on TV for one night (even four hours of MTV).

• *For the student who is "sooo bored."* Help her think of reasons why she might need to know something about different subjects. Make a game of fantastic futures: If she were a set designer for the ballet (her passion), she might have to recreate eighteenth-century London (this week's history lesson) on stage; if she were to sail around the world with a group of friends, she'd need geometry to read charts; if she had a career in fashion, it would help to speak French. Her reward for working hard (doing her homework regularly, turning in assignments and papers on time) in history, geometry, and French might be a ticket to the ballet, a day of sailing, or an afternoon shopping in town.

• *For the student who just doesn't care.* Get him to write down a list of reasons why he should study (to get into college, to get you off his back, to stop feeling guilty . . .) and the reasons why he doesn't. Or ask him to imagine what his life would be like if he did or did not go to college (working as a messenger vs. playing lacrosse at Tulane and later becoming a coach). If he agrees school is important, work out a plan: If he studies an hour and a half each night this week, he'll get to practice lacrosse for an hour every afternoon the next week; if he keeps it up the next week, he can invite his friends over for a Saturday practice and burgers the following week; and so on.

The aim of these exercises is not to bribe adolescents into working but to teach them how to make unpleasant tasks less painful and even rewarding. Post a list of desired privileges where the adolescent can add ideas as they occur to her, but take the studying two weeks or one quiz at a time. At first, walk her through the process, helping set goals, monitoring her progress, and providing some of the rewards. Later, she should do this for herself (with you providing support—your okay to an activity, transportation, and above all, praise). Be prepared for occasional anger, backsliding, and slumps. Don't dwell on these lapses; just do your best to get the adolescent back on track.

Step 4: Getting Help   If none of these strategies work, parents should make an appointment with the school guidance counselor or a private psychologist. The psychologist will probably do further testing, meet with you and the child (separately and together), and then recommend a course of action.

This does *not* mean that the underachieving adolescent is "mentally ill." Adolescents who are chronically anxious or depressed have difficulty concentrating on their work (as do adults). The adolescent may not know what is bothering him, or be too ashamed to discuss his problem with anyone. Adolescent psychologists are trained to uncover the reasons why the student is having problems and to help correct self-defeating patterns of thought and behavior.

A Word of Hope

It's not unheard of for an underachiever to simply outgrow the problem. Middle- and junior-high-school students are betwixt and between. Too old to work hard in school simply to please their parents and teachers, they are too young to be thinking about college admissions and future careers. Some "wake up" in ninth or tenth grade. In the meantime, do what you can, and try not to nag.

RESOURCES

For more on helping your teenager with school, see Julia Hahn's *"Have You Done Your Homework?": A Parent's Guide to Helping Teenagers Succeed in School* (New York: Wiley, 1985).

The following organizations publish information and/or answer questions about parents and schools.

Council for Basic Education
725 15th Street, N.W.
Washington, DC 20005

For a manual, *How to Form a Families in Action Group in Your Community:*

Families in Action (FIA)
Suite 300
3845 North Druid Hills Road
Decatur, GA 30333
404-325-5799

National Committee for Citizens in Education
410 Wilde Lake Village Green
Columbia, MD 21044

National PTA
700 N. Rush Street
Chicago, IL 60611

National School Volunteer Program
300 N. Washington Street
Alexandria, VA 22314

THE TEENS
From 14 to 17

PHYSICAL HEALTH
AND DEVELOPMENT

CHAPTER 12

Sex and the
High-School Student

*B*y the time they graduate, half of today's teenagers will have engaged in sexual intercourse. About a quarter will have their first experience during their sophomore year of high school. What do these facts mean for parents?

First, you shouldn't judge today's teenagers by yesterday's standards. When you were in high school, sexually active teenagers were the exception, not the rule. Many psychologists then held that early sexual activity (before age 18) was a symptom of low self-esteem, rebelliousness, psychological problems, and/or family problems.

But the cultural environment has changed. Teenagers who engage in intimate relationships today are well within the norms of a large segment of the population who believe that sex is a normal and healthy part of close relationships, whether or not the couple are married. Today many psychologists agree that teenage sexual activity, in and of itself, is not a cause for alarm. To be sure, some teenagers do embark on sexual relationships to compensate for low self-esteem, escape from their problems, or get back at their parents. Some get in over their heads. But all sexually active teenagers aren't "bad" or "troubled" kids.

Second, a parent's role in the young person's sexual development has increased, not decreased. The facts of teenage sexuality mean that it is more important than ever for parents to keep the lines of communication on sexual matters open. Helping teenagers deal with experiences you didn't have yourself (or not until you were in your twenties), and accepting that your adolescent's values are not a carbon copy of your own, aren't easy. But they are important.

ATTITUDES AND BEHAVIOR

Teenage boys have always sought sexual experience, with greater or lesser success. The biggest change has been in girls' behavior (especially middle-class, college-bound girls). In the past, 18- and 19-year-old boys were three or four times more likely to have had sexual intercourse than were girls their age. Today, 19-year-old girls are just as *un*likely to be virgins as are boys their age. The double standard has faded. So has the belief that 16 is too young.

Contrary to what some parents believe, however, today's teenagers are *not* obsessed with sex. When teenagers were asked to rank dating, friends, music, school, sex, and sports in order of importance, both sexes said school and friends were far more important to them than sex. Girls put sex at the bottom of the list; boys rated sex as more important than music but less important than sports. When teenagers who had a steady girl- or boyfriend were asked how important sex was to their relationship, most said "moderately" important (as opposed to "very" or "not very" important). A 16-year-old girl explained, "I think in a relationship it's important to be satisfied emotionally and physically. But the emotional part is stronger and more important." An 18-year-old boy felt the same way: "Sex came in second place for me. If I *had* to choose, I would rather have the love and affection and companionship than the sex."

One common complaint among adolescents is that their *parents* are preoccupied with teenage sexuality: "My folks think sex is the only thing on my mind. If I ask about anything, they think it's because I'm doing it. That's not true."

Teenagers do *not* see sex as a casual affair. They do not believe that anything goes. And they do not approve of sleeping around. Today, as twenty-five years ago, teenagers subscribe to "permissiveness with affection." Sexual intimacy is permissible if, and only if, the couple care for one another. Love carries considerable moral weight. In the words of a 17-year-old girl: "I think that if you really love somebody, that [sexual intercourse] is okay. Now, you know, I know a lot of people who just go out for the fun of it and have sex, but I don't put them down for that, because they believe what they want to believe, and I have a different set of values, but I have to really love somebody before I can do anything with him." This girl was not a virgin, but neither was she promiscuous. She had had sex only with her current boyfriend, whom she had been going with for almost three years. And like many teenagers, she did not see sex as a moral issue for *other* people, but applied stricter standards to herself.

The belief that love makes sex permissible is not new. What has changed is that today's teenagers are more likely to believe that love can be temporary, that their first love may not be their last, and that commitments are not necessarily forever. Simply put, they do not see sex as a step in the direction of marriage. But neither do they approve of having sex "just for the fun of it."

Many teenagers find it easier to preach than to practice these ideals, however. Sex has become a status symbol for teenagers. Other symbols of maturity (supporting oneself, living independently, marrying) have been postponed, leaving sex as one of the only available rites of passage to adulthood: If you have had intercourse, you are an adult; if you are still a virgin, you are just a child. Some teenagers see virginity as a "ball and chain of innocence" they want to cast off as quickly as possible. Many believe that a relationship isn't real or meaningful if it doesn't include sex.

YOUR ROLE AS PARENT

How can parents guide teenagers toward healthy sexual attitudes and behavior?

- Face facts. If you imagine that *your* child will not feel pressured into sex, or that she would *never* be stupid enough to get into trouble, think again.
- Help teenagers to anticipate internal and external pressure to have sex and to make responsible decisions.
- Make sure that teenagers know how to protect themselves (and their partners) from pregnancy and sexually transmitted diseases (STDs).

• Communicate that you will *be there* if the teenager gets in trouble. One mother told her daughter, "No matter what you do, no matter how terrible you might think it is, I want you to feel that you can come and talk to me about it." To make her point she added, "Even if you were to kill someone." That's what parents are for.

In discussing sexual decisions with your adolescent, remember that teenagers live for the present. If they think about the future, it is usually in abstract, hypothetical, idealized terms. Intellectually, they may know that this is not Mr. or Ms. Right, that pregnancy would create all kinds of problems, and that STDs can cause sterility. But emotionally, they may forget. Surely you remember the first time a member of the opposite sex paid attention to you. It may have been someone you secretly worshipped from afar; you never imagined that this person was interested in you. Suddenly you felt attractive, life had new meaning, you were walking on air. The first time you kissed, you thought you would melt. In the grip of such strong emotions, it is difficult to think clearly. If you talk to teenagers *before* they are involved in a serious relationship (say, at age 13 or 14), you will have more influence than if you wait until sex seems imminent.

Talking about Sexual Decisions

In early adolescence, youngsters are concerned about who they are sexually, where these new sensations and feelings are coming from, and what to think about sex. In middle adolescence, young people worry about what they personally should *do* about sex, about what role sex should play in their lives.

Teenagers don't want to be *told* whether having sexual intercourse is right or wrong; this is a judgment they want to make for themselves. When parents assert or demand that adolescents must wait until they are older or until they are married, the teenagers get a message, but it is often the wrong message: "I can't talk to my parents about sex."

The laissez-faire attitude of a small number of "liberal" parents can also backfire. A 15-year-old girl's description of her conversations with her mother suggests why.

[S]he was curious about me because she knew I'd been going out with him and she kept on saying, "Listen, you need birth control."

And I was going "No, no," and I kept putting it off myself. Like, "No, I don't need it"—very upset, you know. Like, "Mom, what do you think I am?" [But she did tell her mother when she lost her virginity.] It was really funny because she had just come home from vacation afterwards. She was, "So what did you do?" I didn't want to say, "Well [my boyfriend] was here," so I kinda said, "Well, I was with [my boyfriend] most of the weekend. And, Mom," I said, "I'm not a virgin." And she was like, "Wha-a-at?" And I said, "Mom, I'm not a virgin," and she said, "Oh, was it good? Did you like it?" I was like, "Is *that* all you're gonna say?"

This young woman took her mother's permissiveness first as an accusation and later as indifference.

There is a middle ground between lectures and laissez-faire; namely, talking about how to make the right decisions.

Right and Wrong Reasons for Sex   Few teenagers tell their parents directly that they are thinking about having sexual intercourse. But they may ask an indirect question, such as "How do you know when you are in love?" or "How can you tell when a relationship is real?" No one (not even a parent) can answer these questions for another person. But parents and teens can talk about right and wrong reasons for having sex.

Point out that *sex doesn't make or break a relationship.* The real test of a relationship is whether you can talk openly and honestly with each other, you enjoy doing things together and just being together, and the relationship makes you feel good about yourself (not jealous and insecure, restricted and hemmed in, or wanted too little or too much). There is nothing wrong with physical expressions of affection, of course, but you do not need to have sexual intercourse to be affectionate or even to feel sexually satisfied. If sex is the only way to maintain a relationship, it isn't much of a relationship.

Suggest, gently, that being in love may not be a good enough reason for adding sex to a relationship either. About two-thirds of teenagers say that they have been in love. But in most cases that love was either short-lived or one-sided. Falling in love is grand. But sex implies (or should imply) an emotional commitment that few high-school students are prepared to make.

Your adolescent might ask, How do you know if the time and the person are right? A couple *might* be ready if they

- Are sure that they are not exploiting each other
- Feel comfortable talking to one another about precautions

against pregnancy and STDs, and willing to share responsibility for them
- Are able to deal with the possible consequences of intercourse, including pregnancy and STDs
- Respect and like one another as individuals
- Are ready to make an emotional commitment to one another.

The general rule should be, When in doubt, wait.

How to Say No   For teenage girls, saying no *gracefully* is one of the most difficult aspects of a relationship. Often they tell Planned Parenthood counselors that they had sex not because they really wanted to, but because they didn't know how to refuse. A girl may worry that saying no will make her seem immature and babyish, or that she will be seen as a tease (especially if she and the boy have been petting). She may be afraid of hurting the boy's feelings (a more frequent reason for intercourse than you might imagine). A girl might also feel pressured to have sex because she believes she is the only one of her friends who is still a virgin. But the pressure usually comes from the boy.

Ideally, all a girl should have to say is, "I'm not ready." But many girls lack the confidence to stick to their principles. One way to build sexual self-confidence is to stress *assertiveness* and *freedom of choice*. Parents need to communicate to teenagers that what they do with their bodies is their own business and nobody else's. Girls, especially, need to know that they have the right to refuse to have sex at any time, for any reason, no matter how far they have gone necking and petting, whether or not they have had sex before, and even (when they are older) with their husbands. The choice is theirs alone. In stressing freedom of choice, parents are acknowledging that the teenager might decide to say yes. Teenagers are more likely to make responsible decisions, and to discuss decisions with their parents or another adult, if they are treated as mature enough to make up their own minds.

Another way to build sexual self-confidence is to talk about *self-respect*. Parents used to tell their daughters that boys would respect them more if they said no. This may have been accurate at the time, but it also implied that girls should base their decisions about sex on boys' opinions; that a girl's role was to please boys, even if that meant "frustrating" them in the short run. The real question is not what the boy will think, but *self*-respect and how *she* will feel the morning after. Girls who believe that their only attraction is their sex appeal, or who only feel good about themselves when they have a steady boyfriend, are especially vulnerable to exploitation.

Having sexual intercourse is a big step, one that can lead to pleasure and tenderness—or to disappointment, anxiety, and guilt. Sex shouldn't be something that "just happens."

Not for Girls Only   Coping with peer pressure is not a problem for girls only. Few boys feel pressured into sex by their girlfriends. But most do feel pressure from their male friends. "How was it last night?" "Did she treat you right?" "Have you made it with Susy yet?" "Are you getting any?" "You don't mean you're *still* a virgin?" Friendly banter is fine. But constant hassling can make a boy who isn't on the make, or who hasn't made it to "home plate," wonder if there is something wrong with him. A boy may let his friends think he is going all the way with a girl, when he is not, and later feel guilty that he has damaged her reputation. Surveys find that most teenage boys lie a little about their sexual experience (if only by not saying what they haven't done). Yet they believe that their friends are telling the truth! Boys as well as girls need to know that having sex to please someone else (in this case, their friends) won't make them feel good about themselves.

Date Rape

Many teenage boys try to talk a girl into sex before she is ready. Some do more than talk. They may believe that forcing themselves on a date isn't "really" rape because the girl has agreed to go out with them and allowed necking; that a girl who has had sex with one boy is (or should be) willing to have sex with all boys; or that boys are *supposed* to press for sex and that girls expect and even enjoy this (the old myth that when females say no, they really mean yes). Afterward, they tell themselves, "She wanted it as much as I did." Most would be surprised to hear what they did labeled as rape. But it is.

Young girls are especially vulnerable to this form of exploitation and assault. They may believe that they are in love or that sex is the only way to maintain the relationship; be too inexperienced to recognize when a boy has crossed the line from seduction to coercion; or believe that they have brought the attack on themselves. Some are more afraid of their parents' reaction to their having gotten into a tight situation than they are of giving in. This is especially true when they have broken rules—for example, by going out with an older boy their parents had forbidden them to see or by inviting a boy to the house when their parents were away.

Parents need to give boys a clear message that coercive or exploitive sex is *inexcusable,* whoever the girl, whatever the circumstances. Sex is not something you give or take; it is something two people share, willingly.

Girls need to know, first, that rape can happen within a relationship: Boys can get carried away, especially if they are highly aroused and/or have been drinking.

Second, girls need to decide what their limits are before they get involved; trust their feelings; and say what they feel. If a boy sits or stands closer to her than she wants, if she feels uncomfortable when a certain boy corners her in the hall or puts a "friendly" arm around her shoulder, she should say so, even if it means being rude. If a boys offers to drive her home, then takes a route she doesn't know, she should ask where he is going. If he suggests a walk on a lonely beach and she says yes, she should make sure he knows that a walk doesn't mean she wants to mess around. Remaining silent in any of these situations may make a boy feel that she welcomes his advances or that she is afraid to defend herself.

Third, girls need to take precautions. It is not a good idea to go to a secluded place, including her own home when no adult is around, with a boy she doesn't know very well or a boy who has been pressuring her. If she thinks she may be getting in over her head, she should be extra careful not to say or do things a boy might interpret as come-ons. If a boy is going too far, she should tell him to stop, tactfully but unambiguously: "Look, I like you a lot, but if you don't stop I'm going to leave." If he doesn't stop, she should leave. If she can't get away, she might say, "You'd better stop now. I told all my friends that I was going out with you; if you hurt me you're going to be in big trouble."

If a girl who has been assaulted, by someone she knows or by a stranger, does not feel she can talk to her parents, she should speak to another adult she trusts (a relative, minister, or physician) or call one of the rape hotlines listed in the Yellow Pages. Such calls are confidential, and the people who answer are trained to help deal with the emotional as well as the physical aftermath of date rape.

CONTRACEPTION

Virtually all teenagers regard pregnancy as a disaster. Yet very few practice birth control. In one recent survey, only 40 percent of the teenagers said they had used contraception the first time they had intercourse—and almost half of *them* had relied on withdrawal or timing. Other surveys have found that only a third of the teenagers who are involved in ongoing relationships use birth control regularly, and almost the same percentage *never* use contraception. About a third of the teenagers go to a family planning clinic for the first time because they suspect they are pregnant.

Why Teenagers Take Chances

These are the most common reasons why teenagers do not use birth control:

• *The personal fable.* Although they know that other girls get pregnant, most teenagers believe "It can't happen to *me.*" This kind of magical thinking is common in adolescence (see chapter 7), especially with regard to sex.

• *Ambivalence and guilt.* Many teenagers feel ambivalent or guilty about their sexual behavior and neutralize these feelings through denial. To admit that they are sexually active by obtaining birth control would mean a major revision in self-image. So they rationalize their first experience (or experiences) as an accident, an experiment, or a moment of passion or weakness that will not be repeated. Denial enables a teenager to maintain the fiction of sexual innocence. Among other things, this means that parents who make their adolescents feel guilty about sex may unwittingly contribute to their failure to use contraception.

• *Ignorance and misinformation.* Myths about pregnancy and contraception abound (see Common Myths, chapter 5). Some teenagers believe you can't get pregnant the first time you have intercourse, if you douche after sex, if you have sex standing up, if you don't kiss, or if you wear high heels during intercourse (these beliefs were offered by Michigan high-school students). Some actually believe that you won't get pregnant if you don't want to! Myths about contraception are just as common: Douching after intercourse prevents pregnancy, condoms are unreliable, the pill causes cancer, or you can take a single pill the morning after. Most teenagers don't know at what point during their menstrual cycle they are most likely to conceive, and many have unfounded fears about the side effects of contraceptives.

• *Interference with sex.* Teenagers often believe that contraception interferes with sexual pleasure and spontaneity. Stopping to put on a condom (especially if you're not sure how to use one) or excusing yourself to insert a diaphragm or vaginal foam destroys the magic of the moment. Some adults feel this way, too. But teenagers are especially likely to find birth control awkward—in part because of lack of experience, in part because they don't want to think of themselves as sexually prepared, and in part because teenage sex often *is* spontaneous.

• *Infrequent sex.* Most teenagers do not have sexual intercourse regularly, if only because it is difficult for them to find privacy. So-called "sexually active" teenagers may have intercourse as infrequently as three or four times a year. As a result, they may not be prepared when the rare occasion arises. Or they may believe that they don't need contraception because they don't have sex often enough.

• *Lack of access.* Many teenagers believe (incorrectly) that birth control devices are expensive, difficult to obtain, and/or cannot be acquired without parental permission. Some are just too embarrassed to ask, even in a pharmacy where they are not known or at a clinic where confidentiality is guaranteed.

• *Fear of discovery.* Most teens worry that if they do obtain condoms, birth control pills, or another contraceptive, their parents will find out. The immediate, concrete risk of discovery may outweigh the seemingly remote and abstract risk of pregnancy. This fear operates not only on adolescents who have been forbidden to engage in sexual relations, but also on those who have been told the choice is theirs. If your parents know, it's all but impossible to maintain a myth of sexual innocence.

• *The double standard of (ir)responsibility.* Teenagers find it difficult to communicate with their partner about sexual responsibility, especially the first few times they have sex. They've never been in this situation before; what are they supposed to say? The availability of birth control pills has convinced many boys that the girl will (or should) assume responsibility. After all, she is the one who might get pregnant. The girl may feel that if she is prepared, the boy will assume she is "easy"; if a boy is prepared, the girl may be offended ("He expected it"). The result is a conspiracy of silence: Neither says anything, and they go on having unprotected sex.

How to Talk to Your Teenager about Contraception

Boys often report that all their parents ever said about birth control was "Be careful." While this is not bad advice, it is not enough: Boys need to know *how* to be careful. Girls sometimes say their mothers told them "If you have intercourse, tell me and we'll make an appointment with the doctor right away." But even if a girl does tell her mother the morning after—something surveys tell us is unlikely—it may be too late. A 1987 Harris poll found that two out of three teenagers had *never* talked with their parents about birth control.

Hesitancy on the part of parents is understandable. Talking with a teenager about birth control may sound like condoning or even encouraging them to be sexually active. But at the risk of repeating ourselves, there is *no* evidence that sex education of any kind increases sexual activity, and a good deal of evidence that it decreases sexual irresponsibility.

How can parents say that they do *not* approve of premarital or teenage sex but they *do* want a teenager to use birth control? Isn't that sending a mixed message? Not at all: You are saying that you consider your child's *welfare* more important than obedience or endorsement of your values. The simplest approach is to be direct.

- "You know how I feel about your getting involved with sex right now, so it may sound funny for me to be talking to you about birth control. But someday you will be ready, and when that time comes I want you to have the information you need."
- "You know I think you are too young to complicate your life with sex. But if and when you decide you're ready, I expect you to be responsible. Here is what you should know."
- "Your mother and I think you are mature enough to make your own decisions about sex. But we want to know how much you know about birth control and whether you have any questions."

The earlier you begin talking about contraception, the less likely your teenager will be to take what you say either as an

invasion of privacy or as an accusation. Age 12 or 13 is not too
soon; age 17 or 18 may be too late.

What Teenagers Should Know   When you talk to your teenager about contraception, your main messages should be:

• *Pregnancy is always a possibility.* Don't think that because you
are young, or because you don't have sex very often, or because
you have sex standing on your head (or some other myth that
sounds laughable to parents but not to an uninformed teenager),
you can't get pregnant. You can. Teenagers are approaching the
years of peak fertility, when it is easiest for a girl to get pregnant
or a boy to impregnate a girl. Don't fall for home remedies (such
as douching with Coke or improvising a condom from plastic
wrap). And don't count on withdrawal or the rhythm method.
Withdrawal is risky because the fluid that lubricates a boy's penis
so that it can slip into the vagina usually contains some sperm,
and it only takes one sperm to make a girl pregnant. The rhythm
or calendar method is also a gamble because a teenage girl's periods are often irregular, so that it is impossible to predict when
she will ovulate in a particular cycle. The only way a girl can know
whether she has ovulated is to take her temperature daily, but a
slight cold can throw the best-kept temperature chart off.

There are several reliable methods of birth control for teenagers, including condoms (preferably used in conjunction with an
additional method, such as a spermicide, diaphragm, vaginal
sponge, or cervical cap) and oral contraceptives ("the Pill"). But
the only sure way to avoid pregnancy is to abstain from intercourse. Parents should point out that this does not mean abstaining from sexual intimacy, only from intercourse.

• *The risks and inconveniences of pregnancy are much greater than the
risks and inconveniences of using birth control.* Your teenager may
have heard that the Pill causes cancer, sterility, or birth deformi-
ties. All of these beliefs are false. While any medication can have
side effects, the risks of the birth control pill are quite small,
especially for young women. A doctor can tell you if you are one
of the few who should not use the Pill. The risks from other forms
of birth control are minimal. The complications that can arise
during a pregnancy are far greater than all these risks combined.

Using contraceptives does not interfere with sexual pleasure;
in most cases, you can't even feel them. Married couples who are
not ready for a child, or another child, often find their sex life

improves when they use reliable contraception, because they are more relaxed.

You may be embarrassed to ask if your boyfriend has a condom or your girlfriend is on the Pill. But think how much more embarrassing it would be to have to tell your boyfriend that you were pregnant, or to learn that a girl you had talked into the withdrawal method was pregnant. What would you say *then?* A little courage now can prevent anguish and heartbreak in the future.

Your friends or your partner may say it is "macho" or a sign of "true love" to have sex without protection. Both are nonsense. Remember, you are the one who will have to live with the consequences if you gamble and lose.

• *Both sexes are responsible for birth control.* Never assume that your partner will take care of everything. (To girls) A boy may get swept away by emotion, assume that you are taking the Pill or using another method, or be misinformed about contraception. It is up to you to protect yourself. (To boys) You are just as responsible for birth control as the girl is: If she gets pregnant, it is your problem, too. Girls are even more embarrassed to purchase contraceptives than boys are. The Pill may seem great to you, but you don't have to go to the clinic, have an examination, remember to take one each day, or worry about your parents finding them. It is up to you to protect your partner as well as yourself. (To both sexes) The best protection against pregnancy is to abstain from intercourse. The second best method is for both of you to use contraception (say, a condom and a vaginal sponge). If you can't talk to each other about contraception, you aren't ready for sex.

• *The boy should always use a condom.* Condoms provide protection not only from pregnancy, but also from sexually transmitted diseases (as discussed later in this chapter). Many teenage girls are reluctant to ask their boyfriends to use condoms because they assume boys don't like them. In fact, surveys show that boys have more positive attitudes toward condoms than girls do.

• *When you need contraceptives, here is how to get them.* Many contraceptives are sold over the counter at pharmacies. They aren't very expensive. There is no law about minors purchasing them: You won't have to prove you are 16 or 18. And they are easy to use (just read the directions). Planned Parenthood and other health clinics are not required to notify the parents if a young person asks for contraceptives. The adults who work at these clinics are concerned about teenagers' health and will respect your wishes. Most charge only modest fees, or no fee if you are unable to pay.

Access to Birth Control   Lack of access is one of the main reasons teenagers give for not using birth control. How you choose to handle this subject depends on your values, attitudes, and style. Some parents make an appointment with a doctor or family planning clinic when their youngster is 14 or 15 or beginning to date seriously. To do this without seeming to endorse sexual activity or to accuse the teenager of being sexually active, a parent might say, "You're growing up and it's time you learned about birth control. I think a doctor can explain things better than I can." Some parents talk to the teenager themselves, then leave a box of condoms or chemical contraceptives (vaginal foam or suppositories) in a place where the teenager is likely to discover them and "borrow" if the need arises. Parents who feel that either of these strategies is too forward can simply say, "I want you to feel free to discuss anything you want with your doctor/our family physician. I've told her that whatever you discuss with her is between the two of you."

Most parents feel funny when they discover that their "child" is using birth control. Sexual activity is a sign that the young person is no longer a child, that he or she will be leaving home and starting an independent life and new family in the not too distant future. Some parents feel sad when they make this discovery; some get angry. We hope that, whatever your values and attitudes, you will be pleased (or at least relieved) to know that the young person is acting responsibly. If you are not, read on. The threat of pregnancy is not the only reason for using contraceptives.

SEXUALLY TRANSMITTED DISEASES (STDs)

Everyone has heard about the dangers of herpes and AIDS. But did you know that the U.S. Centers for Disease Control estimate that eight million Americans are suffering from gonorrhea? That there are three to ten million new cases of chlamydia each year? That as many as three-quarters of the victims of these STDs are between the ages of 15 and 24?

We do not mean to scare parents or teenagers, but facts are facts. The incidence of STDs (what used to be called venereal diseases) is much higher today than it was when parents were teenagers and young adults. And the diseases themselves have changed. Many exhibit no symptoms. A person may not know that he or she had an STD, and transmitted it to others, until years later, when complications develop, especially sterility.

Because they are so often reluctant to admit that they are sexually active (to themselves as well as others), because they find it difficult to talk about sex (even though they are doing it), and because they often feel invulnerable (the personal fable again), teenagers are especially susceptible to STDs. Talking about STDs is as important as talking about contraception. Parents should be firm ("You *must* protect yourself") but also reassuring ("You *can* protect yourself").

What Every Teenager Should Know

• *Anyone who is sexually active can contract an STD.* Teenagers who come from poor or troubled families and teenagers who sleep around or who get mixed up with "the wrong crowd" are not the only ones at risk. Like a cold or flu, STDs can strike anyone who is having sex. Adolescents are more likely to be exposed to STDs than any other age group in our society, so it is vitally important that a teenager protect him- or herself *now*.

• *The most common way STDs are transmitted is through sexual intercourse.* Sex doesn't cause STDs; germs do. But these particular germs live in the human reproductive tract and are passed from one person to another through the prolonged, skin-to-skin contact that occurs during intercourse. Some types (especially gonorrhea) may be contracted through oral sex as well. But there is no evidence that you can get an STD from kissing or petting.

• *AIDS is not the only dangerous STD.* To date, most cases of AIDS have occurred in homosexuals or intravenous drug users; a smaller number have been traced to blood transfusions. This may lead adolescents who are heterosexual and drug-free to conclude that they are safe. For the moment they may be *relatively* safe from AIDS, but not from other STDs. (See A Note on AIDS, on page 251.) For girls, untreated gonorrhea and chlamydia can lead to pelvic inflammatory disease, or PID (an infection that spreads from the vagina or cervix, through the uterus, into the fallopian tubes and sometimes to the ovaries). PID is dangerous in itself and may also cause sterility. In boys, untreated gonorrhea and chlamydia can cause problems with urination, difficulties getting an erection, and sterility. The couple are not the only ones who are affected. If a woman who has either of these STDs gets pregnant, she may have a miscarriage or stillbirth, or her baby may be born with infections serious enough to cause blindness.

• *Many STDs do not have obvious symptoms.* In some cases, a victim may have only slight discomfort urinating, minor irritation in the genital area, or a discharge that goes away after a few days. It is extremely important that adolescents know that the fact that these symptoms went away does not mean they are cured. In this, STDs are *not* like a cold or the flu: They remain in your body even when you can't feel their effects. The only way to get rid of an STD is to get treatment. In many cases, STDs have *no* symptoms. (Among other things, this means your partner may not have known he or she was infected when you had sex.) This is a clear case where "an ounce of prevention is worth a pound of cure."

• *After celibacy and "mutual monogamy" (having sex only with one partner who is not having sex with anyone else), the best protection against STDs is a condom.* Some contraceptives for females offer partial protection, but not enough. Couples should routinely use condoms whenever they have intercourse. Urinating and washing the genital area with soap and water after intercourse may also reduce the risk of infection. Getting up to go to the bathroom after making love may not be very romantic, but neither are STDs.

• *A teenager who experiences any of the following symptoms should not have sex and should go to a doctor or clinic immediately:*

> Painful, burning sensations during urination or dark-colored urine
>
> A discharge from the vagina or penis that itches, burns, or has a strong odor
>
> Sores, redness, persistent irritation, or a persistent pimple in the genital area
>
> A persistent sore throat

• *When one person has an STD, so may his or her partner.* In many cases, an STD can only be cured if *both* partners are treated. It is not only wrong not to tell your partner; you will be reinfected if you have sex with him or her again (or someone else will be).

• *Treatment for STDs is free and confidential.* Parental consent and notification are *not* required. If a teenager does not feel comfortable about going to his or her personal physician, the local Department of Health (listed under Community Service Numbers in the phone book), a Planned Parenthood clinic, or the National STD hotline (800-227-8922) will tell a teenager where to go, no questions asked.

• *Almost all STDs can be cured easily and painlessly if caught in time.* (The exceptions are AIDS and herpes.) Treating most STDs is no more difficult than treating bronchitis: In most cases, the doctor will prescribe antibiotics. If you take these as directed, your worries are over. The complications from untreated STDs are far more difficult to treat: PID may require hospitalization and surgery. Given the possibility that a person with an STD may have no symptoms, sexually active teenagers should ask their physicians about an annual test.

Today, the most common STDs among adolescents are gonorrhea, chlamydia, and herpes. If your adolescent, or your adolescent's sexual partner, reports any unusual discharge, painful urination, or genital sores or blisters, a physician should be consulted immediately.

A Note on AIDS

Because relatively few cases of AIDS have been reported among teenagers, adolescents may believe they are safe. This is only partially true and may well change in the future. People who die of AIDS in their 20s usually contracted the virus in their teens, and the number of AIDS cases among heterosexuals is on the rise. Here is what teenagers should know.

• *AIDS is not a homosexual disease.* The first cases of AIDS in this country were reported among homosexuals, and for a time most cases did occur in the homosexual community. Today, however, the rate of infection among heterosexuals is higher than among gays. The greatest increase has been among intravenous drug users (and their partners). But this may soon change. It's easy to see how. Unknowingly, a female may have sex with a male who is bisexual or an intravenous drug user who has contracted AIDS; with no reason to think she might be infected, she may have unprotected sex with another partner; with no reason to suspect he might be infected, he may have sex with other partners; and so on.

• *AIDS can be transmitted through heterosexual intercourse.* The chances of contracting AIDS may be slightly higher with anal intercourse, but studies clearly show that AIDS can be transmitted from male to female or female to male through vaginal intercourse as well.

• *AIDS may be transmitted through oral sex or deep kissing.* From what we know about the transmission of AIDS, it is possible that the AIDS virus can enter the body through small cuts in the mouth. No such cases have been documented, however.

• *To date, there is no cure for AIDS.* The U.S. Centers for Disease Control estimate that 20 to 30 percent of all individuals infected with AIDS will develop symptoms within five years. How many other AIDS carriers will develop AIDS or related afflictions at a later stage is not known. Researchers have been studying this disease for only about ten years. At present, there is no treatment for those who do develop AIDS.

• *The only real protection against AIDS is abstinence.*

• *The second best protection against AIDS is a condom.* Laboratory tests have shown that the AIDS virus does not pass through a rubber condom. Because the virus may be present in the male's preejaculation secretions or the female's vaginal secretions, condoms should be used throughout the sex act (not just before ejaculation). But condoms can break or slip. Cases where AIDS was transmitted even though the man always used a condom *have* been documented.

• *Know your partner.* Having sex with someone you just met, at a party or a bar, can be hazardous to your health. If you don't know the person, or don't feel comfortable asking someone you do know about his or her sexual history, don't take a chance.

• *The more partners you have, the greater the risk.* This is a simple matter of statistics. Individuals who play the field sexually have a greater chance of contracting AIDS than individuals who have one or two partners before settling down into monogamy.

• *Do not use intravenous drugs, under any circumstances.* There are many other reasons for not using drugs, of course. But the primary sources of AIDS infection today are, first, sharing a needle, and second, having sex with someone who uses intravenous drugs.

PREGNANCY

Every year more than a million American teenage girls become pregnant. The problem is not confined to poor, inner-city youth.

One in ten sexually active girls becomes pregnant at least once before her 19th birthday. About half of the time, the pregnancy occurs within six months of the initiation of sexual activity. An unwanted pregnancy has ripple effects. Almost inevitably, the girl's relationship with her boyfriend changes; in most cases, they break up. Her relationship with her parents may also change, especially if they did not know she was sexually active until she became pregnant. If she becomes a mother, her chances of finishing high school, getting a college degree, pursuing an exciting, financially rewarding career, and being happily married to her baby's father decline dramatically.

Teenage pregnancies are more common today than they were a generation or two ago; they are also less likely to be "legitimized" through marriage. When today's parents were teenagers, a pregnant girl had few options. Abortions were illegal in the United States. If a girl wanted to terminate her pregnancy, she had to go abroad (an expensive undertaking) or seek an illegal abortion at great risk to her own health and ability to have children in the future. Becoming a single parent was not a socially acceptable option for most girls; indeed, the term *single parent* was never heard. Many forced ("shotgun") marriages and sudden disappearances (living in a home for unwed mothers or with a relative in a distant place and giving up the baby for adoption) probably occurred, but nobody talked about this. Much has changed.

Today a girl can get a safe, legal abortion almost anywhere in the U.S., but there is heated debate about the morality of abortions. Single motherhood has lost much of its social stigma. Women of all ages and social classes (and not just celebrities) are openly having babies without marrying the fathers, and hardly anyone refers to their children as "illegitimate." Here, too, there is much debate about whether this is a good or bad trend. Finally, the number of infertile married couples looking for a baby to adopt has grown enormously. As a result of these cultural changes, there is no ready-made "solution" to teenage pregnancy. A girl has many more options, but in some ways a more complicated decision.

Given the statistics and the social and emotional implications, pregnancy is something you and your teenager should talk about, even if there is no immediate threat.

"Am I Pregnant?"

It is not unusual for an adolescent girl who began to menstruate within the preceding two years to skip periods (see chapter 4), and many teenage girls worry that they are pregnant when they are not. But just as many deny the possibility when they are. They may not know when their period is due. Or they may not recognize the early symptoms of pregnancy, including tenderness in the breasts, frequent need to urinate, and tiredness. Or they may believe that it just can't happen to them.

Early knowledge is important. If the teenager decides to have her baby, she needs to begin prenatal care as soon as possible. One of the reasons teenagers have more complications during pregnancy and childbirth than older women do is that they put off seeing an obstetrician and do not take proper care of themselves. Should the teenager decide not to have the baby, abortions are much simpler, safer, and less expensive if they are performed early in the pregnancy.

If a teenager thinks her period is as much as a week late, and she has had sex after the day her last period started, she should go to her physician or a family planning clinic as soon as possible, even if she was using birth control; no contraception is 100 percent effective. A simple blood or urine test can tell a trained technician whether a girl is pregnant within days after her period was due. These tests are confidential: The law does not require a clinic to notify her parents if she is pregnant. Teenagers should be warned *not* to rely on over-the-counter pregnancy tests, which can give false positives (indicate she is pregnant when she is not) as well as false negatives (indicate she is not pregnant when she is). Why sweat it out if she has nothing to worry about?

If parents suspect their daughter is pregnant, the same advice applies: Don't wait for her to speak up; ask, and tell her why it is important for her to know one way or the other.

A Parent's Role

When teenagers learn that they are pregnant, their first reaction is "How am I going to tell my parents?" Planned Parenthood counselors advise pregnant teenagers to talk to their parents, however difficult and painful this may be. They warn girls to expect their parents to be very upset and angry but suggest that once their parents work through their anger they will want to help.

Anger is only one of the emotions parents feel when they learn their daughter is pregnant. Feelings of righteousness ("I warned you . . ."), betrayal ("How could you do this to me?"), guilt ("Where did we go wrong?"), and fear ("What is going to happen to my baby?") are also common. Some parents regain their composure quickly; others need time to adjust to the bad news. If you are deeply upset, wait until you have calmed down to talk to your daughter about what she is going to do. Keep reminding yourself that blaming her (or her boyfriend or yourself) won't solve the problem. If you feel that the pregnancy is tearing the family apart —if you are fighting with your daughter and/or your spouse rather than dealing with the problem—we strongly recommend family counseling.

The parent's role in teenage pregnancy should be a supportive one. You may have definite ideas about what your daughter should do. *But the decision is, and must be, hers.* When girls are pressured into a decision, their relationship with their parents may be permanently damaged. Girls who have been psychologically (if not physically) forced to have an abortion or give a baby up for adoption often become pregnant again soon after, "replacing" the baby (and the decision) that was taken from them. Your role is to help your daughter to consider her options carefully so that she can make the right decision for herself.

A woman in her 30s fondly remembers her mother's response:

> Once in high school I thought I was pregnant. My mother discovered my dilemma when she overheard me talking to a friend on the phone.
>
> Her immediate reaction was to take me for a pregnancy test. On the way, she discussed alternatives to going away to college if I was pregnant. I could go to one closer to home, for example. At work that afternoon I received a vase of flowers. The card said simply, "I love you, Mom."
>
> Though I knew she was terribly disappointed, not once did she say any words of judgment. Her conversation was both practical and sympathetic.
>
> I will never forget this. I want to try to be as understanding, loving, and forgiving with my own children.

She wasn't pregnant, but other girls are not so lucky.

The Teenager's Decision

There are no easy solutions to teenage pregnancy and few completely happy endings. A girl has three basic choices: She can decide to keep the baby, give the baby up for adoption, or have an abortion. Some teenagers (and their parents) may think abortion is the only realistic option; others may consider abortion unacceptable under any circumstances. These are value judgments, and we would not presume to tell you or your teenager which is the right decision. But we can give you the best information available on the consequences of these three choices. Most research in this area has focused on the pregnant girl. In the best of all possible worlds, the boy would play an equal role in the decision. We consider his feelings and role at the end of this section.

The decision to become a teenage mother has far-reaching consequences. Parenthood is a twenty-year commitment or more, and few teenagers have thought that far into the future when a pregnancy occurs.

If a girl thinks she wants to become a mother, parents should encourage her to think about why. Teenage girls often have unrealistic ideas about motherhood. Their minds may be filled with images of holding a cuddly, happy baby in their arms, basking in the "ooohs" and "ahhhs" of relatives, finally being recognized as an adult by their parents, having a home of their own, and perhaps marrying the baby's father. Few think about late night feedings, diaper changes, teething, or the "terrible twos." In their minds, motherhood is associated with independence and maturity, not with the dependence and immaturity of an infant.

Planned Parenthood suggests a number of ways parents can help a teenage girl form a more realistic picture of her life as a single mother. When girls say they want to become mothers, it is usually for one of the following reasons:

- To be treated as an adult (the infant as a badge of maturity)
- To have someone to love and be loved by (the infant as a toy or pet)
- To get the attention given to a mother and baby, even by strangers (the infant as an identity)
- To break away from her family (the infant as a banner of independence)

- To win her boyfriend's commitment (the infant as a lure)
- To make up for the guilt she feels for becoming pregnant (the infant as repayment)

If your daughter recognizes any of these feelings, ask her to think about other ways of filling her needs. (How else can she prove that she is a grown-up? become independent? keep her boyfriend?) Suggest that she think about what her immediate future will be like, with a baby and without. She might write out the two scenarios. How will she feel when her friends are busy getting ready for the prom and she is stuck at home? When they are leaving home for college? Urge her to visit a local program for school-age mothers and talk to other teenagers who made this choice.

It may be easier for your daughter to sort out her feelings with a minister, a trusted relative, or a family counselor who doesn't have an emotional interest in her decision.

Keeping the Baby   If, after sorting out her feelings, she decides to keep and raise the baby, there are steps she should take to help minimize the disruptive consequences of early parenthood:

- *Stay in school.* The best thing a teenage mother can do for herself and her child is to complete high school and, if possible, go on to college. Without a diploma, the chances of establishing a secure family life are very slim. The penalty for dropping out of school can be minimum wages for the rest of her life. Pregnant teenagers and teenage mothers have a legal right to a high-school education. Some big-city school districts have special programs for such girls that include day-care for the baby.
- *Consider living at home with parents.* Studies show that most successful young mothers lived with their parents while they completed school. The young mothers would not have been able to graduate without their help. Conflicts over authority were common in these households. The question, Whose baby is this? was not resolved easily. In some cases, the teenage mother expected her mother to take charge, in effect abdicating her role as the baby's mother. In some, the mother/grandmother took charge uninvited, on the grounds that she knew more about babies than her daughter did. But in others, the teenage mother and new grandmother were able to establish a happy medium, with the young mother as apprentice and the grandmother as adviser. For

this arrangement to work, both generations must recognize that it is temporary and that the goal is to help the mother move toward independence. Young mothers who remain in their parents' household indefinitely remain dependent; in effect, they never grow up. Those who have to fight for their right to be mothers are likely to leave their parents' home in anger, and perhaps before they are ready.

Despite these qualifications, living with their parents (temporarily) creates fewer problems for teenage mothers than marrying the baby's father. The divorce rate for teenage marriages in general is high (about 60 percent); separation and divorce are even more likely if the couple gets married because the girl is pregnant. It's not difficult to see why: Giving up your dreams for the future, setting up house, getting a job, adjusting to a new marriage *and* a new baby, all ahead of schedule and at a time when most of your friends are enjoying more freedom than they ever had before, is bound to cause strain. The chances of a teenage family succeeding are better than average if the father has a steady income, but this is rarely the case. One of the biggest risks is that the couple will have another child, making plans to complete their educations all but impossible.

• *Obtain and use a reliable method of birth control.* Finally, successful teenage mothers are typically those who do not become pregnant again while they are completing their schooling and getting established in a job. Birth control is almost as important as education in shaping their futures.

Adoption The second option for a pregnant teenager is adoption. If a girl is opposed to abortion on moral or religious grounds, this may be the best choice. There are many more couples looking for a baby to adopt than there are babies available for adoption today. A teenager can be reasonably certain that her infant will be adopted, especially if the baby is Caucasian and healthy. (Unfortunately, the same cannot be said for black or hispanic babies, or for babies with physical or mental handicaps.) The girl might talk to her physician about arranging a private adoption or arrange for an interview with an adoption agency. In general, adoption through a licensed agency, where couples are carefully screened, is the safest route. Most agencies take the birth mother's background and ideas about child-rearing into account in selecting adoptive parents. Also, if the mother or child want to meet later in life, their whereabouts will be easier to trace. The infant will be placed with a couple who very much want a child and are able to give it the love and care a baby needs.

Although the final decision about adoption is not made until the baby is born, a girl who thinks this is what she wants to do should get in touch with an adoption agency early in her pregnancy. (Licensed agencies can be found through a physician, a minister or rabbi, Planned Parenthood, or the Yellow Pages.) If she is unhappy at home, or embarrassed about being pregnant, they will help her find a home where she can live with other girls in her situation during her pregnancy. They will advise her about legal and medical procedures, and many offer psychological counseling as well. If a girl is 18 or older, she does not need her parent's consent to put the baby up for adoption, but she will need the father's. Coping with the emotional and practical considerations will be much easier if her family and boyfriend support her.

A girl who decides to put her baby up for adoption should be warned that she is likely to have mixed emotions over the course of her pregnancy. Some days she will be convinced that she has made the right decision: "A baby deserves two parents and a stable home; I'm not old enough to care for a child; both our lives would be wrecked." But other days she may wonder how she can give up her own flesh and blood. Visiting a couple with an adopted child may help her to see parenthood as more than a biological relationship and reassure her that the baby will be loved as much as a "natural" child.

A girl who chooses adoption will also be responsible for the baby's health, and this means visiting an obstetrician regularly; abstaining from alcohol, cigarettes, and drugs, including most prescription and over-the-counter drugs; and eating a balanced diet, getting enough sleep, and generally taking good care of herself. For teenagers, who tend to take their health for granted, giving a baby a healthy start in life usually entails significant changes in life-style.

Abortion   The third option for a pregnant teenager is abortion: ending the pregnancy after conception has taken place but before the developing embryo or fetus is able to survive outside the mother's body. Few adults in our society are neutral on the subject of abortion, and chances are your daughter knows where you stand. The question is, How does *she* feel about this option? Federal law guarantees the female's right to decide whether to continue a pregnancy or to have an abortion by a licensed physician. In some states, a girl under the age of 18 is required to obtain parental consent. However, even in these states, she can request a confidential court hearing to determine whether she is mature enough to make this decision for herself. In other states, parental consent is not necessary. A Planned Parenthood or community health service clinic can tell you what the law is in your state.

A girl considering this option should know that the risks associated with an abortion are small, especially if the abortion is performed early in the pregnancy. The main danger for teenagers is that they may delay having an abortion because they haven't faced the fact that they are pregnant or are frightened by the procedure. A parent might point out that visiting a family planning clinic and talking to a counselor won't hurt; she can always change her mind. Taking her best friend along might make her feel more comfortable.

What exactly are the procedures? During the first three months of a pregnancy (counting from the day her last period started), the most common method of terminating a pregnancy is vacuum aspiration: inserting a blunt tube through the cervix and clearing the uterus through suction. This takes about fifteen minutes, requires only local anesthesia, and is performed on an outpatient basis. The girl may experience some menstrual-like cramps during the procedure and some bleeding and tiredness afterward. Most clinics recommend that the patient bring a friend and take a cab home. There is a slight risk of infection after this procedure, and patients are advised to take showers, not baths, use sanitary napkins, not tampons, and abstain from sexual intercourse for several weeks. A follow-up examination should be scheduled two to three weeks later.

Beginning in the fourth month, a two-part procedure called dilation and evacuation (D&E) is usually recommended. The first step is the insertion of slim rolls of material that gradually dilate the cervix. These are left in place for several hours or overnight. The second step is cleaning the uterus through a suction tube. This procedure can also be performed in a clinic, but may involve an overnight stay, may cause some pain and bleeding, and requires a longer recovery period (at least one to two hours). Because the pregnancy is farther along, there is a greater risk of infection, incomplete abortion, or perforation of the uterus.

By the fifth month, terminating a pregnancy through the vagina is no longer possible. An abortion at this stage requires hospitalization at least overnight. Drugs to induce miscarriage are injected into the uterus through the lower abdomen; the contractions that expel the fetus and placenta may begin from twelve to seventy-two hours later. The chances of complications are greater than with either of the earlier methods (though still less than those with full-term delivery). Late abortions are also substantially more expensive than early procedures. Abortions usually are not performed after the sixth month unless the mother's health is endangered.

No medical procedure is 100 percent risk-free. But if an abortion is performed early in the pregnancy at a reliable clinic and if the girl follows instructions for aftercare and has a checkup two to three weeks later, she should not experience problems at the time or in the future. (Repeated abortions, however, may increase the risk of miscarriage later, when she wants to have children.) The names of established abortion clinics can be obtained through your physician, Planned Parenthood, or the National Abortion Federation (NAF).

Most girls do not experience intense guilt, prolonged mourning, or any other psychological damage as the result of an abortion unless they were pressured into the decision. But nonjudgmental concern and support from parents can be especially important in helping the adolescent with her emotions.

Unless a girl has religious or moral objections to abortion, this is often the best decision for everyone involved. When a teenage girl becomes a mother, her own childhood is cut short, her hopes and ambitions (and perhaps those of the father) are postponed or abandoned, and the baby may suffer as a result. To be sure, there are exceptions; some teenage couples and their babies overcome these obstacles. But the stakes are high: The futures of three young people—mother, father, and baby—are on the line.

Whatever decision a girl makes, her next step should be to visit a family planning center and obtain reliable contraceptives. Having survived the trauma of a pregnancy, most teenagers vow they will never take risks again. But vows are not enough: The girl needs to be prepared.

Teenage Fathers

The pregnant girl is not the only one who needs love, forgiveness, and understanding in this situation. Often, the boy is as upset and confused as the girl is. The girl's parents may blame him for getting her pregnant and forbid her to speak to him again. His parents may blame him for being irresponsible. His friends may treat him as if he were a criminal or a hero ("macho-man"—"It's her problem, why are you upset?"). Hardly anyone stops to consider how *he* feels—and this includes researchers, who until recently paid little or no attention to teenage fathers. Everyone just assumed that most teenage mothers were single mothers because the boy walked away. In fact, studies show that many boys want to be involved, but the girls, often under pressure from their parents, send them away.

There are both legal and emotional reasons why the father should have a say in decisions about a pregnancy. No matter how young the father is, he is legally responsible for child support—from the baby's birth to age 18. (In Wisconsin, the law now requires the parents of a minor boy to contribute to child support.) If the mother refuses to identify the father, her child will not be eligible for veteran's or Social Security benefits, or for any inheritance. If she chooses adoption, the father's permission is required. Besides, it is his baby, too.

A teenage boy may want to be responsible but not know how. The pregnancy may be a painful reminder of his immaturity and the fact that he probably couldn't support a wife and child if he wanted to. He may feel angry at the girl for getting pregnant, even though he knows it was both their faults, and guilty for feeling angry. He may feel jealous of all the attention the girl is getting. He may be surprised and hurt that she doesn't want to see him any more. He may want "to do the right thing" by getting married.

The advice for girls considering marriage can also be applied to boys. The best thing he can do for his child is to complete his education. This may mean living with his parents and maintaining a visiting relationship with the mother and baby, with the idea of getting married in the future. Getting married now is risky, as we suggested earlier. But it might work *if* both sets of grandparents are willing and able to support the couple financially, *if* the grandparents can help with child care while the couple are completing their education, and *if* the couple postpone having another child until they have established their financial independence.

These difficult decisions can be avoided, of course, through abstinence or conscientious use of birth control.

RESOURCES

STDs

TELEPHONE HOTLINES (TOLL-FREE)

Public Health Service AIDS Hotline: 800-342-AIDS

National Sexually Transmitted Diseases Hotline/American Social Health Association: 800-227-8922

Teens Teaching Teens AIDS Prevention: 800-234-TEEN. The volunteers who answer this hotline are teenagers themselves. For teenagers who prefer talking to a peer, this is the number to call. This group also publishes a booklet on starting a local chapter. Call for information.

INFORMATION SOURCES

U.S. Public Health Service Public Affairs Office
Hubert H. Humphrey Building
Room 725-H
200 Independence Avenue, S.W.
Washington, DC 20201

American Red Cross AIDS Education Center
1730 D Street, N.W.
Washington, DC 20006

Pregnancy

The National Abortion Federation provides referrals to member clinics in your area and publishes a free booklet, *How to Choose an Abortion Clinic.* Call their toll-free hotline, 800-772-9100, or write to

National Abortion Federation
900 Pennsylvania Avenue, S.E.
Washington, DC 20003

CHAPTER 13

Drug and Alcohol Use in High School

*I*n chapter 6, we looked at myths and facts about alcohol, cigarettes, and marijuana. In this chapter, we look more closely at these and other drugs, discuss the importance of establishing rules about drug and alcohol use, and suggest steps to take if you suspect that your adolescent has used or abused drugs or alcohol.

In high school, your adolescent is likely to be offered one or more of the drugs described on pages 276—282. It's important that you and your teenager know what these substances are and what their effects can be.

ESTABLISHING A POLICY ON DRUGS AND ALCOHOL

Although the 16- or 17-year-old may seem mature in many ways, the high-school student is still too young—emotionally as well as legally—for beer parties at the beach, cocktails at a nightclub, or sharing a bottle of wine with friends. Using illegal drugs is risky at any age and especially for a young person who is still growing and maturing. *All drugs, including alcohol, should be declared off-limits for the teenager,* at least until after high-school graduation.

Studies show that one of the best predictors of alcohol and drug use in adolescence is the extent to which adolescents believe their parents tolerate these activities, so the message you send your adolescent about drug and alcohol use—even occasional use

—is important. For this reason we encourage parents to send a clear and consistent message to their high-school-age child: *No drugs, no alcohol, no exceptions*. If this is the méssage your adolescent hears, he will be less likely to get into situations where alcohol and drugs are present, and more likely to walk away from situations in which they are. If the message you send is mixed (e.g., alcohol is okay, but marijuana is not; it's okay to drink on some occasions but not others), you are increasing the likelihood that your adolescent will experiment with alcohol or marijuana, or become an occasional or even a frequent user.

At the same time, parents must face facts. The older teenager will be in many more situations where her friends are drinking. In early adolescence, drug use of any kind is usually secretive (modern variations on the old stolen cigarettes behind the garage). In middle and late adolescence, drinking is often out in the open. So are cigarettes and, in some cases, marijuana. Teenagers are going more places on their own. Even "nice" kids participate.

We do not believe that parents should fly into a rage if they discover that their son has had a beer with his buddies or their daughter tried a joint once at a party. Surveys indicate that nearly all teenagers will try alcohol before graduating from high school and that a majority of today's adolescents will try marijuana once before the end of their senior year. There is no evidence that experiments with alcohol or marijuana during high school inevitably lead to patterns of alcohol or drug dependence in adolescence or later, in adulthood. While these statistics certainly do not justify alcohol and marijuana use among teenagers, they should help to put experimentation with these substances into perspective. Experimenting with alcohol or marijuana merits a response from you, but it is important that your response distinguish between experimentation and regular or frequent use, and between these substances and other, more serious and more dangerous ones.

There is another reason not to be too heavy-handed. Many parents know adults who have used (or use) alcohol or marijuana in moderation with no ill effects on themselves or their offspring. Likewise, your adolescent may know teenagers who drink or smoke marijuana occasionally but have not become "alkies" or "potheads." If you want to discourage use of alcohol or marijuana, you should emphasize the real reasons for avoiding them (it's illegal; it's bad for your health; it impairs your coordination and judgment; you don't know what you're smoking), not false reasons (you'll get hooked; it will lead to harder drugs; you'll wind up in jail). Scare tactics will only convince the teenager you don't know what you're talking about.

In stating your drug policy, be *firm and reasonable*. Explain why you will not permit the teenager to drink or use drugs. For example:

"Drinking is still illegal at your age."

"I worry about your safety. So many teenagers get into accidents when they've been drinking. I want you to grow up."

"You are still growing, and your mind and body are still developing. You take care of your health in other ways. Using alcohol and drugs aren't healthy things to do."

"Our family doesn't drink, and while you are still living with us, we expect you to follow our rules."

Encourage the teenager to supply reasons of his own. "Why do you think we are asking you not to drink?" "What do you think is wrong with using marijuana?" Be clear about what the penalties will be for breaking the rules. And be sure to praise the adolescent who abstains.

Talking about Alcohol

It's a good idea to discuss responsible drinking with your teenager—as preparation for the young person's adult years and insurance against his having his own ideas about what is acceptable. Responsible drinkers

- Are *occasional* drinkers. They consume alcohol infrequently—not every weekend, not at every party, and certainly not every day.
- Select the *right time and place* to consume alcohol. They may drink at a party or with friends on weekends, but never at work, on school days, or when they are planning to engage in a potentially dangerous activity, such as boating.
- Are *social* drinkers. They drink with friends or family, not when they are alone and bored or blue, and not before they go out, to "build up their courage."
- *Regulate the amount* they drink (sipping, not gulping a drink, and eating while they drink) so that they do not get drunk.

- *Never mix alcohol with other drugs.* This applies not only to marijuana and other illegal drugs, but also to many prescription drugs (such as Valium) and over-the-counter drugs (such as cold or allergy medicines).
- Drink for the *right reasons*—because they like the taste or to enhance good feelings—not to drown their troubles, frustrations, or anger or to pick themselves up when they are feeling down.
- *Do not drink and drive.* This is one of the most important messages to communicate to teenagers.

Many parents avoid discussing drinking and driving because they believe that this topic is covered implicitly, when an alcohol-free policy is laid down. But drinking and driving is so dangerous that it *must* be handled *explicitly*. Teenagers must be told in no uncertain terms *"Never drive when you've been drinking."* Emphasize that you are not talking just about drunken driving but about *any* drinking and driving. An adult who has had more than two drinks in two hours isn't 100 percent safe behind the wheel of a car; a teenager, who has less experience with both driving and alcohol, doesn't know when he or she has had too much. Teenagers shouldn't drink and drive, period. A second rule is *"Never accept a ride with people who have been drinking,"* no matter how sober they think they are.

Having set these rules, you should anticipate occasions when the teenager doesn't plan to drink but does. Here are some ways to handle this:

- *Mothers Against Drunk Driving* (MADD, an organization founded by a mother whose teenager was killed in an accident involving alcohol) recommends that parents make a contract with their teenagers: "If you are not in shape to drive, you can call home at any hour and we will come and pick you up, *no questions asked.*" In other words, you will waive your penalties for drinking too much or staying out too late if the teenager demonstrates the good sense to call you.
- Provide the teenager with the number of a reliable cab service and leave twenty dollars in the front hall for emergencies. Again, the teenager will not be punished if he recognizes that driving would be a mistake.
- *Students Against Drunk Driving* (SADD) looks at this problem from a teenager's point of view. To avoid embarrassment in front of their parents, SADD advises teens who are going out

in a group to designate one person, who will not drink any-thing that night, to be the driver. Alternatively, teenagers who are not going out that night but have access to a car can vol-unteer to chauffeur classmates who have been drinking.

· In some communities, parents take turns being the designated driver for Saturday nights, again no questions asked.

· If there is a party at your house and you suspect that one or more teenagers has had more than a few beers, do not hesitate to take away their keys, arrange for someone who hasn't been drinking to drive them home, drive them yourself, or call their parents. (If the teenager were to get into an accident, you could be held liable, even if you didn't supply the beer.)

The same rules apply to adults. You can't expect a teenager to take the dangers of drinking and driving seriously if you stag-ger out of the car yourself some nights, or if you allow a friend who has had one too many to drive home.

Parents cannot overemphasize the dangers of drinking and driving. When your teenager gets a driver's license, establish the ground rules and the penalties for breaking them: If the teenager drives when he has been drinking, you will confiscate his license for a month, two months, or even six months, depending on the incident; if she doesn't call you or find another ride when her date is drunk, she won't be allowed to go out with that boy for a month; ditto for a boy with older friends who drive. Make sure teenagers understand what losing their license means. If there's a party, they will either have to hitch a ride with friends, depend on you, spend their allowance on cab fare, walk, or stay home. You should also point out that if the teenager is stopped by the police when she has been drinking, she may lose her license for as long as a year (depending on local laws), her insurance rates will be raised, and you will expect her to pay the increase.

DRUG USE AND ABUSE: HOW TO SPOT A DRUG PROBLEM

Your daughter has a group of friends over to watch a video; the next morning you find a half-empty bottle of vodka in the TV room. Your son spends most of his time in his room; the smell of incense creeps through the house; you're sure he's smoking pot. You find a package of rolling papers in your daughter's wastebasket. Your son comes home from a party smashed. Beers keep disappearing from your refrigerator. What should you do?

Don't Overreact. Many teenagers experiment with drugs in the same spirit that they experiment with clothing styles and political views. Experimentation does not necessarily mean a teenager is becoming a "user." Nor does it mean that your son is defying your authority; he is at an age where he wants to find out for himself how alcohol tastes and smoking pot feels. If you blow up at the slightest indication that a teenager tried a drug, your teenager will see you as dictatorial.

Suppose you find evidence that the adolescent has been drinking or has tried marijuana. If this is the first occasion, try to express concern without angry accusations, labeling, or name-calling. Ask what happened and listen to what the teenager feels about the incident. It's possible your son got drunk on screwdrivers before he realized how strong they were. He may be upset about losing control and want your help in setting limits. Perhaps your daughter's friends brought the vodka to her party and she didn't know how to ask them not to drink in her house. She may need your help in dealing with peer pressure. How can she say "not in my house" without being a drag? The rolling papers in her wastebasket may belong to her older sister, and she doesn't want to snitch, but she is worried about her sister. Your son may, indeed, be smoking pot in his room (and waiting to see what you're going to do) or drinking daily (and thinking you won't notice).

Patterns of Drug Use

Your next step depends on which drug or drugs the teenager is using, how often, and under what circumstances. Although there are no set patterns, it is possible to distinguish different levels of teenage drug use.

• *Nonusers* have never tried drugs and never plan to. They don't like the idea of polluting their bodies or confusing their minds.

• *Experimenters* may try drugs once or twice for kicks but decide they don't like the effects. Or they may take a token sip or puff for show at a party, but no more. They rarely try anything "harder" than alcohol or marijuana and don't particularly like either one.

• *Recreational users* can take or leave drugs. They may have a few drinks or share a joint at a weekend party, but do not party every weekend. They generally don't purchase drugs themselves and do not (intentionally) get drunk or stoned. They are not interested in anything stronger than alcohol or marijuana. The main difference between a teenage recreational user and an adult social drinker is that many teenagers see little or no difference between alcohol and marijuana.

• *Regular users* have shifted from passively accepting to actively seeking drugs. They party most weekends; frequently get drunk or stoned; prefer friends and activities they associate with getting high; and buy their own. They are willing to try other drugs (uppers, downers, cocaine). But they still care about their reputation and their parents' approval. They limit drug use to weekends and vacations, keep up their grades, and make a point of never missing a class or athletic practice. This "dual life-style" means that they sometimes lie to their parents about where they've been and what they did.

• *Abusers* begin by getting drunk or stoned almost every weekend and end by extending the "weekend" to weekday afternoons and evenings. They use drugs as medication (to gain relief from stress, build up their self-confidence) and often get high by themselves. Drugs organize their lives. They lose interest in activities they used to enjoy, stop trying in school, drop (or are dropped by) their straight friends, and fight with their parents. Most use harder drugs than alcohol or marijuana, or combinations of drugs, to get high. To pay for their high, they may steal from their parents or sell drugs to their peers. Abusers lie to themselves as well as to others: Most deny that they have a problem and tell themselves that they could always stop if they wanted to.

• *Alcoholics/addicts* live for drugs. They use drugs, not to feel good or high, but just to feel normal. They don't just take drugs, they find ways to get immediate effects (shooting up, smoking crack). Alcoholics and addicts stop caring about how they look or what other people think; their health deteriorates; if they try to stop drugs without help, they experience severe withdrawal symptoms.

Different levels of drug use call for different responses.

Nonusers should not be taken for granted; they deserve applause.

In our view, experimentation is not a cause for serious con-

DANGER SIGNS

DRUGS AND DRUG PARAPHERNALIA

- Possession of pipes, rolling papers, small decongestant bottles, small butane torches, or other drug-related items
- Possession or evidence of drugs, such as butts, seeds, or leaves in ashtrays or clothing pockets or unidentified pills or powders in plastic bags
- Odor of drugs or use of cover-ups (incense, sprays)

IDENTIFICATION WITH DRUG CULTURE

- Possession of drug-related magazines, slogans on clothing
- Preoccupation with drugs in conversations and jokes
- Hostility in discussing drugs

SIGNS OF PHYSICAL DETERIORATION

- Memory lapses, short attention span, difficulty concentrating
- Poor physical coordination, slurred and incoherent speech (incomplete sentences, forgotten thoughts, bizarre statements)
- Unhealthy appearance; changes in appetite and weight
- Bloodshot eyes, dilated pupils, runny nose, hacking cough, increased susceptibility to colds and infections
- Changes in activity levels (periods of lethargy and fatigue and/or periods of hyperactivity)

DRAMATIC CHANGES IN SCHOOL PERFORMANCE

- Distinct downward turn in grades, not just from *C*s to *F*s, but also from *A*s and *B*s to *C*s; assignments not completed
- Increased absenteeism or tardiness

CHANGES IN BEHAVIOR

- Chronic dishonesty (lying, stealing, cheating); trouble with police
- Changes in friends, evasiveness in talking about new ones
- Possession of large amounts of money
- Increasing and inappropriate anger, hostility, irritability, secretiveness
- Mood swings—from overly happy and gregarious to morose and withdrawn
- Reduced motivation, self-discipline, self-esteem
- Indifference to hygiene and grooming
- Loss of interest in favorite extracurricular activities and hobbies

cern, especially if the teenager "confesses" and seems generally willing to talk with you about drugs. We should note, however, that some alcoholics and addicts say they were hooked the first time they tried drugs. Something "clicked," and they never looked back. There is no reliable, scientific way to test these memories. But it is *possible* that some individuals have an instant, uncontrollable reaction to drugs. There is clear evidence that alcoholism runs in families. If this is the case in your family, alert the teenager to the possibility that he or she may be one of those people who can't handle alcohol, in any amount, at any age.

How you react to recreational use of alcohol depends on your family's personal rules and values. If you believe that teenagers should not drink under any circumstances, as we advise, explain why you feel as you do and enforce the rules and penalties you have established. If you feel recreational drinking is acceptable for older teens, review the principles of responsible drinking and be clear that you will impose strict penalties for irresponsible behavior. Permitting recreational use of marijuana is not advisable, for both legal and health reasons. And recreational use of cocaine (especially, but not exclusively, crack) can lead to addiction sooner than the adolescent realizes. This drug should be banned.

Regular use of drugs, drug abuse, and addiction clearly are cause for concern. The problem here is that teenagers who are abusing drugs are highly unlikely to tell their parents that they have a problem. How can you know? A list of the danger signs is given on page 271. Some of the symptoms of drug use overlap with symptoms of other problems, such as depression, (see chapter 8). If three or more of the danger signs describe your teenager, and you have seen or overheard evidence of drug use (drugs and drug paraphernalia), it is time to investigate.

WHAT TO DO IF YOUR TEENAGER HAS A PROBLEM

The first rule for dealing with a teenage drug problem is: Don't pretend that nothing is wrong. This may sound like a contradiction of the advice we gave earlier (Don't overreact). But it's important for parents to distinguish between occasional, social use of alcohol and experimentation with marijuana, and regular, heavy use of these and/or harder drugs. Again, see Danger Signs.

When parents are confronted with evidence that their child has a drug problem (that is, three or more danger signs), the most common reaction is not anger or panic or sorrow; it's denial. They ignore changes for the worse in the child's behavior ("He's going through a phase") and accept the lamest excuses ("My teachers don't like me"; "I was only keeping drugs for a friend"). If someone outside the immediate family (a grandparent, teacher, or even the police) suggests their child has a drug problem, the parents become indignant. They make up alibis when the teenager doesn't show up at work or can't make it to school. They tell themselves "All kids do it" or "At least my teenager isn't _____" (fill in the blank). They blame themselves or their spouse ("I should have been stricter"; "You never spend any time with her"). They would rather believe almost anything (the teenager is sick, suffering from a learning disability, or even mentally ill) than face the fact that their teenager has a drug problem. By pretending that nothing is wrong, parents slip into the role of "enabler." Alcoholics Anonymous coined this term to describe a family member who unconsciously enables an alcoholic to continue drinking by protecting him or her from the consequences.

The reason parents go to such lengths to deny that their child has a drug problem is clear: Recognizing the problem makes them feel that they have failed as parents. In the words of one mother, "I wanted to be a good parent, not a failure. I wanted her to be a happy kid, not a kid with a problem like this." But *parents do not make kids take drugs*. It was the teenager, not the parent, who decided to drink or get stoned or shoot up. And he made this decision of his own free will, knowing that alcohol and drugs can be dangerous, that he was crossing the line from acceptable to disreputable behavior, that he would probably get in trouble at home, at school, and perhaps with the law, and that he might hurt the people who love him. Perhaps you and the teenager did not have the best relationship in the world, your family life wasn't as warm and fun-loving as the Cosbys', your child had difficulty with schoolwork and problems making friends. But right now the cause of his problem is drugs. The first step toward helping the teenager become a "happy kid" again is recognizing that it is your teenager who has a problem, and the problem is drugs.

Whether you try to handle the problem yourself or seek professional help depends on how deeply involved the teenager is with alcohol and/or drugs.

Handling the Problem Yourself

If the teenager acknowledges that she is using drugs you consider off-limits or drinking frequently, and you don't think she is psychologically or physically dependent on drugs yet, you may be able to handle the problem yourself. You should explain why you are concerned ("You're playing with dangerous drugs"; "Your drinking is becoming a problem") and what you expect ("This must stop, now"). If you catch the problem very early, you may be able to negotiate (see chapter 2). Your contract should state that the teenager will not use any drugs under any circumstances, not spend time with friends who are using drugs or go places where others will be using drugs, and keep you informed of her whereabouts and activities. As in all negotiations, ask her what she thinks the consequences of her drinking or drug use should be, in terms of reduced privileges. This contract should be reviewed weekly.

When a teenager has a drug problem, however, negotiation may not be possible. She may abide by the contract for a week or two but slip at the first temptation and/or lie about her behavior. Drug problems are one case where you very likely will have to lay down the law. Remind the teenager that health and safety are not negotiable. The teenager has shown she can't set responsible limits for herself; you will have to set them for her. These might include the following:

- *Suspending driving privileges* until she has been drug-free for several months. This is a *must*.
- *Cutting her allowance* to a bare minimum and requiring her to deposit all earnings from a job and cash gifts in a bank account and to get your permission when she wants to make a withdrawal.
- *Monitoring her activities*. Set up a schedule for her afternoons and weekends that states where she is going, what she is doing, with whom, and when she will be home. Any changes in the schedule have to be cleared with you in advance. Ideally, she should not be home alone, with nothing in particular to do, for the next few months.
- *Removing temptations to use drugs*. If the teenager exercised self-control during the week but frequently got blasted at weekend

parties, ban parties for at least a month (but try to provide substitute activities that do not recall drinking, such as long hikes with the family or redecorating her room). After a month, allow her to have a small party at your house or to go to a party at the home of someone you know, with the understanding that she will not drink or use any other drug and will abide by your curfew. Similarly, if she was drinking at home, remove or lock up all liquor. If she was smoking pot in her room, institute an open door policy.

· *Changing friends.* If you know that a boy she was dating, one particular friend, a group of friends, or her co-workers introduced her to drugs or encouraged her to drink, declare them off-limits. At the same time, make a list of straight friends she is permitted to see.

· *Repairing damage.* If her schoolwork has fallen off, insist that she bring her grades up to her previous level before she is granted some of the privileges you have taken away. If she "borrowed" (stole) money from you to buy drugs, she should be required to pay you back.

· *Imposing strict penalties.* If she breaks any of these rules, she will have to pay. Be specific, and don't accept excuses: If she spends an afternoon with people who are off-limits, she will not be allowed to make or receive phone calls after 5 P.M. for two weeks; if she says she is going to a friend's house but you learn she went to a party, she will have to give something she prizes (her stereo, a piece of jewelry) to charity; and so on.

Expect the teenager to be angry and resentful at first. Just remind her (and yourself) that you aren't trying to wreck her life, you are trying to save it.

The teenager should not be the only member of the family who is held to high standards during this period. These strategies are more likely to be effective if everyone in the family takes a vow to be drug-free. This means no alcohol use by minority-age kids; no smoking by minority-age kids; no regular, nightly use of alcohol by adults; no intoxication (getting drunk) by adults; no use of illegal drugs by anyone (including parents' use of marijuana); no misuse of prescription or over-the-counter drugs; and no use of drugs to lose weight, go to sleep, wake up, or relax (that is, no amphetamines, sleeping pills, stimulants, or tranquilizers in the medicine cabinet). If you have other children, be sure to discuss the problem with them. Young people often report that they were "turned on" for the first time by an older sibling.

Getting Professional Help

If you have reason to believe the teenager is abusing drugs or if, after a month or two, your own efforts fail, you should seek professional help—through your physician, a school counselor, or one of the organizations listed in the following Resources. (See also Getting Professional Help, in Chapter 2.) In some cases, a drug counselor will recommend that the adolescent attend daily sessions of a special program for teenage drug abusers (during and/or after school hours), or that the teenager receive residential (in-patient) treatment at a drug clinic, leaving home and school for a period of weeks or even months. These may seem like drastic measures, but the teenager's future is at stake. Check the program's reputation with your physician, school counselors, and others who have experience with chemically dependent adolescents. Be prepared for the teenager to resist getting help, but don't give up. If a teenage drug problem is detected and treated early, the chances are good that your adolescent can become a healthy, happy kid again.

MAJOR DRUGS: THEIR USES AND EFFECTS

Habituation refers to psychological dependence on a drug: The user feels psychologically unprotected and vulnerable without it. *Addiction* refers to physiological dependence on a drug: The user feels sick without it (presumably because the drug has altered the body's biochemistry in some way). *Tolerance* refers to dosage: The longer the drug is used, the more is needed to obtain the original effects. The ratings given here are averages. Individuals vary in their response to drugs. For example, some people become addicted to alcohol but others do not, and some people can tolerate much larger amounts than others without becoming drunk, hung over, or addicted.

DEPRESSANTS

ALCOHOL
(beer, wine, distilled spirits)

How taken: swallowed

Short-term effects of average amount: relaxation, breakdown of inhibitions, euphoria, depression, decreased alertness (duration 2–4 hours)

Short-term effects of large amount: stupor, nausea, unconsciousness, hangover, death

Risk of dependence:
- Habituation: high
- Addiction: moderate
- Tolerance: yes

Long-term effects of continued excessive use: obesity, impotence, psychosis, ulcers, malnutrition, liver and brain damage, delirium tremens, death

Legal restrictions and penalties: Federal law restricts the advertising of distilled spirits; state and local laws prohibit sale to minors.

BARBITURATES ("DOWNERS")
(chloral hydrate, Doridan, Nembutal, Phenobarbital, Seconal)

How taken: swallowed

Short-term effects of average amount: relaxation, euphoria, decreased alertness, drowsiness, impaired coordination, sleep (duration 4–8 hours)

Short-term effects of large amount: slurred speech, stupor, hangover, death

Risk of dependence:
- Habituation: high
- Addiction: high
- Tolerance: yes

Long-term effects of continued excessive use: sleepiness, confusion, irritability, severe withdrawal sickness

Legal restrictions and penalties: Possession is legal only if prescribed.

INHALANTS
(aerosols, airplane glue, amyl nitrite, nitrous oxide)

How taken: inhaled

Short-term effects of average amount: relaxation, euphoria, impaired coordination (duration 1–3 hours)

Short-term effects of large amount: stupor, death

Risk of dependence:
- Habituation: high
- Addiction: none
- Tolerance: possibly

Long-term effects of continued excessive use: hallucinations; liver, kidney, bone marrow, and brain damage; death

Legal restrictions and penalties: There are no restrictions, except for amyl nitrite and nitrous oxide, which require prescriptions.

NARCOTICS
(codeine, Demerol, heroin, methadone, morphine, opium, Percodan)

How taken: swallowed, injected, inhaled, or sniffed

Short-term effects of average amount: relaxation, relief of pain and anxiety, decreased alertness, euphoria, hallucinations (duration 4 hours)

Short-term effects of large amount: stupor, death

Risk of dependence:
- Habituation: high
- Addiction: high
- Tolerance: yes

Long-term effects of continued excessive use: lethargy, constipation, weight loss, temporary sterility and impotence, withdrawal sickness; risk of infection with AIDS if user shares needle

Legal restrictions and penalties: There is no legal use of heroin; other narcotics may be used in prescription drugs.

TRANQUILIZERS
(Valium, Librium, Miltown/Equanil, Thorazine)

How taken: swallowed

Short-term effects of average amount: relief of anxiety and tension, suppression of hallucinations and aggression, sleep (duration 12–24 hours); effects amplified when combined with alcohol

Short-term effects of large amount: drowsiness, blurred vision, dizziness, slurred speech, allergic reaction, stupor; the combination of Valium and alcohol may cause coma and death

Risk of dependence:
- Habituation: moderate
- Addiction: none for Thorazine; high for Valium; moderate for others
- Tolerance: yes

Long-term effects of continued excessive use: destruction of red blood cells, jaundice, coma, death

Legal restrictions and penalties: Possession is illegal unless prescribed.

P S Y C H E D E L I C S

CANNABIS
(marijuana ["grass"], hashish, THC)

How taken: smoked, swallowed, injected

Short-term effects of average amount: relaxation, breakdown of inhibitions, alteration of perceptions, euphoria, increased appetite, impaired coordination (duration 2–4 hours)

Short-term effects of large amount: trancelike states, panic, stupor

Risk of dependence:
- Habituation: high
- Addiction: moderate
- Tolerance: yes

Long-term effects of continued excessive use: not entirely known; may include anxiety, panic, paranoia, psychosis, infertility

Legal restrictions and penalties: All are illegal. Penalties for sale or possession vary according to state and local law.

HALLUCINOGENS
(DMT, LSD ["acid"], mescaline, psilocybin ["PBC"], scopolamine, STP)

How taken: swallowed, inhaled, injected, sniffed

Short-term effects of average amount: perceptual changes, especially visual; increased energy; hallucinations; panic (duration highly variable)

Short-term effects of large amount: anxiety, hallucinations, psychosis, exhaustion, tremors, vomiting, panic

Risk of dependence:
- Habituation: low
- Addiction: none
- Tolerance: yes

Long-term effects of continued excessive use: increased delusions and panic, psychosis

Legal restrictions and penalties: All are illegal.

S T I M U L A N T S

AMPHETAMINES ("UPPERS")
(Benzedrine, Dexedrine, Methadrine, Preludin)

How taken: swallowed, injected

Short-term effects of average amount: increased alertness, excitation, euphoria, decreased appetite (duration 4–8 hours)

Short-term effects of large amount: restlessness, rapid speech, irritability, insomnia, stomach disorders, convulsions

Risk of dependence:
- Habituation: high
- Addiction: high
- Tolerance: yes

Long-term effects of continued excessive use: insomnia, excitability, skin disorders, malnutrition, delusions, hallucinations, psychosis

Legal restrictions and penalties: All are legal only if prescribed.

ANTIDEPRESSANTS
(Elavil, Ritalin, Tofranil)

How taken: swallowed, injected

Short-term effects of average amount: relief of anxiety and depression, temporary impotence (duration 12–24 hours)

Short-term effects of large amount: nausea, hypertension, weight loss, insomnia

Risk of dependence:
- Habituation: low
- Addiction: none
- Tolerance: yes for Ritalin only

Long-term effects of continued excessive use: stupor, coma, convulsions, congestive heart failure, damage to liver and white blood cells, death

Legal restrictions and penalties: All are legal only if prescribed.

CAFFEINE
(coffee, cola, tea, NoDoz)

How taken: swallowed

Short-term effects of average amount: increased alertness (duration 2–4 hours)

Short-term effects of large amount: restlessness, upset stomach, insomnia

Risk of dependence:
- Habituation: high
- Addiction: yes
- Tolerance: yes

Long-term effects of continued excessive use: restlessness, irritability, insomnia, stomach disorders

Legal restrictions and penalties: none

COCAINE
(coke, crack)

How taken: sniffed, injected, smoked

Short-term effects of average amount: feelings of self-confidence and power, intense exhilaration (duration 4 hours)

Short-term effects of large amount: irritability, depression, psychosis, heart failure, fever, respiratory collapse, death

Risk of dependence:
- Habituation: high
- Addiction: high
- Tolerance: yes

Long-term effects of continued excessive use: damage to nasal septum and blood vessels, impotence, anxiety, depression, psychosis, heart ailments; damage to lungs if smoked; risk of infection with AIDS if injected with shared needle

Legal restrictions and penalties: Cocaine is illegal except when used as local anesthetic by a physician.

NICOTINE
(cigarettes, cigars, pipes, snuff)

How taken: smoked, sniffed

Short-term effects of average amount: relaxation, constriction of blood vessels (duration ¼–½ hour)

Short-term effects of large amount: headache, loss of appetite, nausea

Risk of dependence:
- Habituation: high
- Addiction: high
- Tolerance: yes

Long-term effects of continued excessive use: impaired breathing, heart and lung disease, cancer, death

Legal restrictions and penalties: Federal law restricts advertising; state and local laws prohibit sale to minors.

RESOURCES

The following organizations publish information and/or answer questions about alcohol and drugs.

General Information

The American Council for Drug Education
5820 Hubbard Drive
Rockville, MD 20852

American Lung Association
1740 Broadway
New York, NY 10019

National Clearinghouse for Alcohol Information
1776 Jefferson Street, 4th floor
Rockville, MD 20852

National Clearinghouse for Drug Abuse Information
Room 10A56, Parklawn Building
5600 Fishers Lane
Rockville, MD 20857

National Council on Alcoholism
733 Third Avenue
New York, NY 10017

Parent Organizations

Families in Action
Suite 300
3845 North Druid Hills Road
Decatur, GA 30333
404-325-5799

FIA publishes a manual, *How to Form a Families in Action Group in Your Community.*

Mothers Against Drunk Driving (MADD)
P.O. Box 18200
Fort Worth, TX 76118

National Federation of Parents for Drug-Free Youth (NFP)
Suite 200
8730 Georgia Avenue
Silver Spring, MD 20910
800-544-KIDS

A membership, costing $15 a year, includes educational brochures for parents and teens and a quarterly newsletter. Other information available.

Parents Resource Institute on Drug Education (PRIDE)
Suite 1216
100 Edgewood Avenue
Atlanta, GA 30303
800-241-9746

PRIDE publishes a quarterly newsletter and has a library, films, and printed materials.

Self-Help Groups

Write to these organizations, or look for local chapters in your Yellow Pages.

Alcoholics Anonymous World Services
Box 459, Grand Central Station
New York, NY 10163

Al-Anon and Alateen
AFG, Inc.
P.O. Box 862, Midtown Station
New York, NY 10018

Narcotics Anonymous World Services Office, Inc.
P.O. Box 622
Sun Valley, CA 91352

Hotlines

Alcohol and Drug Helpline: 800-252-6465

Clearinghouse Prevention Line: 800-336-4797

Cocaine (and crack): 800-COCAINE and 800-662-HELP

"Just Say No": 800-258-2766

NFP Drug Information Line: 800-544-KIDS

NIDA Prevention Information Line: 800-638-2045

PRIDE Drug Information Hotline: 800-241-9746

PSYCHOLOGICAL HEALTH AND DEVELOPMENT

CHAPTER 14

The Search for Identity

*I*dentity becomes a central concern in middle adolescence, for a variety of overlapping reasons. Puberty makes adolescents acutely aware of change. Looking in the mirror, the adolescent knows he is no longer the child he used to be—but not what sort of adult he will become. Sexual awakening invites a new type of intimate relationship with members of the opposite sex, unlike any the adolescent has known before. Preparing for adulthood is no longer a game. Decisions about education that will have long-term consequences (especially, whether to go to college and, if so, where) will have to be made in the near future. The array of occupations and life-styles available to adults in our society is vast. How can a teenager choose? Finally, teenagers have the intellectual capacity to reflect on themselves and their future. They can imagine being someone other than who they are now and living a life that is quite different from that of their parents or the one their parents imagine for them. They are also aware that their parents and peers see them in different lights; that they behave differently in different situations; and that how they appear to others doesn't always reflect how they feel inside.

The challenge for adolescents is to assemble these different pieces of the self into a working whole that serves both the self and society. They must connect the skills and talents they developed in childhood to realistic adult goals; reconcile their private images of themselves with what other people see in them and expect from them. They need to feel unique and special, on the one hand, and to belong or fit in, on the other.

A period of exploration, of trying on different roles and identities, is a necessary part of this process. Adolescents need a moratorium—a time out, when they are relatively free from the kinds of adult responsibilities and obligations that restrict experimentation and can investigate possible futures without making irrevocable decisions. Ideally, exploration will lead to commitment. The young person has achieved an identity when he or she is able to make at least tentative commitments to an occupation, a lifestyle, a sexual orientation, and to political and religious beliefs.

TRYING ON IDENTITIES

For most adolescents, the development of identity is a gradual, cumulative, and relatively peaceful process that begins in early adolescence and continues into young adulthood. Most adolescents are able to "find themselves" without losing the values and standards they acquired in childhood; to "get it together" without getting into trouble. Only a minority of adolescents experience a full-blown identity crisis. Nevertheless, many go through spells of brooding, indecision, and self-doubt. Although sometimes painful, this self-searching is normal, healthy, and desirable. An adolescent who never questions what she is taught, never wonders where she is headed, and never explores different identities is likely to be inflexible, dogmatic, and overbearing—or shallow, conforming, and other-directed—as an adult.

In early adolescence the search for identity often leads to overidentification with peers, clannishness, and conformity. The youth culture provides a ready-made identity that sets the new adolescent apart from his former identity as a child and from his identification with his parents. For a time, the adolescent may become a stereotypical teenager.

If early adolescence is a time for distinguishing oneself from one's parents, middle adolescence is a time for distinguishing oneself from the crowd. The quest for identity now takes the form of exploration and experimentation. The teenager tries on a variety of different political attitudes, religious persuasions, occupational commitments, and romantic involvements. At the time, these tentative identities have an all-or-nothing, do-or-die quality. Today's political cause will change the world; today's boy- or girlfriend is the one and only. In fact, they are poses, and the adolescent may change his plans and passions almost as often as he changes clothes.

In late adolescence and young adulthood the search becomes more introspective ("Who am I *really*?" "What do I believe?" "What do I want in life?") and also more pragmatic ("How can I achieve my goals?" "Where am I willing to compromise?"). Typically this is a period of "de-illusionment" (though not necessarily disillusionment). The young person must give up the childlike faith that he can be or do anything he wants for a more realistic assessment of his capabilities and opportunities. He must also face the fact that settling on one direction means abandoning others, at least temporarily.

What should parents expect during the high-school years? Many adolescents test themselves (and others) by

• *Changing interests, plans, and friends.* Commitments made at this stage are tentative, with no strings attached. A girl who has taken ballet classes for years may suddenly decide that this phase of her life is over. Often-expressed plans to become an architect may be displaced by a newfound interest in poetry. Two best friends may drift apart as one seeks identification with the jock crowd and the other with the theater group.

• *Obsessing about appearances.* To the adolescent who is exploring different social roles, looking the part may seem all-important. The teenager may suddenly develop mannerisms that seem phony and affected, such as changing the spelling of his name or adopting a new accent and vocabulary. Or he may dress in ways that seem bizarre to you but are vital to his fragile identity-of-the-moment.

• *Falling in love.* As psychoanalyst Erik Erikson has pointed out, sex is not the only, or even the most important, motive for teenage romance: "To a considerable extent, adolescent love is an attempt to arrive at a definition of one's identity by projecting one's diffuse [self-image] on another and by seeing it thus reflected and gradually clarified. This is why so much of young love is conversation."

• *Taking up causes.* Campaigning to save the whales, raising money for public television, walkathons for the March of Dimes, and other causes give teenagers both the feeling of being special and important and the feeling of belonging to a group. The teenager can stand out *with* a crowd. Devotion to causes may be motivated as much by the desire to be somebody notable as by interest in the cause.

• *Doing "nothing."* Some of the most important experiments in identity take place in fantasy and daydreams—imagining what different social roles and identities would be like, pondering one's place in society, and thinking about relationships with friends, family members, and teachers. Doing "nothing" (listening to music, fooling around with the family dog, staring into space) can be valuable. A certain amount of solitude is related to healthy adjustment in adolescence, and perhaps at any age.

HOW PARENTS CAN HELP (OR HINDER)

As we have said, the achievement of identity depends on a period of exploration and experimentation. Unless the adolescent has tried on different ways of looking, acting, thinking, and being, she cannot know who she *really* is (as distinct from the person other people want or expect her to be). Many parents accept this principle with regard to dating. "Play the field," they tell the adolescent. The same parents may balk, however, when the adolescent "plays the field" with regard to religious beliefs, political ideas, or activities and interests that might affect her future.

Mistakes Parents Make

Identity is an area where parents may, with the best of intentions, do more harm than good. One danger is parental *overidentification* with the adolescent. All parents have hopes and dreams for their children. When the adolescent makes a sudden unexpected detour, it is easy for parents to feel disappointed, even hurt. A mother who is a nurse may dream her daughter will become a physician and be devastated when the teenager announces plans to go to acting school. ("Half the waitresses in New York call themselves actresses! You're so bright; don't throw your life away.") A father may feel alienated when his son, who showed promise of becoming a star basketball player, begins to spend all his time at his computer. ("Great! My son the nerd.") Parents may not understand why their daughter dresses "punk" when they've filled her closet with the very best preppy skirts and sweaters. ("Purple hair just isn't you, Muffy. What will people think?")

There is nothing wrong with wanting the best for your child. But parents who feel threatened and angry about an adolescent's search for identity need to examine their own motives. The nurse-mother may be asking her daughter to redeem her frustrations at taking orders from physicians; the jock-father may feel he is losing his best buddy; the preppy parents may need their daughter to confirm their shaky social status. All of these parents are asking their adolescent to help them with their own unfinished business.

On one level, these parents may be right, of course. A medical degree does offer more security than acting classes; exercising only your brain and not your body isn't healthy; and purple hair might make the wrong impression at a job or college interview. But it's not a parent's job to *tell* adolescents who they are or to *dictate* their interests and tastes. It's one thing to suggest that your daughter test her talent for acting in summer stock, or keep her options open by looking at colleges that have good programs in biology *and* acting; another to tell her that she is a fool. The father might rekindle his friendship with his son by challenging him to design a program for keeping track of sports statistics and predicting the outcome of games. As for the girl with purple hair, the best advice is for parents to tell her they think her hair looks ridiculous (not that *she* is ridiculous), but that it's her decision.

The second danger is parental *overcontrol*. All parents want to protect their children. But the time has come to step back, to offer advice when asked (but not interfere), to suggest alternatives to the adolescent's plans (but not to plan her life for her), to present your thoughts and judgments as your own and recognize the adolescent's right to ideas and dreams of her own. Letting go isn't easy. No parent wants to see an adolescent make foolish decisions, get hurt unnecessarily, invite failure, or spin her wheels. The temptation to step in and take over is strong. But adolescents need to make their own mistakes and develop their own resources for dealing with frustration, disappointment, and pain.

Overcontrol can be insidious and disguised. A controlling parent may let an adolescent set his own curfews, choose his own clothes, decide when to do his homework—but also finish his sentences, solve his personal problems, constantly remind him of the way *we* do things, and thus subtly build an iron cage of expectations.

Adolescent Responses

Adolescents tend to react to overidentification and overcontrol in one of two ways. The first is what Erikson called *identity foreclosure*. The adolescent accepts his parents' plans and dreams for him without question. He plans to go to law school, not because he is interested in the law, but because everyone has always expected him to be a lawyer. He attends the Baptist church because his family have always been Baptists; supports Republicans because they have always been Republican. On a first date, he imagines what his parents would think of the girl. Seeing things through their eyes is reflexive. In effect, this young man has bypassed adolescence. Instead of seeking his own identity, he has received his identification from others. The result later in life may be feelings of emptiness and depression, or simply "adjusted blandness."

The second response to parental overidentification and overcontrol is the development of what Erikson called a *negative identity*. The adolescent goes out of her way to reject her parents' standards and values, adopting an identity designed to oppose or negate everything they consider important. Suppose the adolescent is a talented musician and her parents are pushing her toward a career as a cellist. She resents the long hours of practice; she wants time to explore other interests, time to be an ordinary teenager. Ignoring her wishes, her parents plan a summer trip to European music festivals and talk to the school counselor about early admission to Juilliard. She responds by becoming involved in drugs and the druggie crowd. To paraphrase Erikson, it is better to be somebody bad than to be nobody at all.

Parents are not the only reason why adolescents foreclose on identity or develop a negative identity. An adolescent who is shy or low in self-esteem, one who is having difficulty making friends at a new school or having problems with schoolwork, might adopt one of these strategies. But if these descriptions fit their adolescent, parents should examine their own attitudes and behavior. Are you allowing the adolescent to experiment and explore?

Encouragement and Support

Parents can *help* adolescents in their search for identity by accepting the teenager as a separate person, encouraging experimentation, and providing psychological space. The search for identity is most likely to follow a healthy course when parents are warm but not smothering; when they encourage adolescents to assert their individuality but also to remain connected to the family. How can parents guide the adolescent without interfering?

• *Help the teenager develop a clearer picture of him- or herself.* Parents tend to take the fact that a young person has always been good at math, shown leadership, and other strong points for granted, speaking up only when the young person has problems. Look for opportunities to point out the adolescent's strengths. A teenager with no particular academic specialty may be exceptionally good at resolving disputes among friends and siblings and have a future in careers that require interpersonal skills. You cannot praise an adolescent too much.

Encourage the teenager's special interests. Hobbies are not pastimes (in the literal sense of passing or filling time). They provide young people with experience in setting and achieving their own goals and with opportunities to develop competence and mastery. They are important not only for self-discovery, but also for self-esteem. A trip to an art or natural history museum, a biography of a writer or scientist, or an adult-level book on photography or chess will be a special treat to a teenager whose interests lie in these areas. The key is to focus on the teenager's own interests, not those that you think are worthwhile and likely to lead to the "right" occupational choices.

Extracurricular activities can also be important in the development of an occupational identity. Teenagers who are active in high-school clubs and organizations tend to have higher occupational ambitions than those who are not. The specific skills a teenager acquires working on the school newspaper or yearbook may not be as important as learning how to work with one's peers and seeing a product (the yearbook, a concert) develop from start to finish. These experiences build adolescents' confidence in their occupational futures.

• *Help the teenager gather information about real-world occupations.* Most young people have little contact with the adult world of work. Many don't even know what their parents do, beyond their job titles. Much of their information comes from the limited selection, and stereotyped portrayal, of careers on TV. A girl may believe that the only career open to someone who is interested in science is medicine. (How many research scientists do you see on

TV?) A boy may dismiss his interest in art because he doesn't think he is good enough to become a painter and has never heard of such careers as professor of art history, museum conservator, gallery director, or graphic designer.

If a friend or relative works in a field that interests your child, encourage the teenager to talk to that person about what it takes to become a symphony musician or a stockbroker. Better still, help the teenager get a job in an area that interests her. Most government offices, hospitals, and social service agencies have after-school volunteer programs and summer internships for young people. For example, the New York State YMCAs run a Youth and Government Program, which enables high-school students to work with lawyers, politicians, and lobbyists in formulating bills of special interest to teenagers for presentation to the state legislature. In New York City, the Mayor's Voluntary Association Center has a variety of positions for teens 14 and older. On the day we called, a theater club was looking for someone to help with props; the U.S. Committee for UNICEF was seeking clerical help; an art center needed gallery guides; and there were requests for Korean, Russian, Spanish, and Chinese translators. Other cities and states have similar programs and centers. Many small and large businesses also offer on-the-job training to teenagers. With persistence, a student might find a position at a law firm, newspaper, museum, theater company, political campaign, radio station, or animal hospital. School guidance offices usually have lists of positions and programs for teenagers.

Most of the better career-oriented jobs available to teenagers do not pay (and most of the paying jobs available to teens are not career-oriented; see chapter 17). The value of such nonpaying jobs lies in the first-hand experience they provide and the contact with adults who have chosen a particular line of work. A teenager who works at an animal hospital will discover that there is more to being a veterinarian than loving animals and get an idea of whether she can handle the physical and emotional demands of the job. If she decides she does want to become a vet, her former employer can help her with inside information on different veterinary schools and with letters of recommendation.

• *Reassure the teenager who can't decide what he wants to do that this is normal and common and that decisions are seldom carved in stone.* Many successful adults didn't discover their true vocation until college or later. Many adults who specialized early regret that they didn't take time to explore different fields, through college courses and summer and part-time employment, before settling on one. And many adults change careers later in life. College admissions offices won't think less of a teenager because he hasn't settled on a major, much less formed career plans. Most colleges have liberal arts or general studies majors designed specifically for students who haven't made early career decisions (see chapter 18). Many undergraduates change majors during college.

School guidance counselors may offer vocational aptitude tests to teenagers who do not know what they want to do. While these tests are useful for students who do not plan to go to college, they may lead to career foreclosure in students who do not have to make immediate decisions. The teenager may take the results too literally and stop exploring.

Having "too many" interests is common and normal in adolescence. A teenager who has *no* hobbies, *no* favorite activities, *no* fantasies about the future, and *no* plans may be suffering from depression, or abusing drugs or alcohol (see chapters 8 and 13, respectively).

WHEN TO WORRY

Some confusion and turmoil are a normal part of the search for identity. But intense or lasting distress are not. Psychologists refer to the former as a "normal identity crisis." This phrase sounds contradictory. In everyday conversation, we use the word *crisis* when something has gone terribly wrong; by definition, a crisis isn't normal. But psychologists use this term to refer to a turning point in the individual's psychological development; a point when old ways of thinking about the self in relation to others are no longer adequate, and new ways must be developed before the person can get on with his or her life. From this perspective, a normal identity crisis is a sign that the adolescent is working toward a healthy adjustment; an identity disorder is a sign that the young person is heading toward unhealthy patterns. How can parents tell the difference?

Normal Identity Crises

Adolescents in the throes of a normal identity crisis feel an urgent need to make decisions but an inability to do so. They make plans one week (to enroll in a course, break up with a boy- or girlfriend, look for a job), only to abandon them the next. The religious, political, and moral certainties of their childhood have deserted them, but they haven't yet developed standards of their own. Distrustful of their own judgment, they feel unable to evaluate their value as student, friend, or lover. Uncertain of their own talents and abilities, they look to others for direction. At the same time, they resist overt attempts at guidance. Although painful for family and friends, as well as for the adolescent, an identity crisis of this magnitude is not a cause for serious concern. These adolescents have good days as well as bad days, triumphs as well as defeats, and generally are able to maintain friendships, hold their own in school, and otherwise carry on with their lives. As a rule, their uncertainties resolve themselves over time.

Identity Disorders

In some cases, however, identity problems run deeper. Parents should be concerned if an identity crisis is

- *Acute.* The teenager is not just worried about who she is, but seriously distressed.
- *Pervasive.* The teenager's distress extends to three or more of the following areas: long-term goals, career choices, friendship patterns, sexuality, religious identity, moral values, and group loyalties.
- *Paralyzing.* The teenager is so obsessed with identity questions that she performs poorly at school and is unable to enjoy friends and social activities.
- *Persistent.* The distress and confusion continue for weeks, even months, with little relief.

The difference between a normal identity crisis and an identity disorder are *intensity* and *duration.* Identity disorders do not resolve themselves over time. The danger is that the young person will not be able to make career commitments and form lasting emotional attachments later in life, and so drift or jump from job to job, relationship to relationship, and often, therapist to therapist. Early intervention (in the high school or college years) can prevent chronic aimlessness.

The idea that all adolescents experience an identity crisis has become a cultural cliché. As a result, other potentially serious problems—including depression (chapter 8), an eating disorder (chapter 4), or a problem with drugs (chapter 13)—may be written off as part of the adolescent's search for identity. These are psychological disturbances requiring treatment.

IDENTITY AND MORALITY

Advances in Moral Reasoning

Young adolescents have a personalized sense of moral obligations, based on their desire to be liked. They don't need to be bribed or threatened into good behavior. Earning social approval, maintaining relationships, and feeling like a nice person are their rewards (see chapter 7). They are capable of greater empathy, loyalty, and caring than they were as children. But they don't have their own ideas about right and wrong, and they are easily swayed by the argument "Everybody is doing it." In their middle teens, adolescents begin to move toward a higher level of moral reasoning.

The high-school moralist sees the bigger picture. Looking beyond the immediate situation, beyond friendship and family, the older adolescent asks "What if everybody did it [stole, cheated, lied]? It would be impossible to function; society would fall apart." This insight leads to a new appreciation of social rules and expectations. Where the young adolescent saw rules as something adults impose on young people, often arbitrarily, the older adolescent sees rules as coming from society and serving a necessary function. Where a 12-year-old felt good about breaking the rules for a friend, a 16-year-old feels bad about a friend who breaks the rules. Social approval came first in early adolescence and conscience second; in high school, social order and self-respect come before popularity. The high-school moralist sees doing right not just as a private matter, but as a social obligation. At this age, adolescents are able to take the perspective of people who are not their personal friends (the storeowner) and to think through the social implications of rule-breaking (tighter security, higher prices, ultimately chaos). They realize that it is sometimes necessary to sacrifice immediate gratification and personal freedom for the common good. The feeling that they are playing by the rules, doing their duty, and being good citizens is their reward. They stand for law and order.

Some readers may balk at the suggestion that teenagers are advocates of law and order. By reputation, they are the opposite (advocates of *out*lawed behavior and social *dis*order). There are two reasons for this apparent contradiction. First, the development of society-oriented morality is not as regular or predictable as the emergence of the less mature, "good boy/nice girl" morality. Some adolescents have flashes of "law and order" reasoning as early as junior high school; others only arrive at this stage in college. Some young people shift back and forth between the two in middle adolescence. Most teenagers (perhaps 80 percent) use "good boy/nice girl" reasoning most of the time, and some never show more advanced thinking. This doesn't mean that the young person is "bad," or that his or her moral development is arrested. Our culture often applauds people who put loyalty to family and friends before law and order. Teenagers are not the only ones who cheer when Sylvester Stallone as Rambo takes the law into his own hands.

The second reason for the perception that teenagers are moral renegades is that they may not feel loyal to the social system their parents and most other adults support. An adolescent may denounce "American imperialism" and embrace a radical leftist ideology, or decry "American weakness" and endorse a political stance to the far right. Or she may reject her parent's "materialism" to join a new religious group. The best known example of adolescents breaking with the accepted system was the hippie movement of the 1960s and 1970s, when *teenager* became synonymous with *protester*. The flamboyance of that era was due in part to numbers: The baby boom generation (one-third of our total population) was moving through adolescence. The result, in the words of the demographer Landon Jones, was "a critical mass of teenagers that was as fissionable as any nuclear pile." The memory of those times still colors our image of teenagers. It's worth noting that subsequent studies have found that most of the young radicals of the 1960s came from politically active, liberal homes. They were not so much rebelling against their parents' morality as practicing, perhaps a bit too literally, what their parents preached. The byword of the counterculture was "Do your own thing." But in fact, hippies did the same things in the same ways. In Erikson's phrase, there was a "uniformity of differing." The break with convention was less than met the eye.

Whatever their particular beliefs and values, "law and order" moralists feel a sense of duty and obligation to something larger than themselves. The drawback is that these moralists tend to be rigid and literal in their adherence to the rules. Psychologists call this *conventional morality;* at this stage, adolescents (and adults) go by the book—whether that book is the Bible, the Constitution, or *The Thoughts of Chairman Mao.* They may have the courage to stand up to their parents and peers, but not to stand alone. Only later in life do people achieve true moral independence.

Changes in Attitudes and Behavior

In many ways, adolescents who have reached the "law and order" stage of moral development are easier to live with. They are more willing to listen to reason. Parents have to push a less mature thinker to consider what would happen if everybody did what the child is requesting or defending. When adolescents turn the tables and challenge parental views by stating "If you follow that to its logical conclusion . . . ," they have reached the "law and order" stage.

Adolescents in this stage are less susceptible to peer pressure. The morality of early adolescence was a moral straightjacket. The adolescent's need for approval prevented him from becoming his own person. The older adolescent's commitment to social order gives her the strength to oppose her peers and parents if she thinks they are wrong. When she takes a stand, it is because *she* believes it is right.

Teenagers who have reached this stage can also be extremely self-righteous. Certain that they have all the answers, they berate adults for making such a mess of the world. From their naive perspective, there are obvious solutions to world hunger, the nuclear arms race, environmental pollution, the homeless, and just about any other problem you can name. Real-world obstacles to achieving social ideals seem immaterial; negotiation and compromise are seen as "selling out." Ever ready to say what is wrong with the adult world, "law and order" moralists are also quick to point out flaws and hypocrisies in their parents' reasoning and behavior.

"Law and order" moralists are the backbone of every society. A society could not exist if most of its members did not feel a sense of commitment to the wider community and a duty to uphold law and order. This stage of morality is also important in the adolescent's personal search for identity and development toward adulthood.

Fostering Moral Development

How can parents encourage and support more advanced moral reasoning?

Encourage Independence Teenagers need to become their own authorities on what *they* believe. They want to feel that they have their own ideas about right and wrong, their own political opinions, their own religious convictions. They need to develop their own plans for the future and feel that they are in charge of their own lives. For parents, this means giving up some of their authority.

Middle adolescents can and should make many of their own decisions. One way to help them make good decisions—without stepping on their toes—is to ask questions that will help them to think a decision through: "What will make you happy in the long run?" "Have you weighed the pros and cons?" "Is there another way to solve the problem?" "What other choices do you have?" The decision may be whether to break a date with a girlfriend to go out with a boy she has long admired, whether to quit the soccer team where he is always left on the bench or hang in, or whether to stay friends with someone who is smoking marijuana. These are important decisions, with moral implications, but not matters of life and death (in which case parents *should* step in). Tell the adolescent what you would do, but let the final decision be his. "I hope you will think about what I've said, but you have to decide what is best for you. If you have given this serious thought, I'll respect what you decide."

Middle adolescents often feel torn between loyalty to a friend and going along with the crowd, abiding by its rules. Say your son discovers that the school's star linebacker has been paying someone to write his term papers. He tries to talk about it with a group of friends, but they say "It's none of our business. Besides, we might win the championship this year." Or your daughter's best friend was sexually assaulted by a senior but managed to get away. She made your daughter swear never to tell anyone. Now another friend is dating the same boy. What should they do?

Conflicts between personal loyalty to the friend or group loyalty to the team and the school and to abstract ideas of right and wrong are not unique to adolescents, but they may be especially painful at this age. Teenagers tend to see these as either/or questions (I can *either* be loyal to my friend *or* I can do what's right). You can help by, first, asking what they would do if none of their friends would know what they decided—what would make them feel good about themselves. Then help them work out a strategy that doesn't violate their sense of loyalty *or* their ideas of right and wrong. The boy might speak to the linebacker: "The team really needs you, and if you get caught you won't be able to play for the rest of the season." The girl might try to convince her friend to tell the other girl what happened: "How are you going to feel if he attacks her, too? If you're embarrassed to talk to her yourself, I'll go with you."

More subtly, but equally important, parents need to grant teenagers intellectual independence, the right to think their own thoughts. Parents are sometimes caught off guard when adolescents begin expressing independent opinions: They feel as if their whole value system is under attack. Some common reactions are "Where do you get such ideas?" "Who told you that?" "You sound just like so-and-so." "You don't mean that." "You're just trying to provoke me." Technically, these parents may be right. A teenager who is entering the "law and order" stage may parrot stock phrases, borrow pat ideas, and seem on the way to becoming less, not more, independent. But pointing this out may undermine the teenager's confidence in his right to disagree.

Suppose your daughter suddenly announces that she is against abortion and may join in a demonstration against a local family planning clinic. As a long-time feminist, you're horrified. You happen to know that her best friend's mother is active in the "right to life" movement and has given your daughter books and pamphlets that you consider pure propaganda. What should you do? First, try not to take her opinions personally ("No daughter of mine is going to be at that march!"). However painful it may be, encourage her to articulate her views: "I know some people think abortion is wrong, but why do *you* think so?" Help her to see that the issue is a complex one and that you did not arrive at your position lightly. By all means say how strongly you disagree, but acknowledge her right to her own opinion. A teenager who agrees with your views needs practice in articulating his positions, too: Take turns playing devil's advocate.

Encourage Activity in the Community While discussion is important to moral development, discussion alone may not be enough. As Lickona suggests, "To feel part of society, [teenagers] need to take part in it." Parents shouldn't push a teenager to be active in the community, but the desire to "do something" should be encouraged.

As noted earlier, most communities have programs that place teenagers in volunteer positions—in nursing homes, day-care centers, hospitals, and institutions for the mentally or physically handicapped—or train teenagers to work as tutors or peer counselors (for example, on drug prevention). A teenager who is concerned about the environment might participate in community cleanups; one who is interested in politics might work for a political candidate. Some schools make community work part of the social studies curriculum.

Volunteer work has the most impact on teenagers' hearts, minds, and moral development when it is combined with structured classroom opportunities for reflection and discussion. Students who participate in these programs show the greatest gains in social responsibility and concern for the welfare of others. They are better able to listen to another person's problems and suggest a workable solution. Their feelings of competence and self-esteem increase. And their attitudes toward adults are more positive. If your school does not have such programs, parents and siblings can fill in. "Home seminars" are most valuable if all members of the family are involved in some kind of community service (even if it's baby-sitting or feeding a neighbor's parakeet) and share their experiences.

CHAPTER 15

Problem Behavior

*T*he line between innocent misbehavior and problem behavior in adolescence can be a fine one. Should parents worry if their son ends an argument by slamming out the door, refusing to say where he is going, and spending the night with a friend? If their daughter is dressing like Madonna? If their son and some friends covered the gym wall with graffiti? When should parents draw the line? How?

Adolescent misconduct ranges from *normal misbehavior* (behavior that is not a cause for serious concern, though it may warrant a serious talk) to *troubled behavior* (acts that indicate the adolescent is troubled, or likely to get into trouble, and needs to reform) to *problem behavior* (attitudes and actions that indicate serious disturbance and call for immediate, professional intervention). We discussed drug and alcohol abuse in chapter 13 and problems with school achievement in chapter 11. Here we will concentrate on sexual acting out, defiance, delinquency, running away, truancy, and school phobia.

SEXUAL ACTING OUT

This refers to inappropriate sexual behavior and/or interest, especially provocative and promiscuous behavior. In general, adolescents follow their peers on such matters as how to dress and when to begin going to mixed-sex parties, dating, necking, going steady, and making love. And peers often feel the adult approval schedule is sadly out of date. To this degree, many if not most adolescents are sexual rebels. Where you personally draw the line depends on your family values (as discussed in chapter 12). Sexual intercourse in early adolescence is not healthy. But in our view, sexual activity in middle adolescence—in the context of love —is *normal*. Fidelity, not chastity, is the rule. If a 16-year-old girl has a steady boyfriend whom she has been seeing for some time, and they seem to genuinely care for one another, you should not be upset if you discover she has a diaphragm. On the contrary, you should be relieved to know that she is protecting herself.

When a teenager flaunts her sexuality, however, and behaves and dresses in ways designed to provoke her parents, it's a sign of *trouble*. Such teenagers often talk an ultraliberal sexual line: "Anything goes." When parents attempt to restrain them ("Don't you think that dress is too tight?" "You are *not* going to that beach party!"), their response is "You can't stop me." Sex is *the* battleground on which they fight for independence. In some cases, sexual sophistication is an act, and the teenager is still sexually innocent. Others see their virginity as their personal Maginot line: Once they've crossed that line, once they've "done it," they can think of themselves as grown-up. The desire to prove something through sex often blinds them to the possibility that they are exploiting, or being exploited by, their partners. Physical intimacy may become a substitute for emotional closeness. The teenager falls in and out of love frequently.

Promiscuity and excessive interest in sex are signs of serious *problems*. In a desperate attempt to affirm her popularity and attractiveness, a girl may sleep with boys she just met or have several partners in a single weekend or even on the same night. To maintain his macho image, a boy may focus on conquest, on "adding notches to his gun." *Not* caring about his partners is part of that image, and sex becomes more compulsive than pleasurable. Through sex, adolescents who feel unloved and unlovable can attain the illusion of closeness, however fleeting. Sadly, this behavior prevents them from obtaining what they want most: love.

One price teenagers pay for this level of sexual rebellion is conflict with parents. Another is alienation from their agemates and from same-sex friends. Such teenagers often go around with an older crowd. But their position in that crowd is usually marginal, and they may have to "pay" for acceptance by supplying alcohol or drugs, by participating in delinquent acts, or by offering and accepting sex. Partial acceptance by older teens does not compensate for estrangement from classmates, who may feel threatened or just turned off by them, or for the lack of same-sex friends in whom they can confide. Early or chronic promiscuity may also lead to sexual disinterest and dysfunction later in life. Sexual enjoyment is not automatic: Young people who use sex for other reasons miss opportunities to learn how to give and receive pleasure. Needless to say, the chances of sexually transmitted diseases and pregnancy in adolescence are greatly increased.

DEFIANCE

Some opposition to parental rules is a *normal* part of growing up, as we have stressed throughout. Debating with parents and other adults is one of the chief ways that teenagers prove to themselves and others that they are becoming independent individuals, with standards, values, and goals of their own. Demanding more personal freedom, asserting contrary opinions, "forgetting" to do household chores now and then, and occasionally goofing off (in school as well as at home) are within the normal range.

Frequent aggressive outbursts, however, are a sign of *trouble*. Violent temper tantrums may be common and normal at age 3 or 4, but not at age 15 or 16. A simple request—to clear the table, do their homework, or be polite to Grandma—causes these teens to fly off the handle. Afterward, they may be filled with remorse and tearfully promise to change. But the outbursts continue. Deliberate contrariness is another sign of trouble. It is one thing to argue about parental requests; another to do the opposite intentionally. Say you ask your son to help with the yard (one of his regular chores), and he chases the dog through the piles of leaves you raked up that morning. Or you ask your daughter to help you prepare for a large family dinner scheduled for 6 that evening, and at 5:55 she wanders in from an afternoon with her friends. For these teenagers, rules exist to be broken. What adults are for, they are against. They take their parents' warnings ("If you keep this up, you're going to be grounded/suspended from school/fired from your job") as a challenge. These teenagers feel misunderstood, unappreciated, even exploited. They complain constantly about being hassled. At the same time, they make it clear that they are not making their best effort. This level of defiance is not against the law, but it frequently escalates into something more serious.

Defiant behavior is *problem* behavior when the teenager's actions lead to chronic or severe conflict at home (especially violent threats or acts), at school (suspension), or at work (dismissal), or when the adolescent's war with authority takes the form of illegal behavior and leads to contact with the law. Highly oppositional teenagers are vindictive and unforgiving: When neighbors ask a boy to keep the family dog off their property, he may empty several bags of garbage on their lawn; when a teacher reprimands a girl for talking in class, she may use lipstick to cover the teacher's car with obscenities. Rage has become part of their personalities. Always on the lookout for insults, they often "strike back first." Schoolmates avoid them, and parents may be secretly relieved when they run away or get into trouble with the law.

DELINQUENCY

Technically, this refers to violations of the law, including such status offenses as running away. We would also include violations of school rules (such as cheating) in this category. Delinquency ranges from relatively trivial misbehavior (trespassing, lying about one's age to get into a disco, Halloween pranks) to hard-core criminal acts (stealing, mugging, dealing drugs).

Normal delinquency is infrequent, spontaneous, and non-violent. Nine out of ten teenagers admit that they have shoplifted, vandalized, cheated, or committed some other delinquent act in the last year. These petty crimes are usually committed with a friend or friends: On a sleep-over, four girls take turns making obscene phone calls; on the first day of school, two boys amuse their classmates (and confound their teachers) by exchanging identities; on a trip to the mall, two girls decide to help themselves to some makeup; having nothing better to do, three boys "borrow" a car and go joyriding. Parents should take such misconduct seriously (see below), but they need not worry that their child is headed for a life of crime.

Repeated, premeditated violations of the law or of school regulations, however, are a sign of *trouble:* Two boys break into the school computer system and scramble the records from the last semester; three girls rig a school election to make sure a girl they don't like isn't elected; a group of boys get their kicks breaking into neighborhood houses and stealing small items (a video tape recorder, a six-pack of beer) that may not be missed; a group of girls meet every Saturday for a shoplifting expedition; when one of the parents goes away for the weekend, members of a clique invite the whole school to the house and ask everyone to bring a bottle. A delinquent spree may continue for three to six months, depending on whether the young people are caught. Parents and teachers are often stunned to discover this level of delinquent behavior, for these adolescents may be school leaders, earn top grades, and in other ways appear to be model teenagers.

Signs of problem behavior include *any* violent act (beating up a boy who makes an innocent comment about the teen's girlfriend; smashing the window of the family car with a baseball bat when he is grounded for a night) or violent crime (holding up a gas station; exacting "protection" money from younger, weaker schoolmates at knifepoint). Nonviolent illegal activities also fall into this category. When a group of prep-school students pool their allowances to send two teens to Bolivia to buy cocaine to sell to their classmates, they have crossed the line from pranks to delinquency. So have a group of teenagers who systematically desecrate a temple or a church. Unlike most adolescents, these teenagers usually have problems with school (poor grades, frequent truancy) and poor relations with their families. Which comes first is difficult to say. Inability to meet adult expectations, in the form of either repeated failure in school or constant criticism at home, may cause a teenager to try "proving" himself through illegal activities. Conversely, involvement in a delinquent crowd may lead a teenager to stop trying in school and fight with her parents.

Petty crimes and school offenses are also signs of a problem *if the teenager commits these acts alone*. Cheating on a test to impress your friends with your daring is one thing; regularly cheating on tests and hiding this from peers as well as adults is another. The loner may take private pleasure in stealing from a popular child's locker or tearing up a better student's notes. A girl who shoplifts compulsively, taking things she doesn't even want, also has a problem. Social delinquency may result in greater damage, but solitary delinquency suggests deeper psychological problems. Social delinquents can explain their behavior, even though their explanation involves deviant norms ("Cocaine is no worse than alcohol"; "The guys dared me"). Solitary delinquents often can't say why they do what they do; nor can they stop themselves.

RUNNING AWAY

Estimates are that more than a million teenagers run away each year. Most return home within a matter of days, but for about half a million, this reunion is temporary. They leave home again, and again.

It is not unusual for teenagers to storm out of the house without telling their parents where they are going. If this is an isolated incident, and if the adolescent either returns home the same day or goes to the home of a friend, neighbor, or relative (someone they know will let you know where he or she is), parents should not be overly concerned. This dramatic act may be designed to call attention to a problem at home that needs to be resolved. However, if the teenager runs away frequently (more than once in three months), even for short periods of time, something is wrong. If the adolescent runs, not to a friend or neighbor, but to the streets, parents should be alarmed.

TRUANCY AND SCHOOL PHOBIA

Truancy is unexcused absences from school, without parental consent. Truant adolescents typically have a history of doing poorly in school. They see their classes as "stupid," their teachers as hostile, and would rather be anywhere *but* school. On days when they are absent, they usually spend their time hanging out with other alienated teenagers. They are more likely than other adolescents to get involved in delinquency and drugs. Psychologists used to believe that the truant's absence from school and negative attitudes toward school led to academic failure. They are now coming to believe that academic failure is often the cause, not the consequence, of truancy. These teenagers see school as a setting in which they repeatedly fail, and so develop antieducation attitudes and beliefs to protect their self-esteem.

School phobia is intense anxiety and fear of going to school. In contrast to truants, school-phobic adolescents usually do average or above-average work in school, like school, and worry about falling behind. Nevertheless, they have compelling reasons for not attending school—either physical complaints (headaches, sore throats, stomach problems) or social circumstances (the teachers dislike them, other students are cruel, and the like). When they are absent, it is usually *with* their parents consent, and they spend their time at *home*. Their symptoms and anxieties often disappear over the weekend, only to reappear Sunday night or Monday morning. Although most often seen in elementary-school children, school phobia is not uncommon during the transition to junior high, high school, or even college.

Skipping class or even a full day of school once in a while falls within the *normal* range of adolescent behavior. To some degree, all teenagers resent the fact that they are forced to attend school, study subjects that seem remote from their daily lives, and remain cooped up all day. Cutting a particularly dull class or going to the beach with friends on an especially beautiful spring day restores their sense of freedom and self-determination. They know it's wrong and don't plan to do it again. Getting the jitters before an exam or performance with the theater club is also normal. Teenagers are not immune from tension headaches and nervous stomachs. Adolescents with normal jitters know why they are feeling below par and are willing to discuss their fears.

Cutting school more than once in three months is a sign that a teenager is moving into the *troubled* zone. Frequent truants don't believe that what they are doing is wrong and argue that school is a waste of time. Getting physically sick on school mornings in the absence of such confirming evidence as a fever is also a sign of trouble. The adolescent knows why she dreads going to school, but the reason is so painful, she won't discuss it ("Can't you see I'm sick?").

Repeated absence from school is *problem* behavior. Negative attitudes toward school and cynicism about adult prescriptions for success have become part of the chronic truant's basic value system. Even if he attends school sporadically, psychologically he has already dropped out. His life revolves around a group of friends who share and reinforce his attitudes. The school-phobic adolescent is chronically sick. The more days she spends out of school, the more difficult it is for her to return. Her phobia may extend beyond school to fear of going places where she might see schoolmates, and even fear of leaving the house.

Although the effect is the same (absence from school), truancy and school phobia have different causes and require different approaches. Parents of a frequent or chronic truant should not attempt to handle this on their own. The problem stems from school and must be solved at school. Many school have special programs for alienated youth (individually designed curricula, work-study programs, and the like). The aim of these programs is to make adolescents feel that they can be successful in school and that the rewards are tangible. School-phobic adolescents usually require individual or family therapy. Developing a pattern of psychosomatic complaints can undermine an adolescent's physical as well as mental health. This pattern is most likely to occur when a child has been overprotected and/or overindulged and so has not developed healthy ways of coping with ordinary stress. If there is a concrete reason for his distress, however, such as bullies (see chapter 10), the school should be brought in.

A summary of adolescent behavior problems, indicating degrees of seriousness, appears on page 308.

WHAT TO DO

The key to dealing with behavior problems is to communicate your disapproval of the behavior without communicating rejection of the teenager. This is not the time for angry accusations, name-calling, or sarcasm.

Communication

Normal misbehavior should not be ignored ("He is just going through a phase"), even if it is relatively harmless. But neither should parents crack down at the first hint of misconduct. The problem with overreaction and overrestriction is that they may lead a teenager who was only experimenting to take greater risks, if only to prove that he is independent. What is called for here is a calm discussion of why the behavior is wrong or, if the behavior isn't necessarily illegal or immoral, why you disapprove of it ("We think you are too young to _____"; "I get very upset when you _____"). Appeal to the teenager's growing ability to apply "what-if-everyone" moral reasoning (see chapter 14). Give the teenager a chance to express his views. Listen between the lines. Look for opportunities to compromise. Ask the teenager to suggest appropriate penalties for breaking the rules. When you think

WARNING SIGNS

"NORMAL" MISBEHAVIOR

- One or two minor, *nonviolent* violations of the law or school regulations
- Occasional arguing with parents and other adults
- Sexual activity in the context of love
- Leaving home for a day, or running away to a familiar home, once
- Skipping school or cutting class once
- Experimentation with alcohol or drugs*

TROUBLE SIGNS

- Repeated or premeditated violations of the law or school regulations, however petty
- Aggressive outbursts; contrariness for the sake of being contrary
- Sexual provocativeness
- Running away more than once in three months
- Skipping school more than once in three months
- Regular use of drugs and/or alcohol*

PROBLEM BEHAVIOR

- Any violent act or crime; solitary delinquent acts
- Oppositionalism that leads to violence at home, suspension from school, getting fired from work, or contact with law enforcement agencies
- Sexual promiscuity
- Running away to the streets
- Chronic absenteeism from school
- Addiction to drugs; drug dealing*

* For alcohol and drug problems, see chapter 13.

---

you understand one another, work out an agreement about what will be allowed in the future. In some cases the decision may be "Never again!"; in others, "You know how we feel, but we'll trust you to use your own judgment." Finally, make sure that everyone —you, your spouse, and the teenager—understands the consequences of violating this agreement. Indicate that you are willing to discuss the rules at any time. But if the teen breaks your agreement without speaking to you first, he will be docked half his allowance, grounded for three weeks, or whatever, no ifs, ands, or buts. (See also Communication, chapter 2.)

Enforcing Limits

Misconduct that falls into the troubled zone calls for sensitive but swift attention. If you and the adolescent have a warm relationship and have been able to talk through problems in the past, you may be able to do so now. Follow the guidelines for dealing with normal misbehavior. In addition, press the teenager to think about the consequences of her behavior: "Have you thought about what you would do if you got pregnant? were suspended from school? got arrested?" Many teenagers do not think beyond today. If they have gotten away with minor misbehavior in the past, they may blithely assume that they will be able to get off the hook in the future. The realization that suspension from school would mean they had to give up a summer trip for summer school, or go to work instead of going to college, might be sobering.

Talk may not be enough with these teenagers; they have already shown a poor sense of judgment and lack of responsibility. If you have not established clear standards for behavior, do so now. Make it clear that if they do not abide by family rules *from now on*, you will invoke strict penalties and monitor their behavior as closely as you did when they were children. (See the discussion of handling a drug problem, chapter 13, for more detailed advice on enforcing limits.)

Getting Professional Help

If you feel that the teenager is not listening, if the teenager's response is defiant ("You can't stop me"), if a brief period of compliance is followed by a return to old patterns, or if you just think things are out of hand, it's time to seek professional help. How do you broach this subject with an adolescent?

If the adolescent is vacillating between defiant outbursts and spells of remorse, you might say "You seem unhappy with me, with school, with your life in general; would you like to talk to someone outside the family?" or "I'm worried about you and think it would be good for you to talk to a counselor. Do you like the counselor at school? Do any of your friends see a therapist you think you'd like?" Many adolescents will agree to this idea, especially if they live in a community where therapy is considered socially acceptable, even chic. Indeed, some welcome the suggestion.

If you and the adolescent have never been very close, or if recent events have made it impossible for you to talk rationally, say so: "Obviously you and I don't see eye to eye on this, and the way we're fighting is making everyone unhappy. I think we should talk to someone who is an expert on family conflicts." You should be clear that therapy is not punishment and that you are not accusing the child of having psychological problems; rather, you are concerned about his or her welfare and about your relationship and think your family needs help.

If the adolescent refuses outright, he or she may be angrier or further estranged than you thought. In this case you should make an appointment for you and your spouse with a therapist who specializes in adolescent-family problems. Invite the teenager to come with you, but be clear that you are going, with or without the adolescent. As we noted in chapter 2, in most cases teenagers will come, if only because they want to tell their side of the story. But if your invitation to help is refused, go by yourself. Family therapists are trained to help you get reluctant teenagers involved in treatment.

If the teenager's behavior has reached the problem level, you should seek professional help immediately. These are problems that parents cannot, and should not, attempt to solve on their own. Do your best to win the adolescent's cooperation, but don't leave the decision to the child. In these cases, a mild threat is in order: "You are grounded until we see a professional counselor. You can decide whether you want to go alone or we all go together, but you *are* going." If the teenager resists, the therapist will help you handle the situation. Be prepared for long-term, intensive treatment, perhaps including a period of residential treatment, especially for drug or alcohol abuse. In the course of therapy, some of your weaknesses, defenses, and fears will be exposed. The teenager is not the only one who will have to change; you will, too. It won't be an easy time, but your whole family may be better for it in the long run.

If your teenager has been arrested, contact a *criminal* lawyer. (Family lawyers deal with such routine matters as wills, setting up trusts, and house closings. When your child is in trouble with the law, you need a specialist. Ask your family lawyer for recommendations.) You may be furious with the teenager for defying you and behaving so stupidly. In time, your anger will fade. But an arrest record (say, for possession of a small amount of an illegal drug) can haunt a young person for life. An attorney will make sure that your child's rights are protected.

Finally, don't give up. Defiant, "super-sexy," and delinquent teenagers are good at driving their parents to the brink. Often parents do their best to reason with the teenager, but when they seem to be getting nowhere, back off in anger: "It's your life. If you want to wreck it, go ahead. But don't expect me to bail you out." Teenagers want to believe it's their life, but they still need to know that you'll be there if they fall. Just remember that the great majority of problem teenagers grow up to be good citizens, hard workers, and valued friends of their parents.

RESOURCES

At the end of chapter 2, we list resources that may be helpful to parents who are seeking professional counseling. At the end of chapter 13, we list resources for parents who need assistance with an adolescent's drug or alcohol problem.

CHAPTER 16

Friends and Social Life

CHANGES IN THE TEENAGER'S SOCIAL LIFE

There are clear, predictable changes in social orientation as adolescents move through high school. Cliques and crowds become less important, and friendship and romance more so. Like a young adult, the high-school senior typically has a large circle of acquaintances and a small circle of intimates.

From Conformity to Individuality

The high-school years are a time of increasing individuality. The teenager may still be known as a preppie, biker, brain, or jock, but many middle adolescents are "free-lancers" or "floaters," at home in different groups and with different kinds of friends. Indeed, most high-school students deny that they belong to a crowd. Crowds that guard their social turf against intruders (often the preppies or elites) are seen as snobs by other teenagers.

The decline of clannishness in middle adolescence reflects changes in the way teenagers think about themselves and others. The young adolescent was a conformist: Her friends were *the* authority on what to do, say, wear, and think. In effect, she traded dependence on the family for dependence on the crowd. The teenager is now able to stand on her own. She doesn't want to be seen as being *like* other people; she wants to be recognized as a unique individual. The often repeated argument "But *everyone* is doing it" is replaced by "*I* want to go," "It's *my* life," and similar assertions of individuality. The teenager chooses friends, clothes, and activities, not because they help her fit in, but because *she* likes them.

Susceptibility to peer pressure declines in the high-school years. This doesn't mean that teenagers aren't influenced by their friends; it means rather, that when they need information or guidance, they seek out experts. On matters of style and taste, teenagers consider their peers expert. This is hardly surprising: You wouldn't ask a teenager what you should wear to a job interview or what to serve to your friends at a party; the teenager doesn't ask you what he should wear to school or what is the best time to arrive at a party. (If he likes your style, though, he may borrow from your closet—something the younger adolescent wouldn't do on principle.) Teenagers also turn to peers with day-to-day concerns about school and friends. As one ninth grader explained, she wouldn't ask her parents for help with homework because it would take too long to teach them the background they would need to solve the problem. Classmates know where she is "coming from." But on the big issues—ethics, schooling, and life decisions—teenagers are more likely to turn to their parents. They recognize that although peers have more knowledge of teen culture, adults are better informed about life beyond high school.

The young adolescent tended to see peers and parents as opposing forces, to take advice at face value, and to follow one or the other. Middle adolescents realize that different people have different points of view, and that advice may be colored by self-interest. On important issues, they seek a second and third opinion and weigh the advice they receive in light of the advisers' biases. In thinking about college, for example, teenagers consider both their parents and their friends as good sources of advice. But they take into account the fact that their parents may underestimate the importance of campus social life, while their friends may underestimate the importance of a good financial aid program. Likewise, the teenager will weigh his friends' and parents' advice on buying a car, dating, summer jobs, or other matters, and then draw his own conclusions. The fact that the adolescent is making his own decisions can be disconcerting for parents, but the fact that he is no longer playing to the crowd should be reassuring.

All in all, the high-school student has matured both in thinking and behavior. Because she *is* more independent, she doesn't have to *prove* her independence by disagreeing with her parents because they are her parents. Unless a parent resents the teenager's independence and tries to run her life for her, she is much easier to get along with. Parent-teen conflicts usually decrease during the high-school years, and cooperation and communication increase.

From Cliques to Couples

Another reason why cliques and crowds break up in high school is that teenagers are becoming more interested in the opposite sex. Doing the same old things with the same old gang seems less attractive.

Heterosexual interest develops gradually, in stages. In the preteens, the adolescent's social life revolves around same-sex cliques. Young adolescents are happiest with small groups of close friends. Somewhat later, boys' and girls' cliques begin to get together for joint activities. There is no dating at this stage; boy-girl interaction is group-to-group, not one-to-one. The presence of same-sex friends makes these early heterosexual contacts less threatening. In about ninth or tenth grade, some members of the group (usually the clique leaders) begin dating. Others follow their example, and mixed-sex cliques begin to take shape. At this stage, parties and other group activities are the center of the adolescent's social life. Even though they are dating, 14- and 15-year-olds find safety in numbers: "Dating in groups is friendlier, more fun, because things are less scary, less embarrassing with a bunch of people; even stupid accidents turn into jokes. It's like getting into trouble after school—if you all have to stay, it doesn't feel so bad."

Toward the end of high school, however, couples become more interested in spending time alone with one another, and mixed-sex cliques gradually dissolve. "If I go on a date, I want to be alone with the guy so I can get to know him better," says a 16-year-old. "Groups are bothersome." Thus adolescents move from tight-knit, same-sex cliques, to loose-knit, mixed-sex groups, to serious relationships with a member of the opposite sex.

PARTIES AND GROUP ACTIVITIES

If cliques are the cornerstone of early adolescence, group activities (parties, group dates, hanging out) are the hallmark of middle adolescence. On weekends, most teenagers want to be with their friends. The activity doesn't matter as much as the mood. With a group of friends, teenagers can let go, blow off steam, do or say anything. They feel excited, friendly, involved, motivated. Everyday restraints are cast aside.

Groups of teenagers on their own have been compared to an engine in which all the stops have been pulled, all signals are Go, and the thermostat that would keep the engine from overheating is broken. While this may be an exaggeration (many teens know when to stop), the group can be a license for misbehavior, ranging from the benign to the delinquent.

How can parents exercise control over the teenager's activities without spoiling the fun?

When Teenagers Go Out

Your son plans to go downtown with a bunch of the guys. Your daughter wants to go to a party at a friend's house, and you know the friend's parents are out of town. Your son talks of celebrating the summer solstice by watching the sunrise on the beach after camping out all night with friends. Your daughter is dying to go to a rock concert.

• The first rule for monitoring a teenager's social life is: *Parents should know where the teenager is going, with whom, and what he or she plans to do.* The fact that your daughter has her driver's license or your son pays for his own entertainment with earnings from a part-time job does not mean that your authority and responsibility as a parent are over. The teenager's whereabouts are your business, especially at night. The public service announcement broadcast on many TV stations each night—"It's 10 P.M.: Do you know where your children are?"—is a good reminder. A teenager should let you know where she is going. If her plans change, she should call you before 10 P.M. If the teenager refuses to say where she is going or lies about where she has been, it's a sign of trouble.

Beyond this, there are few hard-and-fast rules. Whether or

not you permit a teenager to attend a party or another group event depends on these factors:

- *The adolescent's age.* Freshmen need more supervision than seniors.
- *Who else will be there.* Going downtown with friends whom you know to be responsible, law-abiding teenagers is different from going off with strangers. If they are his friends, why haven't you met them? Good friends will support the teenager who doesn't want to get smashed, trash a teacher's lawn, or otherwise get into trouble.
- *The teenager's willingness to go along with your guidelines.* No drugs, no alcohol, no driving with someone who has been drinking, home by curfew, and so on.
- *The teenager's past behavior.* Adolescents who have shown they know how to handle a tricky situation—who left a party when drugs were passed around, refused to go along with vandalizing a cemetery, insisted on driving when a friend got drunk —deserve your trust. A teenager who has gotten into trouble needs closer supervision.
- *The frequency of requests to participate in activities with the potential for trouble.* Going to a club to hear a particular rock group is one thing; going to clubs every weekend, another.

- *How much freedom you grant the teenager also depends on your willingness to bail the adolescent out.* If your daughter calls at midnight and says a party is getting out of hand or her date has been drinking, are you willing to get out of bed and pick her up or to call a taxi service and pay for her ride home? Assuming that you are, discuss emergency plans in advance. A young adolescent might not mind being picked up by a parent, but the older teen will feel embarrassed. Arrange beforehand to meet her at a corner a block from the house. Knowing that you understand her need to save face will make her more likely to call.
- *Parties with no adult supervision are not a good idea.* Young adolescents (under age 16) should not be permitted to attend unsupervised parties. Older teens might be, if you know where they are, have an idea of who else will be there, and trust your adolescent to leave if the party gets rough.

The same cautions apply to hanging out at a friend's house after school, when the friend's parents are still at work. For the older teen, this might be alright on occasion. But spending every day at an "open house" is too much. Apart from issues of supervision, a teenager should have something better to do (studying, extracurricular activities, hobbies) with his time.

When Parents Go Away

You and your spouse have planned a long weekend by yourselves. Your teenager asks if she can have a few friends over on Saturday night. You want her to feel that you trust her, but you know what can happen at unsupervised parties. What do you do?

Tell the adolescent that having *one or two* friends to the house is fine, but that you cannot permit a large party when you are away. Explain why. If anything bad should happen—if a fight broke out, a guest were given "bad dope" that sent him to the hospital, a drunken teenager had an accident driving home—you would be held personally liable. You won't be responsible for what happens when you are not around. Furthermore, you don't think the teenager should bear responsibility for a party alone. What would your daughter do if a large group of undesirable strangers crashed her party? if guests were taunting the family dog? offering a younger sibling marijuana? playing catch with an antique vase? Would your son feel comfortable about declaring that alcohol and marijuana were not allowed at *his* party? opening a bedroom door and telling a couple to come out? How would he feel playing the role of parent? The same rules apply to afternoons when both parents are at work.

Even if the teenager doesn't bring the subject up, parents should discuss the no-party rule before they leave and make sure their policy is clear. Don't worry about putting ideas into the teenager's head; if she hasn't thought about a party while you're away, her friends probably have. Be willing to be the "heavy" (she'll be grounded for a month if she breaks the rules).

Of course, it's possible that the teenager's friends will show up uninvited, bringing a party with them. For this reason, as well as general safety, the teenager should have the number of a neighbor or friend he can call at any time, for any reason, when you are away. Better yet, ask the adult to call and/or stop by the house to see how the teenager is doing. Tell the teenager that you are doing this as a precaution, not because you don't trust him. The possibility that an adult will check in gives him an excuse to turn a group of rowdy friends away.

Teenager are more likely to accept this policy if you allow

them to have parties when you are home. This lets them know that it's not the party or their friends that you object to, but the lack of supervision, the possibility of crashers, and other dangers. The guidelines for supervising a party for teenagers are essentially the same as those for young adolescents (see chapter 9), except that you can expect more dancing and talking, more coupling off and making out, more guests who "bring their own" (liquor or marijuana), and less interest in games, food-throwing, climbing the roof, and other stunts. Make your presence known, but wait for your teenager to ask for help.

DATING

In general, the trend in this country has been toward dating earlier—and marrying later. The median age at which adolescents start dating today is about 14 for girls and 15 for boys. But it is not unusual for adolescent girls to begin going out at 13 or even 12. By age 16, nine out of ten teenagers are dating, about half of them once or twice a week. Most teenagers have had at least one serious relationship before they graduate from high school. But norms vary from community to community and even school to school. Whether, when, and how often your teenager dates will depend in part on what his or her friends are doing.

Is Dating Good or Bad for Teenagers?

Dating is more than just fun; at this age, it's almost a competitive sport, one in which adolescents test themselves and others, and one in which there are winners and losers. The effects on the adolescent can be good and bad.

Some Benefits   *Dating can build self-esteem.* To simplify a bit: A boy works up the courage to ask a pretty girl from his French class to a school dance. To his amazement, she accepts and says she was hoping he would ask her. When they show up together, other teens, who thought he was a bit of a wimp, begin to look at him in a new light. His status among his peers rises, as does his self-image.

Dating can help young people discover who they are, especially with regard to gender identity. A series of dating relationships allows adolescents to try out their ideas about masculinity and femininity. Do girls like a boy who acts macho or one who reveals his vulnerability? Do boys like a girl who acts dependent and emotional, or can she show herself to be strong-willed and self-reliant?

Dating can help teenagers learn social skills: Consideration (how to refuse a date without putting the other person down), responsibility (getting the check in a restaurant, making sure a date is home by curfew), and other interpersonal skills, from small talk and dancing to making up after a fight.

Dating can help teenagers learn more about how to develop close, intimate ties to another person. This lesson is especially important for boys, who may not learn about closeness from each other.

Some Costs   *Dating can lower self-esteem.* Being turned down, stood up, or dropped for another boy- or girlfriend can be devastating for a teenager. (These are not fun for adults, either, but adults have had experience at recovering from rejection; teenagers haven't.) Lack of interest from the opposite sex can make a teenager feel like a nobody. Dating is one of the keys to popularity in high school. A girl who, for one reason or another, isn't ready to start dating when her friends are may find those friends drifting away. Once the life of all-girl pajama parties, now she's a wallflower at dances and parties. A boy who is too shy, or too overbearing, to get anywhere with girls begins to doubt his masculinity.

Dating can reinforce sex-role stereotypes. High-school dates tend to follow fairly rigid, sex-stereotyped scripts. A girl who has always been ready to compete with boys as an equal in math or baseball may suddenly clutch when she begins dating. Although most teenagers today say it is okay for a girl to ask a boy out, the available evidence suggests that very few do so. Rather, girls accept the passive, waiting-by-the-phone role. Unless they are "just friends," girls still expect the boy to pay for everything, and boys may feel put down if their date offers to share.

Dating can foster superficiality rather than intimacy, role-playing more than emotional depth. Teenagers often go through the motions, just to be going out. Members of both sexes may use a date to gain status, enjoy the power trip of leading someone on, lie about their feelings to keep a convenient relationship going, and cheat on a steady. But some experience with the good and bad aspects of dating, before they actually begin looking for a mate, is probably useful for teenagers.

The Bottom Line   All in all, we believe that dating is benign —unless it is very *early* or *excessive*. Adolescents who become seriously involved before age 15 may seem confident and self-assured but in fact are more dependent, more superficial, and less imaginative than their peers. More often than not, early dating interferes with the development of an independent sense of who they are and where they are going. Precocious teenagers base their identity on the dating game rather than viewing dates as an opportunity to learn about who they are. Excessive dating—to the point where the adolescent has little time or energy left for anything else—is also harmful. When dating is the teenager's whole life, other interests, like academics, sports, hobbies, and friendships, suffer. But moderate dating (once or twice a week) in high school is not harmful and may even be beneficial.

Going Steady, Falling in Love, and Breaking Up

In some places, a boy and girl who go out together several times are assumed to be going steady; in others, the boy is supposed to ask the girl to go steady. In either case, the presumption is that they are committed to one another and will not flirt or go out with anyone else. This "fidelity" is usually short-lived: Some adolescent romances last only a week or two; few continue for more than a year. The most common pattern in high school is a series of serious, or semiserious, relationships.

Single adults often follow the same pattern of short-term relationships, but they're more honest with themselves and others. They may say "I'm dating a real winner" or "I met someone terrific," but as a rule they do not talk about commitments until they are ready to make them.

Why do teenagers play this game of mock fidelity? Going steady means status and, at least temporarily, security. To peers, a teenager who has a steady boy- or girlfriend is one of the "haves" (as opposed to the "have-nots"). Being part of a couple validates the teenager's attractiveness to the opposite sex. It confers an aura of maturity. Teenagers who have a steady don't have to worry about whether they will have something to do Saturday night, whether they'll get a date for the prom, or whether an invitation to dance will be given or accepted. Going steady can also mean wanting to be with someone because you have so much fun together; getting all excited because John is coming over; thinking all week about getting it on with Helen. But in many cases the fact of having a steady is as important as the relationship itself. Other times it is not: Teenagers do fall in love.

Few adolescents have what adults would consider a "mature" relationship. Rather, most teenage romances are characterized by "pseudointimacy." The couple tell one another (and themselves) that they trust each other, yet often feel jealous and possessive or restless and tied down. They may say that they are being open with each other, yet fear that the other person will see through their act. They may vow to love each other forever, yet have trouble making future plans that include the other. In effect, they are playing at being lovers, without having the commitment and understanding to *be* lovers in the adult sense. Many teenagers recognize that what they are feeling isn't "true love"; few expect to marry the person they are going with in high school. But this doesn't mean that their feelings of attraction, excitement, and wanting to be together are not real.

Sex may also play a part in teenagers' claims of commitment. As we've said, most teenagers consider sexual intercourse permissible only in the context of love, or at least a steady relationship. If two teenagers have been going together for several months, the subject will almost surely come up. In some cases, affection and closeness lead naturally to sex. But in others, sexual curiosity and desire may lead a couple to say, and even believe, that they are in love when they are not. Declarations of love serve as permission to satisfy their curiosity.

Given the tentative, exploratory, pretend nature of adolescent romance, breakups are almost inevitable. Falling *out* of love is also part of the teenage experience. Some teenagers shift gears with relative ease; others do not. One might expect that boys fall into the former category and girls into the latter—after all, females are supposed to be the romantic sex. Girls are more likely than boys to say they loved their ex-boyfriend. But they are just as likely as boys to have been the one who fell out of love, and less likely than boys to go through a period of "mourning" before starting a new relationship.

Establishing Rules

Dating is a new experience for parents as well as adolescents. It's easy for parents to over- or underreact to this change in their adolescent's social life.

With dating, there is a fine line between interest and intrusion. If you've been close to your adolescent, dating shouldn't be a taboo subject. Many teenagers enjoy talking with a parent about their feelings for a boy- or girlfriend and hearing about the parent's experiences as a teenager and young adult. But a parent should not press or demand that a teenager tell every detail of every date. That's intrusion.

The guidelines for involvement with the adolescent's dates are essentially the same as for involvement in the adolescent's friendships, namely:

• *Know whom your adolescent is dating.* Make a point of meeting the people your adolescent is seeing and trying to get to know them a little, but don't intrude. Do ask your adolescent about the person he or she is going out with and how the date went, and look for opportunities to chat with your adolescent's dates. If you are friendly but not intrusive, the teenager is more likely to bring dates home.

• *Know where your adolescent is going on a date and what they plan to do.* The guidelines you have set for group activities apply to dates as well. Discuss places and activities you consider off-limits, and when you expect the teenager to come home, *beforehand.* Part of the excitement of dating is feeling and appearing adult. Don't embarrass the teenager by treating him or her like a child in front of a date.

• *Set guidelines for where, when, and how often your adolescent goes on dates.* Like any other extracurricular activity, dating needs to be kept in perspective. Schoolwork comes first, of course. But neither should dating displace other important activities, such as sports, hobbies, and time with friends and family. In high school, one or two dates a week, usually on the weekend, is a good limit. This doesn't mean the teenage couple (or a teenager and a prospective date) should be forbidden to study together in the afternoon on occasion or to go for a snack after band practice—if they do study and they are home at a reasonable hour. But a high-school student shouldn't be going out three, four, or five nights a week.

• *Don't jump to conclusions about what dating means.* Parents some-times equate dating with sex. They are wrong. Many teenagers are more interested in studying together, talking, dancing, going to parties, participating in youth groups, and just having the ex-perience of dating than they are in sex. (Today, as in the past, going to the movies is a favorite date.) Your adolescent may feel as awkward and uncomfortable about sex as you feel about the idea of his or her becoming sexually active. Even when a couple do become sexually involved, many never go further than petting.

We don't want to suggest that teenagers are not interested in sex; but sex isn't the only or even the primary motivation for dating. Of course, if you haven't talked to the teenager about sex before, you should now (see chapters 5 and 12). Be sure adoles-cents understand that you are not accusing them of anything, you just want to be sure they are informed and responsible.

What if the relationship is serious? Parents who have no problems about dating may get nervous when teenagers announce that they are "serious," "going steady," or "in love." Such announcements conjure up images of premature commitment, premature sex, limited futures, and mistakes that will be difficult to correct. In most cases, however, there is little reason for concern.

Going steady in junior high school can be a problem. Young adolescents who go steady limit their acquaintances, risk getting pushed to go too far sexually, and miss out on a lot of fun. Later they often regret their decision.

But going steady in high school, by itself, is not a problem. The main danger is that the adolescent will invest too much time and energy in the relationship and neglect other important activ-ities. But the same might be true of a teenager who dates a differ-ent person every weekend. Going steady is not a problem if the teenager abides by your guidelines for when and how much. Going steady probably does increase the likelihood that the teen-ager will consider sexual intercourse. But banning serious rela-tionships is not likely to make sexual attraction go away.

What if you dislike the person your adolescent is seeing? Trying to fathom the reasons for your adolescent's choice is largely futile. In adolescence, as in adulthood, love is often blind.

What should you do if you truly dislike the person your ado-lescent is seeing—if you disapprove of that person's behavior, background, or appearance? The answer is, probably nothing. A number of studies have documented a Romeo-and-Juliet effect:

The more parents oppose an adolescent romance, the more intense that relationship becomes. It's easy to see why. Dating is part of becoming an adult, an expression of growing independence. When parents pressure a teenager to break up with a boy- or girlfriend, they are threatening the adolescent's sense of autonomy. The most common response is defiance ("I'll show you how adult I am!") by continuing to date the forbidden person on the sly.

The best strategy in this situation is to say very little unless asked, and then to be honest but tactful: "I don't know him very well; why are you so fond of him?" "He seems awfully hung up on football to me; am I missing something?" "She's a pretty girl, but very quiet; what do you two talk about?" "She acts very sophisticated; what do you think of her smoking and drinking? the way she dresses?" "You two seem very different to me, but tell me what you think" and the like. Remember, most teenage romances are transitory. If you let nature run its course, the two are likely to drift apart; but if you back the adolescent into a corner, she may cling to the undesirable person as an act of self-assertion.

There are exceptions to this rule, however. You should step in if

• *You are convinced your adolescent is being mistreated.* If you have good reason to believe that your child is being taken advantage of, dominated, or exploited, it's time for a talk about why a person can feel attracted to someone who makes them feel bad. For example: When a boy takes you out but constantly puts you down, you may begin to feel that everything about you—the way you dress, the way you walk, the way you think—is wrong and try your hardest to please him. In fact, there's nothing wrong with you; you're with the wrong boy. Or, if a girl keeps doing things that hurt you (making jokes about you to other people, leaving you at a party for someone else), then calling the next morning to say how sorry she is and how much she really likes you, you may want to believe her. But you wouldn't behave as she does; why should you take such mistreatment from her? These are difficult lessons for adults to learn, and adolescents won't see the light the first time you talk. But talking helps.

• *The boyfriend or girlfriend is in trouble with the law, uses drugs, drinks excessively, or drives and drinks.* In these cases, you should not hesitate to forbid the relationship and say why. At the same time, ask yourself whether the reason your adolescent is seeing this person is that he or she is also using drugs or drinking heavily (see Danger Signs in chapter 13). If not, the teenager may have "savior" fantasies: "I'll be the one who will help this person stop." Talk to the teenager about how hard it is for an adult to deal with such behavior, much less an adolescent.

• *Your adolescent has been verbally or physically abused or sexually coerced.* If you see or overhear something that makes you suspect your adolescent has been the victim of date rape, try to learn the truth. Many girls are afraid to tell their parents. Assure your daughter that you won't blame her if this is what happened (see chapter 12). If she has been coerced into sex, forbid her to see the boy again and call his parents immediately. Do the same if your daughter comes home with unexplained bruises and later confesses that her boyfriend beat her up.

• *Your daughter is dating someone much older than she is.* Girls usually date boys who are a year or two older than they are, but dating someone who is five or six or more years older than she is can be a problem. If part of the excitement about dating is feeling and looking adult, dating an "older man" (someone 25 or 26) may seem like the ultimate. At this age, a gap of five or six years is more like a decade in terms of dating experience, sexual confidence, and other aspects of maturity. He's a young adult; she is only a would-be adult. She may do things to make herself appear mature (drinking, going to nightclubs, agreeing to sex) that she wouldn't do with someone closer to her age. (Studies of pregnant teenagers find that the father is often in his mid-20s.) If your daughter is very mature, if you know the boy well, and if he is willing to abide by teenage guidelines for dating, you might make an exception. But in most cases, dating much older boys should be discouraged.

• *Your adolescent is talking seriously about getting married.* Many teenagers make "casual" comments about getting married just to see how their parents react, as part of the "I'll-show-you" response. But some are serious. Teenage marriages are nearly always troubled marriages (as we discussed in chapter 12). Although in most states you cannot prevent an adolescent who is 16 years old from getting married, you can and should actively discourage this.

Start by finding out why they want to get married. Most teenagers think 16 or 17 is much too young to settle down. If a couple is planning to get married, there is a reason. The most common reason probably is that the couple know or suspect the girl is pregnant. Another common reason is that one or both are being verbally, physically, or sexually abused at home and they are desperate to get away. Their common problem may draw them together, or the one may want to save the other from these ordeals. In either case, your goal should be to help the teenagers find another way of dealing with their problem. (See chapter 12 for what to do if a girl becomes pregnant and chapter 5 for dealing with sexual abuse.)

If the teenager is talking about getting married at some point in the distant future, and thoughts of marriage are not interfering with his or her educational plans and occupational goals, parents should not be concerned, even if they don't like the person. Some individuals do marry their childhood sweethearts, but most high-school romances do not survive the adolescent's first year in college.

What if your adolescent won't agree to your rules? Some teenagers can take or leave dating. They are as happy on the sports field as they are at a dance and see benefits in being unattached as well as in being attached. Other teens invest a good deal of themselves in dating: Their self-esteem is tied up with popularity, they equate being in love with being mature, and they see their steady as their best friend. These are the teens who are most likely to quarrel with their parents about dating, especially if they feel their parents don't understand.

The most effective approach to resolving conflicts over dating is the same as that for other conflicts: negotiation (see Resolving Conflicts, chapter 2). First ask yourself whether you are bothered by the adolescent's behavior or by the challenge to your authority. Is what she is doing, or wants to do, dangerous (going to a questionable part of town)? unhealthy (she's involved in a serious relationship but won't talk to you or anyone else about contraception)? interfering with important activities (going out school nights when she needs to study)? age-inappropriate (involvement in a serious relationship at age 13)? If you can't think of a reason for being upset, the teenager probably has a point when she says you're being unfair.

Then take issues one at a time, and try to compromise. Ask what she would propose. If she wants her curfew moved up, you might compromise on a midnight curfew on weekends for a period of a month. Discuss what the consequences will be if she does not abide by this new rule. If she wants to go to a college fraternity party, you might agree that she can if her date picks her up at your house and brings her home by curfew (and no drinking). If she thinks your rule against dating on school nights is totally unfair (she is getting *B*s in most of her classes, and she and her boyfriend like studying together), you might agree to one date a week at your house or two midweek dates out per month. Be sure that you both understand the consequences of breaking these new rules and that you enforce them if she does.

On the other hand, if your teenager *regularly* breaks curfew, refuses to say where he is going or with whom, sneaks out of the house when he's been grounded, lies about going to choir practice or a friend's house, the problem isn't dating, it's defiance. In this case, you should consider seeking professional help. (And see Sexual Acting Out and Defiance in chapter 15.)

What if your teenager is not dating? Some parents worry more about the adolescent who isn't dating than about the one who is. Is there something wrong with the 15- or 16-year-old who has never been on a date? In almost all cases, no. Most Europeans don't begin dating until their late teens, and many psychologists believe they are better off as a result. If the teenager is socially active otherwise (has friends, goes out with groups, participates in extracurriculars) and doesn't seem unhappy, there is no cause for concern. If the adolescent is unhappy about not dating, the problem may be shyness (see chapter 9). You might be able to help him work up his courage to ask someone out. If the adolescent doesn't seem interested in friends of either sex, you should be concerned, however. Friendlessness can be a sign of depression (chapter 8), involvement with drugs (chapter 13), or other problems (chapter 15).

THE IMPORTANCE OF FRIENDS

Despite all the interest in dating, friends are still the most important people in the adolescent's social world. The trend toward intimate friendships based on empathy, trust, and self-disclosure, which began in early adolescence, continues in middle adolescence. Because they are maturing intellectually, middle adolescents are better able to deal with ambiguities and apparent contradictions in other people—for example, that someone who *seems* snobbish or loud may actually be shy, or that someone who seems shy may be iron-willed underneath. They realize that the same person may behave differently in different situations, and begin to recognize the stable core of traits we call "personality."

Middle adolescents are more tolerant, and appreciative, of individual idiosyncrasies. They know friends don't have to like all of the same people, have the same opinions, or share each and every interest. They are also beginning to understand that friendship is based on a balance of dependence and independence: Friends need to trust one another, but they also need to give one another room to breathe—they don't have to go everywhere and do everything together. As a result of these advances in personal understanding, friendships deepen in middle adolescence. Indeed, the friends young people make now may be friends for life.

Platonic friendships, or friendships between boys and girls— rare to nonexistent in early adolescence—become more common now. Such friendships, which allow males and females to get to know one another without all the posturing and preening that typically go into dating, probably do more to teach adolescents about the opposite sex, and what they might look for in a serious, adult relationship, than the ritual of dating does.

Both sexes list trust and loyalty as two of the most important characteristics of friendship. More and more, they turn to their friends when they are angry, disappointed, or in trouble. Like adults, they build a network of support. This doesn't mean that the teenager will stop talking to you. But there are times when you are not around; when a friend knows more about the problem (how to break up with a particular boyfriend) than you do; when the adolescent wants more than one opinion (where to apply to college); and when the problem he or she needs to discuss is *you.*

Heading to a friend's house when you were looking forward to a family evening together, endless phone calls that suddenly stop when you enter the room, and late-night talks behind closed doors are all part of this process. Don't assume that the closed door means adolescents are discussing drug deals, abortion, or running away from home. In all likelihood, they are talking girl- or boytalk (who's going with whom, what they think of so-and-so, how they really feel about this or that, what they dream of becoming), just as you did at their age. And don't feel that greater closeness to friends means greater distance from you. The quality of adolescent friendships reflects the quality of parent-child relationships—that is, the closer your daughter or son feels to you, the closer she or he will also feel to friends.

You may find that you have to work a little harder to stay close, however. A heart-to-heart talk often means staying up beyond your bedtime (the adolescent is busy all day but bursting with news at 12 P.M. after a date) or getting away from home (taking a weekend camping trip or vacation together). You may also find that you're becoming close to one or more of your adolescent's friends. Likewise, your adolescent may become close with one of your friends. Because they are more self-confident, middle adolescents are less wary of adults than they were before. Talking with adults other than their parents, adults who don't know (or think they know) everything about the adolescent, is a way of consolidating and confirming their developing identity. It's fun for adults to keep up to date with the latest trends and fashions, and fun for adolescents to be admitted to an adult's circle of friends.

RELATED ISSUES

The teenager's increasing social independence raises a host of side issues. Parents and their adolescent may agree about the big issues (the importance of school, guidelines for parties and dating, responsible sex, and avoidance of alcohol and drugs), yet quarrel about little things to the point where they don't seem little anymore. Earlier (in chapter 9) we discussed telephone use, spending money, dress and grooming, and tastes in music. Here, we turn to two issues more likely to surface during the high-school years and directly tied to the growth of social independence: driving and leisure time.

Driving

Getting a driver's license is a rite of passage in our society, a clear signal that you are moving toward adulthood and independence. How should parents handle this chapter of their teenager's coming of age?

In general, it is easier and safer to let a professional teach the adolescent how to drive than to give the lessons yourself. Because teenagers associate driving with maturity, the slightest criticism from a parent is likely to send them into a funk; and because parents associate driving with letting go in a very concrete way, and with the possibility of accidents and serious injury, they are likely to overreact to the slightest mistake. Most schools have driver's education programs; if your adolescent's school doesn't, look into a driver's training school.

Before the adolescent gets his license, you should come to an agreement on when, how often, and for what purposes he will be allowed the keys to the car. There are no set standards for this. What you decide depends on your community (and the availability of public transportation), your family's life-style and leisure interests, and your teenager's activities. Let's suppose your daughter has a reasonable amount of experience driving with you and by herself and has shown herself responsible at the wheel and in other ways. You might agree that she will have use of the car one weekend night, Saturday afternoons to drive to bowling, and on Sundays when the church youth club meets, assuming you don't need the car at these times. In exchange, you should expect the new driver to share some of the responsibilities that have always been yours, such as running errands and picking up a younger sibling. There may be exceptions to these rules, but if you have set up guidelines in advance, you are much less likely to be bombarded with requests, and she is less likely to feel you are depriving her of the car unfairly.

You and the adolescent should also discuss who will pay for gas, insurance, parking tickets, and other car expenses. Again, depending on your situation and the teenager's finances and activities, you might decide to carry all of the cost during high school or require him to contribute to some of these expenses. Whatever you decide, the adolescent should know that insurance premiums increase sharply when a young driver is added to the policy. If the adolescent gets a ticket for a moving violation, the cost of insurance will rise even more. One way to bring home the importance of safe driving is to point out that if the teenager gets a speeding ticket or has an accident, you may not be able to afford to insure him.

Owning a car of their own is the stuff of teenage dreams. But these fantasies rarely include the cost of insurance, repairs, and maintenance. If the teenager has factored these costs into her dreams, can afford a car, and is a safe driver, you might consider allowing her to own one. If the teenager actually needs a car (it would enable her to enroll in an enrichment program at a nearby college, to attend daily ballet classes without missing school, or some other good reason), you might consider helping with the costs. But beware of the teenager who says she needs a car to get to work, when all of her earnings will go toward the car. (See Working during the School Year, chapter 17.) Also beware of the parent who spent his adolescence dreaming of a car and now wants to live vicariously through his son by giving him what he couldn't afford. A car won't make a responsible adolescent irresponsible. But for one who isn't very mature and who hasn't yet acquired a sense of personal responsibility and self-regulation, a car can be an invitation to trouble.

Leisure Time

Adolescence is, or should be, a time to explore one's interests, discover one's talents, and develop one's skills—not only in school, but in art, music, dance, athletics, crafts, reading, collecting, computers, automechanics, volunteer activities (the list is virtually endless). Middle adolescents are in a unique position. Unlike children, they have what it takes—intellectually and physically—to pursue a hobby or interest to the utmost. Unlike adults, they have relatively few responsibilities. And most high schools offer them an array of extracurricular opportunities.

Problems over leisure-time activities arise when parents dismiss their adolescent's interests as trivial or tasteless or when parents push adolescents into the activities that *they* consider worthwhile. The wise parent is alert to the teenager's developing interests; encourages him or her to pursue those interests, by allowing time, providing supplies and lessons, and applauding the results; but does not dictate what those interests should be. The fact that varsity wrestling, writing for the school paper, working in Barry Goldwater's or George McGovern's presidential campaigns, or having your own pottery kiln was the highlight of your high-school years does not mean that your adolescent will or should share your enthusiasm. Adolescents should be well rounded, in the sense that they have interests outside school and beyond socializing. But what the interests are should be up to them.

CHAPTER 17

School and Work

A PARENT'S ROLE

All too often parents assume that the high school will look out for their adolescent's best interests. (It won't necessarily.) Or they are afraid of being too pushy. (You have a legitimate right to make appointments with counselors and teachers, to ask questions about school programs, and to play a role in your adolescent's placement.) Or they are just too busy to get involved. High school is a clear case where apathy can be harmful to your adolescent's future.

Why Parental Involvement Is Critical

There are three main reasons why parents need to be involved in planning and overseeing their adolescent's high-school career.

• *Graduation requirements are minimal.* A typical four-year high school requires four years of English, two of social studies, one of mathematics, one of science, one of American history or government, and one to four of physical education. The remaining credits can be earned with virtually anything the adolescent likes. Students who follow this minimal academic course will receive a high-school diploma, but many doors will be closed to them. Colleges often require at least three years of mathematics, science, including one laboratory course, and competence in at least one foreign language. Graduation requirements do not come close to meeting these standards.

• *School guidance counselors and teachers are overloaded.* As long as students are meeting graduation requirements, no one has to approve their course selection. It is not uncommon for a counselor to be responsible for 300 to 400 students. Typically, the counselor schedules one meeting a year with each student. An average meeting lasts about ten minutes. The counselor may recommend that the student take certain courses but doesn't have the time or authority to follow up. Many counselors manage case overload by adopting a reactive stance. If a student seeks them out, they are happy to help; if a student doesn't, that's fine, too. The average student's relationship with teachers (who often see 125 to 150 students a day) may be equally anonymous. The English teacher doesn't know how the teenager is doing in math, and the math teacher barely knows the French teacher. In short, no one at school is responsible for knowing the adolescent as an individual, developing a picture of the whole child, and guiding his or her academic career.

• *Adolescents pick courses for the wrong reasons.* To be sure, some high-school students know where they want to go and how to get there. But many do not. With graduation requirements at a minimum and no one to guide them, they pick courses for all kinds of reasons, many irrelevant or even antithetical to the goal of getting a good education. The most common reasons are: They've heard from other students that the course is easy and the teacher "neat"; the class meets at a convenient time (it doesn't interfere with important extracurricular activities or their job); and they will be with their friends.

What Parents Can and Should Do

The bottom line is that *adolescents who plan to go to college should take the most challenging course of study the school offers that they can handle and continue on this course through graduation, with no slacking off.* How can parents help their adolescent stay on the right track?

• *Schedule a meeting for you and your teenager with the school guidance counselor at the beginning of high school.* Ninth grade is not too soon to be thinking about college. The adolescent may not be looking this far ahead, but you should. Some subjects, especially math and science, are cumulative: If your adolescent doesn't take algebra in ninth grade, he will be shut out of geometry and trig the following years. If he opts for a low-level English course in ninth grade, it will be difficult to move to a higher level in tenth or eleventh grade should he decide to get serious.

Talk to the counselor about several colleges your adolescent might be interested in. What are the entrance requirements for these colleges? (How many years of math do they expect? Do they require a foreign language? and so on.) What course of study does the high school recommend for college-bound students? for your particular child? Make sure you understand what the different level designations for high-school classes mean and what your adolescent's options are. Take notes.

• *Follow up.* The best way to keep your adolescent from becoming invisible is to be visible yourself. In the words of one guidance counselor, "If parents come pounding on the door, then [the school makes] sure that those kids get the best programs. And if parents won't be pounding at the door, they get what's left." A student was even more candid: If you want to get into a particular class or program, "You get your mother to call up the school and bitch." In high school, as elsewhere, the squeaky wheel gets the grease.

Following up does *not* mean that you call to complain each time your adolescent gets a grade that is lower than you would like. Badgering school personnel about grades may convince them to put your adolescent into lower level classes to get you off their back. But you should schedule regular appointments with the adolescent's counselor and teachers, find out how your adolescent is doing, and if there seems to be a problem, ask for help in solving it. As a rule, high schools do not reach out to parents, but they do respond to parents who reach out to them.

• *If your adolescent is offered an honors or advanced placement program, insist that he or she accept.* Students must be invited to enroll in advanced placement (AP) or honors classes (invitations based on past record, teacher recommendations, and test scores—see chapter 11). But they are not required to accept the invitation.

These programs can be tough. At one school, AP students were required to read eight books, write three short (three-page) papers and one long (fifteen page) paper, and take a full-fledged exam every six weeks. But this hard work pays off in a number of ways. Colleges give more serious consideration to students who have chosen a difficult course of study than to those who have taken the easy route through high school. The classroom atmosphere and the assignments in honors programs are more like those in college, so that adolescents are better prepared when they get to college. In addition, students who take AP courses take a national examination. If their scores on this exam are high enough, they may receive college credit for some of the classes they took in high school and be allowed to take more advanced classes in college right away. If your high school does not have an AP program, your adolescent may be able to take courses at a local two- or four-year college.

The high school won't push a student to take honors or advanced placement, but you should. If your adolescent is reluctant (not sure she can handle the work or worried that her friends will write her off as a "brain"), compromise: If she takes advanced classes for one year, you will let her make her own decision the next year. Honors programs attract highly motivated students and create an atmosphere of specialness. Peer pressure from bright classmates and special attention from teachers may turn a reluctant honors student into an enthusiastic young scholar. If your adolescent has good reasons for not wanting AP (for example, he's an exceptionally talented dancer and needs to practice several hours every day), suggest that he take one or two honors courses and the next level in other subjects.

• *If your adolescent is not eligible for honors or advanced placement, still insist that he or she take a strong academic program.* Only a small percentage of students are admitted to honors and AP programs. An adolescent can still get a solid education by concentrating on academic subjects (English, history, math, science, social studies, and language) rather than general courses (personal growth and the like), academic substitutes (consumer math), and nifty electives (the history of automobiles).

Urge the teenager to take the most rigorous courses offered to him and to follow them as far as he can. Some adolescents don't want to push themselves. But many are simply misinformed. They may assume that meeting graduation requirements is enough to get into college. (Except for community colleges, it isn't. More on this in chapter 18.) Or they may believe that the way to gain admission to a more selective college is to accumulate as many As and Bs as they can and that taking "gut" courses will allow them to earn high grades. (In reality, colleges pay as much or more attention to a course's level of difficulty as they do to grades. They are much more impressed by a student who stayed with math through calculus, even though she only earned Cs, than they are with a student who dropped math and got As in chorus and jewelry-making.)

• *Discuss electives with the adolescent.* In choosing electives, urge the adolescent to pick courses that are exciting *and* academically relevant—an English course on the contemporary short story, a history course on the Vietnam War, a science course in psychology. If the adolescent has a burning interest in pottery, photography, or sailing (and these are offered for credit), that's fine. But she should treat these courses as extracurriculars, as something she takes *in addition* to her academic courses, not as a substitute for serious classes. She should be choosing electives because they are interesting, not because they are easy.

• *Convince the adolescent that his or her senior year counts.* When the adolescent has worked hard for the first three years of high school and established a credible record, there's a natural tendency to ease off in the senior year. This is a mistake. Colleges look at the student's most recent work first, and most ask for midyear senior grades. If the student cuts back in his senior year, they may conclude that his earlier efforts were all designed to build a college resumé and he isn't a serious student after all, or that he peaked in eleventh grade and isn't ready to handle work beyond that level. Moreover, if the student does not get into the colleges of his choice and decides to take a year off and reapply, his senior year will be critical.

• *If the adolescent is not planning to go to college, similar rules apply.* Say your adolescent has no plans to go to college, and you agree. He or she wants to join the military or to go right to work for an uncle's construction company or spend time in your church's social action program. This is not a reason to treat high school as a lark. These adolescents should be encouraged to take as much academic coursework as possible. High school may be their last formal exposure to the arts and sciences. On the other hand, they may later change their minds about college. Unless they take college preparatory courses now, they may have to go back to high school as young adults.

The adolescent who everyone (including you) agrees is not "college material" should be encouraged to develop competency in basic academic skills (reading, writing, and arithmetic) and perhaps devote the rest of his or her time to a vocational/technical program. Many school districts offer programs in science and technology, modern electronics, fashion and merchandising, performing arts, communications, agribusiness, hotel-hospitality, aircraft trades, and other specialties. These programs usually do not have the prestige of an academic program (to the dismay of their directors). But students who performed poorly in regular classrooms may improve when their efforts are rewarded with a visible product or public performance. Many also need training in the work habits other students know without instruction, like showing up on time and wearing appropriate clothes. We should caution that there is little evidence that voc/tech programs lead to better jobs. The student who can do regular academic work should do so. But for other students, they are an excellent alternative.

PUBLIC VS. PRIVATE SCHOOL

One alternative to the public high school is private school. If parents feel that their child needs special attention or that the schools in their area do not offer the quality education they want for their child, private school is something they should consider.

If you believe private school might be the right choice for your child, look carefully at the individual child and at the specific schools under consideration. Don't go by the school's name, reputation, or price. The "best" (most prestigious) school around might not be the best for your particular child. For example, recent studies of parochial schools indicate that they are strong on discipline and demand hard work. For a student who is not self-disciplined or highly motivated, these schools may provide the structure he or she needs. But for a student who is a self-starter, who likes to take the ball and run with it, or a student who is independent-minded and creative, these schools may be stultifying. These students might do better in nonreligious private schools, which are usually less structured and prefer talking to discipline.

Start by looking at one or more handbooks that describe both the schools in your area and ways of financing private school (see Resources). Ask those that look interesting for brochures, and choose several to call for interviews. At the interview, ask about the school's educational philosophy, the curriculum, and the faculty. How would they handle a hypothetical problem? What course of study do they offer to the bright, or slow, student? How would they describe their faculty? What do they consider their weak points? Will they permit you to sit in on a few classes? Be sure to ask about your adolescent's special interests and needs. If you have a budding scientist, for example, look into prospective schools' lab facilities. If your child is musical, what does the school offer in the way of classes in theory and harmony as well as extracurriculars (band, orchestra, chorus)? You should also ask for basic information on the school's past and present performance. If your adolescent is college-bound, ask what proportion of graduates go on to college. Does the school have a list of colleges recent graduates have attended? Ask about the average standardized test scores, including the SATs. This won't tell you anything about methods of instruction, but it will give you an idea of the academic level of the school. The school with the highest average test scores is not necessarily the best school for your child. If your child is an average student, this school might be too competitive.

Finally, arrange for you and your adolescent to visit the school and observe one or preferably several classes. When you return home, compare notes. Was the instruction stimulating or humdrum? Were the students engaged or turned off? Most important, how would *your* child respond in *this* learning environment? The key to successful private education is finding the right fit between your child and a school.

EXTRACURRICULAR ACTIVITIES

The word *extracurricular* is somewhat misleading. Educators, parents, and students alike see sports, the band, and the student council as anything but extra. These activities are thought to teach important lessons in life not available in the academic curriculum. Indeed, some schools now call nonacademic activities *cocurriculars* and award credit for participation. Often they are the highlight of the adolescent's high-school career. Adults look back on the year their team won the state football championship or their spell as a high-school newspaper reporter with nostalgia. Children and junior-high-school students watch the marching band come onto the field and dream of the day when they will be carrying the bass drum or twirling a baton. Sports, in particular, provide the most visible connection between the school and the community. In small towns, high-school football is often the most popular form of local entertainment: Thousands turn out for a big game.

Today's high schools usually offer a wide range of extracurricular activities, including sports (both intramural and interscholastic), performing arts (theater, orchestra, chorus), special interest clubs with an academic focus (language and science clubs) or a nonacademic focus (chess, debating, photography), journalism (a newspaper, yearbook, literary magazine, and radio station), and service organizations (student government, community service clubs). High-school students should be encouraged to participate in at least one of these activities.

The Benefits

Participation in extracurriculars can add important dimensions to the adolescent's social and psychological development.

Expanding horizons. Most extracurriculars cultivate interests and teach skills that are rarely touched on in academic classes (getting into shape, playing in tune, using a light meter to get special effects, and conducting an interview, to name a few). They provide opportunities for initiative, independent decision-making, and creativity that are often missing in the highly structured, adult-run classroom. For the average student, they offer an opportunity to excel: On the field or the stage, the "unspecial" student becomes special. The cheers and applause are concrete rewards for hard work. All of this contributes to self-esteem.

• *Encouraging teamwork.* Most are group activities, requiring cooperation. Teamwork is not encouraged in most classes. Rather, academics are individualistic and competitive. In class, students succeed by doing better than their peers; indeed, cooperation on a test or homework assignment may be defined as cheating. In most extracurricular activities, adolescents succeed by working *with* their peers. The individual who attempts to star at the expense of the team is shunned by his teammates (and often benched by the coach).

• *Developing interest in school.* Extracurriculars can build a bridge between the school and the student who is not particularly interested in, or successful at, academics. The visible, public nature of a performance on the basketball court or a solo with the chorus can be a powerful incentive for the student who is not motivated by grades or praise from teachers. Some teenagers show up at school because of their commitment to a team, not because of their interest in classes. But involvement in the school through extracurriculars can spill over into the classroom.

• *Leading to valuable relationships with adults.* Adolescents often develop close, supportive relationships with the adults who supervise extracurriculars. When a student has a problem at home or with schoolwork, she may turn to the coach before the counselor who barely knows her. The adviser to the student newspaper can be a powerful model for an aspiring writer and a more valuable source of information on future careers in writing than the guidance counselor who majored in psychology.

• *Opening social doors.* Extracurriculars allow teenagers to meet schoolmates who are not in their classes, and thus expand their pool of potential friends. This is particularly helpful to the shy adolescent, who has trouble meeting people, and the new student, who doesn't know anyone.

The Costs

Like any good thing, extracurriculars can be carried too far.

• *Time and energy.* The main danger is that the time and energy a student puts into extracurriculars may subtract from the time and energy available for academic work. Sports, in particular, can be very demanding, with frequent practices and games or meets away from school. Good schools, and good coaches, recognize the potential conflict. Some require that a student maintain a good academic record to remain on the team. But others do not. If this is the case, parents need to take charge.

Participation in extracurriculars should not exceed fifteen to twenty hours a week. If your son spends all afternoon at practice, he should devote his evenings to homework, not to lifting weights; if your daughter spends her afternoons in rehearsal, she should not spend the evening learning lines. You do not want to undermine the adolescent's commitment to excellence on the playing fields or the stage. But the teenager can just as easily train or memorize lines on the weekends. Talk to the teenager about potential conflicts in advance, before he is two months into the season or she is five weeks into rehearsal. Make it clear that schoolwork comes first. If the teenager's schoolwork is slipping because of investment in extracurriculars, he or she will have to cut back.

• *Exclusion.* A second danger is exclusion. In a highly sports-minded school, the in-crowd is composed of athletes and their support groups (cheerleaders and the pep band). Adults as well as peers see them as the school leaders. This inner circle is closed to students who are not directly or indirectly involved in sports. The fact that the nonathlete won a chess tournament or a poetry prize or is doing superior work in history or chemistry may go unnoticed. Parents of adolescents on the outside need to help them put things in perspective. Most high-school varsity players do not make college varsity teams, and only a tiny percentage of college players go on to play professional sports. Yes, they are having their moment of glory, but that moment is brief. Skills in other areas can last a lifetime.

• *Failure.* A third danger is failure. When a student fails biology, it's a private matter. When an adolescent fails to make the team or allows the goal that costs the game, when the teenager is not given a part in the play or blows a line on opening night, the failure is public. *Everyone* knows. Such experiences are devastating for teenagers, at least temporarily. Parents should not dismiss the adolescent's feelings ("So you missed a shot/tripped over a prop, big deal"). Nor should they support the adolescent's decision to stop trying. When the pain has begun to subside, talk to the teenager about what he or she can do to get in shape for the next season or another sport, prepare for the next tryouts or the debating team. Autobiographies by athletes and performing artists are a good addition to your library. Even Laurence Olivier flubbed lines.

All in all, the evidence suggests that the benefits of participation in extracurriculars outweigh the costs, *if* they are kept in perspective. Students who are active in extracurricular activities tend to have higher occupational ambitions than those who do not. Persistence and success at extracurriculars in high school are associated with academic success, leadership, and social accomplishments in college. Teenagers are also happiest when they are at work on these freely chosen activities. Encourage your adolescent to get involved in at least one extracurricular that engages his or her interest.

Team Sports: The Pros and Cons

The most popular extracurricular is athletics, but many adults disagree about the costs and benefits of participation in team sports. Advocates argue that team sports build character by teaching the importance of effort ("Hustle," "Give it everything you've got"), sportsmanship (playing by the rules, being fair), teamwork (the necessity of working together and ridicule of "hot dogs" and "prima donnas"), and how to deal gracefully with both winning and losing. Critics argue that team sports undermine character by teaching that winning is everything, promoting aggression ("Knock 'em, dead," "Wipe 'em out"), modeling poor sportsmanship ("Forget your glasses, Ump?"), creating a class system within schools (athletes are *it,* and nonathletes, nerds), and detracting from the more important business of learning. The best evidence suggests that the truth lies between these extremes. Parents shouldn't count on team sports, by themselves, to build character; neither should they worry that team sports, by themselves, will undermine character.

A well-run team sports program can

- Contribute to physical fitness and coordination
- Occupy the adolescent in healthy activity during after-school hours
- Teach skills that will be valuable later on
- Contribute to self-esteem by enhancing the adolescent's status among peers

On the other hand, a poorly run team sports program can

- Lead to fatigue and injury if training is excessive and the coach expects players to ignore pain
- Teach the wrong lessons, such as the importance of winning, instead of the importance of trying hard and doing something well
- Distract the adolescent from other, equally valuable activities, including schoolwork, other extracurriculars, and hobbies
- Take the fun out of an activity that would otherwise be intrinsically enjoyable, through undue pressure to win from parents and coaches, mockery of mediocre players, and the like

A lot depends on the attitudes and action of the adults on the sidelines.

Team sports can be valuable, and should be fun. But they are not for everyone. An adolescent who isn't athletic, doesn't enjoy competition, or just isn't interested in sports can learn the same lessons in other ways. Individual sports (hiking, biking, riding, swimming for fun), a program of aerobics, and/or informal games with friends can maintain physical fitness. Playing the piano or juggling will develop eye-hand coordination, and dancing will enhance footwork, as well as sports do. And working on the school newspaper, joining the debating team, indeed, most extracurricular activities, require teamwork.

With teenagers who do participate in organized sports, these are the most important considerations:

• *Does the coach/supervisor put athletics in the proper perspective?* Most coaches recognize that team sports are an extracurricular activity, not a career. Some keep an eye on their players' academic performance and even act as unofficial advisers. But some put the team first and expect players to do the same. Actually, studies find that it is usually *parents,* not coaches, who apply the wrong kinds of pressure to young athletes.

• *Is the coaching staff safety-conscious?* Are players given a medical screening before being accepted on a team? Are workouts designed to build strength and flexibility and so minimize the risk of injury? Is the proper equipment being used? Do coaches treat injuries seriously or expect players to be tough and play even when they are in pain? Most school programs are quite conscientious, if only because they want to avoid lawsuits, but informal sports leagues may not be.

• *How much enjoyment is the adolescent getting out of the activity?* Don't assume that just because your adolescent is on the starting team, he is loving football—or that just because he's on the bench, he is not. Adolescents participate in team sports for a variety of reasons. Some like the camaraderie; some enjoy the status that accompanies a varsity jacket; others love the game. But competition and high visibility make some adolescents intensely anxious. A teenager shouldn't feel that she has to participate in an extracurricular activity that makes her miserable.

• *Is your adolescent playing on a team because she wants to or because you want her to?* Sports is an arena where parents are especially prone to projecting their fantasies onto their adolescents. A father who misses the glory days of his athletic stardom may live vicariously through his son, ignoring hints that the teenager wants out. A mother who was a total klutz may feel vindicated when her daughter wins a tennis tournament. If her daughter works up the courage to say she doesn't want individual lessons every week (she'd rather be with friends or just read) plus five weeks at tennis camp, the mother doesn't hear. There is nothing wrong with being proud of your adolescent's accomplishments, in sports or any other activity. Just be sure you aren't forcing the adolescent into something he or she doesn't enjoy. If you feel that your son's not playing on the basketball team, or your daughter's giving up the swimming team, would leave a hole in your life, you are probably overinvolved.

• *Do you or the adolescent have fantasies of a professional sports career?* Do you imagine that your adolescent might earn a sports scholarship? If so, think again. Only an infinitesimal fraction of young people who are athletic stars in high school are good enough to make a college team, much less win an athletic scholarship or have a career in professional sports. And contrary to rumor, athletics are not a prerequisite for admission to the better colleges. Colleges are much more interested in grade-point averages than in batting averages (see chapter 18).

• *Are sports taking over the adolescent's life?* Putting schoolwork on the back burner the night before a big match is one thing; letting school slide altogether because of athletics is another. If your adolescent is totally wrapped up in athletics to the exclusion of other interests and activities, you might negotiate a time out (one semester without team participation). If hockey or horses are the great love of her life, but she is doing well in school and spending time with friends, relax. With sports, as with anything else, enthusiasm and commitment are fine, but obsession is not.

In smaller schools and some private schools, almost anyone who wants to play on a team can do so. In larger high schools, only a small percentage of students make the teams. When an adolescent whose heart is set on being part of the athletic elite doesn't make it past the cutoff, parents should acknowledge the teenager's disappointment but not reinforce it (by blaming the coach, saying "You'll make it next year," or otherwise defining the experience as a failure). Instead, help the adolescent find other interesting and involving extracurricular activities and other ways of being active and fit.

WORKING DURING THE SCHOOL YEAR

The Impact of Work

Most people assume that having a job is good for adolescents. Work builds character. It promotes responsibility and self-discipline. It teaches young people the value of money. It gives them experience in the "real world." At the very least, jobs keep teen-agers off the streets and out of trouble.

Recent research has questioned all of these assumptions. Teenagers do learn from their work experience, but not necessarily lessons that adults would endorse. In fact, employment can cause adolescents more harm than good, especially if the teenager works more than ten or fifteen hours a week.

• *Working may undermine school.* Students who work long hours tend to disengage from school. To balance the demands of work and school, many take the minimum number of courses required for graduation, choose the easiest courses available, and do only enough work to get by. (Indeed, a common reason why students quit their jobs is that they want to take advanced courses and electives.) Student workers spend less time than nonworkers on homework, are less prepared for class, cut corners on assignments, have trouble staying alert during classes, and are absent from school more often. Not surprisingly, their grade-point average (GPA) often suffers. They participate in fewer extracurricular activities than nonworkers do and are less likely to say they enjoy school. Some see school as taking a back seat to their job, not the reverse. Said one boy who worked twenty hours a week, "When I have nights off, I study."

• *Working may interfere with family life.* It's normal for teenagers to become less involved with their families during middle adolescence, but working seems to accelerate this process. Adolescents who work long hours don't *see* their parents very much. They are less likely to eat dinner with their families, to spend leisure time with their families, to help around the house, and to say they feel close to their parents. From the adolescent's point of view, working means more independence—in terms of hours (if they work evenings), money, and transportation (if they drive to work). From the parents' point of view, working can mean less control. If the teenager needs to drive to work, for example, it's harder for parents to use the keys to the car as a reward or grounding as a punishment.

• *Working may promote (not prevent) problem behavior.* In particular, working students are more likely than nonworkers to drink and smoke marijuana. There are several reasons for this. The first is money: The working teenager, who earns an average of two hundred to three hundred dollars a month, can afford drugs. The second reason is exposure on the job to older adolescents who have access to alcohol and pot and use both regularly. Many teenagers say that their co-workers, and even their supervisors, come to work stoned and offer to buy liquor for them. The third reason is stress. The kinds of jobs available to teenagers often expose them to heat, dirt, noise, and time pressures; their work schedules interfere with other activities they enjoy; and they have to deal with irate customers, obnoxious co-workers, and bosses who never listen to their suggestions and opinions—all of which lead to stress. Like adults in similar jobs, some turn to alcohol and drugs to relieve the tensions. Working teens may also get into trouble at school, cutting classes, coming late, or cheating to make up for lost study time.

• *Working may teach financial irresponsibility.* Popular wisdom holds that working will teach a teenager that money doesn't grow on trees; in fact, it may do the opposite. Most of today's student workers come from relatively well-off families. (In low-income neighborhoods, rates of teenage *un*employment remain high.) They are working not for necessities, such as housing and groceries, but for luxuries. The result has been called premature affluence: Teenagers have a great deal of pocket money but no real responsibilities, since their parents still provide the necessities. Far from teaching the value of a dollar, teenage employment may be teaching the pleasures of instant gratification.

• *Working may undermine the work ethic.* Most teenagers work at relatively unskilled, minimum-wage, dead-end jobs with few opportunities for initiative or decision-making, few challenges, and no intellectual stimulation. Their tasks are usually dull and repetitive. Moreover, the jobs they hold have little or no bearing on the occupations they will pursue as adults. (How many middle-class youngsters will grow up to wrap hamburgers for a living?) The experience is hardly designed to foster the belief that work can be a meaningful, satisfying part of life. On the contrary, it promotes cynicism.

Of course, work isn't all bad. Some adolescents give their wages to their families and save for the future. Many others help their families indirectly, by paying for their own clothes and entertainment. Teenagers who work say the experience has made them more conscientious, punctual, and dependable. For girls, working increases self-reliance: They feel they are able to "take care of business" without the guidance or approval of others. This sex difference probably reflects the fact that females still see work as a matter of choice, an act of self-assertion, not an obligation, as males do. Students with *C* averages or below often show improvement in practical arithmetic, suggesting that they find learning easier in the workplace than in the schoolroom. Perhaps most important, working enhances social skills. Because they come into contact with many types of people, student workers become more aware of different perspectives and motives, and gain experience in handling sticky situations.

The bottom line is that *moderate involvement in the workplace (less than fifteen hours a week) is usually harmless* and sometimes beneficial, though it is not the panacea many adults imagine. But *intensive involvement in the workplace (more than fifteen hours a week) can and does cause problems*.

Parental Guidance

Your 15-year-old daughter tells you she wants to get a job. What should you do?

• *Discuss the implications of working with the teenager.* Many employers will not hire teenagers unless they are willing to work fifteen or twenty hours a week. Eager for the money, the teenager may not think about what this means. Let's look at a twenty-hour job. The school day usually runs from 8 in the morning to 2 or 3 in the afternoon. Adding twenty hours of work to this schedule would mean working a full day both Saturday and Sunday, plus four additional hours during the week; working one full day on the weekend plus two long (5 to 11 P.M.) shifts on weekday evenings; working two long shifts and two shorter (5 to 9 P.M.) shifts on weekdays; or some other combination. If teenagers are involved in an extracurricular activity—sports or the school band—practice will occupy some or all of their afternoons. Then, of course, there is homework (a minimum of one to two hours a day). In taking a twenty-hour job, teenagers are committing themselves to a sixty- to seventy-hour work week (counting school and extracurriculars). Clearly, something has to give.

Parents may need to press adolescents to think about what they will be giving up if they take a job. Won't she miss playing basketball, writing for the school paper, taking jazz dancing classes, spending Saturday afternoon with friends? How will he feel when he can't attend the school play, a championship game, or a demonstration because he has to work? Will she really be able to complete her papers during the week if she's working weekends? Will he want to study on the weekends if he's working weekday evenings? Will she be able to stay awake in class the next day when she gets home from work at 11:40 P.M.?

In discussing work, parents need to make it clear that school is the teenager's first job. Lowering her academic ambitions to build up her wardrobe or stereo system is short-sighted: She is borrowing from her future to pay for the present. The same applies to artistic and athletic interests. Young people who give up horseback riding or guitar lessons at this age are less likely to pursue these interests in later life. Besides, overloading their schedules—trying to do it all—is unhealthy. Everyone needs some free time for rest and relaxation, especially adolescents.

Talk with the teenager about how working will affect family routines. Will the teenager monopolize the family car on work nights or weekends, or can he find other means of transportation? What about household chores? Will he expect you to subsidize his job by taking over some of his former chores (baby-sitting with younger siblings, cooking, yardwork, or whatever)? If he is working weekday evenings, will he eat with the family on weekends?

Talk about potential problems and conflicts and come to a mutual understanding *before* the teenager makes a final decision about getting a job.

• *Discuss different job opportunities.* If the teenager is determined to work, and you agree that he or she can handle a job, the next step is talking about what kind. Teenagers often fall into jobs. A friend tells them there is an opening where he works, they see a sign in a window, or they apply at a place they know employs teenagers. The result is the routine, boring, menial job we described earlier, with few if any opportunities for learning and career exploration. The thought of looking for something more exciting may not occur to the teenager. Your teenager may think "A job is a job," but you know better.

Encourage adolescents to find jobs that offer more than money, jobs that will enable them to acquire skills and information about occupations they might pursue in the future and expose them to adults who are positive role models. A good job is one that helps the adolescent figure out what she is good at and interested in. It may give her an opportunity to observe, first hand, what goes on in a law office, an art gallery, or a health clinic. And it should enable her to develop a network of adults who can give her "real world" advice on educational choices and

occupational opportunities in the future. (For concrete suggestions on how to get a job, see pages 352 to 355.)

Finally, parents and teenagers should not dismiss such traditional teenage jobs as baby-sitting, yardwork, housecleaning for a
neighbor, and golf caddying. Although not career-oriented or
terribly stimulating, these jobs allow the teenager more flexibility
in terms of time commitments than does formal employment.
Then there are small businesses that teenage entrepreneurs can
run themselves: One high-school junior tie-died T-shirts in his
basement for sale at flea markets and school games. A group of
sophomore girls hired themselves out to serve and clean up at
parties given by family friends and neighbors.

• *No matter what kind of job the teenager gets, limit the hours.* All of
the negative effects of working we described earlier are related to
time. The more hours a student works, the more likely he is to
lose interest in school, become a visitor in your family, get involved with drugs, and become cynical about work. Sophomores
should be limited to ten hours a week; juniors and seniors, to
fifteen hours a week. If they complain, point out that working ten
hours a week allows them to earn more than a hundred and fifty
dollars a month at the current minimum wage, and fifteen hours
a week, almost two hundred dollars a month. Surely this is more
than enough to support a high-school student's social life.

• *Discuss how the adolescent will use the money he or she earns.* The
following scene is all too common: The adolescent gets a paycheck
for seventy-five dollars on Friday afternoon. By Sunday evening,
he has only a ten-dollar bill and some change in his pocket and
doesn't know where the money went. We discuss money management below. For working teenagers, the basic rule is, insist that
they work out a sensible budget, one that you approve, before
they begin working. It's much easier to control the teenager's
spending if you have set guidelines in advance than it is to impose
controls after the fact.

• *If possible, visit the workplace and meet your adolescent's future supervisor.* The teenager may see this as prying. But it is your business to know where the adolescent goes and what she does. The
teenager will spend more hours a week with her supervisor than
she does with many of her teachers. Try to find out what this
person is like. Make sure the place of business is appropriate and
safe. A smoke-filled room with a motley assortment of people
trying to push goods and services on consumers by phone isn't a
good environment for an adolescent.

• *Finally, keep an eye on how working is affecting your adolescent.* This means, first, talking to the teenager about what's happening at work, just as you do with your spouse. Discussions about how to handle conflicts with a co-worker or boss, why an inventory is being taken and how that information will be used, how prices are determined, and the like can turn even a routine job into a learning experience. Second, periodically assess the impact of work on your adolescent's attitudes and behavior. Does the job seem to occupy more of his time and energy than you think it should? Is she becoming preoccupied with money and material possessions? Are there any signs that he is losing interest in school, extracurricular activities he used to value, or close friends? If the answer to any of these questions is yes, the teenager should not be working, or should be working fewer hours.

Money and Money Management

In the past, when adolescents begged for designer clothes, stereo equipment, a racing bike, or a car, parents would say "No, you don't need that" or "No, we can't afford it." Today parents are more likely to respond, "If you want it so badly, why don't you go out and get a job?" Let's face it, it's easier to let adolescents go to work than to convince them that they can survive without a CD player, a drawer full of cashmere sweaters, and front-row seats for every rock concert.

When teenagers work, parents tend to back off. If the teenager has earned the money himself, they don't feel they have the right to tell him how to spend it. One mother explained, "I would like to have my son give me the money and let me dole it out. But I'm afraid to say that, because that tells him that somebody is governing [his] spending . . . You can't do that." Most parents are surprised to learn that in most states they have a *legal right to a minor child's earnings* (if they inform the employer that this is their wish before the adolescent starts to work). We are not suggesting that parents invoke the law. You shouldn't tell a teenager, unilaterally, how to spend his or her money, whether that money comes from a job or an allowance. But neither should you abdicate your authority.

Wherever the adolescent's money comes from—work, an allowance, gifts from grandparents and others—you should discuss its management together. Your discussion should include

• *Savings.* By high school, all teenagers should have a savings account. Teens who work should be encouraged to bank a portion of their earnings (half or more) for college and other future expenditures, even if their parents can afford these things without the teenager's contribution. Establishing a habit of saving now will be important when the teenager becomes an adult and wants to make major purchases that require long-term savings. Teenagers generally do not think very far ahead, so this may take a little prodding on your part.

• *Budgeting.* Teenagers should be encouraged to make a weekly or monthly budget. Money for necessities (lunches, school supplies, transportation) should be set aside first. Then the teenager should decide what proportion of his "free money" he wants to spend on clothes, entertainment, equipment for hobbies, gifts, and the like. Budgeting helps teens realize that if you want to attend a rock concert that costs twenty dollars, you may have to give up movies and magazines for a week or two; if you use a birthday check to buy a compact disc, you should know that a CD may cost twice as much as a standard record. (For more on budgeting, see the discussion of allowances in Chapter 9.)

• *Purchases.* A high-school student should not be required to account to you for every nickel and dime; that is too controlling. But if she plans a major purchase (a hundred dollars or more), she must consult with you first. Why? Because you have more experience as a consumer and are better able to distinguish between a bargain and a rip-off. You are also better able to take the long view (the teenager may be dying for a guitar today but lose interest after a month or two and regret having spent most of his savings on a whim). Finally, as a parent, you have a right to veto purchases that might be dangerous (such as a motorcycle).

• *Other considerations.* If your daughter is saving substantial amounts, she should know about different interest rates for different types of accounts, such as savings, money market funds, and CDs, so that she can make the most of her savings. If your son is handling many expenses for himself, he might need a checking account. Some banks have special accounts for teenagers, with a ceiling so that the teenager cannot withdraw a large amount without your approval. If your family is interested in investments, you might buy your son or daughter a few shares to follow in the newspaper. We don't think teenagers should have their own credit cards, however, except under special circumstances (she's going on a long trip and you want her to have a card temporarily, for emergencies).

Many parents feel it is inappropriate to discuss family finances with their children. But teenagers are more likely to think about money management, and to accept controls on their own spending, if they have some idea of the cost of family living. If they knew what you spent for groceries each week, for example, they would understand why you get upset about wasting food. If they knew what your monthly mortgage payments were, they might understand why you are so "obsessed" with keeping the house in good shape. As we have said many times, teenagers are more likely to go along with your rules if they understand why they are necessary.

SUMMER ACTIVITIES

Summer Jobs

A summer job is a way for teenagers to earn money without shortchanging schoolwork. There is no reason why adolescents shouldn't work full time during the summer and save some of their earnings for pocket money during the school year. Otherwise, everything we said about part-time jobs during the school year applies to summer jobs:

- Urge adolescents to look for jobs that will enable them to acquire knowledge and skills that will be valuable in the future and bring them into contact with adults who will serve as positive occupational role models.
- Insist that teenagers have a financial plan that includes savings (see Money and Money Management, above).

Getting a good job will require more initiative, more digging, than getting a typical teenage job in a fast food restaurant or department store. This is one area where adolescents welcome their parents' advice and help, but the teenager should be in charge.

The Job Search   Start by brainstorming to identify a field in which the teenager might want to work someday (for example, medicine, law, publishing, advertising). If he doesn't know what he wants to do, he should list his special interests and favorite activities. A boy who is interested in sports might look for a job at a health club or coaching younger children; one who likes carpentry might look for work at a construction company or a firm that restores old furniture.

Next the teenager should try to think of all the adults he knows who work or might have contacts in these fields, including family friends, relatives, and school friends' parents; then call and ask whether they know of an organization that hires students during the summer. At the same time, the teenager should ask the school guidance office for a list of summer jobs. If your city has a youth employment office, he should call there to see what is available. The teenager might also write to major employers in the area, enclosing a resumé.

Often the best jobs, in terms of intrinsic interest and career experience, do not pay. Hospitals, government agencies, newspapers, social service agencies, political campaigns, and cultural institutions often have positions for student volunteers. Researchers at colleges and universities may also employ volunteers. If the adolescent does an exceptional job, the volunteer position may lead to a paying job down the line. Even if this is not a possibility, volunteer work pays off in terms of contacts and experience. If the teenager doesn't actually need to earn money, look into these. You might point out that when he applies to college, a letter from a museum director, hospital administrator, or city legislator will count more than a recommendation from the manager of a supermarket.

Jobs at summer camps and resorts may not help the teenager form plans for future careers, but the opportunity to be outdoors and make new friends can be its own reward.

Preparing for Interviews   The teenager should rehearse upcoming interviews with a parent or another adult, anticipating questions she might be asked and practicing her answers. Some likely questions are: Tell me a little about yourself. What do you like to do in your spare time? Why are you interested in this job? What are your qualifications? Have you ever done this type of work before? What are your future plans? What are your greatest strengths? Your weaknesses? The teen should ask the adult who is role-playing the employer to evaluate her performance.

The teenager should also prepare a list of questions for the employer. What exactly will her responsibilities be? Who will she

GUIDELINES FOR A RESUMÉ

A teenager's resumé should include

Education: What school the teenager currently attends, any other educational experiences he or she has had, and any honors he or she has received.

Work Experience: Although teenagers don't have much *job* experience, they may have more *work* experience than they realize. The teenager should include anything he or she has done, with or without pay, that required following directions, assuming responsibility, and being prompt, efficient, and courteous. Such activities as baby-sitting, mother's helper, a paper route, volunteer work, secretary for the school government, or managing a high school's guest lecture program fall into this category.

Special Skills: Here the teenager should list any special abilities he or she has developed, such as typing, using a computer, fluency in a second language, doing layouts for the school paper, supervising a group of young children, and so on. The teenager should also think about activities that are related to the job he or she is applying for and unusual experiences that might catch the employer's eye.

Personal Information: This is a brief description of the teenager, including birth date, background, and interests.

References: A resumé should include the names of two nonrelatives who know the teen well enough to describe his or her abilities, talents, and character (or reliability). The adolescent should ask for their permission before using them as references.

The resumé should be neatly typed, checked carefully for errors in spelling and grammar, and clearly photocopied. When sending the resumé to potential employers, the teenager should write a brief letter stating why he or she is applying to this establishment. The resumé may also be taken to job interviews for reference in filling out a job application form.

---

report to? Where will she be working? What are the hours? Will she be paid an hourly or weekly salary, and how much?

If the teenager has prepared a resumé, she should bring a copy along. If not, she should think of three facts about herself that might impress the employer (previous work experience, her school record, interests and activities that relate to this particular job). If the employer doesn't ask about these, she should look for opportunities to bring them up.

Perhaps this goes without saying, but appearance counts. The teenager who appears in clean, neatly pressed, conservative clothes looks like a serious candidate. Even if the job will not require a suit and tie or a dress (the teenager will be working in construction or on the beach), the teenager shouldn't go to an interview in tattered jeans.

Getting the Most Out of a Job   Even in the best possible work environment, a teenage employee is likely to be assigned low-level, rote work. To get the most out of a job, the teenager should make an effort to be friendly toward co-workers, volunteer to do more than she is required to do, and ask questions ("May I watch . . . ?" "How do you know . . . ?" "Would you teach me . . . ?"). Parents can reinforce on-the-job learning by asking about the people she is working with, what she's learning, and what actually goes on in that particular workplace.

If your adolescent has a good relationship with a supervisor, she should ask for a letter of recommendation at the end of the summer, when the job is nearly over. Two years from now, when she's applying to college, her boss may have moved across the country.

The New Summer Schools

In the old days, summer school was considered a form of punishment for young people who didn't work hard enough during the school year. No longer. Many high schools offer advanced courses and electives, as well as the traditional remedial programs, in the summer. These are a relaxed, low-cost way for adolescents to explore subjects they don't have time for during the regular school year.

Many boarding schools and colleges also run summer programs for high-school students. Some of these programs are designed to give them a taste of college: The teenagers live in dormitories, take a short version of several college courses, and meet with some of the college's undergraduates. Others are enrichment programs, offering courses not generally available in high school (foreign policy, medical ethics, Eastern philosophy, computer applications, and the like). Still others are designed for

RIGHTS AND RESPONSIBILITIES OF
YOUNG WORKERS

In most cases, the laws governing the rights and responsibilities of adult workers apply to teenagers who work in similar jobs. But there are a few exceptions and special rules that you should know about.

WORK PERMITS

Generally, most jobs require that the adolescent have a work permit, and in most states, a work permit cannot be issued to adolescents younger than 14. An exception is made for entertainers, who may obtain a special work permit at a younger age.

A work permit may be obtained from the guidance office of the adolescent's school. To apply for one, your teenager will need your permission and some proof of age, such as a birth certificate. Permits to leave school before graduation to work full time require special parental consent.

A few states do not issue work permits, but employers of adolescents will nevertheless require proof of age before hiring a young worker to ensure that they are complying with child labor laws.

SOCIAL SECURITY

The Internal Revenue Service now requires that all school-age dependents declared on their parents' income tax forms have a Social Security number. In the unlikely event that your adolescent does not, an application can be made at the local office of the Social Security Administration. Look in the phone book, or inquire at your post office, for the address of the office nearest you.

CHILD LABOR REGULATIONS

The kinds of jobs that teenagers may hold are regulated by both federal and state laws. These laws also limit the number of hours students may work, especially during the school year. Regulations may vary from state to state, so check with your state labor department for specifics.

Prohibited jobs: Generally, adolescents under the age of 18 may not work in jobs that require them to drive or use dangerous power-driven machinery; in jobs that might place them near explosives or radioactive substances; or in such potentially hazardous occupations as mining, roofing, or meat processing. There is an additional list of agricultural jobs that teenagers under 16 are prohibited from doing, including working with many different kinds of power-driven machinery used on farms and handling certain types of agricultural chemicals.

Work hours: Students under 16 are prohibited by federal law from working during school hours unless they are enrolled in a special work training program. They are also forbidden by federal law from working between the hours of 7 P.M. and 7 A.M. During the school year, they may not work more than three hours on any school day and no more than eighteen hours a week. During vacations, students under 16 may work as late as 9 P.M., as many as eight hours a day, and up to forty hours a week. Although there aren't any federal restrictions on the work hours of students who are over 16, many states limit the work hours of older adolescents who are still in school. In any case where the state laws are stricter than the federal ones, the state laws prevail.

Child labor laws exist to protect teenagers from work that may be dangerous or that may jeopardize their schooling. If your adolescent is employed and is asked to perform a job or to work during hours that you think may violate child labor laws, you should contact the nearest office of the Wage and Hour Division of the U.S. Department of Labor. Reports can be made anonymously. Employers who have violated the child labor provisions will be fined. Your child will not be fined for working illegally but will probably lose the job if an investigation reveals that it was in violation of the law.

DISCRIMINATION ON THE JOB

Student workers are protected against discrimination in employment on the basis of sex, race, nationality, religion, or disability by the same laws that protect adults. Adolescents who feel that they have been discriminated against on the job should file a complaint with the U.S. Equal Opportunities Commission or the state commission on fair employment practices. Adolescents who are minors will need parental consent to file a complaint.

WAGES

Everyone whose work is covered by the federal Fair Labor Standards Act must be paid at least the minimum wage—*no matter how old the worker is.* Casual jobs, such as baby-sitting, yardwork, or golf caddying, are exempt, but most jobs that teenagers work in are not. Unfortunately, many students accept wages that are lower than the prevailing minimum wage because they are unaware that the law applies to them as well as to adults. If you or your child believes that an employer is not paying the minimum wage for work that should, contact the nearest office of the state labor commission or the Wage and Hour Division of the U.S. Department of Labor. Of course, the minimum wage is just that—a minimum. There is nothing preventing an employer from paying a teenager more than this, and if your adolescent feels that she is entitled to a higher wage than she is being paid, she should speak up.

TAXES

Teenage workers, like adults, are required to pay income taxes on any earnings above the minimum taxable income in effect during the tax year of employment. In many jobs, taxes are automatically withheld from the adolescent's paycheck. The teenager will have to file for an income tax refund if one is owed. If a student anticipates that his earnings will not exceed the minimum taxable income, he may file a W-4 form when he begins working to ensure that taxes are not withheld.

WORKMEN'S COMPENSATION AND UNEMPLOYMENT INSURANCE

In general, adolescents working in jobs covered by workmen's compensation insurance—even if they are working part time—have the same right as adults to claim compensation for any injuries or illnesses suffered as a result of their employment, no matter who is at fault. Not all workers are covered by workmen's compensation. Laws vary from state to state, but often workers who are employed casually or irregularly, or who work for an employer with a small number of employees may not be covered.

Typically, employees who work part time are not covered by government unemployment insurance. In effect, this means that most teenagers will not be covered if they lose their jobs.

---

students with a special interest in, and talent for, math, science, or the arts. A recent listing in *The New York Times* included a field school at an archaeological site in Colorado, where students could work on an ongoing dig; a journalism program in New Jersey, in which students took classes in writing, reporting, and layout from professional journalists, attended press conferences, and produced a weekly paper; and a sea camp in Florida that combined marine biology with scuba diving lessons. Most of these programs offer classes in the morning and sports and recreation in the afternoons. In some cases the adolescent can earn high-school or college credit for classes. These programs tend to be expensive, but scholarships are sometimes available. (See Resources at the end of the chapter.)

Camps, Tours, and Trips

Camps are not for children only today. There are special camps for teenagers who want to work at a particular sport, teenagers who are interested in computers, teenagers who want to meet young people from other countries, teenagers who want to lose weight, and countless other special interests.

Any number of private and public organizations (such as the Y) organize trips and tours for teenagers. Depending on the teenager's interests and your budget, an adolescent might bike from Seattle, Washington, to New York City (a tour organized by the 92nd Street Y in Manhattan, which cost $2,495 in the summer of 1988) or live with a family in France or Sweden through the American Field Service or the Experiment in International Living (the cost varying with the place and the amount of time the American student spends there). With the American Field Service, parents or sponsor groups pay the young person's air fare and pocket money, and the host family provides room and board. With the Experiment in International Living, the student receives room, board, and usually a small salary in exchange for work. Whether the student or the host family pays air fare varies.

The key to a good summer at this age is finding something that is both fun and stimulating, something that adds to the adolescent's range of experience. Parents should encourage their adolescent to explore the possibilities, but, again, not dictate what choice he makes. If the adolescent is interested in a trip, however, make sure it is sponsored by a well-established, reputable organization, such as those we've mentioned.

COLLEGE-BOUND

Handbooks and guidance counselors are fond of saying "College is not for everyone." We question this. In today's labor market, a college degree is essential for anyone who wants a white-collar or professional job (and the number of blue-collar jobs is shrinking). Those young people who want to go into a craft or trade usually need a two-year course of study at a vocational/technical college for credentials and licensing.

Getting a job is not the only reason for going to college, of course. College plays an irreplaceable role in a young person's psychological development. College fosters the development of identity by giving young people the freedom to experiment with different roles and personas. It stimulates intellectual curiosity by exposing them to professors and peers with different interests and ideas. It helps them develop a sense of responsibility by placing them in situations where they have to make decisions without parental guidance. It enhances the capacity for intimacy by extending the period of exploration through dating. It is the only opportunity most of us ever have to be part of a community of young people who are living on their own, yet relatively free from serious responsibilities. Going to college affects not only what kind of job young adults will be able to get after graduation, but also where they will live, who they will marry, who their lifelong friends will be, and most important, who they are.

There are many detailed handbooks on college selection, application, and admissions (some of which are listed in Resources at the end of this chapter). We cannot duplicate their coverage here. Rather, we will focus on helping you and your adolescent understand what colleges look for when they consider applications.

What Do Colleges Look For?

Although procedures and standards vary from one school to the next, most competitive colleges make two evaluations of a candidate: an academic evaluation and a personal one. Of the two, the academic evaluation is by far the most important.

The Academic Evaluation In evaluating a candidate's academic record, college admissions committees look first at how difficult the applicant's course load was and at his or her grade-point average. *B*s in difficult academic subjects count more than *A*s in easy electives, and *B*s in honors and advanced placement courses, even more. Competitive colleges are looking for students who are motivated to work hard.

Second, admissions committees look at the candidate's class rank. The college may not know how difficult it is to get an *A* or *B* at a given high school. If a candidate who got two *A*s, two *B*s, and a *C* (GPA 3.2) is near the top of his or her class, it means the high school is a demanding one; if a candidate with the same record is nearer the middle in class rank, it means *A*s and *B*s were relatively easy to achieve at that school. Class rank tells the college how competitive the school, and the candidate, are.

Finally, colleges look at standardized test scores—especially the Scholastic Aptitude Test (SAT) and/or American College Testing Program (ACT). Scores on these tests give the college an idea of how the candidate ranks nationally. Some colleges assign test scores more importance than others, but in general they are used to determine whether a candidate falls within the normal range for that school. Scores well above this range may prompt the admissions committee to take a second look at a candidate whose academic record was not very distinguished. Was she deeply involved in extracurricular activities? adjusting to a new school and a very different environment? Scores well below this range will prompt second thoughts.

On the basis of this combined evaluation, the admissions committee may decide that a candidate is "very likely," "possible," or "unlikely," or—in schools that process thousands of applications —assign the candidate a numerical rating (say, on a scale from 1 to 5).

The Personal Evaluation Competitive colleges strive to put together a diverse freshman class composed of young people with varied backgrounds, talents, and interests. Each applicant competes, not against all the students who applied to the college, but against the other students who fit his or her personal profile. If hockey is a major sport at the college, for example, a superior goalie may be competing against the 2 or 3 other superior goalies who apply to that college, not all 3,500 applicants for the school's 375 freshman slots. A National Merit Scholar may be competing against 25 or 100 other candidates with academic honors. And so on. The personal evaluation helps the admissions committee fit a candidate into this scheme and decide among its very likely and possible candidates. Sometimes, but only sometimes, it can lead to reconsideration of an unlikely candidate.

The personal evaluation is based on the candidate's application essay, extracurricular record, personal recommendations, and interview. Of these, the application essay is by far the most important. This personal statement tells the admissions committee not only what a candidate has to say about herself, but also how well she writes, something standardized tests do not measure. Students are well advised to put time and thought into this essay. A first-rate essay can save a near-reject from rejection, and a poor essay loaded with misspellings and grammatical errors can send a qualified candidate's application into the reject box. The essay should be original, personal, clear, and strong.

One of the most common myths circulating among high-school students and their parents is that colleges are looking for well-rounded students who have participated in the whole range of extracurricular activities (sports and politics and the arts and social service). Not so. Admissions committees are more interested in depth than breadth. Participation in extracurriculars makes a difference if, and only if, it shows that a candidate has the talent and drive to rise to a position of leadership or demonstrates excellence in a chosen activity. Admissions committees distrust joiners. The "lopsided" individual, who put his all into the orchestra or a community drive, may receive special consideration; the jack of all trades but master of none will not.

Most colleges require letters of recommendation. Unfortunately, these letters are often written by people who barely know the candidate. They may describe the candidate in terms that could apply to almost anyone or simply restate the information on the application. How much weight the admissions committee assigns a given letter depends in large part on the quality of the letter. In general, recommendations from teachers or the headmaster count most; a letter from a senator who knows the candidate's father casually adds little.

If possible, the adolescent should have a personal interview at colleges that are top on her list. If the conversation is not a memorable one, the interviewer may put something like "seems okay" in the candidate's file. If, on the other hand, the adolescent stands out from the hundred other candidates the admissions officer interviewed, the recommendation will be stronger, and she may have an advocate on the admissions committee. In other words, an interview can't hurt, and may help.

It is unusual for the personal evaluation to override a poor or shallow academic record. Competitive schools receive applications from dozens of varsity players, newspaper editors, and class presidents, many of whom are A students as well. An extracurricular may push a candidate over the top only if the athlete is all-city or all-state, the newspaper editor won an award for student journalism, or the class president made a special contribution to the school or community. But for students who are on an academic par with many other candidates, a special essay, strong and personal letter of recommendation, memorable interview, or special success in an extracurricular activity can provide an edge.

RESOURCES

Summer Programs

Among the better guidebooks are

Peterson's Summer Opportunities for Kids and Teen-Agers (published by Peterson's Guides, available in bookstores)

Summer on Campus: College Experiences for High School Students by Shirley Levin and Ann Utterback (Transemantics Inc., 1601 Connecticut Avenue, N.W., Suite 500, Washington, DC 20009)

Boarding Schools: Special Programs (National Associaton of Independent Schools, 18 Tremont Street, Boston, MA 01208)

Exploroptions (30 Alcott Street, Acton, MA 01720)

Parent's Guide to Accredited Camps (American Camping Association, 100 Bradford Woods, Martinsville, IN 46151)

College Handbooks

COMPREHENSIVE LISTINGS

Baron's Profiles of American Colleges (Woodbury, N.Y.: Barron's Educational Series)

Lovejoy's College Guide (New York: Monarch Press)

Peterson's Guide to Four-Year Colleges (Princeton, N.J.: Peterson's Guides)

The Right Colleges: 1988 (College Research Group. Englewood Cliffs, N.J.: Prentice-Hall)

OTHER GOOD SOURCES

Edward H. Fiske's *Selective Guide to Colleges* (New York: Times Books)

Yale Daily News's Insider's Guide to Colleges, 15th edition (New York: St. Martins Press, 1988)

College Admissions Tests

SAT—For a registration booklet, write to

College Board Admission Testing Program
Box 592
Princeton, NJ 085641

ACT—For information, write to

American College Testing Program
2201 North Dodge Street
P.O. Box 168
Iowa City, IA 52243

On Applying to College

Most handbooks walk the student (and parent) through this process, offering advice for every stage. Richard Moll's *Playing the Private College Admissions Game* (New York: Penguin Books, 1986) also describes the process from the inside. In the first chapter, Moll recreates a college admissions meeting at which six candidates are considered and three accepted. Chapter 3 of the book include samples of several good application essays (and one awful one). *Peterson's Guide to College Admissions* (Princeton, N.J.: Peterson's Guides, 1987) also has essay examples.

Financial Assistance

Most high-school guidance offices stock both information and applications for financial assistance. If yours does not have up-to-date information, here are other sources.

Many colleges and scholarship programs request applicants to complete the Financial Aid Form (FAF) and/or the Family Financial Statement (FFS). For the FAF application, write to

College Scholarship Service
CN 6300
Princeton, NJ 08541

For the FFS application, write to

ACT Student Assistance Program
2201 North Dodge Street
P.O. Box 1000
Iowa City, IA 52243

For a free booklet called *The Student Guide: Five Federal Financial Programs,* which describes current federal scholarship, grant, and loan programs, write to

The Department of Education
400 Maryland Avenue, S.W.
Room 1059
Washington, DC 20202

Comprehensive listings of grants, scholarships, and loans include

The College Blue Book (New York: Macmillan)
The College Cost Book (New York: The College Board)
The College Money Handbook (Princeton, N.J.: Peterson's Guides)
Financial Aids for Higher Education (Dubuque, Iowa: Wm. C. Brown)
Financing College Education (New York: Harper & Row)
Lovejoy's Guide to Financial Aid (New York: Monarch Press)

Two helpful, creative guides to cutting college costs are

Edward B. Fiske's *The Best Buys in College Education* (New York: Monarch Press)
Richard Moll's *The Public Ivies* (New York: Viking Penguin)

TOWARD ADULTHOOD
From 18 to 20

CHAPTER 18

You and Your Young Adult

*L*ike early adolescence, young adulthood is a transitional period. Between the ages of 18 and 20, the young person probably will be leaving home, shouldering grown-up responsibilities, getting started on a career path, and perhaps meeting the person with whom he will one day start a family. His behavior will become more and more like that of an adult during these years, and he will expect to be treated more like an adult by his parents. Yet much of the work of adolescence remains to be done. His identity is still up in the air; if he goes to college, his independence will depend on his parents' financial support; his values and moral stance are still being tested; and his relationships with the opposite sex are still tentative. At times he will seem admirably mature, but at times parents will catch glimpses of the egocentrism, conformity, poor judgment, and oppositionalism of his earlier years.

Young adulthood is a transitional period for parents as well as for their adolescents. Your relationship with the young person doesn't end when she leaves home, but your role in her life does change. Giving up your position of authority, learning to deal with your child as an equal, and adapting to the resulting changes in your own life aren't always easy. But the sighs of relief some parents heave when their adolescent packs her bags, or the tears other parents shed when she disappears into the freshman dorm, are premature. Parenthood isn't over yet.

In this final chapter, we look at several issues likely to arise as you and your young adult child negotiate the transition out of adolescence.

ISSUES RELATED TO INDEPENDENCE

Living Away vs. Remaining at Home

It is much easier for young adults to feel and act independent when they are living away from home. A large part of forging an identity and achieving independence is establishing a life-style of one's own. This is difficult to do when you are living in your parents' home and still subject to their rules. Parent–young adult relationships are smoother *and closer* when the young adult has a separate residence. This should not come as a surprise. If your mother has ever come for an extended visit, you know how difficult it can be to assert "But this is how *I* do it" when everything you do provokes a suggestion, a critique, or a pained look. Self-assertion is even more difficult for the young adult, who isn't sure how she would do it, given free choice.

Even if the young adult is attending college or working in your community, it is usually better to arrange separate residences. If this is not possible, you and the young adult need to work out new ground rules for peaceful cohabitation (see When Adult Children Move Back, page 382).

It is natural to worry about how the adolescent who goes away to school will handle her new-found freedom. If you have been responsive all along and have a warm relationship with the adolescent, chances are she will not depart from your upbringing in any significant or long-lasting way. Some experimentation with life-styles is part of the identity-seeking process; just remember that an experiment is not a commitment. The boy who pledges a fraternity is not destined to be a "clubby" for the rest of his life; nor is the girl who falls in and out of love weekly heading for a series of marriages and divorces.

Going to college does not mean that the young adult will be living in an environment where there are no controls on behavior. Colleges grant young people more freedom than they did twenty-five years ago, but they still provide a safety net. Dorm curfews are as obsolete as swallowing goldfish, but freshman residence halls nearly always have one or more resident advisers (older students, faculty members, or both) whose job is to look for problems. Many colleges give freshmen and sophomores much more freedom in selecting courses than was true in the past, but most also require students to clear their programs with an adviser. It is not as if the young adult were heading off into the desert alone with no compass and only a few day's water supply.

Purse Strings

For college students, the move toward independence is complicated by the fact that almost all remain financially dependent on their parents. Putting one or more children through college is a strain on parents. What parents might not realize is that financial dependence can also be a strain on the young adult, who feels grown-up in other ways but still has to go to Mommy and Daddy for money.

Consciously or unconsciously, parents sometimes feel that their financial support of the young person gives them the right to regulate his life. They may threaten to withdraw the support if the young adult does not develop career plans of which they approve, refuse to pay for a share in a house off campus, fine her for not calling once a week as they have requested, or cut her spending money if she doesn't vow to stop smoking or drinking. Parents who find themselves using the purse strings to control their young adult need to remind themselves that *authority derives from reason, warmth, and affection, not from power*. Using money to regulate an adolescent's behavior is bullying—the grown-up equivalent of using physical force to control a small child. This doesn't mean that you shouldn't speak up if you believe the young adult is making a serious mistake, or if you object to the way he is behaving. But financial support should not be the *basis* for your concern and involvement in your adolescent's life. It's better to object to a steady diet of not-too-challenging courses because it isn't stimulating than because you are paying the tuition bill.

Parents who can support their young adult through college should do so, *with no strings attached*. By the same token, the fact that you're supporting your son does not give him the right to act like a juvenile. In return for financial autonomy, the young adult needs to demonstrate financial responsibility. An occasional desperate appeal for money is to be expected, especially in the first semesters of college. But constant overdrafts show that he is not taking his financial independence seriously.

How can you encourage financial independence and responsibility when you are supplying the cash? Let's assume that the young adult's major expenses—tuition, room, and board—are taken care of, and that you are also able to provide spending money.

• The college student should have a monthly budget for personal expenses, which parents will only replenish in emergencies. Decide in advance whether this sum is to include such items as textbooks, clothing, fees for campus activities, and trips home, or whether you will treat these as separate. The adolescent should not have to account to you for every penny of this money, but she should be expected to live within this budget. If she feels the amount you have decided on isn't enough, however, you might ask her to keep an expense record for a month or two, and then decide whether she needs more.

Once they've settled in and feel confident about handling their expenses, many students prefer a lump sum at the beginning of the semester to a monthly check. If you can afford this, it's probably a good idea: One deposit encourages long-term budgeting. Most college students do *not* like being told to call whenever they need cash, even if their credit line with their parents is unlimited: Asking for money is a painful reminder of their financial dependence.

• Many college students have to work, because they have not received adequate financial assistance or because their scholarship requires them to make a contribution. Others want to work, because they want to have extra money, to be less dependent on their parents, or both. In general, everything we said about working during high school applies here (see chapter 17). A moderate work schedule (about ten hours a week) is fine, but trying to work twenty hours or more a week can interfere with the student's academic schedule, not to mention rest and sleep.

College students probably should work during the summer, unless they have some other exciting opportunity. The only qualification is that you and the student should decide in advance whether she will be free to spend her earnings as she chooses or will take on some of the expenses you would cover otherwise, such as clothes, textbooks, and the extra cost of an apartment off campus. Many young adults prefer to pay their own way, at least in part.

• The adolescent should have a checking account in his own

name. This is not merely a convenience; having a checking account is part of being an adult. If the student earns substantial amounts from a summer job and part-time employment, he should also have a savings account and a plan for saving.

• You might consider getting the adolescent a credit card, for use in emergencies and for major expenses. Some credit companies have special accounts for college students, with low credit limits to protect themselves as well as their young customers. Even if the adolescent has a special account, she should understand the uses and abuses of credit and the importance of building a good credit record. If you decide this is a good idea, be sure to include monthly payments in the adolescent's budget. You might want to stipulate that the card will be canceled if the young adult fails to make regular payments that keep her debt level low.

"Why Don't You Call/Write?"

It's natural for parents to feel left out when their adolescent leaves home and doesn't report back regularly. But some decrease in communication is normal and healthy. The plain fact is that the young adult doesn't, and shouldn't, need you as much as he used to. Part of learning to take care of yourself is learning how to get help in your immediate environment and how to identify the best source of advice on a particular problem.

The time has come for parents to "butt out" of the adolescent's daily life. Calling every Saturday, going over everything that has happened to her that week, and offering advice on each and every problem will undermine her feeling of being adult. Now more than ever your daughter needs the freedom to make mistakes. Yes, she may take too many difficult courses, bounce a few checks, get hung over, or sleep with someone she doesn't like all that much. Almost everyone does sooner or later, and most learn from these experiences how to manage their schedule and work load better, keep closer control over their budget, drink in moderation, and choose boyfriends more selectively. But the young adult needs to learn how to bail *herself* out. Putting a little distance between herself and her family is part of this process.

What if your college student asks for help? You don't want to turn him away, of course; you want him to know that he can turn to you if he runs into problems he can't handle. But you also want to communicate that in many cases you aren't the only or the best person for the young adult to turn to—or at least, that your opinion is only one possible view of the matter. Say your son is upset because he flunked a history exam. Has he talked to the professor about where he went wrong? Looked into the possibility of a student tutor? Say your daughter is worried about her roommate's drinking. Has she talked to a dorm adviser about the problem? Does the campus health service have a program for students with alcohol problems? Maybe your son's best friend got a girl pregnant and is talking about getting married. Personally, you think getting married at this age is a mistake, but it's really the couple's decision. Have they considered talking to a counselor? You want your adolescent to know that you're concerned. But you are not an expert on history, alcoholism, or helping people resolve moral dilemmas. Almost certainly, there are people close by who can offer more informed advice and help.

Vacations

Conflicts over the young adult's growing independence often surface, not in phone calls, but during vacations. Typically, college students can't wait to get home, and parents can't wait to see them. But the actual visit sometimes leaves everyone disappointed. The main reason is that parents and their young adult have different agendas.

Parents may be looking forward to special family outings and long, heart-to-heart talks. Their daughter may be looking forward to catching up with her high-school friends and spending every night out or to catching up on her sleep and spending her few waking hours in front of the TV.

A father may ask his son, "How's it going?" expecting to be regaled with tales of thought-provoking seminars, all-night bull sessions, football parties, and girls. All his son can manage is a bland "Okay" as he tries to fight back memories of the night his roommate threw up all over the room, the discovery that a friend saw nothing wrong with cheating on exams, the day he was humiliated by a professor, the night he slept with a girl he never knew, and other unmentionables.

Parents expect their child to have matured, and the returning college student expects to be treated as mature. But the similarity stops there. To parents, *mature* means being more considerate, more responsible, more willing to say where you are going and when you'll be home. To the young adult, it means being trusted, left alone, and *not* having to account for your whereabouts.

Especially on their first visits home, young adults are eager to impress their parents with just how independent and adult they've become. Your son may wear clothes and a hair style you never saw before; affect an accent you can't identify; stay out until 4 A.M.; criticize your family's habits ("Why does the whole family have to go to church?" "If you don't like cousin Marcia, why do you invite her to the house?"); and bait you with newfound social consciousness ("Don't you know that bank has investments in South Africa" or "Can't you see what the Russians are up to?"). Your daughter may smoke and drink openly, even though she knows you disapprove. You may try to act nonchalant about all this—until she casually announces that her boyfriend is staying in her room.

How should parents handle these challenges? You can't expect your college-age son to accept being treated like a high-school student. But neither should your son expect you to change your values and standards just because he has different ideas. Both of you need to compromise. In effect, you should treat the young adult as a guest who has his own values, tastes, and habits, and expect the same courtesy in return. If he has special "dietary requirements," he should tell you in advance, as a guest would, and you should accommodate him if possible, as a host would. If he won't be home for dinner and may not get in until 4 A.M., he should tell you in advance (again, as a house guest would). If no one in your household smokes, don't berate him about his filthy habit, but ask him to confine his smoking to his room. If you don't approve of his sleeping with his girlfriend, give them separate rooms, but try to get the family out of the house now and then so that they can have some privacy, and point out that you treat unmarried adult guests the same way, if you do.

Compromise doesn't mean that you stop caring. If the young adult is coming home drunk every night, speak to him the way you would speak to a friend who was engaging in self-destructive behavior: "We're concerned. Don't you think you're going too far?"

Problems with Independence

It is not at all uncommon for a freshman to call home during the first weeks or months at college and say she is miserable, or to arrive home for her first vacation with a long list of woes: Her classes are boring, the professors are wierdos, her classmates are all nerds and crazies, her dorm is a dump, she *hates* college. Parents' reactions to their adolescent's misery range from worry ("Other kids adjust; why is she so unhappy? Is there something she isn't telling me?") to anger ("We're spending a fortune; how dare she say she hates college!"), confusion ("I can't understand; I loved Wellesley"), and frustration ("What can I do? She's 500 miles away").

Homesickness is a common phenomenon, especially during the first semester of college. Many freshmen mourn the loss of their room, their parents, and their old friends. In most cases, homesickness is an expression of anxiety over independence. What freshmen miss is not their homes, per se, or particular people, but the security and familiarity of the environment they left behind. Homesickness does not mean that the adolescent is immature or overly dependent. This phase usually passes with time. Freshmen are often surprised at how glad they are to get back to their dorm rooms and see their new friends after their first winter break, or to return to college for their sophomore year.

Getting used to college isn't easy, but adolescents who can talk about why they are unhappy are probably on the way to adjusting to their new life. Don't discount their feelings ("You'll get over it"), but reassure them that many people find their freshman year especially difficult. Remind them that when they are feeling overwhelmed, there are students and adults they can turn to for advice and bucking up (see Getting Help on Campus, page 378).

RELATIONSHIPS

Getting Serious

In high school, the teenager wanted you to disappear into the woodwork when she had a date. Your son was furious when his little sister wandered in and out of the TV room while his girlfriend was there; your daughter cringed when her father insisted on greeting her dates at the door. Now, suddenly, young adults want their boy- or girlfriends to be included in family activities, even treated like members of the family. Part of the reason is that young adults want you to take their relationships seriously; part, that they want your assessment of the person, although they won't ask directly; and part, that they want to see whether the person fits in.

Some parents are taken aback by the apparent seriousness of college romances. Parental overreations are especially strong when the boyfriend or girlfriend comes from a different background or ethnic group or seems to have very different values and tastes than those the parents associate with their young adult. Even if the person seems a perfect match, parents may be upset that their child is making a commitment so soon.

It is important to take the young adult's relationships seriously, in the sense that this is a significant person in your son's or daughter's life. But it is equally important not to overreact, in either a positive or a negative way. Marriage and parenthood are probably the farthest things from the young couple's minds. Most college women and men today plan to get started on their careers before they even think about family life. And most relationships are trial runs, especially during the first years of college. But they are important experiences for your adolescent, and you should try to bear this in mind.

Whether your first impression is good or bad, assume that your child has a good reason for liking this person and try to get to know him or her better. If your child asks your opinion, be honest but gentle. If you're not asked, keep quiet. Trying to steer the young person one way or another won't help, and may hurt your relationship (remember the Romeo-and-Juliet effect, chapter 16). If need be, remind yourself that freshman romances often dissolve over vacations, and that although opposites attract, people who are very different from one another rarely stay together.

Living Together

Most studies show that living together has little effect on a couple's present or future. There is no evidence that cohabitation undermines marriage, by taking some of the romance and anticipation out of courtship. But neither is there any evidence that living together improves marriage, by giving the couple a chance to find out whether they are suited to one another and to work out their problems before tying the knot. Couples who live together are no more or less likely to get married than are couples who maintain separate residences. If they do stay together, they are no more or less likely to be happily married or remain married.

There is little a parent can do to prevent a young adult from living with a boyfriend or girlfriend, and little reason to try. If you think the live-in lover is good for your son or daughter, relax. If you think your child has made a poor choice, be patient. Most couples either get married or break up within two or three years of moving in together. Trust them to discover for themselves whether they are happy or unhappy together.

GETTING HELP ON CAMPUS

Today's colleges offer students a wide range of services, almost always free of charge, designed to deal with normal developmental problems as well as more serious concerns. These usually include

- *Mental health services:* general counseling, support groups, workshops, programs for specific problems, such as eating disorders or alcoholism, and programs for specific groups of students, such as ethnic minorities or students with physical handicaps or learning disabilities
- *Physical health services:* access to physicians, other practitioners, and infirmaries
- *Vocational/career services:* individual counseling, career resource libraries, interest testing, interview workshops, and placement services
- *Financial services:* advice on student loans, scholarships, fellowships, and other sources of financial aid
- *Study skill services:* labs in writing, note-taking, and other skills, time management workshops, courses on test preparation and test-taking strategies, test anxiety support groups, and more

There are also a number of people the student can go to for advice or assistance, including

Coming Out of the Closet

"Mom, Dad, I'm gay."

The revelation that a young adult is homosexual may be blurted over the phone, written in a long and carefully worded letter, announced at a family gathering ("There is something I have to tell you . . ."), or discovered by accident.

No parents are prepared for the idea that their child is a homosexual. Some react with anger and hostility: They forbid the young person to associate with her new friends, march her directly to a shrink, or kick her out of their house and their life. Some pretend the situation doesn't exist: They flatly refuse to discuss the matter. Others decide that it will go away: They convince themselves that the young adult will come to his senses or

---

- *Resident advisers (RAs):* RAs are upperclassmen or faculty who live in or near freshmen dormitories, have received training in dealing with student problems, and are available 24 hours a day. Their job is to help a student figure out what to do when things aren't going right.
- *An academic adviser:* Many colleges assign each student a faculty member or member of an advising office to help them plan their course of study. Although their primary job is to advise students on academic matters, they are familiar with the variety of services available on campus.
- *The office of student affairs or dean of students:* All colleges have one or more offices set up to help students with nonacademic concerns (the clue is the word *student* in the title). Most freshman problems do not require a meeting with the dean, but members of the dean's staff will be able to tell a student where to find help.
- *Professors:* Students may fail to realize that professors choose college teaching in part because they like working with college students. Most keep regular office hours when they are available for consultations, list their phone numbers in the college directory, and can be approached before or after class. They *expect* to spend part of their time advising and working with individual students. If they can help, they will; if not, they will be able to tell the student where to find help.

that when the right woman comes along, this bad dream will be over. They plead with their child, in the mistaken belief that he could return to his "true" heterosexual self if he would just try. They pray. Even the most open-minded parents, who count homosexuals among their personal friends and think themselves unbiased, are distressed. They can't help asking themselves "Where did we go wrong?" and in darker moments, "Why is my child betraying me?"

Ideally, parents overcome these first negative reactions and come to accept, even admire, their homosexual child. But just as it takes time for young people to accept themselves, so it takes time for parents to adjust.

How do you get to that point? The first step is to *tell yourself that this is not the end of the world.* The fact that a young person is homosexual does not mean that he or she is doomed to a life of pain and unhappiness. Neither are you. Moreover, the fact that your son or daughter is gay does not mean that the child you knew has suddenly become a stranger.

The second step is to *reassure your son or daughter that you still love him or her and will help in any way you can.* If you are shocked, confused, scared, or all of the above, say so—but with love. Those young homosexuals who work up the courage to tell their parents are terrified of their response. Many (perhaps the majority) never tell their parents. The fact that your son or daughter told you was an act of enormous trust, and you should be grateful that your child had so much faith in your love and understanding.

The third step is to *try to understand your child's feelings and life-style.* Consciously or unconsciously, all of us harbor misconceptions about homosexuality, most of them negative. Perhaps the most common myth is that homosexuality is a matter of choice, something a person can (and should) overcome and outgrow. Not so. (For other common myths, see the discussion of homosexuality in chapter 5.) The best way to come to understand your gay son or daughter is to talk to other parents of gays, ask them and your child to recommend books for you to read (see also Resources at the end of this chapter), and meet your child's friends. If you are like most parents, you will be pleasantly surprised at how unlike your stereotyped image of homosexuals these young gays are, and also at how varied they are in looks, behavior, and interests.

A fourth step is to *meet your son's or daughter's lover.* After the initial shock, this is often the most difficult step for parents. It's one thing to know in the abstract that your child is gay; another to meet the person with whom he or she is living and sleeping. All of you will be nervous. It's useful to remind yourself that sex is not the only or even the central feature of intimate homosexual relationships, any more than it is the only reason for intimate heterosexual relationships. This is a person your son or daughter triumphs with, and wants you to like. Some parents are never able to use the word *lover* to refer to their child's long-term "friend"; others come to think of this person as another son or daughter. Give yourself time.

THE TRANSITION TO ADULTHOOD

Parents' Feelings about "Launching" Their Child

How parents will feel when their child grows up and moves out— especially their youngest and last child—is unpredictable. Some welcome their new freedom, and feel a bit guilty as a result. Some feel proud about having successfully guided their child to adulthood, but unhappy about losing the role of parent. Being responsible for children gave their life purpose; what now? Still others regret not having spent more time with the young adult while he was growing up: Now it's too late (or so it seems).

A good deal has been written about the "empty nest" syndrome. According to this theory, women are especially likely to feel a deep sense of loss when their children depart. Most studies show that this notion has been greatly exaggerated. In fact, mothers are more likely to feel liberated than bereft. One reason women are happy to see their children establish homes of their own is that it means less work for them. Even when they have careers, women bear primary responsibility for housework. When children move out, there are fewer people to shop for, cook for, and clean up after. If you are a mother who has become a "liberated" woman via your child's departure, there is no reason to feel guilty about being pleased.

In contrast, studies find that a surprising number of men feel regretful and saddened when their children leave home—what we might call the "empty den" syndrome. The reason seems to be that men were so busy with their careers, so burdened by the financial responsibilities of fatherhood, so wrapped up in the role of head of household, that they didn't spend as much heart-to-heart time as they might have with their children. Now that the children are gone, they wonder about their priorities. Stories they didn't read, balls they didn't throw, and advice on dating they didn't give begin to haunt them. Whereas mothers are often relieved that the marathon of child-rearing has been run, men may feel that the sprint ended too soon. But there are many different patterns.

All in all, how parents feel about their child's departure depends in part on how they define the event. Mixed feelings are common. But parents who focus on their new freedom are likely to feel happy, for themselves and their child; parents who focus on their loss are likely to feel sad for themselves, if happy for their child. Adjustment to the empty nest/empty den also depends on having other areas of interest and involvement, including their marriage, work, friends, and hobbies. Parents who have let these slide are the most likely to mourn.

The fact that your child has grown up and left home does not mean that your relationship with your child will end, only that it will change. If what parents miss is not so much their relationship with their child, which is ongoing, but having kids around, there are many other ways to keep in touch with children and teenagers. Volunteer to coach a Little League team, head a Scout troop, direct a theatrical group, work in the local high-school library, tutor, become a Big Brother or a foster parent. Organizations that serve youth are always short of volunteers.

When Adult Children Move Back

Today, the number of young adults who return to the nest is growing. More than half of all 20- to 24-year-olds are either living with their parents or being supported by them (up from 40 percent in 1960), and 11 percent of all 25- to 34-year-olds have either never left home or returned home (up from 9 percent in 1960). Many others in this age group have their own place but count on their parents to help pay the rent or buy the condo. Most of the increase in young adults living with their parents has been in middle- and upper-middle-class families. In working-class and ethnic communities, as in Europe, young people have always been expected to live with their parents until they got married.

When children return home, they are no longer adolescents but adults who are used to being on their own and not having to answer to anyone. At the same time, their parents have grown accustomed to living on *their* own and not having to share their living quarters, dinner hour, car, and other resources. Adjustments are necessary on both sides. While there are no right or wrong ways to handle this situation, it is important that you discuss and agree on certain ground rules.

Defining Your Relationship The first decision is whether you will function as a family group or whether the young adult will come and go like a tenant or boarder. Different ideas about what returning home means are a common source of misunderstandings. Will the grown-up child eat with the family or prepare his own meals? Will she be expected to pitch in around the house or only be responsible for her own room? What about laundry? The family car? What you decide isn't as important as the fact that you have a clear agreement.

The Young Adult's Personal Life When your child was an adolescent, you had the final say on such matters as curfew and drinking; you certainly didn't allow high-school students to have boy- or girlfriends spend the night. But it is not appropriate for you to intervene in the young adult's personal life. When she comes home, whether she drinks, who her friends are, and whom she sleeps with are her own decisions. You should expect common courtesy, however. If she may not be home until 3 A.M. she should let you know so that you won't think someone is breaking into the house in the middle of the night. If he's having an overnight guest, you should know in advance so you'll put on a robe before you head for the bathroom. If you don't approve of premarital sex, you have the right to ask your daughter not to sleep with a lover in your house. But you shouldn't forbid her to spend the night at her boyfriend's apartment, even if you think he is not the right man for her. Young adults must be allowed to make their own mistakes and to recover from mistakes by themselves.

Handling Finances If the young adult is working, he certainly should be expected to pay for his own clothing, car expenses, recreation, and the like. It is also reasonable for the young adult to make a contribution toward household expenses such as food, gas and electricity, phone bills, and rent. How large a contribution depends on the situation. If the young person is saving to go back to school or to make a down payment on an apartment, or working only part-time while attending college or going to acting school, you might want to subsidize her living expenses. If your grown child is neither working nor studying and has no immediate plans to do either, you might offer an allowance for a limited time, specifying the cutoff date, and expect her to do extra work around the house that you would otherwise pay an outsider to do, like housecleaning, car or garage repairs, and gardening. When young adults are drifting, the best thing parents can do for them is be emotionally supportive but also make real-world demands. And the real world demands that adults earn their keep.

Setting a Time Limit   Young people who are 20 or older should not live with their parents for an indefinite period. Living with parents makes growing up, solidifying one's identity, becoming autonomous, and establishing intimate relations with the opposite sex more difficult. Unless there are extraordinary circumstances, such as illness, the parents and young adult should establish a schedule for tapering off financial support and set a deadline for moving out. This gives a goal to the young adult who feels lost and encourages planning in the young adult who tends to be muddled and disorganized. Parents should be prepared to give the young adult one final boost, such as the deposit for an apartment or down payment on a car, if they can afford this. But insist on the time limit.

SEEING YOUR GROWN CHILD AS A FRIEND

Having an adult child who is your friend and equal is one of the rewards of parenthood. No matter how close you were with your adolescent, there was always some tension between your legitimate concern for her well-being and the adolescent's equally legitimate need for increasing independence. Now you can begin to put this power struggle behind you. The healthy young adult has worked through her need to establish herself as different from her parents. Because she knows who she is, she isn't so defensive around you. As Mark Twain observed, "When I was a boy of 14, my father was so ignorant I could hardly stand to have the old man around. But when I got to be 21, I was astonished at how much the old man had learned in seven years." Likewise, healthy parents have worked through their need to control their child's behavior and manage her life. Now they can face one another as equals.

Parents sometimes equate growing up with growing apart. In fact, the opposite seems to be true: Parents and children usually become closer when the latter reach their 20s. One reason is that, in their 20s, young people begin to appreciate their parents as people, not just as parents. They don't need to idealize their parents, as was true in childhood, or to de-idealize them, as was the case in adolescence. From their more adult perspective, habits that once drove them up the wall now seem endearing; the fights you had about how the teenager dressed, and whether the college student could move off campus, become humorous in retrospect, part of your family lore. Seeing parents as people is an important step. Parents can help by talking more openly about their feelings, the good and bad decisions they made along the way, the things they worry about, and what makes them proud.

In exchange for being open, parents gain a special friend. Few people have known you as long or as intimately as your children have, and few relationships have been as close. If you are able to see the young adult as an equal, and to give up some of the prerogatives of parenthood, you'll find your child a source of emotional support, a good listener, a good teacher who knows a good deal more than you do about many things, and a good companion.

In short, the end of adolescence can be the beginning of a long and special friendship.

RESOURCES

One of the best known national organizations, Friends of Lesbians and Gays (FLAG), organizes support groups for parents, called Parents FLAG, or P-FLAG. Most college counseling services can provide information on how to locate a chapter near you.

Among the most thoughtful books on the subject is Betty Fairchild and Nancy Hayward's *Now that You Know: What Every Parent Should Know about Homosexuality* (San Diego: Harcourt Brace Jovanovich, 1979).

Notes

Chapter 1

parental styles Eleanor E. Maccoby and John A. Martin, "Socialization in the Context of the Family: Parent-Child Interaction" in P. H. Mussen, ed., *The Handbook of Child Psychology*, 4th ed. (New York: Wiley, 1983) vol. 4, 1–102.

conversations teens crave Torey L. Hayden, "Conversations Kids Crave," *Families*, June 1982, summarized in Thomas Lickona's *Raising Good Children: From Birth through the Teenage Years*. (New York: Bantam, 1985), 255–56.

parents are reasonable Daniel Offer, Eric Ostrov, and Kenneth I. Howard, *The Adolescent: A Psychological Self-Portrait* (New York: Basic Books, 1981), 66–69.

parents who are willing to discuss Catherine Cooper, Harold D. Grotevant, and Sherri Condon, "Individuality and Connectedness in the Family as a Context for Adolescent Identity Formation and Role-taking Skill" in H. D. Grotevant and C.R. Cooper, eds., *Adolescent Development in the Family* (San Francisco: Jossey-Bass, 1983), 56.

negotiable and non-negotiable rules For additional guidelines, see Gayle Dorman et al., *Living with 10- to 15-Year-Olds: A Parent Education Curriculum* (Carrboro, N.C.: Center for Early Adolescence, University of North Carolina-Chapel Hill, 1982).

"A punishment is . . ." Quote from Lickona, *Raising Good Children*, 290.

Chapter 2

communication Our discussion draws on Robert Bolton's classic text *People Skills: How to Assert Yourself, Listen to Others and Resolve Conflicts*

(Englewood Cliffs, N.J.: 1979). Bolton discusses roadblocks in chapter 2, door openers in chapter 3, reflective listening in chapter 4, I-messages in chapter 9, and resistance in chapter 10.

conflict resolution This discussion draws on Bolton's *People Skills*; research from Kathleen M. Galvin and Bernard J. Brommel's *Family Communication: Cohesion and Change*, 2d ed. (Glenview, Ill. Scott, Foresman, 1986); and practical applications from Anne K. Soderman, Barbara M. Rhode, Margaret Bubolz, and David Imig's *Communicating during Conflict: Leader's Guide* (Ames: Iowa State University Cooperative Extension Service, Feb. 1986) and Thomas Lickona's *Raising Good Children: From Birth through the Teenage Years* (New York: Bantam, 1985), chapter 13.

"a dangerous opportunity" Bolton, *People Skills*, 207.

"If you want to hate your child . . ." Bolton, *People Skills*, 234.

the messy room Example adapted from Lickona, *Raising Good Children*, 272–77.

charlatans and quacks These warning signs are adapted from John W. Engel, Luon J. Mathews, and Vivian Halverson's *Marriage and Family Counseling and Therapy in Hawaii: A Consumer's Guide* (Manoa: University of Hawaii, 1985).

Chapter 3

working mothers Urie Bronfenbrenner and Ann Crouter, "Work and Family through Time and Space" in S. Kammerman and C. Hayes, eds., *Families that Work: Children in a Changing World* (Washington, D.C.: National Academy Press, 1982).

divorce For parents who want to learn more about the impact of divorce, we recommend child psychiatrist Richard A. Gardner's *The Parents Book about Divorce* (New York: Bantam, 1979). Many of the examples and much of the advice given here reflect this book. See also Linda Francke, *Growing Up Divorced* (New York: Fawcett Crest, 1983). A good scholarly review of studies on the effects of divorce and remarriage on children is in E. M. Hetherington and K. Camara's "Families in Transition: The Processes of Divorce and Reconstitution" in vol. 7 of R. Parke, ed., *Review of Child Development Research* (Chicago: University of Chicago Press, 1984). For case studies, see J. S. Wallerstein and Sandra Blakesee's *Second Chance: Men, Women and Children a Decade after Divorce* (New York: Ticknor & Fields, 1989).

two-household children See G. Kolata, "Child Splitting," *Psychology Today*, October 1988, 34. Quotations in this section are from Clare Ansberry, "Kids are Often Losers in Joint Custody," *The Wall Street Journal*, 22 September 1988, 41.

single parents See Fitzhugh Dodson's *How to Single Parent* (New York: Harper & Row, 1987). Although written primarily for parents of younger children, this has helpful information for single parents of adolescents.

stepfamilies Many insights in this discussion are from Claire Berman's *Making It as a Stepparent: New Roles/New Rules* (New York: Harper & Row, 1986).

noncustodial parents For helpful advice, see Mark Rosin's *Stepfathering* (New York: Ballantine, 1988).

Chapter 4

ignorance is not bliss J. Brooks-Gunn and D. Ruble, "The Development of Menstrual-related Beliefs and Behavior during Early Adolescence," *Child Development* 53 (1982): 1567–77.

questions about menstruation Adapted from Planned Parenthood's *How to Talk with Your Child about Sexuality,* by Faye Wattleton with Elizabeth Keiffer (Garden City, N.Y.: Doubleday, 1986).

fear of ejaculation A. Shipman, "The Psychodynamics of Sex Education" in R. E. Muss, ed., *Adolescent Behavior and Society: A Book of Readings* (New York: Random House, 1971).

early vs. late maturation Laurence Steinberg, *Adolescence,* 2nd ed. (New York: Knopf, 1989).

adolescent subnutrition W. McGanity, "Problems of Nutritional Evaluation of the Adolescent" in J. McKigney and H. Munro, eds., *Nutritional Requirements in Adolescence* (Cambridge, Mass.: MIT Press, 1976).

normal weight charts Developed by the National Center for Health Statistics. Reprinted in John E. Schowalter and Walter R. Anyan, *The Family Handbook of Adolescence* (New York: Knopf, 1981), 140–43.

physical fitness Lack of fitness among American youth from Emily Greenspan Kelting, "Learning to Love Gym," *The New York Times Magazine/The Good Health Magazine,* 27 September 1987, 20.

fitness and mood Mihaly Csikszentmihalyi and Reed Larson, *Being Adolescent: Conflict and Growth in the Teenage Years* (New York: Basic Books, 1984).

basal metabolism E. Paulsen, "Obesity in Children and Adolescents" in H. Barnett and A. Einhorn, eds., *Pediatrics* (New York: Appleton-Century-Crofts, 1972).

current thinking on obesity Reported by Gina Kolata, "New Obesity Studies Indicate Metabolism Is Often to Blame," *The New York Times,* 25 February 1988, A1, B5.

guidelines for home weight management Jane E. Brody's "Personal Health" column, *The New York Times,* 3 June 1987. See also Ellyn Satter, *Child of Mine* (Palo Alto: Bull Publishing, 1986).

Chapter 5

fantasies Data from a survey of 1,067 teenagers analyzed by Robert Coles and Geoffrey Stokes in *Sex and the American Teenager* (New York: Harper & Row, 1985).

"I want out" Ibid., 17–24.

Woody Allen Quoted in Sol Gordon and Judith Gordon, *Raising a Child Conservatively in a Sexually Permissive World* (New York: Simon & Schuster, 1983), 120.

indirect questions Faye Wattleton with Elizabeth Keiffer, *How to Talk with Your Child about Sexuality* (Garden City, N.Y.: Doubleday, 1986), 75–76.

"homosexual confession" From Gordon and Gordon, *Raising a Child Conservatively*, 132–33.

homosexuality For both research on homosexuality and first-person discussions by gay adults and their parents, see Betty Fairchild and Nancy Hayward's *Now That You Know: What Every Parent Should Know about Homosexuality* (San Diego: Harcourt Brace Jovanovich, 1979).

"latent pregnancy" Gordon and Gordon, *Raising a Child Conservatively*, 133.

teenagers want more information Wattleton with Keiffer, *How to Talk with Your Child*, 25.

sex education in schools Ibid., 10.

common myths Adapted from the pamphlet "How to Talk with Your Child about Sexuality: A Parent's Guide" (New York: Planned Parenthood Federation of America, 1986), 11.

questions about intercourse Wattleton with Keiffer, *How to Talk with Your Child*, 78–79.

real risks Ibid., 60.

data on sexual abuse Ibid., 125–26.

Chapter 6

why adolescents try drugs Quotations are from Beth Polson and Miller Newton's *Not My Kid: A Parent's Guide to Kids and Drugs* (New York: Arbor House/Avon, 1984), 48–50. The explanation of continuing use of drugs is based on G. A. Marlatt and D. M. Donovan's "Alcoholism and Drug Dependence: Cognitive Social-learning Factors in Addictive Behaviors" in W. E. Craighead, A. E. Kazdin, and M. J. Mahoney, eds., *Behavior Modification: Principles, Issues, and Applications*, 2d ed. (Boston: Houghton Mifflin, 1981), 264–85.

research on marijuana Summarized in Peggy Mann, "Marijuana Alert: Brain and Sex Damage" in *Raising Kids* (New York: Berkeley Books, 1981).

"bummed out" Ibid.

reasons for young adolescents to say no Adapted from *10 Steps to Help Your Pre-Teen Say "No"* (Rockville, Md.: National Institute on Alcohol Abuse and Alcoholism, 1986).

one father The father was Leonard Holmes.

Chapter 7

adolescent thinking Today's ideas about cognitive development in general, and adolescent thinking in particular, rest on the foundation laid by the Swiss psychologist Jean Piaget. For a summary and evaluation of his contribution, see John H. Flavell's *Cognitive Development*, 2d. ed. (Englewood Cliffs, N.J.: Prentice-Hall, 1985).

influences on cognitive development C. Holstein, "The Relation of Children's Moral Judgment Level to That of Their Parents and to Communication Patterns in the Family" in R. Smart and M. Smart, eds., *Readings in Child Development and Relationships* (New York: Macmillan, 1972); F. Danner and M. Day, "Eliciting Formal Operations," *Child Development* 48, (1977): 1600–1606.

teens hate fighting with their parents M. Czikszentmihalyi and R. Larson, *Being Adolescent: Conflict and Growth in the Teenage Years* (New York: Basic Books, 1984).

adolescent egocentrism This section is based on David Elkind's "Understanding the Young Adolescent," *Adolescence* 13 (1978): 127–34. See Elkind's books *The Child's Reality* (Hillsdale, N.J.: Erlbaum, 1978); *The Hurried Child* (New York: Addison-Wesley, 1982); and *All Grown Up and No Place to Go* (New York: Addison-Wesley, 1984). See also Susan Harter, "Developmental Perspectives on the Self-System" in P. H. Mussen, ed., *The Handbook of Child Psychology*, 4th ed. (New York: Wiley, 1983), vol. 4: 275–83.

"Our teenager . . ." Ellen Karsh, "A Teen-Ager Is a Ton of Worry," *The New York Times*, 3 January 1987, A23.

right and wrong See Lawrence Kohlberg, "The Development of Children's Orientations toward a Moral Order: Sequence of Development of Moral Thought," *Vita Humana* 6 (1963): 11–13. For a more general discussion of the different stages of moral development, see Thomas Lickona's *Raising Good Children: From Birth through the Teenage Years* (New York: Bantam, 1985).

fostering moral development This section is based on the work of Thomas Lickona, who translated Kohlberg's ideas into practical advice on how parents can encourage moral development in *Raising Good Children*.

appeals to the adolescent's better self Selected and adapted from Lickona, *Raising Good Children*, 178–79.

"statistical morality" Lickona, *Raising Good Children*, 188.

"If you have the approval of someone" Ibid., 185.

a friend is someone who likes you *10 Steps to Help Your Pre-Teen Say*

"No" (Rockville, Md.: National Institute on Alcohol Abuse and Alcoholism, 1986), 16.

Chapter 8

prevalence of emotional problems in adolescence D. Offer and J. Offer, *From Teenager to Manhood: A Psychological Study* (New York: Basic Books, 1975). Also see D. Offer, E. Ostrov, K. Howard, and K. Atkinson, *The Teenage World: Adolescent Self-Image in Ten Countries* (New York: Plenum, 1988).

individuation P. Blos, *The Adolescent Passage* (New York: International University Press, 1979).

disequilibrium J. Hill, "The Family" in *Yearbook of the National Society for Secondary Education.* (Chicago: University of Chicago Press, 1982).

agreement between parents and offspring R. Montemayor, "Parents and Adolescents in Conflict," *Journal of Early Adolescence* 3 (1983): 83–103.

"yes when you can, no when you have to" Thomas Lickona, *Raising Good Children: From Birth through the Teenage Years* (New York: Bantam Books, 1985), 192.

"worry is the result . . ." Search Institute, "The Worries of Adolescents," *Source* 3 (October 1987): 1.

What Worries Young Adolescents [table] P. Benson, D. Williams, and A. Johnson, *The Quicksilver Years: The Hopes and Fears of Adolescents* (San Francisco: Harper & Row, 1986). As reprinted in *Source* 3 (October 1987): 1.

age and sex differences in self-esteem R. Simmons et al., "Disturbance in the Self-Image at Adolescence," *American Sociological Review* 39 (1973): 553–68 and Simmons et al., "Entry into Early Adolescence," *American Sociological Review* 44 (1979): 948–67.

society sends girls mixed messages See J. Bardwick and E. Douvan's "Ambivalence: The Socialization of Women" in V. Gernick and B. Moran, eds., *Women in Sexist Society* (New York: Basic Books, 1971).

Psychological Problems: Danger Signs [table] Adapted from *Parenting Young Adolescents* (Chapel Hill, N.C.: Center for Early Adolescence, 1983), 13.

depression among teenagers G. Chartier and D. Raineiri, "Adolescent Depression: Concepts, Treatments, and Prevention" in P. Karoly and J. Steffen, eds., *Adolescent Behavior Disorders: Foundations and Contemporary Concerns* (Lexington, Mass.: D.C. Heath, 1984).

"I'd just like to go back to bed . . ." Quoted in M. Scarf, *Unfinished Business* (New York: Doubleday, 1980), 5.

Symptoms of Depression [table] *Diagnostic and Statistical Manual of Mental Disorders,* 3rd ed. (Washington: American Psychiatric Association, 1980), 223.

depression in early adolescence For a description and explanation, see I. Weiner's "Psychopathology in Adolescence" in J. Adelson, ed., *Handbook of Adolescent Psychology* (New York: Wiley, 1980).

adolescent suicide C. Holden, "Youth Suicide," *Science* 233 (1986): 839–41; National Center for Health Statistics, *Vital Statistics of the United States* (Washington, D.C.: U.S. Government Printing Office, 1982); M. Shafii et al., "Psychological Autopsy of Completed Suicides in Children and Adolescents," *American Journal of Psychiatry* 142 (1985): 1061; and I. Weiner, "Psychopathology" in Adolescence.

copy-cat suicides D. P. Phillips and L. L. Carstensen, "The Effect of Suicide Stories on Various Demographic Groups, 1968–1985," *Suicide and Life-threatening Behavior* 18 (1988): 100–114; and "Clustering of Teenage Suicides after Television News Stories about Suicide," *The New England Journal of Medicine* 315 (1986): 685–89.

anorexia nervosa and bulimia Descriptions and statistics from Michael E. Mitchell, ed., *Anorexia Nervosa and Bulimia: Diagnosis and Treatment* (Minneapolis: University of Minnesota Press, 1985). New estimates of the incidence of bulimia come from G. Kolata, "Epidemic of Dangerous Eating Disorder May Be False Alarm," *The New York Times*, 25 August 1988, B16.

"I feel as if everyone is making decisions for me . . ." Quoted in Allan M. Josephson, "Psychodynamics of Anorexia Nervosa and Bulimia" in Mitchell, *Anorexia Nervosa and Bulimia*, 78.

"I felt empty and angry . . ." Ibid.

Danger Signs [table] Adapted from *Diagnostic and Statistical Manual of Mental Disorders*, 3rd ed. (Washington, D.C.: American Psychiatric Association, 1980) 69–71.

Chapter 9

cliques and crowds For a summary and review, see B. Bradford Brown, "The Role of Peer Groups in Adolescents' Adjustment to Secondary School" in T. Berndt and G. Ladd, eds., *Peer Relations in Child Development* (New York: Academic Press, in press).

popularity and early identity crisis P. R. Newman and B. M. Newman, "Early Adolescence and Its Conflicts: Group Identity versus Alienation," *Adolescence* 11 (1976): 261–74.

who is popular? For a review of the literature on peer relations, see Willard W. Hartup, "Peer Relations" in P. H. Mussen, ed., *The Handbook of Child Psychology*, 4th ed. (New York: Wiley, 1983) vol. 4, 274–385.

popularity and adjustment M. Putallaz and J. Gottman, "Social Skills and Group Acceptance" in S. Asher and J. Gottman, eds., *The Development of Children's Friendships* (New York: Cambridge University Press, 1981).

Carol Burnett Quoted in Philip G. Zimbardo, *Shyness* (New York: Jove, 1978), 107.

youth culture D. M. Smith, "Peers, Subcultures, and Schools" in D.

Marsland, ed., *Education and Youth* (London: Falmer Press, 1987), 41–64.

the generation gap Areas of parent-adolescent *agreement* are discussed in R. M. Lerner and J. A. Shea's "Social Behavior in Adolescence" in B. B. Wolman, ed., *Handbook of Developmental Psychology* (Englewood Cliffs, N.J.: Prentice-Hall, 1982), 503–25 and J. Conger and A. Peterson's "Adolescence and Youth" in J. Adelson, ed., *Handbook of Adolescent Psychology*, 4th ed. (New York: Harper & Row, 1984).

circular peer influences See D. B. Kandel, "Homophily, Selection, and Socialization," *American Journal of Sociology* 84 (1978): 427–38 and J. L. Epstein, "The Influence of Friends on Achievement and Affective Outcomes" in J. L. Epstein and N. Karweit, eds., *Friends in School* (New York: Academic Press, 1983), 177–200.

variations in susceptibility to peer pressure T. J. Berndt, "Developmental Changes in Conformity to Peers and Adults," *Developmental Psychology* 15 (1979): 608–16.

parental relationships and susceptibility to peer pressure Laurence Steinberg, "The Impact of Puberty on Family Relations: Effects of Pubertal Status and Timing," *Developmental Psychology* 23 (1987): 451–60.

friendlessness and mental health Hartup, "Peer Relations."

parties Survey reported by Eric W. Johnson in *How to Live through Junior High School* (Philadelphia: J. B. Lippincott, 1975), 202–21; guidelines adapted from Johnson.

Chapter 10

victimization Marjory Roberts, "Schoolyard Menace," *Psychology Today,* February 1988, 55–56; Murray M. Kappelman and Paul R. Ackerman, *Between Parent and School* (New York: Dial Press/James Wade, 1977), 152–4.

effects of tracking For a summary see C. Persell, *Education and Inequality* (New York: Free Press, 1977).

testing Ann E. Boehm and Mary Alice White, *The Parent's Handbook in School Testing* (New York: Teacher's College, Columbia University, 1982).

stability of IQ N. Baley, "Consistency and Variability in the Growth of Intelligence from Birth to Eighteen Years," *Journal of Genetic Psychology* 75 (1949): 165–96.

what parents should ask The questions and examples here are adapted from Boehm and White, *Parents Handbook,* chapter 5.

Parents' Legal Rights [table] Adapted from Bruce Baron, Christine Baron, and Bonnie MacDonald, *What Did You Learn in School Today?* (New York: Warner Books, 1983) 264–66.

gifted adolescents Murray M. Kappelman and Paul R. Ackerman, *Between Parent and School* (New York: Dial Press/James Wade, 1977), chapter 20; three questions paraphrased from page 322. Eric W. Johnson discusses the problem of boredom in *How to Live through Junior High School* (Philadelphia: J. B. Lippincott, 1975) 146–51.

learning disabled adolescents Kappelman and Ackerman, *Between Parent and School,* chapter 12; Baron et al., *What Did You Learn,* Boehm and White, *Parent's Handbook,* chapter 10.

Chapter 11

contacts with the school Bruce Baron, Christine Baron, and Bonnie MacDonald, *What Did You Learn in School Today?* (New York: Warner Books, 1983), 261–3.

homework Reasons why parents shouldn't *do* homework for a child are from Eric W. Johnson's *How to Live through Junior High School* (Philadelphia: J. B. Lippincott, 1975), 105–7.

grades For a discussion of the importance of beliefs about success and failure, see C. Dweck and B. Light's "Learned Helplessness and Intellectual Achievement" in J. Garber and M. Seligman, eds., *Human Helplessness* (New York: Academic Press, 1980).

reading problems Based on Johnson, *How to Live through Junior High School* and Baron et al., 98–102.

adult reading patterns Johnson, *How to Live through Junior High School,* 122.

math problems Ibid., 130–7.

math anxiety See Sheila Tobias, "Math Anxiety: Why Is a Smart Girl Like You Counting on Her Fingers?" *Ms.,* September 1976, 5; Sheila Tobias, *Overcoming Math Anxiety* (New York: Norton, 1978).

parental pressures For further discussion of the negative impact of certain types of parental pressure, see I. Weiner's *Psychological Disturbance in Adolescence* (New York: Wiley, 1970), chapter 7.

"Paul smiled broadly . . ." Weiner, *Psychological Disturbance,* 268.

underachievement in school Johnson, *How to Live through Junior High School,* 138–45; Weiner, *Psychological Disturbance,* chapter 7; and Douglas H. Powell, *Teenagers: When to Worry, What to Do* (Garden City, N.Y.: Doubleday, 1986), chapter 7.

Chapter 12

data on intercourse P. H. Dreyer, "Sexuality during Adolescence" in B. B. Wolman, ed., *Handbook of Developmental Psychology* (Englewood Cliffs, N.J.: Prentice-Hall, 1982).

how important is sex to teenagers? A. M. Juhasz, B. Kaufman, and H. Meyer, "Adolescent Attitudes and Beliefs about Sexual Behavior," *Child and Adolescent Social Work* 3 (1986): 177–93; Aaron Hass, *Teenage Sexuality: A Survey of Teenage Behavior* (New York: Macmillan, 1979), 21–22.

permissiveness with affection Ira Reiss coined this phrase in *The*

Social Context of Sexual Permissiveness (New York: Holt, Rinehart & Winston, 1967).

"I think that if . . ." Quoted in Robert Coles and Geoffrey Stokes, *Sex and the American Teenager* (New York: Harper & Row, 1985), 48.

"Even if you were to kill somebody" Quoted in Thomas Lickona, *Raising Good Children: From Birth through the Teenage Years* (New York: Bantam, 1985), 382.

"she was curious about me . . ." Quoted in Coles and Stokes, *Sex and the American Teenager,* 97.

good and bad reasons for sex Adapted from Planned Parenthood's *How to Talk with Your Child about Sexuality,* by Faye Wattleton with Elizabeth Keiffer (Garden City, N.Y.: Doubleday, 1986), 98.

how to say no Ibid., 100–101.

bragging about sex Coles and Stokes, *Sex and the American Teenager.*

statistics on date rape Wattleton with Keiffer, *How to Talk with Your Child,* 133.

teenage use of contraceptives Coles and Stokes, *Sex and the American Teenager,* 121; 1987 Harris poll reported in "Kids and Contraceptives," *Newsweek,* 16 February 1987, 56; *Fact Sheet,* Planned Parenthood Federation of America, 1986.

why teenagers take chances For more details, see Coles and Stokes, *Sex and the American Teenager,* chapter 12.

personal fable applied to sex Dreyer, "Sexuality during Adolescence."

ignorance and misinformation "Kids and Contraceptives," *Newsweek,* 16 Feb. 1987, 57.

1987 Harris poll Ibid.

attitudes toward condoms Survey by Susan Kegeles of the Center for AIDS Prevention Studies at the University of California, San Francisco. Reported in *Psychology Today,* October 1988, 14.

data on STDs F. Maloney, *Human Sexuality* (New York: McGraw-Hill, 1983).

a note on AIDS Based in part on Lawrence K. Altman, "Fact, Theory and Myth on the Spread of AIDS," *The New York Times,* 15 February 1987, A1.

pregnancy Much of the information and advice in this section is drawn from Wattleton and Keiffer's *How to Talk with Your Child,* 112–24.

facts of teenage pregnancy in America National Research Council, *Risking the Future* (Washington, D.C.: National Academy press, 1987).

"Once in high school . . ." Quoted in Lickona, *Raising Good Children,* 382.

economic problems of teenage mothers Frank F. Furstenberg, Jr., et al., *Adolescent Mothers in Later Life* (New York: Cambridge University Press, 1987).

reasons for becoming a mother Adapted from David Elkind, *All Grown Up and No Place to Go: Teenagers in Crisis* (Reading, Mass.: Addison-Wesley, 1984), 131.

attitudes toward abortion Coles and Stokes, *Sex and the American Teenager*, 127–34.

abortion procedures Planned Parenthood Federation of America, *Pregnancy Resource Book 3: Deciding on Abortion*, 1981.

teenage fathers Furstenberg, *Adolescent Mothers*.

Chapter 13

major drugs [table] Adapted from *Playboy*, May 1987, 5.

data on drugs and drug use L. D. Johnston, P. M. O'Malley, and J. G. Bachman, *Use of Licit and Illicit Drugs by America's High School Students 1975–1984* (Washington, D.C.: U.S. Government Printing Office, 1985) and *Drug Use among American High School Students, College Students, and Other Young Adults: National Trends through 1985* (The University of Michigan Institute for Social Research and U.S. Department of Health and Human Services, 1986).

long-term consequences of adolescent drug use M. Newcomb and P. Bentler, *Consequences of Adolescent Drug Use: Impact on the Lives of Young Adults* (Newbury Park, Calif.: Sage, 1988).

teenage deaths in alcohol-related accidents Anne Swany Harrity and Ann Brey Christensen, *Kids, Drugs, and Alcohol: A Parent's Guide to Prevention and Intervention* (White Hall, Va.: Betterhall Publications, 1987), 60.

danger signs [table] From *Schools without Drugs*, (Washington, D.C.: U.S. Department of Education, 1986), 16.

parent denial For a more complete discussion, see Beth Polson and Miller Newton's *Not My Kid: A Parent's Guide to Kids and Drugs* (New York: Avon, 1984), chapters 1 and 4.

Handling the Problem Yourself Adapted from Polson and Newton, *Not My Kid*, 153.

Chapter 14

adolescent identity See especially Erik H. Erikson, *Childhood and Society* (New York: Norton, 1963) and *Identity: Youth and Crisis* (New York: Norton, 1968). For more contemporary research, see J. B. Dusek and J. F. Flaherty, "The Development of the Self-Concept during the Adolescent Years," *Monographs of the Society for Research in Child Development*, vol. 46, no. 4, 1981 and Daniel Offer, Eric Ostrov, and Kenneth I. Howard, *The Adolescent: A Psychological Self-Portrait* (New York: Basic Books, 1981).

"de-illusionment" Discussed in Daniel J. Levinson et al., *Seasons of a Man's Life* (New York: Knopf, 1978), 195.

"To a considerable extent . . ." Erikson, *Childhood and Society*, 262.

doing "nothing" Mihaly Csikszentmihalyi and Reed Larson, *Being Adolescent* (New York: Basic Books, 1984).

"identity foreclosure" and "negative identity" Terms coined by Erikson in *Identity: Youth and Crisis.*

"adjusted blandness" This phrase comes from David Reisman, *The Lonely Crowd: A Study of the Changing American Character* (New Haven: Yale University Press, 1950), 11.

extracurricular activities and ambitions Douglas Kleiber and William Rickards, "Leisure and Recreation in Adolescence: Limitation and Potential" in Michael G. Wade, ed., *Constraints on Leisure* (Springfield, Ill.: Charles C. Thomas, 1985), 289–317.

identity disorders This description of severe identity problems is based on the diagnosis of identity disorder in *Diagnostic and Statistical Manual of Mental Disorders,* 3rd ed. (Washington, D.C.: American Psychiatric Association, 1980). One criterion of this diagnosis is "duration of the disturbance of at least three months." However, we do not believe parents should wait three months to seek counseling if a young person seems severely distressed.

studies of young radicals R. J. Braungart, "Youth Movements" in J. Adelson, ed., *Handbook of Adolescent Psychology* (New York: Wiley, 1980), 560–97.

"uniformity of differing" Erikson, *Identity: Youth and Crisis.*

moral straightjacket The phrase is from Thomas Lickona's *Raising Good Children: From Birth through the Teenage Years* (New York: Bantam, 1985), 197

fostering moral development The general outline for this section and some of the examples are from Lickona, *Raising Good Children,* chapter 10.

help them make good decisions Questions adapted from ibid., 206.

"To feel part of society" Ibid., 213.

volunteer work and moral development David Conrad and Diane Hedin, *National Assessment of Experimental Education: A Final Report* (St. Paul, Minn.: Center for Youth Development and Research, University of Minnesota, 1981) and Richard Danzig and Peter Szantom, *National Service: What Would It Mean?* (Lexington, Mass.: Heath, 1986).

Chapter 15

problem behavior More detailed descriptions of various types of problem behavior in adolescence may be found in Douglas H. Powell's excellent book *Teenagers: When to Worry and What to Do* (Garden City, N.Y.: Doubleday, 1986).

sex as *the* battleground Ibid., chapter 6.

rules exist to be broken Ibid., chapter 8.

delinquency M. Gold and R. Petronio "Delinquent Behavior in Adolescence" in J. Adelson, ed., *Handbook of Adolescent Psychology* (New York: Wiley, 1980).

running away Statistics from Patricia Hersch, "Coming of Age on City Streets," *Psychology Today,* January 1988, 28–37.

truancy B. Sommer, "Truancy in Early Adolescence," *Journal of Early Adolescence* (1985): 145–60; D. Kimmel and B. Weiner, *Adolescence: A Developmental Transition* (Hillsdale, N.J.: Erlbaum, 1985); I. B. Weiner, "Psychopathology in Adolescence" in J. Adelson, ed., *Handbook of Adolescent Psychology* (New York: Wiley, 1980).

Chapter 16

the breakup of cliques and crowds D. Dunphy, "The Social Structure of Urban Adolescent Peer Groups," *Sociometry* 87 (1963): 230–46. For an update and critique, see B. Bradford Brown, "The Role of Peer Groups in Adolescents' Adjustment to Secondary School" in T. Berndt and G. Ladd, eds., *Peer Relations in Child Development* (New York: Academic Press, in press).

"Dating in groups . . ." Quotes are from Leslie Jane Nonkin, *I Wish My Parents Understood: A Report on the Teenage Female* (New York: Penguin Books, 1985), 91–92.

age of first dates M. P. McCabe, "Toward a Theory of Adolescent Dating," *Adolescence* 19 (1985): 150–70.

duration of adolescent relationships Robert Coles and Geoffrey Stokes, *Sex and the American Teenager,* (New York: Harper & Row, 1985), 101.

pseudointimacy This perception was developed by Erik Erikson in *Identity: Youth and Crisis* (New York: Norton, 1968).

sex differences in breaking up Coles and Stokes, *Sex and the American Teenager,* 101.

going steady Data on the duration of teenage romance from Coles and Stokes, *Sex and the American Teenager,* 101. Comments on going steady in junior high adapted from Eric W. Johnson, *How to Live through Junior High School* (Philadelphia: J. B. Lippincott, 1975), 231.

friendship E. Douvan and J. Adelson, *The Adolescent Experience* (New York: Wiley, 1966). See also B. J. Bigelow, "Children's Friendship Expectations: A Cognitive-Developmental Study," *Child Development* 48 (1977): 246–50.

closeness to friends *and* parents M. Gold and D. S. Yanof, "Mothers, Daughters, and Girlfriends," *Journal of Personality and Social Psychology* 49 (1985): 654–9.

Chapter 17

comments on guidance counselors Arthur G. Powell, Eleanor Farrar, and David C. Cohen, *The Shopping Mall High School: Winners and*

Losers in the Educational Market Place (Boston: Houghton Mifflin, 1985), 48.

parents who push Quotes from ibid., 146.

pros and cons of team sports The basic issues are described and analyzed in Gary Alan Fine's *With the Boys: Little League Baseball and Preadolescent Culture* (Chicago: University of Chicago Press, 1987).

working during the school year This discussion is based on Ellen Greenberger and Laurence Steinberg's *When Teenagers Work: The Psychological and Social Costs of Adolescent Employment* (New York: Basic Books, 1986).

rights and responsibilities of young workers Material adapted from *Young People and Work: Things to Know,* an unpublished manual from the Adolescent Work Project of the University of California, Irvine.

premature affluence See Jerald Bachman, "Premature Affluence: Do High School Students Earn Too Much?" *Economic Outlook USA* (Summer 1983): 64–67.

the job search The suggestions for role playing in the text and guidelines for a resumé are adapted from *Family Times,* developed by the 4-H Youth Development and Family Living Education Programs, University of Wisconsin-Extension (University of Wisconsin-Madison: Wisconsin Clearing House, 1987), 89–90.

what colleges look for See especially Richard Moll, *Playing the Private College Admissions Game* (New York: Penguin Books, 1986), chapter 3.

Chapter 18

new dimensions of independence Arthur W. Chickering, *Education and Identity* (San Francisco: Jossey-Bass, 1972).

independence and living away from home during college K. Sullivan and A. Sullivan, "Adolescent-Parent Separation," *Developmental Psychology* 16 (1980): 93–99.

vacations Some ideas about vacations are drawn from Karen Levin Coburn and Madge Lawrence Treeger's *Letting Go: A Parent's Guide to Today's College Experience* (Bethesda, Md.: Adler & Adler, 1988).

homesickness Aaron Brower, University of Wisconsin, Madison, personal communication.

homosexuality The descriptions and advice in this section are drawn from a book written by two mothers of gay children, Betty Fairchild and Nancy Hayward, *Now that You Know: What Every Parent Should Know about Homosexuality* (San Diego: Harcourt Brace Jovanovich, 1979). Though ten years old, this book is highly recommended by young adult homosexuals and their parents.

studies of the "empty nest" syndrome See S. McLanahan and J.

Adams, "Parenthood and Psychological Well-Being," *Annual Review of Immunology* 5 (1987): 237–57.

the "empty den" syndrome M. Farrell and S. Rosenberg, *Men at Midlife* (Boston: Auburn Press, 1981).

living with adult children Data from Denise M. Topolniki, "What You Really Owe Your Kids," *Money*, June 1988, 157–62 and Lawrence Kutner, "When Young Adults Head Back Home," *The New York Times*, 14 July 1988. For more details, see Jane Davies Okimoto and Phyllis Jackson Stegall's *Boomerang Kids: How to Live with Adult Children Who Return Home* (Boston: Little Brown, 1987) and Susan Littwin's *The Postponed Generation* (New York: Morrow, 1987).

closeness in young adulthood See F. Hunter and J. Youniss, "Changes in Functions of Three Relations during Adolescence," *Developmental Psychology* 18 (1982): 806–11.

Index

About the Authors

Laurence Steinberg, Ph.D., is professor of psychology at Temple University, where he is also a senior research associate at the Center for Research in Human Development and Education. Dr. Steinberg has taught previously at Cornell University, the University of California at Irvine, and the University of Wisconsin at Madison. A nationally recognized expert on psychological development and family relations during adolescence, he is the author of numerous scholarly articles on adolescence as well as several books on growth and development during the teenage years.

Dr. Steinberg was educated at the Johns Hopkins University and Vassar College, where he was elected to Phi Beta Kappa and graduated with honors and distinction in psychology, and at Cornell University, where he received his Ph.D. in human development and family studies. He is a fellow of the American Psychological Association.

Ann Levine was an editor in the journals department of Rockefeller University and the college department of Prentice-Hall before becoming a freelance writer. In addition to popular articles, she has co-written and contributed chapters to leading college textbooks in psychology, sociology, and anthropology.

Ms. Levine received a B.A. with highest honors in English from New York University.